SOVIET AND NAZI DEFECTORS

When MVD officials are posted to a Soviet Embassy in the West, what measures if any are taken to discourage their defection? Are their children over a certain age held in the Soviet Union? If the official is single, is he allowed abroad? Is [sic] any of his relations nominated as hostages? Does source know of an instance where action has been taken against the relations in the USSR of an MVD official who has defected? Are defections publicized or explained?

MI5 Questionnaire for Vladimir Petrov,
April 1955

It was a classic case where a spur-of-the-moment defection so frequently goes sour. The guys who have done best are those who worked in place for a long period of time and then come over with some preparation.

Bob Gates in *Sell-Out* by James Adams

SOVIET AND NAZI DEFECTORS

COUNTER-INTELLIGENCE IN WW2 AND THE COLD WAR

NIGEL WEST

FRONTLINE
BOOKS

First published in Great Britain in 2024
by Frontline Books
An imprint of
Pen & Sword Books Ltd
Yorkshire - Philadelphia
Copyright © William Nester
ISBN 978 1 03611 388 9

The right of William Nester to be identified as Author of this work has been asserted by him in accordance with the Copyright, Designs and Patents Act 1988.
A CIP catalogue record for this book is available from the
British Library

All rights reserved. No part of this book may be reproduced or transmitted in any form or by any means, electronic or mechanical including photocopying, recording or by any information storage and retrieval system, without permission from the Publisher in writing.

Typeset by Lapiz Digital
Printed and bound in the UK by CPI Group (UK) Ltd,
Croydon, CR0 4YY.

Printed on paper from a sustainable source by
CPI Group (UK) Ltd, Croydon, CR0 4YY

Pen & Sword Books Limited incorporates the imprints of Archaeology, Atlas, Aviation, Battleground, Digital, Discovery, Family History, Fiction, History, Local, Local History, Maritime, Military, Military Classics, Politics, Select, Transport, True Crime, Air World, Claymore Press, Frontline Publishing, Leo Cooper, Remember When, Seaforth Publishing, The Praetorian Press, Wharncliffe Books, Wharncliffe Local History, Wharncliffe Transport, Wharncliffe True Crime and White Owl.

For a complete list of Pen & Sword titles please contact
PEN & SWORD BOOKS LTD
47 Church Street, Barnsley, South Yorkshire, S70 2AS, England
E-mail: enquiries@pen-and-sword.co.uk
Website: www.pen-and-sword.co.uk
or
PEN & SWORD BOOKS
1950 Lawrence Rd, Havertown, PA 19083, USA
E-mail: uspen-and-sword@casematepublishers.com

CONTENTS

Books by Nigel West vii
Acknowledgments.. ix
Glossary and Abbreviations x
Dramatis Personae.. xiii
Introduction xvii

Chapter I	Erich Vermehren 1
Chapter II	Grigori Tokaev........................... 18
Chapter III	Yuri Rastvorov........................... 30
Chapter IV	Vladimit Petrov and Evdokia Petrova 38
Chapter V	Anatoli Golitsyn 85
Chapter VI	Oleg Lyalin........................ 141
Chapter VII	Arkadi Shevchenko........................ 165
Chapter VIII	Vitali Yurchenko 169

Appendix I	SIME Report on Erich Vemehren, March 1944 177
Appendix II	MI5 Study of Defectors, 1948..................... 190
Appendix III	Defector Case Histories 203
Notes 245
Index 249

BOOKS BY NIGEL WEST

Spy! (with Richard Deacon)

MI5: British Security Service Operations 1909–45

MI6: British Secret Intelligence Service Operations 1909–45

A Matter of Trust: MI5 1945–72

Unreliable Witness Espionage Myths of World War II

The Branch: A History of the Metropolitan Police Special Branch

GARBO (with Juan Pujol)

GCHQ: The Secret Wireless War

The Friends: Britain's Postwar Secret Intelligence Operations

Molehunt: The Search for the Soviet Spy in MI5

Games of Intelligence

Seven Spies Who Changed the World

Secret War: The Story of Special Operations Executive

The Faber Book of Espionage (Anthology)

The Illegals

The Faber Book of Treachery (Anthology)

The Secret War for the Falklands

Counterfeit Spies

Crown Jewels (with Oleg Tsarev)

VENONA: The Greatest Secret of the Cold War

The Third Secret: Solidarity, the CIA and the KGB's Plot to Assassinate the Pope

MASK: MI5's Penetration of the Communist Party

The Guy Liddell Diaries (ed. 1939–42; 1942–45)

The Historical Dictionary of British Intelligence

The Historical Dictionary of International Intelligence

At Her Majesty's Secret Service

The Historical Dictionary of Cold War Counterintelligence

The Historical Dictionary of World War II Intelligence

The Historical Dictionary of Sexspionage

TRIPLEX: Secrets from the KGB Archives

The Historical Dictionary of Ian Fleming's James Bond

The Historical Dictionary of Naval Intelligence

SNOW (with Madoc Roberts)

Historical Dictionary of Chinese Intelligence (with I.C. Smith)

Historical Dictionary of Signals Intelligence

MI5 in the Great War

At Her Majesty's Secret Service

Double Cross in Cairo

Black Ops

Cold War Spymaster

Churchill's Spy Files

Spycraft Secrets

Codeword OVERLORD

Spy Swap

Historical Dictionary of Cold War Intelligence

The Kompromat Conspiracy

Spies Who Changed History

Hitler's Nest of Vipers: The Rise of German Intelligence 1933–42

Hitler's Trojan Horse: The Fall of German Intelligence 1942–45

Classified! The Adventures of a Molehunter

ACKNOWLEDGMENTS

The author owes a debt of gratitude to Molly Sasson, Dr Michael Bialuguski, Michael Thwaites, David and Hope Doyle, Nicholas Elliott, John Scarlett, Tony Brooks, Erich Vermehren, David Major, Stephen de Mowbray, Arthur Martin, Peter Wright, David Murphy, Drew Thompson, Peter Deriabin, Ken Millian, Peter Earnest, Vladimir Kuzichkin, Dick Helms, John Symonds, Yuri Modin, George Kisevalter, Pete Bagley, Cleve Cram, Ray Batvinis and Oleg Tsarev.

GLOSSARY AND ABBREVIATIONS

ABM	Anti-Ballistic Missile
ABMT	Anti-Ballistic Missile Treaty
ASIO	Australian Security Intelligence Organisation
BAOR	British Army of the Rhine
BEF	British Expeditionary Force
CIA	Central Intelligence Agency
CIB	Commonwealth Investigation Branch
CPA	Communist Party of Australia
CPGB	Communist Party of Great Britain
CSDIC	Combined Services Detailed Interrogation Centre
D-G	Director-General of MI5
DCI	Director of Central Intelligence
DP	Displaced Person
DST	Direction de la Surveillance du Territoire
FBI	Federal Bureau of Investigation
FCD	First Chief Directorate
FCO	Foreign & Commonwealth Office
GAF	German Air Force
GCHQ	Government Communications Headquarters
GRU	Soviet Intelligence Service
GUGB	Soviet Police and Secret Police

IC	Committee of Information (*see also* KI)
ICBM	Inter-Continental Ballistic Missile
IRD	Information Research Department
ISOS	German Abwehr decrypts
JIC	Joint Intelligence Committee
KGB	Soviet intelligence service
KI	Committee of Information (*see also* IC)
KO	KriegsOrganisation
KONO	KriegsOrganisation NeheOrient
MFA	Ministry of Foreign Affairs
MGB	Ministry of State Security
MGIMO	State Institute of international Relations
MI5	British Security Service
MIT	Turkish Intelligence Service
MVD	Ministry of Internal Affairs
NASA	National Aeronautics and Space Administration
NID	Naval Intelligence Division
NSA	National Security Agency
NYFO	New York Field Office
NATO	North Atlantic Treaty Organization
NKVD	Soviet Intelligence Service
NSDAP	National Socialist German Workers' (Nazi) Party
NTS	Union of Ukrainian Nationalists
NY	New York
OKW	Oberkommando der Wehrmacht (German army)
OSS	Office of Strategic Services
OWI	Office of War Information
RAE	Royal Aircraft Establishment
RAF	Royal Air Force
RCMP	Royal Canadian Mounted Police

SALT	Strategic Arms Limitation Talks
SCD	Second Chief Directoratr
SEATO	South-East Asia Treaty Organisaion
SIA	Soviet Intelligence Agency
UN	United Nations
UPI	United Press International
US	United States
USA	United States of Ameirica
USSR	Union of Soviet Socialist Republics
VM	V-Mann (Abwehr agent)
VOKS	Soviet Film Distribution
WAAF	Women's Auxiliary Air Force
W/T	Wireless Telegraphy
WFO	Washington Field Office

DRAMATIS PERSONAE

Sirioj Abdoolcader	KGB spy in London
AE/LADLE	CIA codename for Anatoli Golitsyn
ARTIST	Abwehr officer Johnnie Jebsen
Ray Batvinis	FBI officer
Dr H.C. Beckett	ASIO source FRANKMAN
Kurt Beigl	Abwehr defector
BLACKGUARD	SIS double agent in the Middle East
Tony Brooks	SIS case officer for Oleg Lyalin
Robin Brook	SIS officer
Frances Bernie	Soviet spy codenamed SISTER
Dr Michael Bialoguski	ASIO source DIABOLO
Ashjorn Bryhn	Chief of Norwegian Security Service
CAPULET	SIS codename for Yuri Tasoev
Anatole Chebotarev	KGB defector from the Brussels *rezidentura*
Wally Clayton	CPA organiser and Soviet spy CLOD
CLOD	Wally Clayton
Bill Colby	Director of Central Intelligence
Kyriacos Costi	KGB spy in London
Felix Cowgill	SIS officer
Allan Dalziel	Private Secretary to Dr Evatt, codenamed TECHNICIAN
Wilfred Dunderdale	SIS officer
DELFTER	Abwehr codename for Erich Vermehren
Peter de Wesselow	MI5 officer
DIABOLO	ASIO source Dr Michael Bialoguski

xiv SOVIET AND NAZI DEFECTORS

Turi Drozdov	KGB *rezident* in New York
DYNAMITE	CIA codename for Arkai Shevchenko
ERIKSON	KGB codename for Erik Gabrielson
Dr Herbert Evatt	Leader of the Australian Labour Party
Wilhelm Evang	Chief of Norwegian Intelligence Service
EXCISE	SIS codename for Grigori Tokaev
FAREWELL	French codename for KGB officer Vladimir Vetrov
Philip F. Fendig	CIA officer
FRANKMAN	ASIO source Dr H.C. Beckett
Frank Friberg	CIA officer
Erik Gabrielson	KGB spy in Helsinki codenamed ERIKSON
GARMASH	KGB mole in the French DST
Paul Garbler	CIA officer
Vasia Gmirkin	CIA officer
George Goldberg	CIA officer
Aantoli Golitsyn	CIA codename AS/LADLE and SAWDUST
GOLDFINCH	KGB defector Oleg Lyalin
Robert Gray	CIA officer
Gunvor Haavik	KGB spy in Norwegian Intelligence Service
Derek Hamblen	MI5 officer
Christopher Herbert	MI5 officer
Jim Hill	Soviet spy inside External Affairs codenamed TOURIST
E. Howard Hunt	CIA officer
Jim Hunt	CIA officer
IRONCLAD	FBI source inside the KGB *reziednuta* in New York
Johnnie Jebsen	Abwehr officer codenamed ARTIST by SIS
Quentin Johnson	CIA officer
JUNIOR	Abwehr defector Hans Ruser
Peter Karlow	CIA officer
Urho Kekkonen	Finnish politician and KGB agent

KIN	NKVD codename for Boris Yartsev
George Kisevalter	CIA officer
KISS	SIS double agent in the Middle East
Fred Kovaleski	CIA officer
Dick Kovich	CIA officer
Nikolai Kuznetsov	KGB officer in New York
Pavel Kuznetsov	KGB officer in London
George Leggett	MI5 officer
Guy Liddell	MI5 officer
Rupert Lockwood	Australian journalist codenamed WARREN
Yuri Loginov	KGB illegal
Oleg Lyalin	KGB defector codenamed GOLDFINCH
Ingeborg Lygren	Norwegian spy suspect
Constantinos Martianon	KGB spy in London
Jack Maury	CIA officer
Ed Miller	Head of the FBI's Domestic Intelligence Division
Ian Milner	Soviet spy inside External Affairs
Vasili Mitrokhin	KGB defector
David Murphy	CIA officer
NINA	Russian immigrant and espionage suspect
Yuri Nosenko	KGB defector
Fedor Nosov	NKVD officer under TASS cover
OLGA	NKVD codename for Rose Marie Ollier
Rose Marie Ollier	Cipher clerk in French embassy, codenamed OLGA
Fergan O'Sullivan	Press Secretary to Dr Evatt, codename TOURIST
Ivan Pakhomov	NKVD officer under diplomatic cover
George Paques	KGB spy at NATO headquarters
PRECIOUS	Abwehr defector Erich Vermehren
Ron Richards	Director, New South Wales ASIO
Alex Rosen	Assistant to FBI Director J. Edgar Hoover

SOVIET AND NAZI DEFECTORS

Hans Ruser	Abwehr defector codenamed JUNIOR
Vladislas Savin	KGB officer in London
SAWDUST	CIA codename for Anatoli Golitsyn
SISTER	Soviet codename for Frances Bernie
Valentin Sadovnikov	NKVD *resident*, Canberra
SASHA	Igor Orlov
Vikenti Sobole	KGB New York *resident*
Arkadi Shevchenko	Soviet mole codenamed DYNAMITE by the CIA
Vladimir Skripkin	Putative GRU defector
Alexander Sogolow	CIA officer
Bruce Solie	CIA officer
Bogdan Stashinsky	KGB defector
STORK	SIS codename for Grigori Tokaev
Bill Sullivan	FBI officer
John Symonds	Former Scotland Yard detective
Yuri Tasoev	GRU defector codenamed CAPULET
TECHNICIAN	NKVD codename for Allan Dalziel
Michael Thwaites	ASIO case officer
Grigori Tokaev	GRU defector codenamed STORK by SIS, EXCISE by SIS
TOURIST	Soviet codename for Jim Hill
John Vassall	KGB spy in the British Admiralty
Erich Vermehren	Abwehr defector codenamed PRECIOUS by SIS and DELFTER by the Abwehr
Vladimir Vetrov	KGB officer codenamed FAREWELL
Yuri Voronin	KGB *resident* in London
WARREN	Soviet codename for Rupert Lockwood
Harry Wharton	MI5 case officer for Lyalin
Pete Wheeler	CIA officer
Boris Yartsev	NKVD officer in Canberra codenamed KIN
Courtenay Young	MI5 officer

INTRODUCTION

Defectors are very strange, complex creatures and their management, like the handling of all human sources, is an immensely challenging occupation because of the many unpredictable complications associated with issues of motivation, loyalty, trust, deception and betrayal. Nevertheless, a well-informed defector is an invaluable asset and will be suitably motivated to cooperate fully with the debriefers and thereby hope to enhance his or her value.

From a counter-intelligence perspective, the first 'pressings' of a defector, like a great vintage wine, are likely to be of top quality, with the remainder being of rather less value. A defector can provide an overview and context of an asset that will provide the detail missing from relatively sterile technical alternatives, such as intercepted communications or comprehensive surveillance. Put simply, an indiscreet conversation in the canteen, the corridor gossip around the water-cooler, may offer a vital clue that no amount of wire-taps, overhead reconnaissance or sophisticated satellite imagery will ever provide.

The principal task of any intelligence agency is to generate reliable information for policymakers, and this is accomplished by developing a matrix or jigsaw puzzle of individual pieces that, when fitted together, reveal a picture on a topic that fulfills a requirement set by ministers and their advisors. The agencies will rely on a variety of sources, including open-source material, intercepted communications, diplomatic gossip, prisoner interrogation reports, tips passed through liaison relationships with friendly nations, aerial observation, technical sensors categorised as measurement and signature intelligence (MASINT) and, of course, human sources. Often categorised as HUMINT, the human factor is the least predictable source of all, but it can be of critical importance when a priority target country, perhaps Iran or North Korea, creates a closed society, and an environment, which is sometimes referred to as 'denied territory' that renders conventional tradecraft redundant.

For example, conditions in the Soviet Union were so adverse with a ubiquitous hostile security apparatus, that it was almost impossible for Western intelligence personnel to recruit or manage agents in Moscow or Leningrad during the Cold War. Virtually every active spy was caught within a few weeks. Similarly, there was precious little information from within the totalitarian regime, and Kremlin-watchers were limited to studying small quantities of signals intelligence and some satellite coverage. Entirely absent were the other components of the overall jigsaw, and in those circumstances the relative value of defectors was greatly enhanced.

It was the British intelligence community, specifically the Security Service (MI5), which was the first institution to recognise the significance of defectors when, in 1937, the former GRU illegal *rezident* in The Hague, Walter Krivitsky, failed to attract the interest of the French or the American authorities in taking him seriously. Alarmed by the purges in Moscow, which had claimed the lives of so many of his friends, Krivitsky abandoned his post in the expectation that his knowledge of clandestine Soviet military intelligence in Western Europe would be received with enthusiasm, but he was greeted with disinterest by the authorities in Paris, Ottawa and Washington DC. Finally, after he had compromised John King, an active Soviet spy and British Foreign Office cipher clerk, he was invited to London and interviewed at length. Krivitsky's bona fides had been established by King's confession, and his information became the foundation for numerous other counter-espionage investigations that followed. Krivitsky would return to the United States where he would die in mysterious circumstances in February 1941, but his information would remain relevant for decades.

In 1948 an unidentified MI5 officer completed *A Study of Defectors from the USSR*, which included an account of Krivitsky's interviews conducted in January 1940, described as having 'provided an enormous body of very valuable information.'

Almost forty years later SIS's Ian Chalmers drafted a report on ten post-war defectors, among them OVATION (Oleg Gordievsky), REDWOOD (Vladimir Kuzichkin) and NORTHSTAR (Mikhail Butkov). Whereas the MI5 document took a positive tone, and concentrated on the success of the individuals concerned, the SIS version did not avoid the hazards of resettlement and the problems of handling these unusual men. Gordievsky underwent a painful (and expensive) divorce, alienation from his two daughters and severe alcoholism. Kuzichkin became one of London's most popular acupuncturists – with actor Alec Guinness as a patient. He married twice before drinking himself to death in Weston-super-Mare. At one point his alcoholism resulted in a protracted stay at SIS's country retreat near Chichester, followed by a period in The Priory, having been sectioned under the Mental Health Act. As for Butkov, the KGB officer who had operated in Oslo under TASS cover until his defection in May 1991, he later set up a fake business school in Berkshire, attracting foreign students with a promise of visas, and was sentenced to three years' imprisonment for fraud.

Outside of the intelligence community the concept of defectors is little known and less understood. *The Daily Telegraph* journalist Gordon Brook-Shepherd, a former wartime SIS agent who died in January 2004, is the only historian to have studied the phenomenon in depth, starting in 1977 with *The Storm Petrels: The First Soviet Defectors 1928–1938*[2], inspired by an interview in Paris with Boris Bajanov, who had defected in 1928, Brook-Shepherd covered George Agabekov, Grigory Bessedovsky, Alexander Orlov and Walter Krivitsky. His second book, *The Storm Birds: Soviet Post-War Defectors*[3], published a decade later, included Oleg Penkovsky and an unidentified FAREWELL, now known to be Vladimir Vetrov, even though neither officer ever defected.

Brook-Shepherd's analysis of post-war defectors was described by the CIA's Cleve Cram as 'not only an exciting read but is accurate in almost every respect.' Cram, whose research was supported by his legendary CIA analyst Carolyn Carpenter, had spent nine years in London as the deputy station chief, retired in 1992, having completed his SAWDUST review of the Golisyn controversy, and embarked on a lengthy study, *Of Moles and Molehunting*, of the contemporary literature devoted to the singular, compelling issue of hostile penetration of MI5. However, during his professional career, which had included a spell as station chief in Ottawa, Cram developed an increasing antipathy for James Angleton, the chief of the CIA's counter-intelligence staff who was accused of having succumbed to Anatoli Golitsyn's 'monster plot', a pejorative term used by Angleton's critics to deride his perception of the Kremlin's Machiavellian schemes to undermine and mislead the West.

Cram lauded Brook-Shepherd who had received 'generous help from the CIA and the British intelligence services'. He was able to interview at least six defectors (Yuri Rastvorov, Piotr Deriabin, Arkadi Shevchenko, Vladimir and Tatiana Rezun, and Stanislav Levchenko) and described, chronologically, the cases of Igor Gouzenko, the GRU cipher clerk who defected in Canada in September 1945, FAREWELL, the KGB Line X (science and technology) officer who was executed in the Lubyanka in January 1985, Nikolai Khokhlov, Yuri Nosenko and Stanislas Levchenko.

In turning his attention to failed defectors, Brook-Shepherd described the cases of Konstantin Volkov, the NKVD deputy *rezident* who had offered to switch sides in Istanbul in September 1945, and Vladimir Skripkin, a GRU officer who had indicated his wish to desert in Tokyo in May 1946. The son of a general, Skripkin had been betrayed by a Soviet mole in London, and then entrapped at his apartment in Moscow when he was visited by a pair of NKVD investigators masquerading as British representatives and, most importantly, armed with a codeword previously agreed with Skripkin and ostensibly known only his British contacts.

The next cases to be examined by Brook-Shepherd were the four NKVD officers who in 1954 independently opted to defect when news of Lavrenti Beria's arrest and execution in Moscow circulated among his subordinates. Yuri Rastvorov sought asylum from the Americans in Tokyo in January 1954; Peter Deriabin abandoned his post in Vienna in February 1954; Nikolai Khokhlov followed his example in Frankfurt, also in February 1954; and in April of the same year, the Canberra *rezident*, Vladimir Petrov, and his wife, Evdokia, sought refuge with the Australian Security Intelligence Organisation.

Brook-Shepherd devoted two chapters to Oleg Penkovsky, who was arrested in Moscow in October 1962, and then turned his attention to the controversy surrounding Golitsyn and Yuri Nosenko. Golitsyn defected in Helsinki in December 1961, while Nosenko made contact with the CIA in Geneva in June 1962 but did not defect until February 1964. Many of the issues raised by these two cases are unresolved, but in 1978 Nosenko, who had been accused of fabricating some aspects of his story – which allegedly included access to the KGB file of the John F. Kennedy assassin Lee Harvey Oswald – was exonerated, compensated for his ill-treatment by the CIA, and employed by them as a consultant. Finally, Yuri Rastvoroov sought asylum from the Americans in Tokyo in January 1954.

Brook-Shepherd's other defectors were Oleg Lyalin, the KGB officer who agreed to work for MI5 before his arrest on a drink-driving charge in August 1971 triggered the expulsion of 105 Soviet intelligence professionals operating in London under various official covers. Another, perhaps rather less significant Soviet was Artush Hovanesian, who slipped over the Turkish frontier in July 1972, but changed his mind a couple of months later and returned home, accompanied by his young wife. His value lay in the KGB border watch-list, which he had brought with him.

In conclusion, Brook-Shepherd gave an account of two important cases, being Arkadi Shevchenko, the Soviet diplomat based at the

United Nations headquarters who was granted political asylum in New York in April 1978. However, Brook-Shepherd appeared unaware that Shevchenko had spied for the CIA for the previous three years. In a curious postscript to Shevchenko's defection, it became the catalyst for another when the GRU's Vladimir Rezun was assigned the task in Geneva of tracking down Shevchenko's son Gennadi, a junior diplomat, and escorting him to Moscow. Though a series of mishaps, Rezun failed in his mission, so he decided with his wife, Tatiana, also a GRU officer, to defect rather than carry the blame. Accordingly, both Rezuns defected spontaneously to the British.

Brook-Shepherd's final case study was that of the KGB officer Oleg Gordievsky, who was exfiltrated from Moscow in July 1985. However, on this occasion Brook-Shepherd received minimal cooperation from SIS, partly because Gordievsky was undergoing a prolonged debriefing, but also because his wife and two daughters were under what amounted to home arrest in Moscow, effectively hostages to ensure the defector did not embarrass the Kremlin.

In retrospect, and with the benefit of declassified MI5, FBI and CIA files, Brook-Shepherd must be acknowledged as a pioneer in his chosen field, although with hindsight he can be seen to have perpetuated some popular myths. For example, he mistakenly attributed the VENONA triumph as having been accomplished by 'analyzing the remains of a Red Army code-book found on the Finnish battle-front.'[4'] Since the National Security Agency had declassified most aspects of the VENONA programme in 1995, three years before *The Storm Bird*s was published, Brook-Shepherd should have known better then to peddle a long-discredited cover-story for one of the greatest cryptanalytical triumphs of all time.

In another momentary lapse Brook-Shepherd recalled how Konstantin Volkov, the NKVD deputy *rezident* in Istanbul had approached the British in August 1945 and attempted to open negotiations for his defection, offering a list of disclosures in return for his resettlement in England with his wife, Zoya. Brook-Shepherd explained that among much else, Volkov had 'offered to name 314 Soviet agents in Turkey and 250 Soviet agents in Britain'.[5] Subsequently this assertion would be reproduced, word for word, by numerous other historians and commentators, although Volkov's actual letter had been couched in rather different terms and had included an offer to reveal:

1. List of 314 agents of the Intelligence Directorate of the NKGB in Turkey. This list includes active agents and also agents on ice. On some agents there are official descriptions.

>   2. List of employees of military and civilian intelligence services of Great Britain known to NKGB. [The] List includes about 250 official and secret employees of mentioned service of whom there are descriptions.[6]

Thus, far from claiming possession of a list of '250 Soviet agents in Britain', Volkov had described a list of *British* intelligence personnel, with no suggestion they were Soviet spies. This is a colossal misrepresentation, so how could it have happened? Why did nobody question the very idea that there were 200 Soviet agents in Britain? Compared to the dozen or so spies mentioned in January 1940 by a previous defector, Walter Krivitsky, Volkov's claim should have appeared downright fanciful.

Brook-Shepherd never explained the source of his information about Volkov, or the circumstances in which he had read the crucial letter, but Cram's endorsement was enough for it to be taken at face value, as described by Brook-Shepherd. Furthermore, Brook-Shepherd had not been the first to misquote Volkov's offer. In *Philby: The Long Road to Moscow*, released in 1978, Philby's *Observer* colleague Patrick Seale said,

> Among the secrets he promised to bring over were the names of three Soviet agents working in Britain,: two, he claimed, were in the Foreign Office, and the third was head of a counter-espionage section in London.[7]

Volkov, of course, never claimed he knew the actual names of the varying number of Soviet spies supposedly active in England; Seale never explained his source for his Volkov material, but evidently it was not the same as the one relied upon seven years later by Brook-Shepherd, who makes no comment on the discrepancy.

Brook-Shepherd's error would be repeated in the 2010 authorised history of the Security Service, *The Defence of the Realm*[8], by Christopher Andrew, who remarked that 'the most reliable account of Volkov's attempted defection is in Gordon Brook-Shepherd's *Storm Birds*.' According to Andrew, Volkov 'under brutal interrogation in Moscow before his execution ... confessed that he planned to reveal the names of no fewer than 314 Soviet agents, probably including Philby.'[9] Since Brook-Shepherd's figure of '250 Soviet agents in Britain' was an invention, Andrew's version is sheer embroidery, and is partly responsible for Ben Macintyre's statement in his 2014 biography of Kim Philby, *A Spy Among Friends*, that Volkov had offered to 'furnish the names of 314 Soviet agents in Turkey, and a further 250 in Britain'.[10] Surprisingly, an equally flawed version would find its way into the paperback edition of another official history, *MI6* by Keith Jeffery, who added an entire chapter to his magisterial history. According to Jeffery, Volkov had

> offered to provide 'a list of the NKGB Intelligence in Turkey numbering 314 men' together with 'a list of the known regular NKGB agents of the military and civil intelligence in Great Britain', comprising about 250 known and less well known agents.[11]

Thus, Brook-Shepherd' original, mistaken assertion, that Volkov possessed a list of '250 Soviet agents in Britain' when he had been referring to British personnel, not Soviet spies, had escalated to 250 'known and less well known' Soviet spies! To create even further muddle, in 1999 Vasili Mitroknn's archive, edited by Christopher Andrew, gave what purported to be an insider's view of the Volkov incident, based not on Volkov's letter, but his confession, allegedly extracted 'under interrogation in Moscow before his execution'.[12] Supposedly Volkov had admitted to having 'planned to reveal the names of no fewer than 314 Soviet agents' but, according to Mitrokhin, had not mentioned they were all in Turkey. What about the other agents in Britain?

Brook-Shepherd's misrepresentation of the Volkov letter included the false assertion that 'of the agents in Britain, two, he claimed, worked in the Foreign Office. Seven more 'inside the British intelligence system.' However, the relevant passage of the actual document reads rather differently:

> In some cases there are duplicates or photocopies which were given to us by NKGB who are employees of the British intelligence organs and Ministry of Foreign Affairs of Great Britain. Judging by the cryptonyms there are nine such agents in London.

Subsequent writers have simply copied Brook-Shepherd's error and, in 1990, Christopher Andrew and Oleg Gordievsky asserted in their *KGB: The Inside Story*, that

> Among the most important war-time Soviet agents, he claimed, were two in the Foreign Office and seven 'inside the British intelligence system'.[13]

A decade later, as MI5's authorised historian, Christopher Andrew, made much the same statement in *The Defence of the Realm*:

> Volkov revealed that among the most highly rated British Soviet agents were two in the Foreign Office (no doubt Burgess and Maclean) and seven 'inside the British intelligence system'.[14]

Curiously, Andrew cites *The Mitrokhin Archive* as his source for this mistaken statement, the relevant passage reading:

> Among the most highly rated Soviet agents, he revealed, were two in the Foreign Office (doubtless Burgess and Maclean), and seven inside the 'British intelligence system'.[15]

Thus, having originally relied on Brook-Shepherd for his account of the Volkov letter, Andrew had credited the same information to Mitrokhin, giving the appearance of validation. In reality, of course, Andrew had relied on Mitrokhin to corroborate his earlier mistakes. As for Macintyre, he cited Jeffery and Andrew as sources in his 2014 biography of Kim Philby when he stated that

> Among the Soviet spies in important positions in Britain, he revealed, were seven in the British intelligence services or the Foreign Office.[16]

Exactly how Brook-Shepherd came to make his original mistakes, which others would replicate remains unclear, but the damage had been done, and the fiction would be perpetuated in innumerable books, such as *Stalin's Agent* by Boris Volodarsky[17], Richard Kerbaj in *The Secret History of the Five Eyes*[18] and Tim Milne *in Kim Philby*.[19]

* * *

During the Cold War, the phenomenon of the intelligence defector became an important part of the counter-intelligence conflict in which the principal adversaries sought to persuade potential defectors to remain in place for as long as possible before making the overt act that would result in long-term resettlement in a host country. Defectors became the principal currency of the counter-espionage profession, with virtually every major spy of the era having been originally identified by an inside source. Although the security authorities, especially in the United States and Britain, have sought to convey the impression that spies are often caught 'by the vigilance of colleagues', or by the use of routine precautions, such as polygraph tests, and background screening, the reality is very different. The overwhelming number of spies arrested in the post-war era in the United States were compromised by a tip given by a defector (or a defector in development). The same goes for the United Kingdom, where the Security Service actively propagated the myth that spies, such as William Marshall in 1952, Harry Houghton in 1961 and Michael Bettaney in 1982, had been exposed due to impressive sleuthing, rather than sheer chance in the first example, and a mole inside the KGB's London *rezidentura* in the second. Marshall, a young radio operator employed by the Diplomatic Wireless Service, had been contaminated when an off-duty MI5 watcher happened to notice a known Soviet intelligence officer, Pavel Kuznetsov, taking a stroll in Kingston-upon-Thames, west London. The encounter was not part of any organised surveillance, but the initiative taken by the watcher led him to witness what was intended to have been a clandestine rendezvous. Kuznetsov's tradecraft had been immaculate, so MI5 promoted the impression that the officer was not a victim of misfortune, but the target of a well-established investigation.

Two issues quickly emerge during any prolonged study of post-war defectors. Firstly, the art of handling such tricky customers was developed during the Second World War, with the classic model being example of Erich Vermehren, the Abwehr officer whose decision to switch sides in January 1944 – which would have the most profound consequences for the organisation – had been driven by his deep commitment to Roman Catholicism, which he could not reconcile with the regime. The second common denominator is the amount of either deliberate or accidental misinformation that has obscured the truth of the dramas that will be examined. Only with the benefit of recently declassified files can we now re-evaluate the eight case histories that follow.

Chapter I

ERICH VERMEHREN

The SIME view of PRECIOUS is that, while anti-Nazi, he appears to retain patriotic German sentiments and they also estimate that he or his wife may later develop patriotic or religious scruples which may interfere with any genuine employment of them by you.

Guy Liddell to Felix Cowgill,
13 March 1944

It might have been imagined that, if the Second World War was an authentic conflict between the clearly delineated forces of good and evil, with the Allies representing democratic values, and the Axis, personifying genocide, atrocities and fascism, that there would have been a constant flow of intelligence defectors seeking to escape Nazi oppression. Yet this was not the case, even though there were plenty of opportunities for German intelligence officers posted in neutral countries, such as Portugal, Spain, Switzerland, Sweden and Turkey, to make contact with their adversaries and negotiate their desertion. In fact, the numbers involved are astonishingly small, with one in Stockholm (Hans Zech-Nantwich), three in Madrid (Hans Ruser, Otto John and Peter Schagen), five in Istanbul (Erich Vermehren, Willi Hamburger, Kurt Beigl and the Kleczkowskis) and none in either Lisbon or Berne. The explanation for these extraordinarily low numbers is likely a combination of factors, such as the impact of the Venlo incident, in which a pair of SIS officers had been duped in November 1939 into meeting a supposed group of anti-Nazi officers, a rendezvous that resulted in their abduction. Understandably, having been deeply shaken by this early *coup-de-main*, the British intelligence community would become extremely risk-averse in its future dealings with alleged political dissidents. The Axis was also cautious in its deployment of well-informed staff on what amounted to the frontlines of the intelligence war, posting only the most reliable of personnel to cities perceived to be teeming with enemy agents and, perhaps most significantly, family members were to be considered potential hostages. In addition to these disincentives, the Allied intelligence agencies themselves were hesitant to enter into discussions with the enemy because the information offered by some putative defectors might prove counter-productive, especially where the individual involved possessed a knowledge of sources who might turn out to be double agents already under Allied control. In those circumstances the Abwehr would be likely to assume that the defector would compromise everything he knew, and would therefore take the appropriate counter-measures, which would probably include terminating the sources thought to have been contaminated.

Born in Lubeck in December 1919, Erich Vermehren was the son of a well-connected Hamburg lawyer whose wife, Petra, was a correspondent for *Das Reich*. After graduating with a law degree, his refusal to join the Hitler Youth movement had prevented him from taking up a Rhodes Scholarship at the University of Oxford, and in 1939 he converted to Roman Catholicism after meeting his future wife, Gräfin Elisabeth von Plettenberg, an anti-Nazi activist, six years his senior, who had been imprisoned briefly by the Gestapo for distributing subversive religious literature.

In late 1942, despite an exemption from military service because of a childhood injury, and following the influence of his diplomat cousin, Adam von Trott, Vermehren joined the Abwehr and worked as an interpreter at Oflag VI-B, a camp for British officer prisoners of war in Dössel. His transfer to Turkey came at the request of his father's friend, Paul Leverkühn, and he arrived in Istanbul in December 1942, ostensibly to negotiate the release of fifty Societé Francais de Navigation Danubienne tugs, which French-built and destined for use on the river Danube, had been interned by the Turkish authorities. In reality, Vermehren was assisting in the management of Abwehr agents active in Iran and Iraq that were run by the local Abwehr headquarters, known as the KriegsOrganisation NeheOrient, which was accommodated in the consulate general.

In summer 1942, Vermehren's request for permission to have his wife join him was refused by Berlin but, undeterred, he made another application while on home leave in November 1943 and obtained a passport for her through the intervention of Monsignore Angelo Roncalli, the Papal Nuncio in Istanbul. Then, following influence exercised by a family friend, Marshal von Bieberstein, she travelled to Sofia where she initially was refused an onward air passage to Turkey. However, on Christmas Day 1943 she completed her journey, despite Leverkühn's disapproval, and was granted two weeks' sick leave by the German ambassador to Turkey, Franz von Papen, who happened to be her cousin.

In January 1944, Vermehren approached the British assistant military attaché who put him in touch with Section V's local representative, Nicholas Elliott, and the two men met for the first time on Monday, 18 January. Over the next three days Vermehren removed a large quantity of secret papers from his office to prove his bona fides and, having been photographed by Elliott and sent to London, they were assessed as authentic. In his report to the head of Section V, Felix Cowgill, Elliott described Vermehren as 'a highly-strung, cultivated, self-confident, extremely clever, logically minded, slightly precious young German of good family'. Accordingly, Vermehren was codenamed PRECIOUS by SIS.

Three days later, Vermehren reported to his office that he was ill and would not return on Monday, also that he was moving to a new address in Istanbul. When he did not appear at the KONO suite as promised a messenger was sent to the new address, which could not be found with the aid of a deliberately misleading map supplied by Vermehren. On 27 January 1944, from the safety of Cairo, a jubilant SIS issued its first assessment, entitled *The German Secret Service in Turkey*,

1. A well placed and reliable source whose previous information has been substantiated by our records, has produced the following information on the organization and personalities of the Abwehr station known as Kriegsorganisation Nahe Osten, the headquarters of which are situated in the German Embassy building in Istanbul. This organisation is usually known in Abwehr circles by the short title 'KO NO'.
2. The Dienstellenleiter Hptm Dr Paul Leverkuehn [Leverkühn], who succeeded Major Shulze-Bennett, is responsible for coordinating the activities of the various Abwehr sections in KO NO and maintaining general supervision over them.
3. The staff directly under the control of Dr Leverkuehn [Leverkühn] consists of two sections known as the Aussendienst which might perhaps be described as an administrative section. The Aussendienst consists of Abw. I Heer officers and the Leiter I/H is Leverkuehn's deputy.

4. The other sections of KO NO, the Abs. I. Marine, Abw. I. Luft, Verwaltung, Abw. III and Abw. II, whilst under the general supervision and coordination of the Dienstellenleiter enjoy a very large measure of autonomy and receive their instructions direct to their own headquarter sections in the Abwehr Amt., and also render their reports direct to their own headquarter sections, only passing a copy to Leverkuehn [Leverkühn] for his information and not necessarily his approval.
5. W/T traffic between KO NO and the OKW is passed by the W/T station in the German Embassy building in Istanbul; the staff of which are under the command, for discipline and administration, of Vice Admiral von der Marwitz whose office is also situated in that building. All incoming and outgoing messages are decoded and encoded by the W/T staff and all messages are handled by the Naval Attaché's office which passes the enclair texts by special office servants (and not by consular officials) to the KO NO. OKW messages which include Abwehr messages are encoded by a special procedure. Messages for the Consulate General, however, are sent in the normal foreign office code which is kept in the safe of the Chancellor.
6. It is the general policy of the Abwehr to appoint the Leiters I/H, I/M, I/Luft to the posts of Assistant Military Attaché, Assistant Naval Attaché and Assistant Air Attaché, respectively. Source has produced a chart shown in Appendix 'D' which is largely self-explanatory. The German Foreign Office naturally provided the staff (diplomatic) for their Embassy in Ankara, Consulate General in Istanbul and various consulates in Turkey. The Attaché Department of the OKW naturally provided the service attachés who have their main offices in the Embassy in Ankara with the exception of the Naval Attaché whose office is situated in Istanbul. The Abwehr appoint officers for the I/H, I/M, and I/Luft to their respective attaché departments under which cover they work. In the case of Turkey, the Abw. II representative works under the cover of the 'Regierungs Rat'. The Abw. III representative works in Istanbul under the cover of 'Konsulats Sekretaer'.
7. Under the control of the Dienstellenleiter there are aussenstellen at Izmir, Ankara, Adana, Iskendeun and Trabzon, for details of which see Appendix 'C'.
8. Source states that the KO NO has the strictest instructions not on any account to engage in espionage against Turkey and that even if sources should offer them information on the Turkish armed forces they should refuse to handle it. Source adds that KO Bulgaria is responsible for espionage against Turkey and as far as the source is aware none of the KO NO representatives in Turkey hold German diplomatic cover.

9. At Appendix 'E' is attached a list of cover names supplied by the source and used by KO NO, Aussenstellen, and officers and at Appendix 'F' is a further list of various Abwehr cover names.

Attached to this summary were four pages of diagrams created by Vermehren to illustrate KONO's internal structure and its links to Berlin. The other appendices included some forty cover names which, when delivered to the Radio Security Service cryptanalysts, opened up the accumulated and current ISOS traffic by identifying each individual referred to. He also listed five Abwehr officers active outside KONO, headed by Willi Hamburger.

This first interrogation report amounted to a significant breakthrough for SIME and its parent agency, MI5, because, for the reasons previously described, SIS had exercised great caution in its direct contact with Abwehr personnel. In fact, such engagement as there had been, was limited to just two individuals. The first was Major Richard Wurmann, who had been captured on the Tunisian border in November 1942 as he fled the Allied liberation of Algiers, where he had headed the local Abwehrstellen. Brought to London for interrogation, Wurmann agreed to cooperate with his captors and in January 1943, codenamed HARLEQUIN, he acquired the status of 'a reference library for all matters affecting the Abwehr'. Much of Wurmann's value lay in the fact that none of his German colleagues had the slightest inkling that he had switched allegiance, and every reason to believe that his cover, as part of the German Armistice Commission in Algiers, had remained intact. Thus, HARLEQUIN became a walking encyclopedia on all aspects of the Abwehr. Indeed, measures were taken to ensure that his subordinates, who had also been taken into custody in North Africa, never learned of Wurmann's defection, and accepted the fiction that he had been hospitalised for medical treatment.

The second Abwehr inside source, Johnny Jebsen, was active from September 1943 until his arrest in May 1944. Codenamed ARTIST, Jebsen was based at the Lisbon KriegsOrganisation where he had handled the Popov brothers, Ivo and Dusan (DREADNOUGHT and TRICYCLE respectively). Jebsen was a delicate source because he had come to suspect that the Popovs were really double agents, working for the Allies. Although Jebsen was never under British control physically, and had been discouraged from defecting, he did hand over 'much useful information', but nothing akin to the material disclosed by Wurmann. Against this background, Vermehren represented a major coup, even if it was anticipated that the Abwehr were bound to take counter-measures to mitigate the damage inflicted on its networks.

On 27 January, the same day that SIS circulated its first interrogation report based on the first round of interviews with Vermehren, the III/F (Abwehr counter-espionage) representative, Thomas Ludwig, learned from a Turkish MIT contact that Leverkühn's subordinate had defected to the British, accompanied by his wife. He immediately reported the incident to Berlin and repeated that, as he had warned previously, he had harboured grave suspicions about the loyalty and intentions of another Abwehr staff member, Willi Hamburger. Ludwig's cable resulted in the arrival of Hans Milo Freund from Berlin who spent two weeks investigating the circumstances of Vermehren's defection, and the subsequent disappearance of both Hamburger and two other III/F agents, Karl and Stella von Kleczkowski. While KONO was in the midst of this crisis, Ludwig Moyzisch's former secretary, Cornelia Kapp, whose father was a German diplomat, defected to the Americans in Ankara. Consequently, Leverkühn was recalled to Berlin and replaced temporarily by Admiral von der Marwitz before the SD took over. In the Gestapo complaint against Leverkühn he was accused of

> having created an Anglo-Saxon atmosphere at the KO, giving too much freedom to his people to make controlled contact with the enemy, and having strong homosexual tendencies.

MI5 was unsure of Leverkühn's fate, as there were rumours that he had been shot in Germany. Naturally, Berlin was stunned by these events and in May 1944 Erich Pfeiffer was appointed as head of KONO. Pfeiffer was a seasoned Abwehr officer whose naval career had begun as a gunnery officer on the battleship *König* at Jutland. At the time, in 1944, Pfeiffer was engaged in negotiating with the Reich Foreign Ministry about Abwehr representation at the German Embassy in Ankara, having been recently promoted to Georg Hansen's deputy at Amt. I. In November 1943, he had conducted a brief four-day inspection tour of KONO at Hansen's request, because of concerns about Leverkühn's leadership style. On that occasion

> he had set out from Zossen well primed with the results achieved in Turkey recently, and he impressed on Leverkuehn [Leverkühn] the need to apply himself exclusively to military intelligence work, pointing out also that he observed a certain lack of coordination in the work of the several sections. It appeared that only the I/H section took direct orders from Leverkuehn; I/M, I/L, II, III, and Vermultung enjoyed considerable independence and took their orders directly from headquarters. The few Aussenstellen worked in a haphazard fashion.

According to the British-controlled double agent BLACKGUARD, who retained his access to KONO, the organisation was 'in pandemonium' with Kurt Zaehringer in particular apparently convinced that there was another traitor at large who had been responsible for the recent arrests of Fotuhi and KISS, threatening to exercise his own discipline and shoot Leverkühn and Ludwig.

After lengthy interrogation Leverkühn and his colleague Gottfried Schenker-Angerer were dismissed from the Abwehr, Leo von Koblensky was posted to Denmark and Eberhardt Momm was returned to the Luftwaffe to serve in an anti-aircraft unit. Meanwhile, Vermehren was undergoing questioning by SIME professionals whose task was to extract maximum information from their prisoner without even hinting at their access to ISOS, or to knowledge gathered by the management of double agents. Any question or approach that might betray a degree of insight had to be attributed to another prisoner, Otto Mayer, an Abwehr officer who had been wounded and captured by Partisans in an ambush near the Dalmatian coast in November 1943 and flown to Brindisi. However, although 40-year-old Mayer had undergone a preliminary interrogation by CSDIC in Bari, where a bullet was removed from a wound in his neck, he had not reached Camp 020, via Algiers and Prestwick, until *after* Vermehren had defected. It turned out that Mayer had also served in Istanbul, so information disclosed by Vermehren's interrogators gave the impression that they were seeking corroboration for his assertions, rather than material from infinitely more sensitive sources. Even better, the Abwehr (and Vermehren) were unaware of Mayer's exact fate and had no idea he had been handed over to the British for questioning, thus setting the scene for a classic triangulation strategy, pitting Mayer against Vermehren, and *vice versa*. Meanwhile, ISOS revealed that Ast Belgrade knew Mayer had been captured by Partisans but planned to negotiate his release in a prisoner exchange, an event then not uncommon in the Balkans.

While the Abwehr imploded in Istanbul, MI5 analysts were able to monitor Berlin's reactions through ISOS intercepts, and MI5's Herbert Hart assembled all the relevant texts in August 1944. The material was often hard to interpret as the original message was usually encrypted employing an internal code to conceal names and places. Staff identities were hidden behind codenames but some of the characters became very familiar to the analysts who translated the German clear text derived from Enigma encipherment. Chronologically, the first message was dated 2 February 1944, and was part of a longer signal from Istanbul to Berlin.

Part 2. For this reason he wished to obtain from country under all circumstances; after our letter of refusal 1196. This was sanctioned through agency of Herrn von Trott zu Sulsa in the AA and Marschall, Chief of Henke service, under pretext of I[ntelligence]. S[ervice]. activity on (corrupt) political sector in Turkey. (5 corrupt) NUNTIUS RONCALLI (6 corrupt) Proselytizer of Greek Orthodox Church. As reported in letter 7085/1464 the [von] Plettenberg woman entered country on 20 December with service passport of AA. Return journey was intended by 6998 on 28/2. Hereby Vermehren saw his plans endangered; he and his wife went over to the English. Was taken to Izmir, intended to fly direct to London by British special plane from neighbourhood of Bandirma. Turks are reported to have prevented his departure up to now, and have ordered closing of frontier. In this connection also VM of 6098 Dr. Hamburger working for British and American I[ntelligence] S[ervices]. Was given assignment by British to take over Vermehren's post with 6998, to carry on deception. According to investigations of VM of AST there also belonged to the traitor clique Herr and Frau Klekzkowski, further VM of SCHENKERA GERER HEROCK, also RIDIGER, In addition to those already reported by) 7082 also (6 corrupt); Director of Deutsche Bank Dr. BARTH, With exception of Vermehren all are Ostmaerker and absolutely opposed to NSDAP. Motive of traitors probably creation of a free Austria under Catholic leadership. Treason of group also for USA I[ntelligence] S[ervice], Hamburger, with Earle and director OWI BIT, with whom Frau Kletchkowski is supposed to have intimate relations and who is continually negotiating with group. BRITT is expected on 3rd February for further meeting with group in Istanbul. If Vermehren and his wife reach London, important political actions may he expected from enemy side, (part of msg. not rec'd.) Ast is trying to get Kleczkowskis to leave on pretext of meeting with MILO in Sofia, then Hamburger also, if necessary by use of special means, 6998 informed OKW today of Vermehren disappearance, will not however communicate above details until further investigation. Urgently request that you do not fail to take this into consideration in evaluation. I warned AST months ago about all those implicated and demanded their expulsion on grounds of unreliability, ALADIN too, applied without success, in Berlin for recall of Hamburger and the Kletczkowskis on basis of cur and other reports. Whole activity of the AST here exposed and nullified as far as Anglo Americans are concerned. Our Stelle is the least incriminated because as you know, we refused from the first to collaborate closely with Buero 6998 for reasons of security. Irresponsible behaviour of AA of HENCKE service. It is highly probably that eventual interplay of certain circles ... (continued).

Although badly fragmented, the text refers to the anti-Nazi diplomat Adam zu Trott and mentions the other defectors, Willi Hamburger (linked to the American minister George Earle) and the Klekzkowskis, but seems ill-informed, perhaps by the Turks, on Vermehren's escape plan as executed by the British. Four days later, on 6 February 1944, Berlin was in touch with Lisbon on the subject of Vermehren's mother, Petra. Doubtless the intention was to get her back to Germany so she could be used against her son as a hostage.

> The mother of the lawyer Dr. Vermehren, who went over to the English in Turkey is a correspondent for Das Reich in Lisbon. By order of Amtschef, Frau V[ermehren] is to be persuaded to cane back to Germany at once by suitable means, BELLING.

The next day, 7 February 1944, Lisbon replied to Berlin, concerning Vermehren's mother:

> No. 217. To PELLIS. 1) As reported confidentially by POLMANN representative here the son of Frau Vermehren in Lisbon has gone over to the English in Turkey. She herself is suspected of being an accessory. Frau Vermehren is as I worker and in contact with Ruser. A subsidiary of Ruser is said to have been arrested and to have declared that Ruser works for the Russian Officers' Committee. 2) Portugal friends warn us against an important V-mann of the English in Berlin who has access to our correspondence. With reference to communication of Portugal friends we think (he has access) to HERKULES's correspondence. Please treat POLMAN report as confidential. Details by courier.

This was the first ISOS intercept to disclose the news of Vermehren's defection, and it warned Berlin that his mother, Petra, then the local *Das Reich* correspondent in Lisbon (and an Abwehr Eins agent), was in contact with Hans Ruser, another newspaperman and putative defector. Codenamed JUNIOR by SIS, Ruser had been dismissed from the Madrid Abwehr in September 1942, and was then exfiltrated to England in November 1943. Perhaps significantly, The Lisbon KO also warned that some past communications had been compromised. On the following day, 8 February 1944, Berlin speculated about the Vermehrens' travel plans informed Lisbon:

> 40. Most secret. For CIRO. Confidential. Vermehren with wife, nee [*sic*] Graefin [von] Plettenberg, is probably flying within the next few days via Lisbon to London from Turkey. V[ermehren] was a solider with German Military Attaché and has taken flight as a traitor. Will probably meet in Lisbon his mother, the German journalist Petro or Carola Vermehren. Arrange for strict observation of the married couple and the mother. Ascertain with what papers V[ermehren] and his wife

are travelling. If it is possible to prevent departure to London by legal means, on the ground that V[ermehren] has embezzled German service funds, use every means possible to obtain this. In any case radio for Freund whatever is ascertained at your end. PELLIS 222.

On 9 February, the Lisbon KO responded to Berlin, warning that Verhehren, now codenamed DELFTER, who had deserted to the British, could compromise an asset, Viktor Bogomolz. The information came from LUDOVICO, actually Ludwig von Auenrode, the head of the KriegsOrgaisation. Evidently, von Auenrode believed Vermehren could endanger Bogomolz, a White Russian who had worked for the British for many years, first in Istanbul, and then in Paris.

(Contd) Vermehren knows [Viktor] BOGM'OLEZ. B[OGMOLEZ] was previously a for (Roman) I. About 2 years ago LUDOVICO received orders from Berlin to resume contact with B[OGMOLEZ]. B[OGMOLEZ] refused. Portugal friends now reveal that GUILLERMO's journeys to Lisbon were reported by B[OGMOLEZ] to the English and the Americans further that HIOBI's intended meeting at the beginning of October last year with important worker at a *quinta* (a country house) at this end when he (HIOB) was in Lisbon with GUILLERMO was betrayed to the Allies by the same route. Place and time of the meeting were transmitted by Berlin by W/T to this end. [The] Meeting place was kept under surveillance by the Allies and the police, but a day later. Activity of the worker BALLHORN I AST II was largely betrayed t the Allies and Portugal friends through the same channel. BALLHORN is in the know about this and (will be) in Berlin in the next few days. (possibly part missing). The journalist Koester who is suspected of espionage and who is being called up at present through Wehrbezirkskommando Ausland in Germany was also in contact at this end with Vermehren's wife.

On 9 February, Berlin sent instructions to Lisbon:

Ref Petra Vermehren. Ref your signal of 8/2. The son of Petra V[ermehren] has gone over to the English in Turkey and they intend to take him to London. This may happen any date. Hence there is no time left to recall Vermehren through the Reich. You are therefore to instruct Vermehren at once from your end to return to the Reich.

Also, on 9 February, the Bucharest to Vienna channel disclosed:

11. For BAUER. Most Secret. Urgently notify SCHILL (ROBERT) that Dr Vermehren has probably deserted. Ast Vienna Liter I.

On the next day, 10 February, Lisbon sent further news:

> Urgent 55. To ERBE for BELLING. Petra Vermehren leaves RODING [Lisbon] by plane on 11/2, arrives TOR 12/2. NERBACK ACHERN has been requested to arrange for her to fly on. I recommend that arrest should not be carried out at either MOENICH, STUTTGART or at ROT. Because of my suggestions to her she is expecting MOENICH Leiter at TOR to indicate a hotel to spend the night. She will therefore not be surprised if a representative of STRAUCH or EICH offers to escort her. I have forbidden her to communicate with relatives beforehand. She has learned through Reuter report of her son's high treason, but in spite of this has declared herself ready for journey to Reich. To allay the greater part of her suspicions I gave her a card of recommendation for STRAUCH-Leiter. ENZMANN.

Also, on 10 February, Berlin was in contact with Sofia:

> Most Secret. No. 43. From VERA No. 13. AST Vienna Leiter I For CARA for Chief personally. The following W/T message has been received from Istanbul. Strictly confidential. Dr Vermehren. POSTER's first Milarbeiter, has probably deserted to the English. He is informed about SCHILL's activity. Checkup (or: We are checking up) to see whether it is advisable, in the circumstances for SCHILL to enter Turkey. All transmissions ISOLIE, MIMI, DIANA, KASSAK stopped until the situation is clarified.

Also, on 10 February 1944, Lisbon confirmed to Berlin that Colonel Hans Milo Freund was to begin his inquiries in Istanbul:

> 257. It is communicated for information that Oberstleutnant Freund is flying to Istanbul on 11/2 in the matter of Vermehren.

On 11 February 1944, Lisbon reported to Berlin:

> To ERBE BELLING. Petra Vermehren left RODING by air at 1500 hours today. Search for Erich Vermehren and wife instituted as early as 7/2. The agents (Agenten) available on the airfields have been ordered to report every air-passenger landing here from Cairo, Halma or Vetschau. Any possibility of preventing Erich V[ermehren] from leaving the country will be by illegal means only. Please radio a personal description of Erich V[ermehren] and wife. ENZMANN.

Also, on 11 February 1944, Berlin to Lisbon:

1. Most Secret. No. 148. For ELCANO. For DON I. Ref. Dr. Vermehren.

Dr. Vermehren is traveling [sic] with his wife, nee [sic] Graefin [von] Plettenberg from Istanbul to London via Spain – Portugal at the beginning of February 1944, on behalf of the English. He will probably meet his mother, the German journalist Petra Vermehren in Lisbon. Vermehren has close (?) personal contacts with worker Jebsen of (ROM.) I, who is controlled by HOEFLINGER. Keep observation on any intercourse between Jebsen and Vermehren. Jebsen should on no account be informed. CIRO has been informed. JUNTA No. 1478 Most Secret of 11/2/44. Berlin-Lisbon, No. 62. For CIRO. Ref. Dr. Vermehren. Ref our W/T message of 8/2/44 (see previous sheet). Dr. Vermehren has personal connections with worker Jebsen of (Rom) I, who is controlled by HOEFINGER. Keep observation of any intercourse between Jebsen and Vermehren. PELLIS No. 337.

On 14 February 1944, Berlin replied:

To ENZMANN. Ref. Married couple Vermehren. Ref above message. SOMMERHAUS has instructed Konto RODING to prevent by all possible means the Vermehrens traveling [sic] on. Compromising of Konto is however to be avoided. On enquiry it was stated that 'by all possible means' everything except the most extreme measures. On ENZER's orders also the married couple are to be prevented from continuing their journey within the limits of the means stated above. Christian name not Erich but Kurt. Following personal description of married couple. Continued ...

Berlin to Lisbon. Dr, V 25 year of age, height 165, slim, medium-fair, long hair, blue eyes. Neither have any special distinguishing marks. Photographs follow with BAUER. TURM.

On 15 February 1944, Lisbon replied:

To RUEM. Ref. Above message. 'Plane air-line Cairo SUND AG (England) did not fly this time via RODING (Lisbon) but direct SUND AG from Gibraltar on 12/2. VM ascertained from British Overseas in RODING that there were in this (plane) SUND AG military commission from Turkey whose personalities are not in hand at British Overseas at this end. It must be expected that the Vermehren couple travelled in this 'plane or are using another 'plane to SUND AG which is not starting from this end. Measures at this end will nevertheless be continued. ENZANNIN JNR.

On 16 February 1944, Sofia to Berlin:

80. ANDREAS HOLM 1) Correct name and activities of BACH given away by Dr. Vermehren to English and Turks. I immediately ordered him to leave country for this end and asked YOK to find some other means of carrying on the network in the meantime.
Addendum to address: For PASA, CARA 618.

Also, on 16 February 1944, Lisbon-Berlin.

257. To PELLIS. Ref. FETUS No. 337 of 11/2/44 (above of 12/2/44). Worker JONNY, after [an] interview with Petra Vermehren who informed him of the affair, reported his personal acquaintance with the Vermehren family. The departure of Petra Vermehren invalidates assignment of shadowing JONNY. HARRY considers JONNY reliable. LUDOVICO CIRO.

On 17 February 1944, British intercept operators monitored a signal on the Zagreb to Prague channel:

To RHSA AMT IV and VI Berlin. Ref. Kleckowsky and Hamburger. Radio Ankara reports om 14/2/44 that according to SSO EXPRESS the 2 German secret agents Kleckowsky and Hamburger, both Austrians, have come over to the enemy. They were working in Istanbul. The alleged head of the German Secret Service in Istanbul, Vermehren, had already fled from Turkey and is said to have gone to Lisbon. According to [an] earlier radio report from Ankara V[ermehren] was deputy Military Attache. His wife is nearly related to ambassador von Papen. After 6 months preparation for flight and making contact with Secret Service he hid for a few days before his flight in the English Embassy. His wife was with him. Ankara further reports that the German Military Attaché has been taken to the Reich by 4 Gestapo agents on account of V[ermehren]'s flight. Sgd. BLUHM.

On 19 February 1944, on the Istanbul-Sofia circuit:

CAA for PASA. 1) If PASA enters the country here, he will be compromised as he has been betrayed by Vermehren. Do not enter under any circumstances. 2) SQUA's journey now impossible. MILO YOK.1120.

On 22 February 1944, Berlin-Istanbul:

To 7085. Please send with this week's courier post detailed collective report about Vermehren case. From this it must be clearly recognisable above all which are your own discoveries and which those from outside. AST, etc. 6986.

To 7085. Paul Sternkowski born 18/7/87 Berlin and his wife Martha Sternkowski born 5/10/90 Berlin formerly domiciled Istanbul, Galata Poste Kutusu 1449, are trying to establish contact with me. I request your estimation of the persons mentioned. DR. SCHMITZ.

On 28 February 1944, Sofia responded to Berlin:

124 for FLETT. RASCHID, SHEIKH and Hamburger in internment camp at Damascus. Vermehren has been in service of England for some considerable time. Source: KAPFEN of GIBSON. MILO. KUKS 777 C.

On 8 March 1944, Istanbul to Sofia:

14. Assignment of SCHILL and BACH betrayed to the Turkish and English I[ntelligence] S[ervices]. by Vermehren. Both were also known exactly to RASCIHD. Grave objections therefore to entry. YOIC 1135.

On 4 September 1944, Lisbon-Madrid 2:

534. To VI Z PELLIS. And DON 1. MARTIN reports that the Allied I[ntelligence] S[ervices] at this end have now received instructions not to accept any more deserters, the Vermehrens mentioned (as an instance – text d'ful). Reich Germans who offer themselves can be interrogated but not supported or taken over. CIRO.

On 12 August 1944, Istanbul signaled Berlin to give an assurance that the recent defection of Kurt Beigl was entirely unexpected:

After the desertion of [Kurt] Beigl KO is trying to make this Dienstelle responsible because of the extension of his sojourn. Beigl came here in connection with AST MOB network. He worked until the last of AST W/T stations which had already been betrayed by Vermehren and built up again with old VM because the police (took) no action. KO attached MOB contacts to these owing to lack of other W/T stations. Attitude of Beigl could not be foreseen even by KO. A fortnight previously, also, he had not returned, it was said, and this was not expected on account of the AST W/T stations, can now be asserted. 504.

Although an Austrian, Beigl had a long history of loyal service to the Abwehr, since his recruitment in 1937, having joined the Brandenburger regiment in February 1940, and had been a party member for many years.

However, as he explained to his SIME interrogators, he had been posted to Abwehr II in Bucharest in February 1942, and then had been selected to build a stay-behind network in Turkey, run from Sofia, and equipped with transmitters in Erzerum, Adana and Istanbul, which he felt certain must have been betrayed by Vermehren. Clearly the rot had set in if men of Beigl's calibre were willing to desert to the Allies. Having made contact with SIS in Istanbul in August 1944, Beigl and his wife, Hildegard, caught a train to Aleppo to be interned. He was then transferred to Cairo and during his interviews with SIME he was asked about his friendship with Vermehren and, specifically, why his controller, Schnick, had left Turkey on 29 January 1944, so soon after Vermehren's defection.

> Beigl replied that Schnick rarely stayed more than eight or ten days in Turkey after which he returned to Bucharest. He did not think this particular journey had anything to do with the Vermehren affair; Schnick had never discussed it, and had not mentioned receiving any special orders to report back to his Headquarters.
> On Feb 21st or 23rd, Beigl received orders from Ludwig to report to Sofia because of Vermehren's defection. In Sofia Beigl was not questioned about Vermehren but was told that he might return to Turkey. He asked if he might visit his father in Grenzen near Vienna.
> DELIUS told him to go for two or three weeks, after which he must report to Abwehr Headquarters in Zossen, near Berlin to speak to Obst Holman (believed to be Abw. I-H).
> Holman asked Beigl if he knew Vermehren. Beigl replied that they had been good friends. Holman said he did not know how things were going. Beigl was to return to his mother, and would receive further instructions through Zvirner, now of Ast-Vienna, as to whether he was to return to Turkey or to remain in Austria. Beigl spent only about ten minutes with Holman and only one day in Berlin, after which he returned to his mother. Sometime in April Zvirner telephoned that Beigl was to report to his office. On his arrival, Zvirner told him to go to Bucharest and pick up Schnick, with whom he would return to Turkey. They arrived in Istanbul on 25 April. Schnick did not say whether he had been in contact with the Abwehr concerning Vermehren, but only mentioned that they had to restart work on their story-behind organisation. [Thomas] Ludwig was very annoyed, with Schnick, and Beigl for returning to Turkey, and said they must return to Bucharest because everything about their W/T network had been discovered. Schnick left Turkey for the last time, after his usual ten or fourteen day sojourn, but Beigl had to wait until his papers had gone through the official closing. They did not arrive until July, when Uppenborm told him to hurry away because they still had to arrange the transfer of one set from Dijatrbekir to Istanbul.

Beigl was not the last of the defectors to be inspired by the haemorrhage from Istanbul. Soon afterwards the German consul general in Geneva, named Kraul, followed their example and defected to the Allies, although this particular episode was never revealed publicly.

Over the next two months Vermehren was questioned by Security Intelligence Middle East in Cairo and provided his interrogators with enough detailed information to complete six lengthy reports, which were circulated and resulted in the identification of virtually every Abwehr asset in the region. Also compromised were their secret writing and other communications techniques. Meanwhile, his mother Petra returned voluntarily to Germany where she was incarcerated at the Oranienburg concentration camp neat Berlin.

Vermehren would not reach England until 13 April 1944, when he landed at RAF Lyneham, beading a British passport in the name of Eric Vollmer, on a flight from Gibraltar, his wife having fallen ill with pneumonia in Algiers. He was escorted to SIS's headquarters in Broadway for a brief interview, and then was accommodated in the Chelsea flat owned by Kim Philby's mother, at 7 Grove Court, Drayton Gardens. There he remained for the next seventeen months until September 1945, initially employed as a consultant by the Political Warfare Executive, and then as a teacher at the Roman Catholic schools at Beaumont College, Crawley and then Worth Priory. At this point, in October 1945, Vermehren made contact with his family in Germany to explain himself and his 'breach of trust'. His sister, Isa, who had become a nun, and elder brother, Michael, had survived imprisonment, as had Elisabeth's youngest sister, Gisela, who later wrote a memoir, *A Journey Through the Final Act*, about her experiences in Ravensbrück, Buchenwald and Dachau concentration camps.

After the Second World War, the Vermehrens acquired British nationality and, changing their surname to de Saventham, lived in Switzerland. When interviewed in April 1982 Vermehren claimed not to have known that many observers considered that his defection had been the catalyst for the SD takeover of the Abwehr, and the momentous events that followed. He seemed reluctant to accept any responsibility for the collapse of the KONO networks across the Middle East, although he remained annoyed at the publicity his defection had received at the time. Evidently he had imagined that he could simply switch sides without attracting any attention, and perhaps had not considered the propaganda value of his desertion. He died in Bonn in April 2005, seven years after losing his wife, and before his extensive SIME file was declassified and released to The National Archives in Kew.

As the Cold War developed, some of the key figures in the British intelligence community drew on their experience gained during the Second World War to cope with other adversaries, directed from Moscow. Maurice Oldfield, Myles Ponsonby, Harry Shergold, Alex Kellar, Bill Magan, Dick White, Arthur Martin and Douglas Roberts, among many others, learned their trade in the Middle East and understood the immense, incomparable value of the self-recruited defector who has accumulated enough information to betray not just a few agents or their networks, but an entire intelligence organisation. Vermehren fatally undermined KONO and in the three months before D-Day the Abwehr was in a state of collapse, its staff distracted by the SD or preoccupied with plotting the Führer's (Adolf Hitler's) assassination.

There were many intelligence lessons learned in the Middle East, such as strategic deception, the management of double agents, and the exploitation of signals intelligence during a ground campaign, and all would be applied with great effect in Normandy, four years after the British Expeditionary Force had been evacuated from the European continent. In the intervening period the conflict in Europe had been fought largely at sea and in the air, so the North African campaign provided the only opportunity to acquire and hone the skills that would become so relevant during and after D-Day, and then be applied against the Soviets.

Chapter II

GRIGORI TOKAEV

Mr Hayter's friends inform us that exhaustive tests have given as near a guarantee as possible that he is not a double agent.

Foreign Office memorandum,
12 June 1948

A lecturer in jet engine technology and rocket propulsion at Moscow's Zhukovsky Air Force Academy, 39-year-old Colonel Grigori Tokaev was a scientist who had spent much of his career at the elite Institute of Engineers and Geodesics. Born in October 1909 and having graduated from the Moscow Higher Technical School in 1932, he underwent training at the Zhukovsky Military Air Academy. However, at the end of the Second World War he was transferred to Berlin with instructions from General Ivan Serov to recruit as many German scientists with a knowledge of missile research as he could find. In this context the NKVD's reference to recruitment meant kidnapping, and when Tokaev discovered that Professor Kurt Tank, Focke-Wulf's chief aircraft designer in Bremen was listed for abduction, he underwent a crisis of conscience.

While serving as a scientific advisor to the Soviet Control Commission, under the direct command of Marshals Georgi Zhukov and then Vasili Sokolovsky, Tokaev was called to the Kremlin in April 1947 to assess the work of the German experts already in harness and complete an evaluation of a rocket-powered bomber designed by Eugen Sänger. For the first time, Tokaev was indoctrinated into a Soviet missile development programme to be targeted against the West.

Appalled by the ruthlessness of the NKVD, Tokaev was also preoccupied by the fear that he himself might be kidnapped by an émigré organisation, and by the worry that the NKVD had learned of his support for Leon Trotsky. Unable to bear the pressure any longer, Tokaev crossed into the British sector with his wife Aza Baeva and their 8-year-old daughter Bella in early November 1947 and surrendered first to the military authorities, and then to the SIS station in Berlin headed by John Bruce Lockhart, who had him flown to RAF Northolt, to be installed with the initial codename STORK in a Kensington safe house.

The British received Tokaev with enthusiasm and elaborate arrangements were made to exploit the coup. The head of the RAF's security branch, Owen de Putron, assigned a linguist, Molly Sasson, to act as case officer and a senior air intelligence officer,[1] Christopher Hartley, was given the task of supervising the defector's resettlement and collating his information. The family, accompanied by Sasson, continued to live in their safe house under MI5's protection until a suspected assassin was detected outside the building, an incident that prompted a swift evacuation to an isolated farmhouse in Kingsbridge, Devon, owned by a retired SIS officer, Fred Winterbotham, who had previously headed the organisation's air intelligence section.

As well as the valuable technical information that Tokaev was willing to disclose, he revealed when questioned a further dimension, claiming to be in contact with a reliable source inside the Politburo's secretariat. From SIS's viewpoint, the prospect of this additional recruitment opportunity was an extra bonus and the source was tentatively identified as a Central Committee official, Petr I. Dubuvoi. When pressed by his interrogator, Tokaev named his intermediary as one Yarotsky, and mentioned involvement with a subversive underground group active across the Soviet Union.

At the end of November 1947, MI5's deputy director-general, Guy Liddell, discussed STORK with a senior RAF officer and recorded the conversation in his diary:

> I had a word with Air Marshal Lawrence Pendred about STORK the Russian defector from the equivalent of RAE Farnborough. He said that a lot of extremely valuable information had already been obtained. He seemed to have the answer to everything. I asked Pendred whether previous estimates about the potentialities of the Russian Air Force were confirmed. He said that from what he had been able to gather so far the Russians were not nearly so far as we thought they were.[2]

Tokaev also played a role in April 1948 in the defection of Colonel Yuri D. Tasoev, head of the Soviet Reparations Committee in Bremen, whom Tokaev had recommended to SIS as a potential agent several months earlier. A period of cultivation followed, codenamed Operation HOUSE PARTY, and then a meeting was convened at which, quite unexpectedly Tasoev, codenamed CAPULET, asked for political asylum.

Contact with Tasoev had been attained initially through an American intermediary, the local United States director of G-2 military intelligence, General Robert Walsh. The final meeting took place on 23 April 1948 at the home of the director of Bremen's United States Port Operations, Stanley A. Clem when, against Tokaev's advice, delivered in their native Ossetian language, Tasoev decided there and then to defect. They drove to Hamburg, where they spent the night together, sleeping in the same room, and then, after sharing a midday meal, drove to a British aircraft for a flight to England. The plane, on temporary loan to SIS, was the personal transport of the Chief of the Imperial General Staff, Field Marshal Bernard Montgomery, and had flown Tokaev to Bremen the previous day.

Tasoev's meeting with Tokaev had been arranged apparently in the hope that both men could boost each other's morale and demonstrate SIS's capacity to attract and protect defectors. It was also hoped that the operation would 'loosen Tokaev's tongue' as he had become increasingly capricious and reticent. However, the encounter was not a success and each accused the other of being a traitor. While Tokaev appeared very shaken by the episode, Tasoev's confidence was completely undermined and on 7 May 1948, at the first opportunity, fled his safe house, a six-roomed flat at 19 Rugby Mansions, in Bishop King's Road, Kensington, managed by SIS's Betty Wiggins, and asked a patrolling police constable in Olympia to take him to the Soviet Embassy. Tasoev was then escorted to Hammersmith police station where he was incarcerated while embarrassed Foreign Office staff arranged for him to be repatriated to Gatow, on 20 May 1948, to the Russian kommandantura in Berlin. SIS concluded that CAPULET's change of heart had been prompted by his fear of retribution against his 20-year-old son Vasili, then a student in Moscow.

The Tasoev debacle proved extremely awkward, especially when the matter was raised in the House of Commons and the TASS news agency reported that the officer had been abducted by Tokaev and British intelligence personnel. On 7 July 1948, a Foreign Office minister, Kenneth Younger, who had himself served in MI5 during the Second World War, undertook the delicate task of fielding mischievous questions from radical backbenchers, among them Geoffrey Bing MP. The SIS Chief, Sir Stewart Menzies, came in for particular opprobrium and was privately accused of having bungled the affair, his line that SIS had no suitable facilities in Germany in which to hold and question Tasoev seemed very thin. He certainly acted outside the JIC's guidelines on the handling of defectors and the ensuing inter-agency spat drew in MI5 too, with the Security Service highly resentful of SIS's behaviour, and its failure to understand that even foreign nationals could not be locked up indefinitely without any legal grounds. To make matters worse, General Lucius Clay expressed his disapproval of the way American personnel had been drawn into the affair. In the aftermath, it emerged that Menzies had orchestrated Tasoev's recruitment largely to placate Tokaev, and that SIS had really intended to support Tokaev's grandiose schemes for establishing and sustaining an underground anti-Soviet movement. By humouring Tokaev, Menzies had sought to extract yet more technical data from the defector who was expressing signs of resentment towards his hosts.

According to his file, Tokaev was much chastened by the fiasco and became considerably more cooperative, evidently conscious that the Soviets had turned the entire event to their advantage, alleging that Tasoev had been assaulted and kidnapped. Both MI5 and SIS could agree that the incident would have a negative impact on future attempts at defection from the eastern bloc.

In London, Tokaev, who adopted the Ossetian version of his name, Tokaty, was codenamed EXCISE and debriefed by a Russian-speaking SIS officer, Wilfred Dunderdale (alias Mr Douglas), at the Special Liaison Centre in Ryder Street where his trenchant political opinions were given wide circulation by the newly created Information Research Department, resulting in a series of articles published by the *Sunday Express* in January 1949. However, his controversial views caused considerable adverse comment in Whitehall where his analysis was largely unwelcome, and there had been widespread dismay concerning a press conference called in September 1948, which had been intended to introduce Tokaev to selected newspaper journalists. Instead, the ill-prepared event, hosted by his literary agent, Cyrus Brooks, of A.M. Heath & Co., descended into a bitter argument between the Russian correspondents and the other attendees. Photographers were not allowed to take his picture, Communists tried to monopolise the proceedings, and the whole affair was regarded as a colossal flop, causing SIS, and Robin Brook in particular, much anxiety.

While SIS regarded Tokaev as a valuable asset, and IRD saw the immense propaganda advantages of publicising his anti-Stalin treatises, the Foreign Office's northern department, responsible for Russian policy, became increasingly alarmed at his potential impact on Anglo-Soviet relations. The IRD had been created by Christopher Mayhew MP to counter Moscow's growing influence, and he had the support of the virulently anti-Communist Foreign Secretary Ernest Bevin, who was entertained to tea by Tokaev, but the day-to-day management of the small group was in the hands of Ralph Murray, who was not then a senior figure. Accordingly, the IRD and its activities were never especially popular in King Charles Street, and even the chairman of the Joint Intelligence Committee, William Hayter, would express reservations about Tokaev's perceived volatility. As Tokaev became increasingly restless at his confinement and continuing interrogation, he spent much time drafting slightly eccentric memoranda on such diverse topics as Soviet meddling in Palestine, the split with Tito and Stalin's policy toward Mao Zedong. He also wrote numerous pamphlets, supposedly for clandestine distribution in the Soviet Union by White Russians, but these initiatives led to him being described by one official as 'becoming a little unbalanced'. Astonishingly, in mid-July 1948, there was speculation in the Foreign Office that Tokaev might be 'a very long-term plant and may be wishing to reassure Moscow'. Hayter was especially critical, remarking 'the more I see of EXCISE's products the more difficult I find it to regard him as a serious character'. Nevertheless, apart from his somewhat odd political views, Tokaev answered questionnaires assiduously and drew up personality profiles of the leading Soviets he had known. These in turn served to enhance SIS's reputation for gathering accurate military, political and technical information.

Undeterred, Tokaev continued to submit unsolicited reports and commentaries on current events for the prime minister and foreign secretary. Discontent about him even extended to his protection. SIS employed a single retired, unarmed Special Branch detective, Inspector Dew, to act as Tokaev's sole bodyguard, but by any standards this provided inadequate coverage.

Despite the setbacks and a deteriorating relationship with Whitehall, SIS proposed another scheme to acquire a Soviet defector, Colonel Tyupanov, who had been identified as likely to be persuaded to seek political asylum, but Tokaev was doubtful about his motives and the project was shelved.

Tokaev's interviews subsequently formed the basis of his two autobiographies, *Betrayal of an Ideal*, published in 1955[3], and *Comrade X*,[4] released the following year. They also attracted adverse comment, which resulted in libel actions being brought against the Communist publications *Daily Worker* and *Russia Today*.

Tokaev subsequently pursued a distinguished academic career at Imperial College London, Cranfield College and City, University of London. He also participated in NASA's Apollo lunar programme and retired from City, University of London in 1975 following allegations that he had given illicit assistance to the examination results of some of his students. He died in Cheam in November 2003, and his British Foreign Office file was declassified two decades later, which contained the following MI5 case summary:

> In August 1948 MI5's Soviet espionage research section completed an analysis of the Tokaev case.[5]
>
> TOKAEV was born on 13.10.1909 near Vladikavkaz in the Caucasus. He is of Ossetian origin which he describes as a small minority of Indo-Iranians living in the Northern Caucasus. Son of a peasant family, he had the normal upbringing of a Caucasian peasant and although he attended the usual village school and later graduated to secondary schools etc., he was in his early years, almost entirely self-educated. He joined the Communist Party in February 1932 having previously been a member of the Komsomol.
>
> In July 1932 he obtained nomination as a student at the Zukhov Military/Air Academy in Moscow where he studied for five years, qualifying as an 'aero-constructor' in 1937. He was appointed an engineer in the aero-dynamics laboratory in the same Academy, eventually becoming the head of the laboratory. In December 1940 he was transferred to the appointment of deputy head of a department in the Academy and on 16.4.41 he became a Doctor of Science which he describes in German as '*Kandidat Technischer Wissenschaften*' of the same Academy. In November 1942 he became '*Dozent im Flugzeugbau*' and was appointed lecturer and in November 1944 he was appointed senior lecturer – honorary title of professor – at the Academy, During this period he lectured to other institutions, and had attained the rank of Engineer Lieutenant-Colonel.
>
> At the end of the [Second World] war, on the 28th June 1945, TOKAEV arrived in Germany on appointment to the Abteilung Luftwaffe at the SIA Karlshorst, Berlin, remaining there, however, only five weeks. On the formation of the Allied Control Authority Secretariat (U.S. Sector of Berlin) he was appointed Joint General Secretary of the Russian element of this Allied Secretariat, where he remained until 6th March 1946. During this period he had occasion to meet a large number of British, American and French officials, and he realised for the first time in his life that these people were human beings and moreover gave an impression of freedom of thought and action which was quite contrary to his Soviet

upbringing. At this time TOKAEV apparently had several conversations with his Western friends about possibilities of visiting their countries.

On the 6th March 1946 he transferred at his own request to the SIA. Although he had been extremely interested in the work of the Allied Secretariat and above all with the contacts he had been able to make there, he realised that he was not a clerk but a technician, hence the request to be returned to the duties with which he was familiar.

In the SIA he had the general assignment of collecting all possible information on German aero-dynamics. In addition he had certain subsidiary tasks from time to time. As examples of these he gave:-

(a) To discover in detail the organisation and structure of the German Luftfahrtforschung Akademie which is next door to the GAF Ministry in Berlin. This task was on direct instructions from MALENKOV in Moscow.
(b) To examine and obtain all available information on the project SANGER. This was a so-called project thought up by SANGER for a supersonic long range very high altitude jet propelled bomber which had been discovered by TOKAEV and a few more engineers in 1945. Moscow expressed great interest in this project.
(c) To try to persuade SANGER and certain of his colleagues to transfer to Moscow; this again was on direct orders from MALENKOV, VOSNESENSKY and General SEROV but TOKAEV was unable to carry out this assignment.
(d) Throughout the whole of his service in Germany he was consultant on air development matters to Marshal SOKOLOVSKY. He was taken to Moscow by the Marshal on two occasions to act as his advisor at conferences in the Politburo.

In October 1946, TOKAEV was called to Moscow by the Soviet Foreign Office as consultant in the preparation of the air clause of a German peace treaty. He was required to prepare a report stating which German aircraft experts were still in Germany and which had been taken to the West.

In April 1947 TOKAEV was again summoned to Moscow where he was told by VOSNESENSKY, a member of the Politburo, Deputy Prime Minister, and chairman of the State Planning Commission:-

Comrade TOKAEV, we have asked you to come in order to have your views on SANGER's project; they say you are opposed to it; is that so or not? Give us your observations.

TOKAEV expressed his views which were briefly that SANGER's project did not exist – that the material described as a project only represented rough notes and an interrupted formulation of an interesting idea. It would require extensive and very serious research to build such an aeroplane as SANGER had visualised. Out of the discussions arising from this meeting a project was formulated which included the following:-

The Soviet of Ministers of the USSR directs:-

A Commission is to be created composed of the following, Colonel General YAKOVLEV, Engineer Lieutenant Colonel TOKAEV, Academican KELDISH and Professor KISHKIN.

This Commission is to proceed to Germany to carry out research for further details and specialists dealing with SANGER's project. On completion of this task the Commission will submit a reasoned report on the practical possibility of realising SANGER's project.

Marshal SOKOLOVSKY is to afford the Commission all possible assistance.

On the following day TOKAEV was taken to see Stalin, MOLOTOV, MALENKOV, ZHKINOV, BULGANIN, VOROSHILOV, MIKOYAN, BERIA, V0SNESENSKY and SHVERNIK.

Stalin asked TOKAEV about SANGER's project and TOKAEV again repeated his reservations. Under Stalin's direction it was there and then arranged that the Commission with General SEROV instead of General YAKOVLEV should be set up and should present its report by the 1st August. While TOKAEV was in the room Stalin telephoned SOKOLOVSKY, told him that TOKAEV's chief in Germany, KUTSEVALOV, was being removed, and said that TOKAEV was to be made deputy to whoever took charge of the Air Department. On the next day, the 10th April 1947, the Commission left for Germany.

General SEROV and TOKAEV immediately had a sharp dispute about the former's treatment of one of the German scientists. Next SEROV on his own initiative appointed to the Commission Stalin's son, a man of whom TOKAEV had a very low opinion. At the end of April a telegram was sent to Stalin stating that the Commission had so far failed to find any further materials or specialists on SANGER's project. TOKAEV at the same time, with the knowledge of the Commission, sent his own telegram to the effect that his attitude to the SANGER project remained unchanged, and that in his opinion the methods of the Commission were all wrong.

TOKAEV was immediately summoned by SOKOLOVSKY who told him that MALENKOV was very displeased by his behaviour and that he was to drop his obstinacy and his personal intrigues.

VORSHNIKOV had instructed SEROV, KELDISH and KISHKIN to proceed to Moscow and the work of the Commission was to be handed over to General ALEXANDROV, TOKAEV refused to work under ALEXANDROV whom he considered quite unsuitable and whom he personally disliked.

Marshal SOKOLOVSKI flew into a terrible rage and in spite of his objections, TOKAEV started work with the Commission under ALEXANDROV on the May 1947.

The burden of the work of the Commission fell on TOKAEV's shoulders. Meanwhile LANGE, one of the German scientists working for the Russians, had drawn up a plan for starting a construction office to design an elaborate supersonic aircraft. TOKAEV protested against this plan as he did not think LANGE and his team were capable of designing such a plane. Moscow, however, approved the aircraft and asked that a Russian report should be provided regarding the LANGE Group's proposals, TOKAEV met the LANGE Group and after a long exchange of ideas, the Group presented an ambitious programme of work. This was forwarded to Moscow together with TOKAEV's comments which were to the effect that he did not consider that the LANGE Group was worthy of any serious attention.

About two weeks later TOKAEV was informed that he was relieved of work on the Commission. He became aware that he was falling under suspicion and furthermore a number of his friends and colleagues were disappearing, lie asked Stalin's son whether he could be received by Stalin to talk about the work of the Commission, but he was told not to worry. He also wrote a request to be allowed to return to the USSR.

In July 1947, General SEROV unexpectedly arrived back in Germany and told TOKAEV that they must start looking for specialists in designing jet-propelled aircraft engines. TOKAEV said that he had been removed from work on the Commission and he again asked to be allowed to return to Russia. SEROV, however, said that he was to stay in Germany and continue work on the LANGE/SANGER project. TOKAEV also became involved with an attempt to get another German scientist, Professor TANK, to cone to Russia, This negotiation was a most complicated one (TANK was a suspected British agent) and as a result of this it seems that TOKAEV fell more and more under suspicion, TANK had in fact been in contact with the British authorities. To suspect TANK was, therefore, reasonable] and it may well have been reasonable for the Russian security authorities to suspect TOKAEV, if they had already evidence that he was disloyal to the regime.

TOKAEV, according to his own statements, had long been anti-Stalin and he had been involved with an anti-Stalin underground movement in Russia and in Germany. He went on leave to Moscow in September 1947 and there he obtained certain information about arrests of fellow conspirators which led him to believe that he would soon be caught himself. It was a matter of time before his underground connections would be discovered and his involvements with the suspect TANK would be another nail in his coffin. He therefore hurried back to Germany and decided to try to defect.

After considerable thought he chose the Canadians to defect to as opposed to the British, Americans or French, for the following reasons:-

1. He is violently against the Potsdam Agreement.
2. He had heard in Russia that the British hand back defectors.
3. He was opposed to the materialistic outlook of the Americans.
4. Among the French there are too many people like Thorez and Duclos.

He therefore chose the Canadians as being ideologically closest to the British and as not having been signatories of the Potsdam Agreement, In about September 1947 he wrote and sent through the ordinary mail a letter to the Canadian Military Mission in which he said that Officer X, a high ranking Russian Officer, asked for asylum for himself and his family and promised to respect Canadian laws. He said that he would telephone on a given day, but no call was received from him. Later he wrote another similar letter which was handed to the Persian Mission with the request that it be delivered to the Canadians.

By October 1947 the net had started to close around TOKAEV. He had been questioned about what he knew of the underground organisation, was under constant surveillance and indeed was more or less under open arrest.

On the 13th October 1947 he again asked in writing to be sent back to the USSR and was told to prepare for his departure. On the 21st October he was informed that he was released from duty. TOKAEV started preparing to leave for Moscow, but in the meantime he was also trying to get in touch with the Canadian Military Mission to whom he had written over a month earlier. An officer who knew of TOKAEV's difficulties went to an address in the French Sector in Berlin and telephoned the Canadians. Two days later he was flown back to the USSR with his family, and TOKAEV never learned the result of the telephone call, He then decided that he would have to take a risk; he asked an unknown German to telephone the Canadians and ask for their decision. An appointment was made for the following day and after various elaborate and efficient arrangements, TOKAEV, his wife and small daughter, were removed by air. It was not until the last minute, after he had entered the plane, that he discovered that in fact it was the British who were in charge of his escape. He was horrified at this discovery and expected at any moment to be put down at a Soviet airport. However, he has expressed the greatest satisfaction at his subsequent treatment by us and says that he now realises that the story that the British hand back defectors must have been Stalinist propaganda.

TOKAEV has been extensively interrogated, has provided a very large amount of technical and political information and his interrogation is still in progress. He has been a very difficult man to exploit. First, he is fanatically anti-Stalin and is anxious that we should immediately carry out his plans to help bring about the downfall of the Stalin government, plans of a propagandist nature whose implementation could not be countenanced. The refusal to carry them out has caused TOKAEV [to] have frequent bouts of annoyance, in which he refuses to cooperate in his interrogation. Secondly, he has consistently refused to cooperate in any atter.pt to contact and use his alleged former fellow conspirators for intelligence purposes.

During his first interrogation TOKAEV was asked why he had defected. He did not reply for some time, saying that he was not really quite clear in his own mind yet as to why he had taken the step. He gave several reasons,

   a. He had belonged to a small Indo-Iranian minority, for many years domiciled in the Caucasus, whose national characteristics and in fact whose existence had been destroyed by the Soviet regime.
   b. He has been fortunate in that he had a good education and obtained a position of importance in his particular profession. He therefore lived in a way far superior to the greater majority of his fellow countrymen. He could not, however, help realising that the majority of the subjects of the USSR lived in a state of complete squalor in order that the aims and objects of the Stalin regime might be carried through – in other words, that his people were being betrayed by their government to further their own ends.
   c. He learned while in Berlin to despise Russian propaganda. He realised its utter falseness. He got to know British, American, French and other Western Europeans, He realised that the propaganda regarding Eastern Europe and the United States as put out in every Russian newspaper, every radio programme, every theatre and in every book was false.
   d. He realises that the Stalin regime has systematically endeavoured to seal off Russian thinkers from all civilizing influences; that

any section of the community which believes in being unable to carry out its tasks efficiently without some contact with the outer world is liquidated. In this connection he mentioned that there has recently been a systematic purge of all scientists of international reputation. That he himself was under suspicion and that unless he took this opportunity of deserting he would not get a second chance,
e. He has a child. He wants her to have a free education, not the hopelessly biased and propagandised one that she would get in a Russian school.

TOKAEV has given all his interrogators the impression that he was fanatically anti-Stalin, He said that he would never do anything against his own people, but that he was prepared to do anything in his power to destroy the present Russian Communist regime; that the Russian nation fought the war in order to destroy Hitlerism and oppression and semi-slavery; they fought it with their allies in the hope that on victory being obtained they would have the same privileges and freedom as their allies. This hope was never realised – their position now is worse even than before the war.

After his defection TOKAEV was anxious to go somewhere where he could live as a free man and where he could work towards the destruction of the present Russian regime in order that someday he may return to Russia and find it a country where man is free.

Tokaev may not have turned out to be all that SIS had hoped for, but his extensive knowledge of Kremlin personalities, and the senior army staff at least proved the point that a single, well-informed defector, however 'difficult', was infinitely more valuable than the hundreds of Red Army line-crossers who deserted their posts to become refugees in the west. Huge resources were devoted to the interrogation of these low-level sources for little practical return, apart from some tactical intelligence that soon became outdated. Both MI5 and SIS, fully committed to the principle of attracting knowledgeable defectors, even if the Soviet authorities had spread the falsehood that 'the British handed back deserters' learned several lessons from Tokaev, particularly in the area of resettlement, but it would be some years before either organisation had another opportunity to embrace a really valuable defector.

Chapter III

YURI RASTVOROV

I will never feel safe.

Yuri Rastvorov

One of the most significant NKVD defectors of the Cold War, Yuri Rastvorov had been a member of the Tokyo *rezidentura* for four and a half years, until he was granted political asylum in the United States on 24 January 1954, after having initially approached the British Secret Intelligence Service.

Born in July 1921 in Dmitriyev. Kursk Oblast, Rastvorov's father had served as a Red Army commander and fought during the Russian Civil War, eventually being appointed military kommissar of the Tagansky District in Moscow. Rastvorov's mother, a physician, died of breast cancer in 1946.

Upon the outbreak of the Second World War, Rastvorov was conscripted into the Red Army and posted to Latvia and Lithuania as part of the Soviet occupation. In December 1940, he was transferred to Moscow to attend a Japanese language course as a GRU officer. He graduated in 1943 and was assigned as a cryptanalyst to the Russian Far East. Between 1944 and 1946 he received further intelligence training in Moscow, and then was sent to the Soviet Embassy in Tokyo under translator cover. However, soon after his arrival at the NKVD *rezidentura* he was recalled to Moscow because his paternal grandfather had been denounced as a kulak landowner. In reality the peasant farmer, who had scraped a living with two cows and two horses, had perished of starvation in the 1932 famine. While still under investigation, Rastvorov had been sent to Khabarovsk where he had screened Japanese internees and interviewed those deemed suitable for recruitment. One of these candidates was Shii Masaji a Japanese interpreter fluent in Russian who was repatriated in November 1948, with instructions to avoid contact with the Communist Party of Japan, and to await instructions. However, in February 1949 Masaji's language skills attracted United States Army G-2 and he was hired to debrief other repatriated Japanese officers. Accordingly, Rastvorov, who was appointed his hander, fortuitously found himself running a source with access to American military intelligence information.

Having been declared politically reliable in 1950, Rastvorov returned to Tokyo as an agent recruiter and operated as a talent spotter, by cultivating contacts made at the upscale Tokyo Lawn Tennis Club. However, in late 1953, following the execution of Lavrenti Beria in December, Rastvorov was ordered back to Moscow, but instead made contact with SIS, represented since November 1952 by Maclachlan Silverwood-Cope. As can be imagined, the prospect of a senior NKVD officer switching sides created great excitement in London as he was the first prospect since Yuri Tasoev, but in spite of British promises regarding resettlement, perhaps in Australia, Rastvorov was uneasy about SIS's plan. One version, recalled by the CIA's E. Howard Hunt, suggests that he was escorted onto an RAF Transport Command aircraft at Hameda airport, destined for Singapore, but when the flight was delayed by a blizzard he demanded to be driven back to Tokyo. The second version, as told by MI5's Peter Wright, was that Rastvorov refused to travel when he learned that he was being flown to London, where he considered he would be in great danger.[1]

In any event, Rastvorov would change his mind about seeking asylum from the British, and in January 1954 approached the CIA through Maude Burris, his Oklahoma-born English language teacher, and met Quentin Johnson. According to Johnson, who retired to Rockport, Maine,

> There were two things that apparently caused him to change his mind: (1) When the British thought they had him in the bag for sure, they made a small celebration in his presence which offended him as he interpreted their regarding him merely as a 'big catch'. He certainly was, but it was unwise for the British to thus have acted in Subject's presence. (2) The British had assured him that he would be settled in Canada, but at the last moment they indicated he would go there by way of England. This frightened Subject because he apparently had some knowledge there was a Russian Intelligence Service penetration of British Intelligence.[2]

The moment of defection had been in the car park of the Suchiro, a popular downtown restaurant, where he held an evening rendezvous with a young CIA case officer, Werner Michel, who was driving a black Chevrolet.

Having been offered political asylum in the United States, and resettlement under the alias Martin Francis Simons, Rastvorov was flown to Okinawa for interrogation. During his interviews Rastvorov revealed that he had changed his mind about defecting to the British because in 1946 a former colleague, Vladimir Skripkin, had been betrayed when he had indicated his intention to defect. According to the CIA's Cleveland Cram, later the CIA deputy station chief in London, Rastvorov

> had been playing tennis in Tokyo with the late Phil Fendig, but the latter played no role in [Rastvorov's] defection. But there was an elderly American school teacher in Tokyo who had been giving Subject English lessons. He liked this person and trusted her and it was his entirely platonic relationship with this school teacher (or English teacher) which caused Subject, when frightened by the British intention to take Subject to England, caused him to seek her advice and assistance. Fortunately, she called the U.S. Embassy and asked for someone to come to see her 'foreign friend' who needed help. The late Pete Wheeler sent Quentin Johnson, then a very young case officer to the teacher's home and there found [Rastvorov].[3]

Rastvorov nearly had second thoughts about defecting at all, as Hunt, one of the CIA officers who accompanied him on the C-47 flight to Okinawa, later recalled he 'was especially ill at ease, saying ... that the Japanese would come aboard and take him off, handing him back to the Soviets.'

During his lengthy debriefing on Okinawa, Rastvorov was cross-examined on his background and intelligence career, which he described in these terms:

> I was born July 11, 1921 in Etaitrovsk, Orlovslcaya Oblast, USSR. My education was received in the Soviet Union, In 1929 I enrolled in the 5th school (middle school) in Voronezh acid completed middle school in 1939 at the 268th school in Moscow. In 1939 I was admitted to Moscow Geodesy Institute (Moakovsky Institut Geodezii), however, after two months was conscripted into the Soviet Army.
>
> In September 1940 I was selected to be a student at the Military Faculty of the Far Eastern Language Institute where I pursued the study of Japanese and English. With the outbreak of [the Second World]

war I was sent to the Office of Military Intelligence at Chita and later to the Seventh Army Area in Outer Mongolia to train in psychological warfare aimed at the Japanese, During this period I was commissioned a Lieutenant in GRU (Glavnoye Razvedyvatelnoye Upravleniye – Chief Intelligence Directorate of the General Staff of the Red Army). Following entry of Japan into the war I was reassigned to the Par Eastern Language Institute, then located in Fergaga, near Tashkent, and later moved to Stavropol, north of the Caucasus.

In February 1943 I was transferred from the Military Intelligence Service to NKGB (Narodny Komissariat Gosudarstvennoye Bezopasnosti – People's Commissariat of State Security) in Moscow. In 1944 I was transferred to the Intelligence Directorate of NKGB and sent to the Causae us un an assignment having to do with the relocation of national minorities from Southern Russia to Siberia, Upon completion of this task I returned to Moscow and received a thorough training in intelligence work and was graduated from the NKGB Intelligence School at the end of 1945.

Following graduation I returned to the First Directorate of NKGB in Moscow. In January, 194£ I was sent to Tokyo as an NKGB Intelligence Officer under the guise of a Foreign Office translator. In November, 1946 I returned to Moscow where I served as desk officer until January, 1948, when I was assigned to a special group engaged in recruiting agents among Japanese war prisoners held in Siberia, At this time I held the rank of Captain of MGB. In August 1948 I was reassigned to Moscow, and remained there until 1950, when I received assignment with the Soviet Mission in Tokyo, By this time I held the rank of Major. In Tokyo my primary objective was the recruitment of Americans as Soviet Intelligence agents, however, due to the difficulties of this task, my time was devoted primarily to the management of Japanese agent.

In January, 1954, while still in Tokyo, I made the decision to break with the Soviet way of life and on January 24, 1934, put this decision into action and requested asylum. At that time I held, the rank of Lieutenant Colonel of MVD (Ministry of Internal Affairs). It is observed that the Foreign Intelligence Directorate in which I was employed as an integral part of the Soviet Government agency having constant jurisdiction over State Security, and under a series of organizational changes, known variously as NKGB (Peoples' Commissariat of State Security), MGB (Ministry of State Security), IC (Committee of Information), and MVD (Ministry of Internal Affairs).

During the interviews, which lasted more than a month, Rastvorov described the Tokyo *rezidentura*, headed by Aleksandr Nosenko and identified several Japanese diplomats as spies, among them Nobinuri Higurashi, Shigeru Takamore and Hiroshi Shoji. Higurashi would commit suicide by jumping out of a window during his interrogation.

Takamore was tried and sentenced to eight months' imprisonment for breaching secrecy as a civil servant under the National Public Service Law. Shoji was released, apparently having been granted the benefit of the doubt by the government.

Rastvorov, who was known to his recruits as UCHIDA, revealed that some of his agents had been Japanese prisoners of war who had been released by the Soviets on condition that they undertook espionage missions in return for their freedom. Some simply disappeared after they reached Japan, but others apparently had felt a duty to fulfill the obligation. The *rezidentura*'s priority was information relating to the deployment or storage of American nuclear weapons in Japan.

Rastvorov also shed light on some unresolved counter-intelligence puzzles, such as the cases in 1952 of Masao Mitsuhashi and the celebrated leftist Japanese writer, Wataru Kaji. The latter had disclosed that he had been recruited as a Soviet agent when he had been held as a prisoner of war in the Soviet Union. He had then agreed to work as a double agent under American control, and he communicated with his Soviet handlers by radio. The issue became controversial when it emerged that Kaji had been kept in custody against his will after Japanese sovereignty had been restored in April 1952. Similarly, when Masao Mitsuhashi was returned to Japan, he provided information about his mission as a radio operator, and implicated Rastvorov.

Another of Rastvorov's 'meal tickets' was John M. Byington, a United States Air Force military policeman whom he had recruited as a source, Byington had been a 'walk-in' at the Soviet mission in April 1953 when he had offered to sell information, and Rastvorov had been assigned as his handler. Rastvorov also named Major Rose Esther Ennis as a *rezidentura* recruitment target in 1952. She was then employed as a Russian language teacher by United States Army G-2 and was thought to be vulnerable because of having family members in the Soviet Union. Another counter-espionage lead was Ernest J. Lissner, a United States Counter-Intelligence Corps officer, who was alleged to have offered to sell classified information to the *rezidentura* in 1947.

Following his defection Rastvorov was invited in October 1954 to record his knowledge of the Petrovs, and this he did in the form of an affidavit:

> I became personally acquainted with this woman during the latter part of 1943; at which time we both attended the Foreign Language School of the Committee of Information in Moscow, and studied the English language in the same group. We occupied adjoining seats in

the classroom at this school. The classes were held three times weekly and we both attended regularly until June 1950 when I discontinued the school and departed Moscow for assignment in Tokyo. I have not seen Mrs Petrova since that time.

The Foreign Language School of the Committee of Information mentioned above, was comprised of intelligence personnel only, and the majority of the students in this school held the status of intelligence officers It is my recollection that Mrs Petrova held the rank of Senior Lieutenant when I first met her and was subsequently promoted to the rank of Captain. I recall her as a carcer officer I have identified a photograph of Evdokia Petrova from the 1954 issue of *Time* Magazine on page 30, as a good likeness of the woman described above. I wish to state that I knew her and she was known in the Soviet Intelligence Service by her maiden name of Evdokia Alexeevka Kartseva, I was aware that she was married to Vladimir Proletarsky (Petrov).

From conversation with Evdokia, I learned that she was employed at an earlier date in the Fifth Directorate (Cipher) of GUGB/NKVD and had worked with Gerasim Balasanov, who was a friend of mine. Evdokia also told me that she and her husband had been assigned to the Soviet Embassy in Stockholm, Sweden, where she was employed as a Cipher Clerk. Both were officers of the Foreign Intelligence Directorate of NKGB, later MGB, during this service in Sweden.

I learned from Evdokia that in 1948 she was not a member of the Communist Party but was a member of the Komsomol (Young Communist League). As a candidate for membership in the Communist Party, she was then in the process of being accepted as a Party Member.

As a matter of interest, Evdokia told me that 3he had a child by a previous marriage who had died. I also have a recollection that she stated that she had learned a little Japanese.

On 15 April 1954 I observed a photograph in *The New York Times* newspaper of that date, which was reported to be of Vladimir Petrov. I recognised this photograph immediately as that of an MVD Intelligence Officer with whom I was previously acquainted. I had known this individual under the name of Vladimir Mikhailovich Proletarsky.

I first met Proletarsky after he returned to Moscow from Sweden, which occurred I believe in 1947. Proletarsky was given an assignment in the Second Directorate of the KI (Committee of Information) which was responsible for positive intelligence operations in Europe. During 1948 and 1994. I saw Proletarsky frequently at KI Headquarters, both in the office area and in the mess hall. Proletarsky was sometimes accompanied by his wife, whom I knew well because of having attended language school with, her, In late 1949 Proletarsky was transferred from the KI to the MVD (Ministry of State Security), I knew of this transfer through conversations with Proletarsky's wife who also told me, on a later occasion, that she and Proletarsky had both performed cipher duties at the Soviet Embassy in Stockholm, Sweden, between 1943 and 1947. I cannot state what names Proletarsky and his wife used in Sweden, I have never known him personally under any name other than Vladimir Mikhailovich Proletarsky.

Proletarsky was a relatively well-known officer among Soviet Intelligence personnel at Moscow in the late 1940s, and he said I had several mutual friends in the Soviet Intelligence Service. It is my best recollection that Proletarsky held the rank of major or Lieutenant-Colonel in 1950,

I last saw Proletarsky at Moscow prior to my departure for Japan. I had no knowledge that Proletarsky or his wife had been transferred to Australia until I recognised his photograph in *The New York Times* in April 1954.

I have carefully read the above statement consisting of four typewritten pages, and hereby certify as to its truthfulness and accuracy.

Rastvorov's defection was not made public until August 1954, by which time he had been safely installed in a safe house in Travilah Road, Potomac, in the guise of a Czech immigrant codenamed DIPPER 19. There he was interrogated by fellow tennis enthusiast, Fred Kovaleski, who would become his lifelong friend.

In 1956 Rastvorov obtained a Mexican divorce from his wife Galina Andreevna Godova, a well-known ballet dancer with whom he had a daughter, Tatyana, in 1945, so he could marry Hope Macartney one of his CIA debriefers, by whom he had two daughters, Alexandra and Jennifer. It would be more than a decade before the girls were told about their father's true antecedents. In 1977, Hope divorced Rastvorov, and began a relationship with an ice-skater, Anne Garnier, but his life went into a decline.

Rastvorov started many businesses, including a restaurant, the Captain's Table, in Georgetown, Washington DC, but none prospered. He died in February 2004, aged 82, having hired a lawyer to extract a belated annuity from the CIA, having easily exhausted his original payment of $25,000, plus a further $25,000 from *Life* magazine. According to the *FBI Counterintelligence Reader*,

> In all, he produced over 1,000 positive and operational intelligence reports, including the identification of about 600 Soviet intelligence officers and agents. The information that he provided was considered to be very important and useful.

During his post-defection interrogations Rastvorov was questioned at length about his Japanese spy-ring, the Skripkin episode and a pair of NKVD colleagues, Vladimir and Evdokia Petrov. The allegation that Skripkin had been betrayed by a mole in London would have a lasting impact as it became part of a matrix of evidence that either MI5 or SIS, or both, had suffered hostile penetration. The issue, which was of the highest sensitivity, meant that both agencies would be considered contaminated, and untrustworthy, until the matter had been fully investigated. At that stage, in 1954, the accumulated evidence amounted to an assertion made by the GRU cipher clerk Igor Gouzenko in September 1945 that he had heard corridor gossip about a spy in London codenamed ELLI. Then, of course, there was the Volkov debacle, which suggested that the NKVD had several assets in London, including someone in a 'counter-intelligence directorate'.

Skripal had made a rather vague approach to the British naval attaché in Tokyo on 9 May 1946, and then gone to the Americans ten days later, again with an offer to go back to Moscow and then defect with his wife on his very next foreign posting. Nothing more had been heard of Skripkin, but Rastvorov explained that Skripkin had been betrayed, and had incriminated himself when two NKVD officers had showed up at his Moscow apartment pretending to be British SIS officers This news caused consternation in London as it suggested that the Soviets had somehow acquired a copy of the original Naval Intelligence Division report of Skripkin's tentative offer, which had included his address in Moscow. Initially, the reaction in London was that the likely source of the leak had been Kim Philby, who had been dismissed from SIS in July 1951, although Philby had never been on the NID report's distribution list. Later, more light would be shed on the incident. Firstly, when the KGB's Anatoli Golitsyn defected in December 1961, he recounted the Skripkin episode and confirmed that he had seen photographs of two NID reports about Skripkin which had come from London. Secondly, when challenged in January 1963, after Philby had accepted immunity from prosecution and written a confession, he denied any knowledge of Skripkin. The inescapable conclusion was that in the summer of 1946 another, as yet unsuspected Soviet mole had been active in London.

The other topic that was of great interest to Rastvorov's interrogators was the Petrovs, recently defected in Australia, who had been known to him since 1943 under their NKVD cover-name of Proletarsky. Indeed, he recalled that he had even attended the same language course as Evdokia.

Chapter IV

VLADIMIR PETROV AND EVDOKIA PETROVA

I saw the sufferings of my own peasant folk under collectivization, and the ruin of my native village of Larikha. After that, the horrors of the purges, the victimization of innocent people, the desperate poverty of the Soviet masses, followed by the striking contrast of conditions in other countries – all these had destroyed my faith in the professions of our regime, long before I came to the point of action.

Vladimir Petrov, *Empire of Fear*[1]

The defection of the Canberra *rezident* Vladimir Petrov in April 1954 was unquestionably one of the great turning-points in the intelligence Cold War, although the entire operation, which included three years of cultivation, before his actual application for political asylum, was really an immense gamble as right up until the last moment, ASIO's management was not entirely certain of the precise nature of his role in the embassy.

The Western intelligence community took the issue of Soviet intelligence operations in Australia very seriously for three reasons. Firstly, British atomic weapons had been tested at Montebello in Western Australia since October 1952, so information from the site could reasonably be expected to be regarded as a collection priority for Moscow. Likewise, the rocket range at Woomera had accommodated British guided missile tests since 1947 and also would have been bound to attract Moscow's attention. Finally, there was the certainty, provided by the VENONA traffic, that the Soviets had already built and exploited the Communist Party of Australia by building a large spy-ring controlled by a succession of intelligence professionals, including Valentin Sudovnikov and Fedor Nosov. Their CPA intermediary was Walter Clayton, who had been in frequent contact with CPA cells inside the Civil Service, academics, journalists and other well-placed sources. The fact that a British classified report, circulated by the Post-Hostilities Planning Committee in Whitehall, had turned up in the Canberra VENONA channel dated 16 March 1946 was eloquent proof of a massive security problem in Australia, and had acted as the trigger for the Australian government to create a security apparatus based on the MI5 model to plug the leaks. Although VENONA had not revealed any specific breaches relating to atomic weapons or guided missiles, the intercepts had proved the existence of a well-organised Soviet spy-ring which had the means to collect secrets and communicate them efficiently to Moscow.

The VENONA material consisted of 329 pages of messages exchanged with Moscow between August 1943 and June 1948, so when MI5's Director-General Sir Percy Sillitoe visited Sydney in mid-February 1948, accompanied by his director of F Division, Roger Hollis, the source was still contemporaneous. Their task was to persuade the (initially reluctant) Australian government to create a security apparatus on British lines so the continuing damage could be properly dealt with. The issue was a delicate one because one of the active VENONA spies had served in the current security unit, the Commonwealth Investigation Branch, was BEN, soon to be identified as Detective Sergeant Alf Hughes of the Vice Squad. Clearly the CIB was not fit for purpose. Furthermore, Sillitoe and Hollis possessed some significant leverage: unless the Australians agreed to the British plan, they would be cut off from all Allied classified information. In particular, the Americans were unwilling to take any risks with delicate information, sources and methods, which included the VENONA secret.

Accordingly, when ASIO came into being in March 1949, it did so with the support from an MI5 security liaison officer, Courtenay Young. He would act as an intermediary, passing the new organisation espionage leads from London without compromising the source, although several ASIO officers would guess the source was likely cryptographic. Thereafter, Young's role would be continued by Derek Hamblen who in April 1952 arranged for ASIO's Ron Richards to visit London in September and be briefed on VENONA.

Apart from the establishment of ASIO, little had been accomplished in terms of plugging the leaks, and it was clear from VENONA that, for example, the country's external affairs department had been thoroughly penetrated, as had the leader of the Opposition's private office. Sir Charles Spry, who had supervised ASIO's development, saw the Petrovs as an opportunity to alert the government and the wider population to the espionage challenge through a Canadian-style Royal Commission, and regarded the defectors as a heaven-sent pretext for exploiting the VENONA leads and thereby neutralising the Soviet threat. However, only a few of the individuals compromised by Petrov's documents (such as Rupert Lockwood and Frank O'Sullivan) had appeared in the VENONA traffic, and the commissioners' remit was far wider than the documents purloined by Petrov. Those items consisted of Russian language papers, known as the G Series; Document H, in English, written by O'Sullivan and Document J, typed by Lockwood.

These documents were the very heart of the Royal Commission and represented the hard evidence of the allegations of espionage under consideration. Oral testimony from the Petrovs might be dismissed as hearsay, exaggeration or embroidery, but the actual sheets of paper were harder to refute, although a sustained effort was made to undermine the Petrovs' credibility, impugn their motives and infer the documents were not to be taken at face value. For example, on 17 January 1955, Petrov was cross-examined at length about the documents, all of which were originals (with one exception, designated G4) that had been placed in a sealed envelope by the previous *rezident*, Valentin Sadovnikov, and then handed over to Ivan Pakhomov, who in turn passed it on to Petrov in February 1952.

Each handover had involved a brief ceremony when the envelope was removed from an inner safe and the wax seal marked with a swan was inspected. The first ten documents, G1 to G10, were in Sadovnikov's handwriting, and the remainder, G11 to G18, had been written by Petrov, who at the end of March 1954 had opened the package, removed all the documents and then replaced them with some allegedly innocuous paperwork that referred to Rose-Marie Ollier, a 47-year-old cipher clerk at the French Embassy codenamed OLGA.

The irrefutable fact was that the handwriting on some of the most incriminating items was Sadovnikov's and not Petrov's, and the envelope had lain undisturbed for two years until Petrov had decided to employ the material as leverage in his defection.

While Petrov's papers were interesting and even embarrassing, they were by themselves inconclusive, and in comparison to the VENONA intercepts, almost irrelevant. However, the secret of VENONA had to be maintained at all costs, so the commission was briefed in private session about some of the VENONA decrypts in order to establish a link between some of the principal suspects, such as Jim Hill, Ian Milner of external affairs, and Wally Clayton, where there was a gap in the evidence. The problem arose in the commission's conclusions, which could hardly condemn the spies without disclosing the evidence or admit that Petrov had failed to deliver the proof required to bring criminal charges. In his testimony Clayton denied ever having met either Hill or Milner and admitted only that he had been shown some low-level papers by a typist, Frances Bernie, who made a limited confession, having accepted immunity from prosecution. Bernie worked for Dr Evatt's secretary, Allan Dalziel, who appeared in the VENONA material as TECHNICIAN, and was also listed on one of the 'Petrov papers', designated G1, as 'Denis'.

To cap it all, Clayton denied on oath that he had ever met any Soviet citizen. This, of course, was a travesty, but both the British and the Americans insisted that VENONA was too important to be jeopardised in an effort to imprison Clayton and his ring. Accordingly, unlike its Canadian equivalent which had resulted in twenty-one prosecutions based on Igor Gouzenko's evidence, not a single charge was brought against a suspect in Australia. Doubtless the outcome would have been rather different if ASIO had been permitted to reveal what had been achieved by the British and American cryptographers over the past decade, but this was never an option, so the Royal Commission confined itself to the various documents that Petrov had removed from his embassy safe. These consisted of a short hand-written list of contacts, inherited from Ivan Pakhomov, that appeared to incriminate those named, and various other items, including a forty-page profile of leading Australian politicians and personalities containing some highly pejorative and controversial observations. Much to Rupert Lockwood's embarrassment, he was identified as the principal author of the notorious 'Document J' and he reluctantly conceded that he had visited the embassy to help compile it, claiming that he had simply acted as a professional journalist, assisting a foreign correspondent who had sought his help on what would now be called 'background'. Such behaviour, while reprehensible, amounted to neither espionage nor criminal conduct, and much the same was true of the others similarly tarnished.

Despite the disappointment of the Royal Commission, which markedly failed to have the same impact as its Canadian counterpart, set up after Gouzenko's defection in September 1945, the Petrovs were nevertheless the most senior Soviet intelligence defectors to the West for two decades, and together they supplied a wealth of information to flesh out the bones already provided by VENONA. For instance, the Petrovs confirmed the composition of the *rezidentura* which, apart from himself and his wife, who had acted as his cipher clerk, included the second secretary, Filipp Kislytsin, who had arrived in 1952, having spent three years at the London *rezidentura* between 1945 and 1948; the TASS correspondent Viktor Antonov, and an attaché from Latvia, Janis Plaitkais, who had arrived early in 1953 and had concentrated on monitoring the very substantial local émigré community. In addition, the *rezident* could rely on a few co-opted workers in the embassy, and these included the press attaché since 1951, Georgi Kharkovetz, and the commercial secretary since 1952, Nikolai Kovaliev (who was also the embassy's party secretary). MI5 was particularly keen to hear about Petrov's friendship with Kislytsin who had confided to his colleague that while in Moscow he had supervised the last-minute escape from London in May 1951 of Guy Burgess and Donald Maclean, who had been resettled in the Soviet Union. His recollection that Burgess and Maclean had been recruited by the NKVD while still at university, would be a considerable shock. Perhaps worse was Kislytsin's assertion that the two diplomats had fled the country because they had spotted MI5's interest in them.

For the past thirty-five months the British public, media, government and intelligence agencies had puzzled over the disappearance of the two diplomats. The last confirmed sighting was of them, on Saturday, 26 May 1951, after they had disembarked from the SS *Falaise*, in St-Malo, attempting to catch a train to Paris. Only MI5 knew that probably both men had been long-term Soviet agents, perhaps since their university days, but the organisation also knew that it had been Maclean who had been under surveillance, and that Burgess had never been an espionage suspect. Yet, according to Petrov, they had been alerted in part by MI5 surveillance on Burgess. The Russian also knew that their escape had involved 'an airlift over the Czech border to Prague' before they reached Kuybyshev (modern day Samara), where they were now living.

The Petrovs also gave valuable information about their previous posting in Stockholm, and revealed that the assumption that Boris N. Yartsev, codenamed KIN in VENONA, had been the NKVD *rezident* was incorrect. In fact, he had been a subordinate of his wife, who was the real *rezident*, a detail that did not emerge from scrutiny of the VENONA texts.

While they may not have had quite the same impact as Gouzenko, the Petrovs did achieve considerable political notoriety because Australian Prime Minister Sir Robert Menzies was accused of having made capital out of the defection, and of having attempted to smear the Labour opposition with disloyalty. When Dr Evatt, formerly the minister for external affairs, but now the leader of the Opposition, appeared before the commission he denounced Petrov's papers as forgeries and accused him of conspiring to undermine the Labour Party. Tactically, his approach was a mistake as the documents were entirely authentic, but he did unite the Australian left against what he claimed was a massive, politically motivated plot. Dr Evatt, of course, had never been indoctrinated into the original VENONA-based enquiry, and therefore never realised that the accusations against Milner, Hill, Throssel and Clayton even predated Petrov's arrival in the country.

The defection of Petrov, and his wife Evdokia, who was also an intelligence officer, holding the rank of senior lieutenant, and who acted as her husband's cipher clerk, took some three years to gestate, and remains an object lesson in how to develop and handle a potential candidate for defection. The beginning of the Petrov story is best told by Michael Thwaites, one of several remarkable Australian case officers who pulled off one the greatest coups of the Cold War. In November 1955, ASIO circulated Thwaites's report:[2]

DEFECTION of Vladimir Mikhailovich PETROV @ PROLETARSKI, and Evdokia Alexeevna Petrova © KARTSEVA

Introduction:
1. The defection of V.M. Petrov and his wife was the culmination of a case conducted by the Australian Security Intelligence Organisation as part of its counter-espionage function. In the account which follows no attempt has been made to summarize the whole case. Only those elements which concern the Petrovs' decision to defect, and the steps by which they arrived at that decision, have been included, together with some general conclusions on the subject of Russian defectors, Some of these conclusions are necessarily tentative at present, and may be modified by subsequent disclosures. Nevertheless, the main outlines of the Petrovs' defection are now fairly clear, and shed considerable light on the internal stresses in a Soviet station in foreign territory, and on the psychological and other factors involved in a defection from the Soviet Intelligence Service abroad.
2. The defection was in each case the free deliberate choice of the person concerned, and this was acknowledged by both Petrovs. On the other hand, it is certain that neither defection would have taken place without careful study, and in the latter stages, detailed planning and vigorous action by ASIO to anticipate difficulties

and facilitate the final step. It must be acknowledged that the Soviet authorities for their part, could hardly have done more than they did to ensure the successful conclusion of the venture. Their part is one of the encouraging aspects of the story.

Arrival in Canberra:

3. V.M. Petrov and his wife arrived in Australia on 5th February, 1951, to join the staff of the Soviet Embassy in Canberra. He was then listed as 'Clerk', and he and his wife travelled on Special (non-Diplomatic) passports. However, on 4th April the Soviet Embassy described Petrov to the Department of External Affairs as 'Third Secretary'; and that remained his official posting up to his defection to the Australian authorities on 3rd April, 1954. Mrs Petrov carried out the duties of Accountant and Chief Secretary at the Embassy until November 1953, when she was relieved by the wife of the new First Secretary, Vislykh.

Study of Soviet Representation:

4. At the time of the Petrovs' arrival in Australia, AS1O. had just embarked on a programme of systematic study of the official Soviet representation designed to build up background information as a basis for, (a) penetration of the Embassy, (b) selection of likely Intelligence operatives, (c) assessment of potential defectors.

5. Background particulars and a photographic register of all Soviet Embassy personnel were compiled and revised at regular intervals; and the collated results were studied in conjunction with the known pattern of Soviet espionage and of Soviet Diplomatic establishments in other countries. Studies supplied by [the] UK Security Service proved to be of the utmost value in this connection.

6. A particular effort was made to maintain surveillance of the interstate travel of Soviet personnel selected for special attention, as it was considered that the larger cities of Sydney and Melbourne provided better opportunities for 'clandestine contacts' than did Canberra. Though exacting, this surveillance paid good dividends.

7. Surveillance in Canberra offered peculiar difficulties because of Canberra's wide, deserted streets, semi-rural atmosphere, and widely-spaced houses. However, though surveillance there was of necessity limited and sporadic, it supplied indispensable evidence of persons in social contact with Russian officials.

8. (Clandestine contacts were in fact carried out by Petrov, and probably other Russian officials in Canberra itself, and a letter-drop was selected by Petrov in a small railway bridge in the nearby countryside. The bigger cities of Sydney and Melbourne were, however, preferred for the purpose of secret contacts.)

9. From the end of 1951 technical aids began to supply a steady stream of information on Soviet Embassy personalities; and from August 1952, when the exploitation of this source was intensified, it became possible to draw up an increasingly accurate Order of Battle, and to select with some confidence the likely candidates for Intelligence functions among Soviet officials.
10. Petrov was soon selected as one of several Russians deserving special study because of – (a) his frequent visits to Sydney and Melbourne (often unaccompanied), (b) the fact that, though he was listed only as Third Secretary, he and his wife occupied a complete house of their own, (c) a report that on a previous tour of duty in Sweden he had had some kind of unspecified Intelligence duties, (d) his claim, as Third Secretary, to diplomatic immunity.
11. His overt functions were obviously such as could provide him with excellent cover for clandestine contacts as Consul he was the point of contact in the Embassy for Soviet and Satellite nationals in Australia; he was found to be active in the Soviet's repatriation drive, and to visit numbers of migrants in this connection; he was a regular visitor to the pro-Soviet Russian Social Club in Sydney; as VOKS representative he was concerned with the distribution of Russian films, and had a natural link with pro-Soviet organisations such as Australia-Russia Societies; he was responsible for meeting the Diplomatic Couriers in Sydney, and seeing them off again; he was in charge of travel arrangements for members of the Embassy to and from Australia; and he was in frequent official touch with the UK Passport officer in Canberra and the protocol officer in the Department of External Affairs.
12. It was debated whether these functions of Petrov's were so many and so open as to preclude secret Intelligence duties; but his freedom of movement was considered to be an overwhelming argument in favour of giving him special attention, A striking feature was the frequency with which he travelled alone on his visits to other cities, and there was some evidence of independence of Ambassadorial control.
13. As a result of this study, together with information from other sources, the Counter-Espionage Section of ASIO was satisfied, by mid-1953, that Petrov was in fact an officer of the MGB (Ministry of State Security), later incorporated in the MVD (Ministry of Internal Affairs).

Role of Source DIABOLO in the Defection:

14. A key part in the cultivation of Petrov and in his ultimate defection was played by DIABOLO. DIABOLO was a Russian-speaking source already working in the pro-Soviet Russian Social Club in Sydney. He was a Pole who arrived in Australia in 1947, 'became

a naturalized British subject in 1947, obtained a medical degree by means of a shortened post-war course, and went into practice in Sydney, his practice consisting to a large extent of migrants who were glad to avail themselves of his language qualifications.'

15. DIABOLO met Petrov in the Russian Social Club, to which Petrov was a regular visitor, and he was frequently in touch with him on his visits to Sydney. The exact nature of this early relationship is 'by no means entirely clear as yet. According to DIABOLO, Petrov and another member of the Club encouraged his interest in NINA, a Russian girl who had recently arrived in Australia as a migrant, with whom DIABOLO soon became intimately associated. For a period of, months DIABOLO reported sensational statements and conspiratorial behaviour by NINA, who claimed that she was a member of a spy ring, produced an NKVD camera, ostentatiously photographed Sydney Harbour and Mascot aerodrome, and generally played the part of the would-be Miata Hari.

16. DIABOLO reported her behaviour with apparent objectivity, but was found to have played up her story in or two small but possibly significant particulars. In general his attitude in reporting to his case officer was that NINA was mysterious and unreliable; but he expressed strong disbelief in her espionage story only when it was clear that his case officer disbelieved it.

17. At an early stage NINA visited Canberra in company with DIABOLO; she called at the Soviet Embassy, and was sent back to her hotel in an Embassy car. Questioned after Petrov's defection, NINA has denied any participation in real espionage and has admitted fabricating her espionage role, but claims that this was with the purely personal objective of interesting DIABOLO. Whether DIABOLO himself was a victim or a conscious participant in the scheme has yet to be resolved.

18. However that may be, as early as May 1951 DIABOLO was briefed to devote himself instead to the cultivation of Petrov and any other members of the Embassy whom he might meet. He established himself as a regular dining and wining companion of Petrov's in Sydney, and on various occasions visited him at his home in Canberra.

19. As early as November 1951 DIABOLO reported that he was sure that Petrov and his wife would not wish to go back to Russia when their term in Australia expired. If this represented more than wishful thinking on his part, it would seem to confirm Petrov's assertion that he had thought about defection even when he was in Sweden. However, when questioned on the point, DIABOLO explained that he had formed this view by observation of Petrov's behaviour in Australia, not from a direct statement by Petrov that he would like to stay; and his report was accordingly received with some caution.

20. Nevertheless, in April 1952 ASIO Headquarters advised State offices that Petrov (along with the TASS agent, Pakhomov) should 'be studied as a possible subject for a planned defection operation'.
21. DIABOLO's association with Petrov continued to be close and regular. He reported in considerable detail on Petrov's movements, overt activities, and relaxations, indicated Mrs. Petrov's position as Ambassador's Secretary and Accountant in the Embassy, and supplied some facts (later confirmed) about their domestic life and background.
22. In September 1952 DIABOLO reported was feared and respected by other members of the Embassy indicating that he was a high-ranking member of the MVD at the Embassy. However, he asserted that all the members of Soviet Embassy staffs are MVD and this, coupled with suspicions concerning the NINA episode, cast some doubt upon his reliability in assessing the importance of his contact.
23. (In fact it became clear when direct contact was established with Petrov that DIABOLO had no precise knowledge Petrov's MGB-MD functions or of his undercover activities and contacts.)
24. Throughout 1952 and into 1953 the convivial association of DIABOLO and Petrov continued. DIABLO would meet Petrov on his arrival at Mascot aerodrome, Sydney; or Petrov would ring DIABOLO at his surgery using the codename of 'Bill'. They dined and drank together, and attended various social gatherings, including meetings at the Russian Social Club, parties given by the Czechoslovakian Consul-General, end gatherings of a pro-Soviet complexion enlivened by variations on the 'peace' theme.
25. DIABOLO reported that Petrov, besides partaking of his hospitality, regularly asked him to perform small commissions, such as obtaining blank official forms (Immigration forms, driving licences, etc.) and several times got him to make enquiries on his behalf about migrants who were Soviet or Satellite nationals. DIABOLO performed many such services for Petrov, as well as driving him about Sydney in his car.
26. Early in 1953 a new and important trend appeared. DIABOLO began to report repeated evidence of open hostility on Petrov's part towards his Embassy colleagues, On one visit Petrov eluded the Chauffeur who had apparently been sent to accompany him as a bodyguard, and swore at 'the Embassy crowd', implying that some of them were jealous of his being on good terms with Australians. According to DIABOLO, Petrov said he would not drink with this mob'; that they were 'a lot of bastards'; that he had no friends at the Embassy; and that he was afraid his house might have been wired by his1 colleagues.
27. On 20th April 1953 DIABOLO reported that Petrov seemed sick, worried and depressed, and was having trouble with his eyes.

Moreover he claimed that he and Petrov had had discussions on the question of Petrov going into partnership with him in a restaurant business in Sydney.

28. (Mrs. Petrov has subsequently confirmed that Petrov hod DIABOLO under study for recruitment, and gave him the code name of GRIGORII in 1951; DIABOLO supplied Immigration forms and gave other help to Petrov, and Petrov had recommended the loan of £500 to DIABOLO to help him buy the restaurant, which could then be used for Illegal work).

29. On 3rd May 1953, a development occurred the importance of which for various reasons was not fully appreciated at the time. Petrov visited DIABOLO at his recently acquired flat and stayed the night there, instead of at an [sic] hotel, as had hitherto been his practice. From this time onwards he frequently stayed at DIABOLO's flat on his visits to Sydney, and showed other signs of laxness and recklessness in regard to caution and security. (See below, Operational Comments, paragraph 140.)

30. Reports were now received that Petrov was due to in late May or early June. On 4th May he told DIABLO he was going to the USSR with his wife for a few months leave, and indicated that he thought it quite on the cards that he might not return.

31. On 19th May Petrov consulted FRANKMAN, an eye specialist, about his eyes, and went into Canberra hospital for treatment; but on 16th June he again stayed at DIABOLO's flat in Sydney; and said that if the condition of his eyes was satisfactory for travel, he would leave for Russia by air early in July. He dismissed the business proposition, saying he was not certain he would be returning to Australia.

32. He was worried about his return to Russia, abused his colleagues and their intrigues, and described an incident at the Soviet National Day celebrations on 7th November of the previous year when he had refused to carry out the Ambassador's order to remove a Duty Officer who had imbibed too freely. At an Embassy meeting next day the Ambassador had charged Petrov with disobedience and drunkenness.

33. Petrov said that he had had a row with the Ambassador over this and also over his wife, who had been charged with insubordination: he suspected that this episode might be behind his recall to Moscow.

34. On the strength of these reported events, DIABOLO suggested various lines of action to get Petrov to defect. He suggested that a prominent Commonwealth official, with whom Petrov had normal business contact, should be asked to approach Petrov with, offers of money and protection; 'alternatively, that some Australian public figure should send Petrov a letter with an offer of

political asylum.' Neither of these proposals was taken up by ASIO since the first would involve the Commonwealth Government in the incitement of a Soviet diplomat to defect, while the other would provide documentary evidence of such an attempt by a prominent Australian if Petrov (as then seemed quite possible), reported the whole matter.

35. Something of a deadlock seemed to have been reached. On the one hand the reality of serious friction between Petrov and the Embassy authorities was not discounted; on the other hand the danger of relying on DIABOLO as an intermediary in defection loomed large in view of (a) his evident ignorance of the diplomatic pitfalls, (b) his personal eagerness and acknowledged mercenary interest in the matter, (c) doubts as to the reliability of his reports, in view of his opportunist character, and the earlier suspicions surrounding the NINA episode (in review, it is apparent that in all main points regarding the defection this suspicion was unjustified, and that his information was substantially accurate. This view was strongly maintained from this point by the officers who were in close personal touch with him), (d) the feeling that, granted the truth of DIABOLO's reports, his unscrupulous character, obvious to ASJO, would not have escaped Petrov's notice, and this, together with the fact that he was so recently naturalized and of Polish origin, would create doubts in Petrov's mind about his real standing and his official Australian connections, points on which a would-be but wavering defector would require the utmost assurance.

36. Two factors combined to break this deadlock, the announcement of Beria's arrest on 10th July, 1953, and the enlistment of the assistance of FRANKMAN. Beria's fall might have important repercussions which could be exploited, particularly at a time when Petrov was under sentence of recall to Moscow.

37. As ASIO were by this time satisfied that Petrov was an MGB officer, it was felt that the news of Beria's fall might have important repercussions which could be exploited, particularly at a time when Petrov was under sentence of recall to Moscow.

38. FRANKMAN was the eye specialist to whom Petrov had been introduced by DIABOLO for the treatment of his eye complaint. It was felt that he could represent a useful new element in the situation. His characteristically Australian manner would be the reverse of conspiratorial, and would carry conviction; at the same time by dealing with him direct a useful cross-check would be obtained on DIABOLO s accuracy.

39. FRANKMAN was approached without DIABOLO's knowledge. It was explained to him that ASIO had reason to believe that his patient, Petrov, wished to remain in Australia instead of returning to Russia, but that there were strong, reasons against any official

sounding out of Petrov's wishes: however, these objections did not apply to enquiries made by a private citizen, FRANKMAN agreed to help. At his own suggestion, he passed a message to Petrov, via DIABOLO, that he would like to examine his eyes again for professional interest in a rather unusual case; and an appointment was made for 23rd July.

40. Meanwhile Petrov again stayed at DIABOLO's flat, that he was not leaving for Russia immediately, the Ambassador (Lifanov) was leaving early in In this connection he expressed the hope that perhaps there were some good people in Russia who saw Lifanov's actions in their true light; and said that he heard that the new Ambassador was a decent fellow.

41. Meanwhile Petrov again stayed at DIABLO's flat and said he was not leaving for Russia immediately but that the Ambassador (Lifanov) was leaving early in August. In this connection he expressed the hope that perhaps there were some good people in Russia who saw Lifanov's actions in their true light; and said that he had heard that the new ambassador was a decent fellow.

42. The next evening from the flat Petrov rang his wife, who was on duty at the Embassy, and enquired how the meeting that evening had gone. He described to DIABOLO the procedure of criticism and counter-criticism, and said he despised the Soviet system of 'putting each other in.'

43. Next morning DIABOLO took Petrov to FRANKMAN's surgery. FRANKMAN indicated that he would be same time with Petrov, and that DIABOLO need not wait. When they were alone and there had been some preliminary talk, the following conversation took place:

FRANKMAN: Are you going back to Moscow?

Petrov: Yes.

FRANKMAN: I don't know that I would want to go back, with all the changes taking place there – Beria.

Petrov: It is my duty.

FRANKMAN: Don't you like this country?

Petrov: Yes, it is a fine country – plenty of food – plenty of everything.

FRANKMAN: Why don't you stay here?

Petrov: It is my duty to go back.

FRANKMAN: If I was in your place I'd stay here.

Petrov: It is very hard to get a job like that.

FRANKMAN: Not if you know the right people – it is traditional that the Diplomatic Corps look after other members of the Diplomatic Corps who are in difficulties or in these circumstances – such as the Czech Consul who was here – I have friends who know about these things.

There was a long pause here, whilst FRANKMAN was busy treating Petrov – then Petrov said:

Petrov: That Czech – yes, he has a restaurant in ... Street. (The Doctor could not recall the street name he mentioned.)

FRANKMAN: Oh, I am sure you could do better than that if helped by the right people.

Petrov did not comment and the matter was not pressed. An appointment was made in a fortnight's time.

44. FRANKMAN described Petrov's manner as quiet, guarded, slow and deliberate. He was quite sure Petrov perfectly understood the import of the conversation and he recorded his impression of three elements in Petrov's reaction – (a) a sense of duty to the Soviet, (b) fear that he would not be able to establish himself in Australia, (c) wistfulness in country, etc.

45. DIABOLO subsequently reported that he had met Petrov after his visit to FRANKMAN, and Petrov had described the conversation. 'The account given by DIABOLO was substantially accurate'; he added that Petrov warned him against FRANKMAN as being a 'security' man. The word 'security' was never used by FRANKMAN: Whether it was introduced by Petrov or by DIABOLO is not clear. DIABOLO also reported that Petrov referred to a Czech consular defector viio had established himself comfortably in Sydney; and that Petrov was very vague about the interview but mentioned that it would be interesting to 'see how it develops'.

46. Petrov saw FRANKMAN a month later on 22nd August, at his surgery. On this occasion Petrov spoke glowingly of and at any attempt by FRANKMAN to steer the conversation towards the advantages of life in Australia, praised Russia even more emphatically. He mentioned that he would not be going back for a while, but that his chief was leaving soon. He was amicable but moved off briskly as soon as the medical examination was completed. FRANKMAN felt that he had completely dismissed any idea of staying.

47. The ASIO assessment was that, while the FRANKMAN approach was probably a 'dead duck', at least a clearly defined line of contact with official quarters had been established for Petrov if at any future time he should feel disposed to make use of it.

48. Petrov's association with DIABOLO continued unbroken on his frequent official visits to Sydney, including drinking, dining, and staying overnight at DIABOLO's flat; and there were further reports of friction between him and Ambassador Lifanov.

49. In late September DIABOLO reported that Petrov had said that he did not believe that the charges against Beria were true. DIABOLO believed that Petrov was still interested in staying in Australia.
50. On 3rd October 1953 the new Ambassador, Generalov, arrived to take over the Embassy in Canberra. (The significance of this in the defection story was not fully appreciated till later, but it would seem that Petrov nourished some hopes that with Lifanov's replacement a more congenial regime might be inaugurated. The reverse proved to be the case.)
51. Early in November there was independent evidence that the new ambassador was taking a severely authoritative attitude to the Petrovs. DIABOLO confirmed this, and early in December reported as follows:

    Petrov was impressed with the prosperity and rapid progress of migrants in Australia, and would like to stay but was a prey to fear. His wife had been recently sacked from her job as Accountant and Secretary. (It was independently confirmed that she had been replaced by the wife of the new First Secretary, Vislykh, and had handed over her duties); this caused Petrov great alarm; he was very upset, hostile to the new ambassador and Soviet officialdom, said he would rather work in the streets than live in fear of his life, and that he and his wife were considering suicide. DIABOLO said that Petrov never talked Communist ideology; he had a good deal of contempt for 'peace' and 'front' organisations; but had never expressed any attitude to the Australian Communist Party.
52. On 28th November DIABOLO reported that he had offered to assist Petrov with the purchase of a chicken farm near Sydney; that Petrov had admitted that he would like that sort of life, but had remained non-committal towards any definite proposal; DIABOLO believed that he was seriously considering the matter. He further reported that Petrov had no close relatives in Russia, as they were all dead; his wife had her family in Russia, but DIABOLO thought that Petrov's main concern would be for his own safety.
53. On 1st December a conference was held to review the defection possibilities; and next day DIABOLO was briefed by Ron Richards (Regional Director for New South Wales) who by this time was handling him personally. He was instructed to pursue the chicken-farm business purely as a private venture, and was given clear instructions as to his course of action if Petrov showed signs of coming to a decision. It was impressed upon him that ASIO could in no circumstances be a party to inciting Petrov to defect but that if Petrov decided he wished to put in direct touch with an ASIO officer and that DIABOLO was in no position to take the official measures indispensable to a diplomatic defection. (Up to

this stage DIABOLO's reported conversations with Petrov had dealt solely with the question of what Petrov might do in Australia. In the absence of feelers in regard and political asylum, doubts persisted intentions.)

54. From this point until Petrov's defection Richards was in constant touch with the Director-General, reporting each development and discussing each stop in the case.
[Paragraph 54 missing in the original.]

55. Throughout December Petrov paid several visits to the flat, DIABOLO reported that he spoke well of Australia, as a country where one could do well, and said that his wife was very ill and might not live very long. (DIABOLO interpreted this as a pretext for unilateral action by Petrov).

56. On 16th December Petrov said he would like to defer any decision about his future until the New Year; the farm was a great opportunity which might not occur again; he might take it without his wife. He said that his disappearance would be a terrible scandal, and spoke about his youth and the hard life he had endured.

57. On 16th December Petrov again called on FRANKMAN at his surgery, and asked for an examination of his eyes. Neither party raised the question of his staying in Australia. However, Petrov suggested to DIABOLO that it would be a good idea to invite FRANKMAN to lunch as soon as possible.

58. On 23rd December tentative arrangements were made on Petrov's next visit, that DIABOLO would take him to FRANKMAN's home, and leave them alone in order that FRANKMAN could confirm his ability to arrange official contacts and protection.

59. Early on the morning of 24th December Petrov was involved in a car accident on the road between Canberra and Cooma. He claimed that he was forced off the road by a lorry; his car overturned and was completely burnt out.

60. A few days later DIABOLO met him by chance in Sydney; he was depressed over the accident, and said that as he had failed to renew the insurance on the car, the ambassador was insisting that he pay for its replacement. He complained of the callousness of his Embassy colleagues to the painful abrasions he received in the accident, and said he got a lot more sympathy from Australians. He told DIABOLO that he would stay in Australia even without his wife, but it was a very hard decision to make because of her. She would not agree to stay because of her family in Russia; but if she went back her head would be cut off in any case; the authorities over there would-not ask any questions as to guilt or otherwise.

61. On 9th January Petrov was again in Sydney, DIABOLO took him out to visit the chicken farm, and he paid a deposit on it. Next day

DIABOLO reported that Petrov, before returning to Canberra, had had a frank discussion with him about the official aspect of defection, and had asked DIABOLO touch with the local authorities.

62. He had been in an overwrought state, and had opened up to DIABOLO about the abject poverty of life in Russia contrasted with the privileges enjoyed by Maenkov and the ruling clique who lived in luxury, just as the Czar did. But you try to go to Russia and say something against them: they will cut your head off'. Three million Russians ran away: Beria was killed, after he himself had killed legions. 'Why shouldn't Russians live and let live, open their frontiers, they can't fool anybody anyway; foreign diplomats can see things for themselves. I will stay here. I will write a true story, I will fix those bastards. I will tell the whole truth'.

63. (There is no reason to doubt the description of Petrov's outburst against the Soviet; he has repeatedly spoken in the same vein since his defection.)

64. DIABOLO promised Petrov to take steps to arrange the necessary official contacts; and was briefed at each step. From this point the business moved swiftly into a new phase. FRANKMAN invited Petrov and DIABOLO to his home for drinks on the evening of 15th January, Petrov did not keep this engagement, but explained later that he had been too busy with the Ambassador and the Commercial Attaché, who were in Sydney on that day.

65. But on the evening of 23rd January Petrov and DIABOLO visited FRANKMAN at his home. From discussion of conditions in Australia and the world the conversation passed to 'doing well' in Australia and what Petrov could do if he were not a diplomat but a resident. Petrov explained that he had no special qualifications and was only a 'country man'; whereupon FRANKMAN suggested the possibility of a chicken farm. (This was in fact pure coincidence, and happened to be a hobby of FRANKMAN's.) Petrov then made clear his need of financial help and personal protection; to which FRANKMAN replied, 'That can be arranged, I think I know the right people to help in that regard'.

66. At this meeting Petrov showed obvious signs of strain and anxiety; but both FRANKMAN and DIABOLO were convinced that he had in fact made up his mind to stay.

67. DIABOLO reported that during this visit to Sydney Petrov had suggested that DIABOLO should visit Canberra and try to persuade his wife of the advantages of staying in Australia, After a briefing by Richards, he went to Canberra and visited the Petrovs at their house on the morning of 31st January.

68. DIABOLO reported that Mrs. Petrov was obviously under great stress. He suggested her remaining in Australia. She said that the

ambassador's wife was not on speaking terms with her; but then launched into a tirade in which she declared that coexistence of different systems was impossible, that the ideas of Marx-Lenin-Stalin still held good for her; that she would go back to Russia even if it meant death; that it was no use trying to talk her into staying. She said that she cared little for her father or brother, but much for her mother and sister. This was her general line when Petrov was present. At other times she ridiculed the unbecoming dress of Soviet women, and expressed her admiration for the Queen (who was then visiting Australia).

69. She said she would like to accept DIABOLO's invitation for them 'both to visit him in Sydney; and a plane seat was booked for a visit on the 24th February.'

70. In Petrov's absence she asked DIABOLO if he were [sic] suggesting she should stay in Australia, expressed the Antonov's (the Sydney TASS Agent and his wife, whom DIABOLO was in touch with), and asked for complete discretion in regard to their conversation. DIABOLO recorded his opinion that the Petrovs did not completely trust each other.

71. On the 2nd February the Australian press carried the story of Yuri Rastvorov's disappearance in Japan; and DIABOLO was instructed to bring it to Petrov's attention. He reported that Petrov had said that his wife had lost her job through being too outspoken; and that the Ambassador had accused her of using her husband as a mouthpiece at meetings in the Embassy.

72. DIABOLO felt that Petrov was playing a waiting game, and was hoping that his wife would make up her mind; he did not seem to be afraid that she would inform the Embassy authorities of his intentions; but he would not commit himself until the last moment. Petrov had recently repeated that his wife's family were the main obstacle to her coming, that she assisted them, and they depended on this to keep them in reasonable material comfort, and she felt wholly responsible for their maintenance and well-being. Petrov agreed that if he stayed in Australia and she returned to Moscow her fate would be sealed, but she still needed to be convinced of that.

73. As instructed, DIABOLO told Petrov that FRANKMAN was pestering him for some clear indication of Petrov's intentions. Petrov commented, 'He is a keen customer' but did not wish to discuss the matter.

74. On 19th February Petrov was again in Sydney; he told DIABOLO that he had been ordered back to Russia in two months, and he thought his wife had decided against staying. DIABOLO urged the necessity for practical steps and definite arrangements. That evening they both visited FRANKMAN's home.

75. FRANKMAN reported that when reference had been made to his influential connections, Petrov took the initiative, showed his alarm ('They could shoot me'), asked to see a high security official with credentials, and emphasized the need for absolute secrecy, especially if there was to be any delay.
76. FRANKMAN replied that he would be glad to introduce Petrov to a personal friend of his, Richards, 'Head of the Security Department here', whom he could vouch for. He made it clear that for international reasons no initiative could come from the Government, but said that the Government would certainly grant protection. He then telephoned Richards, and an unofficial meeting was arranged for 10 a.m. the next morning at DIABOLO's flat; Richards would bring credentials, and absolute discretion would be observed.
77. After some general talk on the enmities of Europe contrasted with the amiable relations of people of different origins in Australia, Petrov and DIABOLO left, DIABOLO commented that FRANKMAN was a decent sort of fellow; to which Petrov replied, 'Yes. He is not out to shoot men of my type', and again expressed his disgust with the system of mutual denunciations.
78. Next morning (20th) DIABOLO, with Petrov at his elbow, rang Richards and said that Petrov would like to postpone the meeting until the 26th, Richards then got DIABOLO to make certain that Petrov understood his position Director of the Security Service in New South Wales, with authority to represent the Commonwealth Government. Asked whether he was serious, Petrov replied, 'Yes, I am serious', Petrov returned to Canberra that evening.
79. On the 26th Petrov rang DIABOLO from Canberra to say that he could not come that day; since Kovaliov (the Commercial Attaché) and Pliatkais, Petrov's assistant in migrant work, were on their way to Sydney.
80. The next day, Saturday 27th February, DIABOLO rang me from his flat to say that he had Petrov with him, and that Petrov would like to see Richards.
81. Richards arrived at the flat at 6.50 p.m. Petrov was sober but acutely nervous and perspiring; he several times laughed loudly without reason. DIABOLO was present most of the time, but left the room while Richards had a short talk with Petrov alone. Richards left at 8 p.m.
82. On arrival Richards introduced himself and showed his credentials and another document giving him authority to grant political asylum on behalf of the Commonwealth. Petrov examined these closely, accepted them and Richards, and gave his own position as Third Secretary and Consul of the Soviet Embassy. He said, 'This is to be between the three of us'. He said he wished to stay in

Australia; his wife was the main difficulty, and he would try to persuade her to stay, but in any case he would stay. He was shown a brief statement that he was voluntarily seeking political asylum in Australia; he said he would sign it when he made the actual break. He asked for assurance of physical protection, and material assistance to establish himself in Australia.

83. For his part, he said that he would, (a) tell all he knew about the work of the Soviet Government in Australia, (b) write a book 'for the world to know the truth'. He would have further discussions, and would probably make the break about mid-March.

84. He discussed the steps that the Embassy would take after his disappearance. They included a request for the police to find him: he hoped they would not be able to. He also predicted that the Embassy would charge him with, 1) mental weakness, 2) suicide, 3) some offence against Soviet law.

85. He attacked the Embassy staff, and confirmed the reports received from DIABOLO that he and his wife had been adversely reported on by the Ambassadors.

86. When asked by Richards what he meant by his promise to toll 'all', he replied, 'I know what you do, Mr. Richards. I know what you want. I can tell you all you want to know, and I will do so, but that is later' (i.e. when he came), Richards terminated the interview on friendly but official terms.

87. Next day, DIABOLO confirmed that Petrov had accepted Richards' assurances was impressed by the offer of safety and assistance, and was confident that he could cope with his Embassy colleagues. But later he had said, 'How do Ido I know that the Government will do what Mr Richards says they will do – then I would he in a mess'.

88. According to DIABOLO, Petrov suggested that he would need six months holiday and a sum of money, say £5,000, to give him time to tell all he knows and write a book; hut DIABOLO should not put up this requirement too bluntly. He repented that he knew what Mr Richards wanted, and would make a plan to 'got together everything': He could manage this during his nights on duty at the embassy.

89. On 19th March Richards again saw Petrov with DIABOLO at the latter's flat. Petrov told Richards that he had definitely decided to stay in Australia; and discussed being made to his wife, possibly through some other woman of her acquaintance. (This proposal was put aside, as being altogether too dangerous, impracticable, and uncertain.)

90. A discussion on finance ensued, on which matter Richards had already sought the advice of the Director-General. As a visual aid and demonstration of the Commonwealth's bona fides, Richards

showed Petrov £5,000 in cash, a sight which, as described by DIABOLO, impressed all, 'including myself'. 'Petrov dismissed proposals for a trusteeship account, saying that he believed the promises would be kept. It was then arranged that he should receive this sum of money after his defection, and should keep it in a safe of which he would have the key.'

91. There was a brief discussion of the information which Petrov could provide; and it was made plain to him that particular value would be attached to matters affecting the security of Australia and any help towards the detection of persons working against Australia.

92. As to the mechanics of his 'disappearance', Petrov rejected the idea of being picked up in Canberra, and proposed instead that he would come to Sydney with very little as if on a normal trip, and simply not return. He was anxious that after his disappearance no information should be given to the Press or the Soviet Embassy until after his wife's departure for Russia, as he felt that would help her.

93. After Richards had left the flat he expressed pleasure at the financial arrangements, and said 'I don't think they are going to put it over me' (meaning the Australian authorities).

94. On the 20th and 21st March, further discussions took place between Petrov, DIABOLO and Richards. (DIABOLO reported that Petrov was badly needing reassurance about the moral basis of his proposed action.) Petrov proposed to come about 3rd April; he would be meeting new arrivals to join the Embassy staff, including his own successor, and he wanted to turn over his work to the new man and leave everything in order. He was still turning over the possibility of another approach to his wife, and even suggested a visit to their home in Canberra by Richards.

95. This suggestion was of course ruled out as foolhardy; but the possibility was mentioned of an approach to her on board ship, while the chance remained of her dis-embarking at some Australian port. Practical details which interested Petrov were the picking up of his sporting gun and fishing rods, and arrangements for his Alsatian dog, Jack, to which he was devoted.

96. Meanwhile on the 20th Richards met Petrov at another flat without DIABOLO's knowledge. Petrov was cool and decisive, watchful 'but not uneasy, He now made clear that he considered DIABOLO his good friend in the matter of assisting his defection; 'but stressed that, (a) in spite of DIABOLO's emphasis on the financial aspect, he, PETROV, was not primarily concerned to bargain about the money ('I trust you to take care of me')', (b) DIABOLO did not know anything about his espionage work.

97. Petrov promised to give all the help he could in regard to current espionage including names of sources and reports: he would give these when he actually defected. He said that Generalov had

demanded to know his contacts; but that he had refused to reveal them. Finally he voiced an apprehension which has evidently been real to both Petrovs at times – 'My wife says we are like the Rosenbergs if we stay; I told her that was stupid'.

98. The next contact with Petrov took the form of three brief meetings between Richards and him in Richards' car at various rendezvous in Canberra, At the first, on 30th March, Petrov was in a hurry, as he was on his way to a reception. He was satisfied that all was safe at the Embassy, and was so confident that he proposed to return to Canberra with the new arrivals from Moscow, and spend a week or so with them, getting valuable recent information before defecting.

99. The rendezvous next evening was for 8.30 p.m.; but Petrov did not turn up till 10.30 p.m. He said that a meeting at the Embassy which he had expected to be over in half an hour had lasted three hours. Generalov had criticized many of the staff, including Mrs Petrov. Following this Petrov had suggested that she should stay; but she was obdurate on account of her family. He felt that she was being stupid: he would stay in any case.

100. Richards again met Petrov the following evening. This time he was very nervous, and said that the previous evening, after he and his wife had left the Embassy, Generalov had carried out a raid on his safe and desk, where a document had been found which should not have been there. The Ambassador had severely reprimanded him, and had said a report would go to Moscow. The documents –which Petrov had secreted were quite safe; but in view of what had happened, he had decided to stay in Sydney on his next visit, and not return to Canberra: he thought there was a chance that his wife now might stay. He gave Richards his gun and a bag for conveyance to Sydney.

101. Petrov travelled to Sydney by next morning's plane, carrying only a light handbag, Richards was a passenger on the same plane.

102. At 2.30 p.m. that day (2nd April) Richards met Petrov at Richards' flat. At 4.30 p.m. Richards left Petrov in the flat and reported the situation to the Director-General. At 6.30 p.m. Richards returned to the flat, and Petrov signed the document requesting of his own free will political asylum in Australia, At 8 p.m. the Director-General arrived at the flat and had a short interview with Petrov. During this interview Petrov showed all the documents he had brought with him, and Soviet espionage in; for the first time gave detailed information about Australia. Petrov then went to stay the night at DIABOLO's flat. Richards called there for a short time later in the evening.

103. On 3rd April Petrov met the new arrivals from Moscow, including his successor Kovalenok, escorted them to Mascot aerodrome, and saw them aboard the plane for Canberra. Then at 11.35 a.m. he

followed Richards out of the passenger lounge of the aerodrome, and into Richards' car, and drove off.

104. On the way to the safe house he asked to be taken to a private hotel where he had some business to complete with one of his Embassy colleagues. He transferred to a taxi some distance from this hotel, and arranged to be picked up again at an agreed time and place. He was late for this rendezvous, but arrived in due course. He explained that on his way he had felt thirsty, and had gone into a bar for a beer.

105. On arrival at the safe house, Petrov was given the promised sum of money, which he put away for him. He handed over the documents to Richards, gave a brief explanation of their contents, and though very distraught and anxious for his own safety, began to give his own statement.

Defection of Mrs. Petrov:

106. Mrs. Petrov's defection took place substantially as by her in considerable detail to the Royal Commission on Espionage, and reported in the Australian press.

107. From ASIO's point of view the desirability of obtaining a double defection had never been in doubt, particularly in view of the important position which Mrs. Petrov clearly held in the Embassy in her own right, reinforced by the reports of her given by DIABOLO, and in the latter stages by Petrov himself. On the other hand there had been nothing like the close and continued contact which had been established in the case of Petrov himself; her own husband was dubious of her ultimate desire to defect; and there was the known factor of her family in Russia. In the circumstances it was decided that no initiative could be risked, and that the most that could be done was to foresee and prepare for every eventuality. What could not be foreseen was the degree of assistance to be provided by the Soviet authorities themselves.

108. Mrs. Petrov told the Royal Commission that her husband had 'infiltrated' the possibility of defection into her mind. Whatever the exact degree of their discussions on this point it seems clear that, (a) she knew that her husband was seriously considering defection, (b) she was by no means fully informed of his plans, and did not know when he left home on Friday, 2nd April, that he had arranged to following day, and not return.

109. On 6th April when Petrov was already several days overdue and nothing had been heard of him, Generalov called Mrs Petrov to his office and said that he feared Petrov would not now return, and had perhaps been kidnapped. He told her that he was asking the Australian authorities to investigate; that meanwhile she must

take up residence in the Embassy building, in case an attempt should be made to kidnap her also.

110. From this point onwards the incredible ineptitude shown in the handling of this intelligent and high-spirited woman played an important, if not a decisive part, in her final decision, confined to one room. She was obviously under virtual arrest, was confined to ne room in the Embassy building under continual supervision, was only provided with bed and food as a result of her own protests, was allowed to see only one newspaper, *The Canberra Times*, and whenever she asked to listen to the wireless, was told that all the sets had 'gone wrong': this even proved to be the case, with the wireless in the official car which drove her to Sydney. She was studiously avoided by all Embassy staff except on official business; and the other Embassy wives showed malicious pleasure at her predicament, She was allowed a short visit to her house under escort to collect clothes and belongings, There she was outraged to find evidence of a hasty search and to see a large pile of her own and her husband's clothes heaped indiscriminately in the middle of the room. She was several times interrogated by Generalov and Kovaliev (Commercial Attaché and Secretary of the Party in the Embassy) about her husband's intentions and movements, but she insisted that she knew nothing beyond the fact that he was greatly distressed by the attacks and adverse reports against him.

111. Meanwhile (in her capacity as MVD cypher clerk) she handed over to Kovalenok all the documents, equipment, and funds of the MVD office: he checked these, accepted them, and signed for them on the 15th, After that she was not allowed into the cypher section.

112. Generalov and Kovaliev interviewed her again, and showed her a letter from her husband which had been received through External Affairs; in it he said he was well and asked her to meet him, Generalov said the letter was obviously written under dictation. She had to write a reply under their supervision, on instruction from Moscow, in which she said that she was unwilling to see him as she was afraid of falling into a trap. She protested against this reference to a trap, but finally gave way, Generalov also insisted that she alter the diminutive 'Volodenka' (her usual form of address to her husband) to the less affectionate 'Volodya'. The stupidity and pettiness of the treatment she received irritated and provoked her greatly.

113. Three other developments caused her even more serious alarm, (a) she discussed with Kovalenok her situation when she returned to Moscow, and be reminded her that she herself must be aware of the provisions in the Soviet penal code for the punishment of relatives of enemies of the people which could mean penal servitude or even death for the wife a voluntary defector, (b) she asked

Generalov to obtain for her a guarantee of immunity from Moscow. On the morning of her departure she again asked about this and he replied that it had not yet arrived. Prom this she inferred the worst, (c) finally, Generalov reminded her that the couriers who would escort her were armed, and if there were any attempts by the Australian authorities to force her to stay, they might use their weapons, (in Mrs. Petrov's mind this aroused the apprehension that there was a plot to do away with her on the journey, under pretext of an attempted escape).

114. On the 8-hours plane trip from Sydney to Darwin, all these episodes added up in Mrs. Petrov's mind to the consideration, 'If they treat me like this in the Embassy here, what will they do when I get to Moscow?' Nevertheless her feelings for her family in Moscow inclined her to take the risk.

115. She was to travel under escort of the two couriers, Jarkov and Karpinsky and Kislytsin, 2nd Secretary at the Canberra Embassy. By this time the Prime Minister's announcement on the evening of 13th April that Petrov had sought asylum, and the subsequent publicity, had aroused great public interest and sympathy for Mrs Petrov, who was believed to be returning to Russia under duress. On the night of 19th April when the party were due to leave Sydney, a demonstration took place at Mascot aerodrome organised by anti-Soviet Russians and Czechs, Mrs. Petrov was assisted through the unruly crowd, losing a shoe in the process, and had to be helped aboard the plane. But she is insistent that at this point, though distressed and anxious, she had every intention of returning to Russia, and would not have responded to an offer of asylum had one been made.

116. (In fact, preparations had been made to grant Mrs. Petrov asylum at Sydney, Darwin and other points along the route if she asked for it, and Petrov was actually waiting in a room at Mascot aerodrome to interview her. But this was not thought likely and the demonstration ruled out the possibility.)

117. The Director-General of Security, Colonel Spry, was by this time in Canberra, in constant touch with the Commonwealth Government; he took personal charge of the operation throughout the night. Wireless communication was established with the Captain of the aircraft, who was asked specific 1 questions; after making enquiries he reported that Mrs Petrov was very much afraid of the couriers, who were armed, (bs; was anxious to know what had happened to her husband, and was interested in the question of staying in Australia.

118. Detailed instructions were then telephoned to Mr Leydin, the Assistant Administrator of the Northern Territory at Darwin. When the plane landed there, before dawn on 20th April, Mr Leydin

approached Mrs. Petrov as soon as she disembarked, and asked her if she wished to remain in Australia. Another Commonwealth official engaged Kislitsyn in conversation, and at the same time a police guard interposed between the couriers and Mrs Petrov, and asked them if they were armed, (it had been ascertained that the carrying of firearms and ammunition in a pressurized aircraft was contrary to International Air Regulations and to the rules of the airline by which they werc travelling). One of the couriers made a move as if to draw a revolver; and both couriers were thereupon disarmed. (One courier offered resistance, the other did not.) Each was found to be carrying a loaded revolver. The weapons were handed to the Captain of the aircraft, for return to the couriers in due course; and the ammunition was sent back to the Soviet Embassy in Canberra. After this no restraint was placed upon the couriers' movements, Kislytsin protested that diplomatic immunity had been violated; but was told that he was completely free to move about as he wished, and appeared satisfied. These events gave Leydin sufficient time with Mrs Petrov for him to inform her that her husband was safe and well, and that if she wished to seek asylum also he was in a position to grant it on behalf of the Commonwealth Government. She would not decide, asked to speak her husband, and eventually rejoined her companions.

119. Then a telephone call was arranged from Petrov in Sydney to his wife in Darwin. Her escort stood by during the conversation. She was laconic, answered, 'No, No', and finally, 'That is not my husband'. After a minute or two she put down the receiver and went back to sit with her companions in the passenger lounge, where six remained, apparently having rejected the offer. However, when the plane crew were already going on board, Leydin again asked if she would like to talk to him; and she said she would. In spite of her companions' protests she went with him to the quarantine office and spoke to him alone. She was acutely nervous, 'but said that she would like to seek asylum.' She admitted that she had heard her husband clearly, that he was well and cheerful, and wanted her to stay. She refused to sign any statement until she saw him.

120. She was then taken to Government House, Darwin, and thence flown back to join her husband at the safe house Sydney, where she signed the statement that she of her own free will requested political asylum in Australia.

121. There is little doubt that Mrs. Petrov was fully awake of the issues involved and the choice before her. The telephone conversation with her husband was almost certainly the deciding factor because – (1) it satisfied her that he was alive and well. (She insists that she was never sure up to that point that he had not been

kidnapped, or was not under committed suicide), (2) he appealed to her not as a husband but as a 'man', because even if she did go back to Russia she would now never see her family again.

Motives for Defection
A Material Inducements:

122. Both Petrovs acknowledge their appreciation of the material attractions of Western life. Petrov has described Sweden as a very good country and admits that the thought of defection crossed his mind as early as their term of service there (1943–47). He likes outdoor life, and frequently went fishing and shooting in the country round Canberra; while in DIABOLO's company he showed a distinct taste for the more convivial pleasures of the city. His observation of the rapid progress of migrants towards an established prosperity also impressed him with the material possibilities of life in Australia.

123. Mrs Petrov was distinguished among the Russian Embassy women in Canberra by her western aptitude for clothes and cosmetics (which was doubtless a factor in their enmity towards her). She is attractive and intelligent, speaks good English, has considerable social aplomb, well qualified to make her way in a Western society.

124. Since their defection they have both taken a keen interest in the question of providing for their future financial security.

125. On the other hand it is certain that material inducements alone, however great, would not have brought about either defection. Both Petrovs had achieved m their own right a successful career in the Soviet Service. From very humble origins both of them by their own efforts had attained the position of privilege and prestige that belongs to officers of the MVD; their combined salaries totalled approximately £8,000 (Australian) per annum. By Russian standards they were prosperous and privileged.

126. At the time of defection neither of the Petrovs were greatly concerned to bargain about actual sums of money; protection, with reasonable comfort and security, bulked larger in their minds than visions of vast wealth. At present Petrov shows most interest in the possibilities for fishing, shooting, and an outdoor life; while Mrs. Petrov shows an appreciation of the greater scope afforded in a Western country for dress, decoration, and house-furnishing.

127. As diplomats and as MVD officers, the Petrovs enjoyed a standard of living that made them privileged persons in the Soviet, and which did not come sufficiently short of Western standards to provide in itself a strong enough motive for defection.

128. Fear was without doubt the prime mover in both cases; without it neither defection would have occurred. For most of their three

years term in Australia, the Petrovs were the subject of a campaign by successive Ambassadors, and the Party Secretary, Kovaliev, to isolate them in Canberra and destroy their credit in Moscow.
129. In the tangled skein of this intrigue against them, certain threads can be distinguished, including, (a) personal malice on the part of the Ambassadors and their wives, (b) a perennial campaign by Ambassadors against the credit of the enclave of independent authority represented by the MVD office, (c) repercussions of the struggle in Moscow between Party, Army and MVD, illustrated dramatically in the fall of Beria. As described by the Petrovs, this campaign included adverse reports to the Ministry of Foreign Affairs and the Central Committee in Moscow, an effort to isolate them socially, attacks upon them in the meetings of Party members in the Embassy, including the accusation that they were forming a 'Beria group', and a search of Petrov's safe and desk, during which a document was found which, he was told, would be reported as an example of negligence.
130. Resentment at these attacks, and fear of what awaited him in Russia, obsessed Petrov over a long and precipitated his defection when the opportunity was presented to him.
131. A similar fear, accentuated by her treatment after her husband's disappearance, finally overcame Mrs. Petrov's strong impulse to return to Russia out of devotion to her family. Every action by the Soviet authorities reinforced this fear and apprehension that nothing but the worst awaited them on their return to Moscow.

Ideological Factors:
Disillusionment with the Soviet:

132. It is doubtful whether either of the Petrovs was ever in the position of the fanatical ideologue or the dedicated revolutionary known in Western Communist Parties. Both are of peasant origin, familiar with the abject poverty which remains the lot of most of their fellow countrymen in city, town, or village. For both of them the Communist party and the MVD have represented a privileged elite, and a road to education, status, and advancement, wherein service of the State went hand in hand with service of their own material interests. Both of them, since their defection, have voiced criticisms of the Soviet which are evidently the fruit of experience and secret reflection rather than opinions hastily adopted to suit their new situation. Their stated desire to 'tell the truth' about the Soviet seems to represent something more than policy, and to reflect a genuine indignation and disillusion.
133. Petrov expresses himself as completely cynical about the Soviet system and Soviet professions, and inveighs against, (a) the ruin of village life by forcible collectivization (which he, as a young

Communist official, helped to carry out), (b) the system of denunciation, (c) the injustice and brutality of the wholesale purges, (d) the growth of a privileged caste, whose luxurious life contrasts with the poverty of the masses, (e) the false propaganda about Soviet superiority, which deceives no-one, (f) the intolerance and suppression of all criticism.

134. Mrs Petrov's criticisms are 'not so unequivocal' as her husband's, but are frank and starching nevertheless. She has led a more sheltered life in the MVD, fold in Moscow, in which she enjoyed considerable personal and professional success. It is likely that, as a woman, her general criticisms would not have greatly influenced her course of action had she herself not been so directly and personally affected. She bitterly resented the campaign against them by the Ambassadors and the Party Secretary, and resisted the attempts to discipline and discredit her and her husband. Her public statements voice her indignation at the local Soviet authorities and their behaviour, rather than any radical criticism of the Soviet system or of Moscow control.

135. However, an obvious motive for this distinction exists in her anxiety for the fate of her family in Russia; and in private she too has spoken with frank dislike of the regimenting of opinion, the constant suspicion, the ruthless and inscrutable regime of terror under which all Soviet citizens live, and the grim poverty of the mosses, particularly widows and old people.

136. She appears to retain some sense of affection and loyalty to Russia as her country, but almost none to the tenets of Communist ideology. Like her husband, she depicts a system which has expended all its idealism and now relies in practice, though not in words, solely on calculated self-interest as a basis for service. A grievance which touched her particularly is the discrepancy between the theory and practice of the right of criticism. Though guaranteed by the Soviet constitution to all Party members equally, and publicly proclaimed by Soviet leaders, this right proved a hollow privilege indeed in their controversy with the Embassy authorities in Canberra.

137. Resentment at the hypocrisy, insecurity, and ruthlessness of life under the Soviet system is apparently a real factor in the outlook of both Petrovs, and certainly weakened any feeling of loyalty which the machine which they may have had to the machine which they had served.

Appeal of Democratic Life:

138. Unlike Igor Gouzenko, the Petrovs have not so far taken any lofty line as to their motives for embracing democracy, They do not conceal the fact that the goading from behind, rather than the

blandishments in front, governed their decision to defect to the West: namely, dread of the Soviet system as they had begun to experience it, rather than attraction to democracy for its own sake. However, this generalization requires qualification as follows:-

139. The Petrovs had had personal experience, in both Sweden and Australia, of life in a democratic Western country, Petrov in particular, even before his defection, expressed his preference for the freedom of Western countries, and the more tolerant human attitudes which this made possible. This accords well with his own easy-going nature, and is believed to have weighed with him at least as much as strictly material considerations. Mrs Petrov, though much more restricted, had a few women friends outside the embassies in both Sweden and Australia. She had acquired a fairly clear idea of the much greater freedom enjoyed by women outside Russia, particularly in family and private life.

140. Both Petrovs were impressed by the firm but humane approach of the Commonwealth officers in relation to their defection: this contrasted notably with the hectic and crude treatment which each of them received from their own superiors in the Embassy. At the first interview Richards succeeded in establishing Petrov's confidence in his authority and competence: Mrs Petrov has described the favourable effect of Leydin's calm but confident manner in his approach to her at Darwin.

141. Since their defection, both Petrovs have expressed their appreciation of the considerate treatment which they have received, and have also commented on the informality, mutual trust, delegation of responsibility end team spirit among the ASIO personnel with whom they have had to deal, contrasted with the timidity and mutual suspicion which pervade their own service, and all Soviet officialdom.

142. (The deep-seated suspicion of the Petrovs that they will be abandoned by the Commonwealth once their usefulness has been exhausted, or that they will later be punished for their work against Australia, has not yet been wholly eradicated. It indicates the influence of anti-Western propaganda in the Soviet even upon persons who have had unusual contact with Western life, like the Petrovs, when added to their experience of the cynical opportunism practised by their own system.)

Operational Comments:

143. The Petrovs assert that Soviet Diplomats generally try to prolong their periods of service abroad, and that many would like to defect but are deterred by, (a) members of their family remaining in Russia as hostages, (b) lack of contacts with the west. The Petrovs' own story illustrates these points clearly enough.

144. The Petrovs are childless, and Petrov has no close relatives left in Russia. His defection was thus the 'trigger' to his wife's defection since the Soviet penal code provides severe penalties for 'enemies of the people'.
145. The value of intensive study of Soviet Embassy personnel appeared in three ways:
    (a) It led to a correct general appreciation of Petrov's functions, and hence of his value as a defector.
    (b) It made possible the exploitation of contemporary events to advance the defection plan.
    (c) It corroborated hostility and jealousy in the Embassy towards Petrov.
146. The length of DIABOLO's intimate association with Petrov enabled a gradual establishment of Petrov's familiarity with at least some aspects of Western life over a long period, and constituted a slow build-up to his ultimate decision.
147. Nevertheless, Petrov has named mid 1953 the time when his contacts with the West had reached a 'good situation'. This was the time of FRANKMAN's intervention. FRANKMAN's entry into the scene evidently –
    (a) Established for Petrov a trustworthy Australian link with Security (representing the Commonwealth).
    (b) Introduced the Beria theme (which appeared later, a curious sequence, when the Petrovs were accused of forming a 'Beria group' in the Embassy).
148. The very closeness of DIABOLO's association with Petrov acted as a brake on ASIO as it was felt that the most likely explanation was that DIABOLO must be under cultivation by Petrov (as was indeed the case), and that the defection project might be a blind on Petrov's part (which happily proved not to be the case).
149. In general, the capacity and efficiency of the Russians' intelligence operations in Australia were over-estimated. Petrov, for example, seems to have been in no real danger from Russian surveillance while he moved about Sydney with such remarkable freedom, (it was not realized that he enjoyed this freedom as senior MVD representative; he himself has reported warning off his MVD colleague Plaityais from making enquiries about his movements).
150. The tactics adopted by the Soviet authorities after Petrov's disappearance followed a stereotyped and expected pattern. They included, (a) suggestions of kidnapping; (b) the accusation that money had been stolen. (Petrov had already returned an air ticket and petty cash; while Mrs. Petrov had officially handed over, without queries being raised, her Embassy accounts to Mrs. Vislykh, and her MVD funds to Kovalenok). Preparations had been made to allow the Russians a closely-controlled interview with Petrov

if they requested it. However, they did not do so, and refused his request to allow his wife to see him, clearly fearing that he would persuade her to defect as well.
151. Administrative arrangements made in advance included –
    (a) Arrangements for the possible defection of either or both Petrovs in Canberra, Sydney or Darwin. i.e. provision of transport, necessary documents, and preparations to brief the necessary local officials.
    (b) Briefing of the necessary Ministers and Heads of Departments when the defection appeared imminent.
    (c) Arrangements for safe houses and physical protection of the Petrovs.
152. Interrogation plans included –
    (a) Detailed briefs on the basis of all that was known of the Petrovs before their defection.
    (b) Arrangements to record intelligence supplied by them in a form suitable for possible legal action and the presentation of evidence.
    (c) A plan for preliminary questioning to ascertain
        (i) Any other potential defectors.
        (ii) Matters affecting the security of Australia or other countries which called for immediate action.
        (iii) The substance of any documents supplied.
153. In conclusion, it seems certain that the defection of the Petrovs would not have occurred if there had not been –
    (a) An unusual combination of circumstances assisting it.
    (b) A vigorous effort to appreciate and take advantage of the opportunities as they occurred.

* * *

The Thwaites report remains the most comprehensive account of a Cold War defection yet declassified, illustrates the complexities of running two intermediaries, DIABOLO and FRANKMAN, against a candidate for defection. Incredibly, we learn that ASIO had very little idea of Petrov's true role in the Soviet Embassy, nor ever guessed that his wife was also an intelligence officer.

What Thwaites omitted from his very readable narrative was the one other aspect of Petrov's statement completed by him on the evening of his defection, and given to Ron Richards. This was Petrov's biography and, perhaps most importantly, details of Soviet agents currently active and managed by the *rezidentura*. Now declassified, the document makes fascinating reading for several reasons. Firstly, although he was unaware of it, the document was validated by the VENONA material already in ASIO's possession. This was the cryptographic material that had already identified Nosov and Antonov as members of the NKVD's *rezidentura*. Petrov, of course, never learned about this very secret source. Secondly, some of the spies named by Petrov, such as Ric Throssel and Wally Clayton, had been compromised already by the VENONA messages, so Petrov's testimony served to authenticate the conclusions reached by the VENONA counter-intelligence analysts. This single document would come to be recognised as one of the most significant of the Cold War, for another reason. Petrov, consciously or not, tarnished Leader of the Opposition Dr Evatt by revealing the penetration represented by O'Sullivan. Evatt's misguided reaction had been to denounce the entire exercise as a political stunt created by Prime Minister Sir Robert Menzies in the critical pre-election period, whereas this had not even been contemplated by ASIO. Evatt's determination to denigrate Petrov, and indeed the ensuing Royal Commission, ensured the Labour Party would remain in opposition for a generation.

One other aspect to this initial Petrov statement, dated 3.00 pm on 3 April 1954, should be noted. His defection was only hours old, and he had not yet come to trust ASIO, so was mindful that the document he had signed might be used as evidence against him in a subsequent prosecution charging him with espionage. Understandably, Petrov exercised considerable circumspection at this early stage in his relationship with ASIO.

> I was born in 1907 in a village called Larikha in the Tumen District, in Central Siberia, approximately 250 kilometers from the city of Omsk and 29 kilometers from Eshim.
>
> My father was a peasant – he could not read or write. I was at school – a primary school – for 2 years in my village. I left school at nine years of age.
>
> After I left school my father was killed by lightening, and I then went to work for my mother, and was helped by my younger brother – this would be about 1914.
>
> I helped my mother until 1921. Following that, I went to work for the village blacksmith. In 1923 I joined the Komsomol – the Young Communist organization – this was whilst I was still working for the village blacksmith.
>
> In 1921 our district had a famine and many people died.
>
> The situation was so bad that we were eating potato plants with tree bark, and were making bread out of this.
>
> The blacksmith was a communist – after the 1917 revolution – he was married twice – his second wife was the daughter of a chanter in the church. Because of this the blacksmith was expelled from the

communist party. I worked for him until 1926. In 1926 I was sent by the Komsomol to the city of Perm to study in the Workers College. I studied mathematics – the Russian literature – and political and social studies. I failed in my first examinations. I made 76 mistakes in the dictation test – I also failed in mathematics. It was a competitive examination and because I failed I was not allowed to continue my studies. I tried to get work in Perm – I asked at the employment bureau – it was difficult to get a job at the time. I managed to get casual jobs on the docks which earned enough for me to buy bread to live. I then returned to my village by traveling [sic] via Sverdlovsk, by train and not paying the fare, as you say in Australia, 'jumping the rattler'.

I was spoken to on the way by an NKVD guard and made to show my papers, which were in order – I was allowed to go on.

At Sverdlovsk I called at the office of the District Committee of the Communist Party asking for money to pay for my fare the rest of the way to the village. At that time I was a candidate member of the Communist Party – it is a probationary period before becoming a full member of the Party. The District Committee paid me 13 roubles with which I bought a railway ticket and I went back to my village.

I again went to work at the same blacksmith's shop.

A few months later I was sent to Sverdlovsk by the Komsomol, to attend a special course for the training of pioneers.

The pioneers were the children selected to be trained as communists.

I had been reading Russian newspapers and literature in order to improve my knowledge of the Russian language and grammar.

I studied the special course for 9 months – this was in 1937.

I then returned to my village after which the Komsomols sent us to another village as a tutor for pioneer communists.

I was there a few months after which I attended a Soviet Party school in Linsl-Tagl in the Urals. It is an industrial area. I studied two years at this school and graduated. The school dealt with Trade Union activities. I then was sent to another industrial city which is now called Sorov, where I worked until 1929. I was the Party youth organizer of the factor – the factory Youth Committee paid my salary.

In October that year I was conscripted to the Red Navy. I served about 4 years in the Navy. I went to Moscow. There I had friends who had served with me in cipher section of the Navy who helped me obtain a position as a code clerk in the NKVD.

I served in a special section which dealt with sending and receiving telegrams to and from Soviet embassies and legations in foreign countries.

At that time there was no connection with the Australian Government.

I have been a member of the NKVD from that time until today.

My first post in the NKVD was assistant to the deputy chief of the operations office. It was the lowest rank in the office. In this rank I served until 1939. In 1938 I was detailed to Tintzin in China where a rebellion was in progress against the government and where Soviet troops were posted. I served there as a cipher clerk for a period of about 9 months. I then returned to Moscow and was transferred to the section which dealt with internal communications. This was a promotion – I became assistant to the Chief Cipher Clerk. This was in 1940. I was still there when Germany attacked the Soviet Union. I was appointed Chief of the Cipher Section of the NKVD. This was in June 1941.

In 1942 I was posted to Stockholm as code clerk in the Soviet Embassy there – my cipher duties included keeping under observation the conduct and associations of members of the Embassy. This was an NKVD function.

The Ambassador at first was Mrs Kolontai and later Mr Semenov (he is now in Berlin) and ten Mr Chenisev (he is now assistant to the General Secretary to the United Nations Organisation in the USA).

In 1947, I think it was in October, I returned to Moscow. I was posted as chief of the Cipher Section; my responsibilities included controlling the NKVD agents who submitted reports as to the political reliability of women on ships plying between the countries of Bulgaria, Romania, Czechoslovakia and Hungary.

The ships plied on the river Danube.

The reports from the agents were submitted to NKVD representatives in those countries who in turn relayed the information to Mr Petrov. The messages were sent sometimes in code, sometimes clear, and by secret diplomatic mail. I considered the reports and arranged for the transfer of politically unreliable women. I made my reports to the head of the Department. Our recommendations were sent to the Central Committee of the Communist Part. In the Central Committee there is a special section which deals with these matters. It is called 'The Special International Department'. It controls all Soviet citizens abroad. I stayed with this section until 2/1/1951 when I was posted to Australia. I arrived in Australia on 5/2/1951 in Sydney. My posting was as 3rd Secretary to the Embassy in Canberra. My responsibilities then were, as a member of the NKVD, to which the conduct of the Soviet Embassy personnel in Australia, and also to investigate cases of the activities of the anti-Soviet organizations in Australia.

A few days after my arrival in Australia I was appointed by Mr Lifanov, the ambassador, as Consul for Australia in the Soviet Embassy. I communicated directly with the NKVD office in Moscow and not through the Ambassador.

At that time there were two separate Ministries – now called the MVD, which was responsible for the internal security of the Soviet, and the other the NKVD which was responsible for control of concentration camps, border control and the conduct of Soviet officials abroad.

The separate functions were combined when Beria was made Minister for the MVD. I then became the officer of the MVD for Australia. When

I arrived in Australia the other agents of the MVD was Mr Valentin Sadovnikov, who was First Secretary to the Embassy and Mr Ivan Mikhailovich Pakhonov who was the TASS agent in Australia.

Before I came here the NKVD agent in the Embassy was Mr Simon Makarov and his contact was Fedor Nosov, the TASS representative in Australia. Nosov was a secret agent of the NKVD – he obtained his information from one man – this man operated a group of agents in Australia, who reported information. I did not see any of this information but I know about it from Pakhomov. I have never seen Mr Nosov. I do not know this man he contacted but I know he was in close contact with Joan Ferguson of the Australian-Russia Society and Rex Chiplin of the *Tribune*.

When Mr Nosov left to return to the Soviet he was replaced by Mr Pakhomov. Pakhomov was MVD agent and he reported to Sadovnikov – who in turn reported his information direct to Moscow.

When Sadovnikov left to return to the Soviet Mr Pakhomov was appointed as temporary chief MVD agent in Australia. Sadovnikov left in about April 1951.

I worked independently of Pakhomov – we had different responsibilities Pakhomov's responsibility as MVD agent was to establish contacts with officers of the Department of External Affairs with a view to obtaining and securing information regarding the policies of the Australian Government – including the plans for possible war by Australia against other countries including the Soviet.

Pakhomov was also responsible for maintaining contact with Press representatives in order to find out similar information.

He developed a contact with a representative of the *Sydney Morning Herald* who supplied him with information in the form of typed documents during a parliamentary session in Canberra about 5 or 6 months before he left. This document id the one I now show to the Australian Security Service. I'd not know [sic] where it was typed. Mr Pakhomov gave me the document – I have had it in my safe. The man's name is Mr Frank O'Sullivan. The man is not a member of the Australian Communist Party but he is a sympathizer of the Party. He is not now a newspaper man – he is now an important man with the Australian Government. He is a responsible secretary to a member of the Opposition. He is the private secretary to Dr Evatt, the leader of the Opposition. I have met him twice – once in Canberra and once in Sydney. The Canberra meeting as about a year ago – the Sydney meeting was about 6 or 7 months ago. We had a meal together at the Adrin Restaurant. From my own knowledge he is a sympathizer towards the Soviet.

After Pakhomov returned to Moscow I received a cable from the MVD in Moscow to make contact with O'Sullivan. O'Sullivan is a young man, he intended to marry the wife of another newspaper correspondent in Canberra with whom he was living – I do not know her name but she attended a preview of Soviet films at the Capitol Theatre Canberra during 1952. I do not think she is attractive. I tried to make a contact with him but it was difficult in my position as 3rd Secretary.

The first introduction to me from Moscow was for Mr Antonov, the TASS agent, to make contact with O'Sullivan but he was unsuccessful. Then I received a cable to make the contact myself with O'Sullivan. Victor Mikhailovish Antonov, the present TASS agent is a cadre MVD officer in Australia.

Filip Vasilievich Kislytsin, the present 2nd Secretary of the embassy in Canberra is also a cadre MVD officer.

Between 1945 and 1948 there was a very serious situation in Australia in the Department of External Affairs. The Communist Party here had a group of External Affairs officers who were giving them information. Two members of the group were bringing out copies of official documents, which they gave to a Communist Party member. This Party man gave the documents to Mr Makarev at the Soviet Embassy. The documents described the Australian foreign policy and also contained a list of information about American and British foreign policy. I do not know the name of the Party man who at that time reported to Makarev, but his codename was 'CLODE' – (phonetically this is CLAUDE). One of CLODE's group was Ric Throssel, an officer of the Department of External Affairs. Throssel had a code name 'FERRO'. Throssel is the son of Katharine Suzannah Pritchard – the Australian writer. He has served abroad for External Affairs in the Soviet and also in South America. He is not active now – he is very still – I think he is afraid.

Moscow sent me a cable to me during 1953 – it was in June – instructing me that he was a very important man, and that I had to arrange personal contact with him for Mr Kislytsin. Kislytsin invited him to the 7th November reception in Canberra in 1953 – he attended but did not stay long – we also invited him to a film night at the Embassy, but he did not answer and did not attend. I do not know how many reports he made but Moscow regarded him as very important to them – I know his information was regarded as important.

In my opinion the Party contact of Ric Throssel was Rex Chiplin – but I am not sure of this.

Rex Chiplin has told me that he has a few friends in External Affairs – he said he [was] using the name of 'Charlie'. About a month ago he told me, in Sydney, about this. About 2 months ago he gave to me a report on the Economic Conference held in Sydney – it was later published in all the newspapers.

About 2 months ago I received an MVD cable not to make any further contact with the Australian Communist Party, except official contact, because of the international situation. This instruction was sent to all countries. For example, I could continue to contact John Rodgers and Jean Ferguson on official matters connected with the Australian-Russian Society but I could not continue to make any secret contact with Party members to obtain information of a secret kind.

I don't know if Chiplin has passed to the Soviet secret Government information. He does not know his code name is 'Charlie'. All Embassy outside contacts have a code name.

I know a member of the Australian Communist Party – his name is Jack Hughes – whose responsibility is to investigate Security Service in Australia – he told us that he had a man working in the Post Office in Sydney who helped to 'tap telephones'. He is the man who informs Hughes that a telephone is being tapped by the Security Service and to be on guard. I don't know his name.

> Hughes is a member of the Central Committee. Hughes also old 'Charlie', before Pakhomov left Australia, that a young woman who worked in the headquarters of the Security Service had fallen in love with a communist; they were intimate with each other and she informed him that Security Service were interested in the people at the Soviet Embassy – she mentioned two names – Mrs Petrov – my wife, and Mrs Koslova.

Later on Hughes told me himself, he said that the girl had left for a holiday in London after she had told the communist this information. Hughes told us this during 1953. I have met Hughes about 3 times. I know he reported to Sadovnikov the development of the peace movement in Australia. Hughes contacted Pakhomov in the Journalists Club, Sydney. I don't know whether he contacts Mr Antonov.

I'm feeling very tired and I think I should rest. But there is a lot more information I have for the Australian Government. I have tonight with no documents from the embassy, which I will briefly describe tonight and explain them in detail later on.

(i) Document headed American Espionage in Australia.

This document was supplied by Mr Rupert Lockwood to Mr Antonov during 1953. Mr Lockwood visited the embassy with Mr Antonov – they arrived separately and stayed there three nights typing the report. He sued an Embassy typewriter but typed it himself. Lockwood has a codename 'WARREN'. Moscow selects all the code names.

2, 3, 4, 5, 6 and 7 are paragraphs of letters from MVD Moscow to me, describing my responsibilities in Australia. Some are in code, but I have brought the code with me. Each letter has a separate code.

8. A document describing two people in whom the embassy authorities would be interested to develop them as spies in Australia – they are Australians. It is in the writing of Sadovnikov.

> Sadovnikov has a codename 'SAEED'.
> My code name is 'MICHAEL'.
> Kislytsin had code name 'GLED'.

Antonov has code name 'IGNAT'.
Jack Hughes had code name 'BASK'

9. A document containing name for references in Sadovnikov's writing.
10. A document in Sadovnikov's writing describing the views of a list of 36 people in Australia.
11. A document concerning Vintoss Vintsossvich.

Divischok – whose code name is PETCHEK. His wife is named Frantislika Volor. wife's sister lives at 16 Holt St., Stanmore – she helped him get to Australia.

Divishok was born 2/22/1907 in Czechoslovakia – he was a good Soviet agent during the [Second World] war, and Moscow has instructed MVD here to contact him – set him up as a manager of an Australian restaurant – encourage his assimilation – so that he could become a good contact for spies. So far as I know, no contact has yet been made with him.

I have made this statement voluntarily and sincerely – it is the truth – I will say more in detail later.

I wish to ask the Australian Government for permission to remain in Australia permanently – I wish to become an Australian citizen as soon as possible – I ask for protection for myself and assistance to establish myself comfortably in this country.

I have no wish to return to the Soviet Union – I know that if [I] did so I would be killed – I know that Mr Lifanov and Mr Kovaliev have sent bad reports about me to Moscow and that Mr Generalov has confirmed these reports to Moscow. By confirmed I mean supported. The reports have been untrue but there is nothing I can do about them, and I would find it difficult to prove my innocence in Moscow – it would have been very dangerous for me to return to Moscow.

I like Australia and the Australian way of life – Lifanov and Generalov have behaved like Hitler towards me and also to my wife.

I no longer believe I the Communism of the Soviet leadership – I no longer believe in Communism since I have seen the Australian way of living.

My wife would like to stay in Australia but also is afraid for her family in Moscow and says that she must go back. There is a possibility that she might change her mind and stay here, but it is very difficult for her.

This statement has been read over to me in English and in Russian. I have read it for myself. It is the truth.

Petrov's statement, formally witnessed by Ron Richards, named Hughes, Throssel, O'Sullivan and Chiplin as Soviet agents, thus confirming the identification of FERRO and CLAUDE who had both appeared in the VENONA traffic. The overlap with VENONA, mentioning Bernie, Throssel, Hill and Hughes, served to validate the VENONA identifications, and to authenticate Petrov.

Petrov, of course, never learned about VENONA, and great care was taken when encryption topics were discussed to avoid giving any clue of the source's existence. Over the years, the couple lost their fear of prosecution and cooperated with their ASIO interrogator, John Elliott, and foreign visitors, such as GCHQ's John Christie; both Petrovs had much to say about Soviet cipher systems and explained that the encipherment of a message usually took place after the clear text had been encoded. Specifically, Mrs Petrov was asked about ENORMOZ, the codeword for atomic weapons development, and in September 1954 the new MI5 D-G, Dick White, informed GCHQ about Mrs Petrov's procedures and the *rezidnetura*'s interest in atomic matters:

> Mrs. Petrov has given the following explanation of the codeword ENOKMAZ which occurs in the documents:-
>> ENORMAX – Code word used for the MVD interest in the matter of research and testing of the atom bomb in Australia, Thus, for instance, we received an instruction to collect information about the last test of the atom bomb in Australia, and also about the persons who were present at this test.
>
> ASIO add the following comments:-
> 1. The codeword does not appear on the lists which were in Mr. Petrov's possession but because of the very Top Secret nature of the word it was coded in a special code which Mr Petrov kept in her possession. This special code was very seldom used. One of the rules concerning it was that it could not be used in cables and when used the message could only go by hand of courier.
> 2. The special code book referred to was published about 1949 and was at the Embassy when Mrs. Petrov arrived in Australia.
> 3. The first time the code word ENORMAZ was used to Mrs. Petrov's knowledge was about 15 days after the last atomic test when a signal was received by Petrov asking him to collect information about the last atomic test in Australia and the people who attended the test.
> 4. The special code book referred to above was destroyed under directions from Moscow last year after the arrest of Beria.

The Petrov interrogations were supervised by ASIO and MI5's Russian expert George Leggett, with occasional visits by MI5 officers such as Pamela Stiebel, and research work in London undertaken by Ronnie

Reed and his senior officer, Squadron Leader Peter de Wesselow, a distinguished wartime Pathfinder pilot.

From a counter-espionage perspective, the priority for ASIO and MI5 was to identify the individuals mentioned in Petrov's papers, the material designated the 'G Series', which consisted of ten pages of lists of names, all in Sadovnikov's handwriting, apart from G.4, which had been written by Petrov.

DOCUMENT G.1
1. 'Denis' [Dalziel]
2. 'Stepan' [Stanley]
3. 'Tikhon' – Tennequist [TENNEKUIST]
4. 'Rafael' – F [Ferguson, see G.3]
5. 'Sister' [SESTRA] – Burney, Francisca, bank

DOCUMENT G.2
K's Contacts:
1. 'Mastercraftsman' [MASTER]
2. 'Tourist' [TURIST]
3. 'Sister' [SESTRA] – Francisca Burney
4. 'Girl Friend' [POIRUGA]
5. 'Ben' – Hughes
6. 'Joe' – bank (archives)
7. Academician, young girl, has finished the school of the bank and is going to work in the bank.
8. – sister of the wife of B
9. 'Don Woods' [UDS] – secretary to the adviser of Dr E. on Rtist [ARTIST] Enormous [ENORMOZ]
10. 'Sailor [MORYak]' McNamara [MCNAMARA] George
11. B. [Burton] – deputy director of the bank.

DOCUMENT G.3
1. WILBUR KRISTIANSON – '[Mastercraftsman] [MASTER]', husband of Tourist's sister.
2. HERBERT WILLIAM TATTERSELL – Artist [ARTIST].

DOCUMENT G.4
Mr C.R. TENANT 'K'
50 BUNDARRA Rd
BELLVIEW HILL,
Sydney
Tel. FW 1267

Kristisen S.B. – 'Crab' [KRAB]
Rogers 'Clever' [LOVKIJ]
Kristisen H.M. 'Eva' [EVA]
Ferguson – Rafael
Koaki – 'Friend' [TRIYaTEL]
Turnbull K. – 'Teodor'
GEORGE McNAMARA – Sailor [MORYaK]

DOCUMENT G.5

Letter No. 2 of 14/6/48

Herewith [or Communicate] additional materials and conclusions drawn therefrom in respect of the following persons:
1. <u>Bruce Millis</u> – progressive labourite, illegally aided the academy. Had the confidence of Chiffley Lived and had a commercial company in the town of Katoomba.
2. <u>Geoffrey Powell</u> (GEOFFREY POWELL) – former doctor of physics in Melbourne University, considered a leading scientist. Member of the academy since 1937. Carried out active work on an assignment of the academy. Went on a duty journey to the island.
3. <u>Eric Burhop</u> – former doctor of physics at Melbourne university. Considered a leading scientist. It was suggested that he change over to work in the club.
4. <u>Dave Morris</u> – born 1910, major, bachelor of science, illegal member of the academy. After graduation from the university studied on the island. During the second world war he worked as a technical expert at Headquarters [GLAVShTAB] in Melbourne. Learned about tanks on the island. In 1948 he was sent to the island for work in the field of military research.
5. <u>Kaiser (F. KAISER)</u> – member of the academy, physicist, worked in the field of atomic energy. Went on a duty journey to the island.

DOCUMENT G.6

6. <u>Don Woods [UDS] (Don Woods)</u> – former secretary to the adviser of Dr. E om ENORMOZ Briggs.

DOCUMENT G.7

App to Letter No. 2 of 10.11.40
1. <u>Joe</u> – born 1921 works in the archives of the bank. Lives in the village [SELO]
2. <u>Taylor</u> – judge and representative of the Arbitration Commission, labourite, until 1943 head of the club in the capital; during that period passed on to the academy a document permitting the uncovering of Mastercraftsman [MASTER] in one of the areas of the academy. President of the Legislation Commission of NSW. 'K' characterizes him as positive.

3. Legge, Jack – scientific chemist. Academician since 1936. In 1939 on an assignment from the academy he worked in a Trotskyite group. When the academy was illegal 'K' used Legge J's house for issuing the paper 'yt'. Carried out an assignment of the academy when he went on a duty journey to the country of the skiers [LYZhNIKI]. L's wife is at present doing scientific work in Melbourne. 'K' considers that N (L.) inspires confidence. A relative of L works in the political intelligence department of the Ministry of Foreign Affairs [MID].
4. Hook, Jack – president of the Sydney trade union – Labour council, labourite, one of the leading members of the Labour Party. Collaborates with the academy. Holds progressive views. 'K' considers N to be a man who merits trust.

DOCUMENT G.8

5. Barras – doctor of economic sciences, an official worker of the club and an expert linguist, a swimmer. Engaged in throwing light upon runners, swimmers, etc. Among the members of the club he is regarded as left. Lives in the village [SELO].
6. Burney, Francisca – born 1923, Australian, worked as secretary-typist in the secretariat of the bank in the capital. Illegal academician since 1943. 'K' was in personal contact with her and received interesting information from her.
7. Miller, Forbes – born 1912, native of Australia, deputy editor of *'The Daily Telegraph'*. Expressed a desire to keep 'T' systematically informed of materials being prepared for going to press. Like himself, his wife is also well disposed towards us.
8. McInnes [MAKINES] – about 40 years old, journalist. Has wide contacts amongst employees of the press, in political and business circles. By conviction he is a left-inclined man.
9. Birtles, B. – about 48 years old, important journalist, has contacts amongst writers and artists. Has traveled [sic] in Europe, known the country of the swimmers well.
10. McLean [MAKLIN] – journalist, sympathetically disposed towards us, a very well-informed man. In the opinion of 'T' he will give information.

DOCUMENT G.9

11. Olsen, C. – promised to help 'T' in learning about the country and in acquiring information passing through the newspaper.
12. Simpson, Colin – positively disposed towards us.
13. Fraser – member of parliament, former correspondent, labourite, very close to Evatt. Likes drinking and in such a condition is very talkative. 'A' used him for obtaining information from Evatt.

14. Finnard – lawyer, graduate of Sydney university, interested in questions of Marxist philosophy. Stated his opinion of the labourites very clearly. To 'A' he prosed getting interesting information. Friendly with Withall, director of the Federal Chamber of Manufacturers.
15. Calwell – minister of information, interested in our country. Expressed a desire to meet 'A'.
16. Brook [sic] – alleged academician. Brother is an academician. Elected to parliament.
17. Falstein – about 40 years old, a Jew, former member of parliament, distinguished by left pronouncements, wanted very much to go to the Soviet Union.
18. McKell – former Prime Minister, was on good terms with SDONOV, first representative of the USSR in Australia. Asked 'A' to apply to him for help.

DOCUMENT G.10
19. Westcott – former employee of the communications branch of the Ministry of Foreign Affairs [MID], his work was secret. Very cautious. Was acquainted with 'Lipskij'. Lives in Manooka circle, Canberra, Tel. B. 173 [sic].
20. Fitzharding – librarian of the national library, knows quite a lot and can give useful advice. Has access to the parliamentary library. Was acquainted with 'Lip'.
21. Hibbard, L.U. – representative of the state of NSW [New South Wales] in the Federal Council, academician.
22. Gutvakh, Aleksandr Mikhailovich – born in Odessa in 1923. Went to the USA and then to Australia. Has relatives in the USSR, with whom he maintains correspondence.

In total there were forty-four suspects to be investigated, which placed an impossible burden on ASIO which found itself chasing leads as Petrov gave his public testimony before the Royal Commission. The fear in Canberra and London was that, having been alerted by the media, many suspects would disappear, and the SLO, Derek Hamblen, came under pressure from both MI5 and the FBI to at least gain access to the interrogation transcripts. Understandably, the impatient Allies had their own agendas, and were appalled by the 'trickle' of information being shared. Indeed, MI5's de Wesselow complained to Hamblen that the newspapers were better informed than he was! Underlying this was the suspicion that ASIO was deliberately milking the situation, having been on the receiving end of fraternal abuse for so long. At the heart of the problem was MI5's concern about Soviet illegals infiltrated into Australia as legitimate immigrants, and the embarrassment of Kislytsin's disclosures about Burgess and Maclean, whereas ASIO had prioritised every individual named in front of the Royal Commission. Added to this volatile mix was Petrov's own mercurial personality, and his apparent tendency to grandstand.

From MI5's standpoint, Petrov's appearance before the Royal Commission represented a daily threat to VENONA, as it was almost impossible to separate information that had originated from the earlier cryptographic source, and the defector himself, as James Robertson articulated:

> To avoid confusion it is absolutely essential that information obtained from Petrov, on the one hand, and the information obtained from BRIDE [VENONA] on the other, should be kept as much as possible separate in all reports and letters.

Administratively, this discipline proved a nightmare because only a handful of indoctrinated officers knew about VENONA, yet there was a large group of staff handling Petrov leads, some of whom were inquisitive about cross-references to some other top secret source.

Predictably, the Royal Commission authenticated what became known as Petrov's papers. and found the couple very credible witnesses. The commissioners also found that the only Australians willing to spy for the Soviets were communists, and that none should be prosecuted.

When the VENONA project came to an end in 1979, analysis of the Canberra traffic showed that a total of forty-seven codenames had been mentioned, of which about a dozen consisted of Australians who were assessed as 'possibly involved in espionage'. In terms of contributing to the then current cryptanalytical programme, the Petrovs contributed little, except in relation to the Stockholm-Moscow channel where he was consulted about cables that he himself had drafted. Indeed, his codename, SEAMAN, appeared in the wartime Stockholm – Moscow traffic.

Initially the Petrovs were accommodated at an ASIO safe house in Palm Beach, Sydney, but they were moved to Sandringham in Victoria, and were given new identities, those of two Swedish immigrants, Sven and Maria Allynson in 1956. They stayed in St Kinda, Windsor for six months, and then bought a house Parkmore Road, in the Melbourne suburb of East Bentleigh, and started work. Petrov found a job as a processor at Ilford Films in Ferntree Gull Road in Waverley, while his wife worked for sixteen years as a typist for William Adams tractors. Petrov would become increasingly morose and descended into alcoholism. He suffered a stroke in 1974 and later moved into a nursing home in Brighton. He died of prostate cancer in the Royal Park Hospital, Waverley, in June 1991.

***

The unexpected bonus of Petrov's defection was his wife's last-moment decision to join him, after she spoke to him on the telephone during a refueling stop at Darwin while being escorted back to Moscow by a pair of burly Soviet couriers. Petrov deliberately had kept her in the dark about his plans because she had both parents, and a brother and sister, living in the Soviet Union, and she believed that if she was declared 'an enemy of the people', her family would probably perish too. The shock was ASIO's discovery that she too was an intelligence professional, had participated in a cryptanalytical attack on a Japanese cipher machine during the Second World War, and had handled agents while at the Stockholm *rezidentura* between 1943 and 1947. As she would explain that her original assignment to Sweden had been as an 'SK' security officer, to monitor the activities of her colleagues in the Soviet Kolony expatriate community. Significantly, upon her return to Moscow she had been at the heart of the 'Committee of Information', a coordinating organisation created by Stalin in July 1947 to supervise all Soviet foreign intelligence operations. The KI would be closed down in 1951, and Petrova was the West's first authoritative source of accurate information about this elusive body.

Known to her friends as Dusia, Mrs Petrov had enjoyed a fascinating career. Born in March 1914 in Ilpki, 120 miles south of Moscow, her family moved to Semipatatinsk in Siberia when she was five, and then went to live in Moscow where, through family connections, she was employed by the GRU as a cipher clerk, working on Japanese intercepts, until 1941 when she transferred to the NKVD and married Vladimir, her first husband Roman Kruvosh having disappeared in a purge, their daughter Irina having died of meningitis at the age of 3.

Early in the Second World War, Petrov worked in the NKVD's cipher section in the Lubyanka, while Dusia's department, recently accommodated in the Hotel Select, was transferred to Kuibychev. They would be reunited in Moscow in 1943 and posted to Stockholm, but in July 1942 were unable to sail from Archangel as planned. They returned to Moscow and eventually were flown to Tehran and then Cairo. Travelling with four other Soviet diplomats, they embarked on a troopship, the SS *Llandaff Castle*, bound for Durban, but the ship was torpedoed by the *U-177* off Dar-es-Salaam in November 1942. They were rescued by a destroyer, HMS *Catterick*, and put ashore in Cape Town where, in March 1943, they completed their voyage to London. Finally, they flew from Aberdeen to Stockholm where they joined the *rezidentura* and remained there until October 1947.

Petrov's appointment to Canberra under consular cover, with the rank of lieutenant colonel, had come about through the intervention of an NKVD friend, and did not take account of the fact that by 1947, the year his widowed mother died, he had no family left in the Soviet Union, both his brothers having been killed in the first months of the Second World War. His lack of relations made his decision to defect much easier, and the fear of what might have happened to her relatives haunted her until 1990 when her younger sister, Tamara, emigrated with her family to Australia. She revealed that their father, a former Moscow trolley-bus conductor turned NKVD agent, had been dismissed from his job.

Desia died in July 2002, still resentful that the book she had co-authored with Vladimir in 1956, *Empire of Fear*, had earned them next to nothing. She remained loyal to her husband, who was cordially disliked by most he met. He suffered from poor health and had a low income. He always regretted his defection. For the Petrovs, defection had not turned out to be the idyllic retirement to a chicken farm they had imagined, but the loss of two such senior officers would have a lasting impact on the NKVD, and on Australian domestic politics. It may also have emboldened Rastvorov.

During that same year of 1954 there had been one other NKVD deserter, Piotr Debiabin, who in February had presented himself to the United States Counterintelligence Corps in Vienna. He had been quietly exfiltrated to Linz, where he was interrogated. A former member of the NKVD's Guard Directorate, responsible for the Kremlin's security, Deriabin was kept under wraps by the CIA, with no public acknowledgment of the defection for a further five years. In December 1961 he played a crucial role in confirming the bona fides of one of his NKVD colleagues in Vienna who, unexpectedly, defected to the CIA in Helsinki.

Chapter V

ANATOLI GOLITSYN

Security Service conspiracy theorists were further encouraged by Golitsyn whose passionately paranoid tendencies made him an increasing liability to the U.S. and British intelligence communities, which had originally welcomed him with open arms.

Christopher Andrew, *The Defence of the Realm*[1]

Within the international counter-intelligence community there is probably no greater divisive individual than Anatoli Golitsyn, the KGB officer who turned up unexpectedly, accompanied by his wife, Svetlana, and 6-year-old daughter, Tanya, at the home in Haapatie Street, in north central Helsinki, of Frank F. Friberg in December 1961.

Golutsyn quickly revealed his true identity, and his true role in the local Soviet Embassy *rezidentura* and persuaded the CIA station chief that he was a genuine defector seeking to trade political asylum in the United States in return for valuable information about KGB plans, personalities and operations.

Having been exfiltrated to New York on a series of flights routed through Stockholm, Frankfurt, London and Bermuda, Golitsyn proved his value by supplying information, which would compromise several important assets, including the French mole in NATO, George Paques, the Admiralty spy John Vassall, and the Finnish president, Uhro Kekkonen. Over the next thirteen years he exercised considerable influence over how American, British and French intelligence agencies conducted their business, and he played a central role in assisting specially indoctrinated counter-intelligence personnel conducting investigations into evidence of Soviet penetration of the West. Specifically, he was the inspiration behind a counter-espionage program, conducted jointly with the FBI, designated HONETOL (a combination of 'Hoover' and 'Anatol').

Golitsyn developed his own system of interpreting intelligence operations from the Kremlin's viewpoint and became a source of controversy when he assessed some major successes, such as the recruitment of Colonel Oleg Penkovsky, as a KGB manipulation. Some of his analysis, including his assertion that the Sino-Soviet split was an example of Moscow-driven strategic deception, or that Yugoslavia had remained a Soviet satellite, would be ridiculed, and his books, *New Lies for Old* and *The Perestroika Deception*, would be subject to much adverse comment.

Golitsyn's principal supporter within the CIA was James Angleton, a seasoned veteran of the wartime OSS's X-2 branch, and head of the CIA's counter-intelligence staff since 1964. During his wartime posting to London Angleton had been indoctrinated into many British techniques, and in the immediate post-war era he had run operations in Rome. Once back at headquarters, he was assigned the task of liaising with the Israelis who sought American help for their security apparatus which they knew to be thoroughly penetrated by the Soviets. The leadership of Mossad, Shin Bet and the military intelligence directorate Aman were very conscious of their vulnerability to refugees from the Soviet Bloc, some of whom had agreed to act as spies in return for an exit visa and were aware of the threat this posed to the country's safety. Angleton's advice and active support for their efforts to rid themselves of the contamination was warmly appreciated by the Israelis, and accordingly elevated his status within the CIA. It also resulted in the Clandestine Service's Israeli desk being removed from the Near East Division to become Angleton's responsibility.

However, as Angleton became increasingly persuaded of the validity of Golitsyn's unrivalled knowledge and experience of the KGB he supervised an unforgiving regime within the organisation to identify suspected moles, a process that would become known as a molehunt. In particular, Angleton was determined to track down a spy with the cryptonym SASHA who was alleged to have operated in Germany before being transferred to a more senior position. Several CIA officers, among them Peter Karlow, Paul Garbler, George Goldberg, David Murphy, Vasia Gfmirkin, George Kisevalter, Richard Kovich, Robert Gray and Alexander Sogolow found their careers wrecked by the fourteen major investigations associated with the search for SASHA.

Further collateral damage as inflicted by the treatment of Yuri Nosenko, a KGB officer who defected in February 1964 in Geneva, but was suspected of being the despatched 'false defector' that Golitsyn had predicted. Accordingly, in April 1964 Nosenko was detained at a safe house for seventeen months, on the authority of the attorney general, and then was transferred to a cellblock specially constructed at the CIA's training facility at Camp Peary in Virginia, where he remained, under continuous hostile interrogation until October 1967. A year later a report sponsored by the CIA's Office of Security concluded that Nosenko was a genuine defector, and he was given an apology for his treatment, $137,062 in compensation and a contract as a consultant.

At the height of the mole hunting a KGB officer, Yuri Loginov, who had been recruited by the CIA, was arrested in South Africa and traded back to the Soviet Union, in the mistaken belief that he was playing a double role for Moscow. Consequently, these perceived excesses Congress sought, in 1980, to compensate the victims though Public Law 96-450, which became known as the Mole Relief Act.

Angleton and Golitsyn would be severely criticised by their ruthless determination to thwart the Soviets, and warnings that Golitsyn would be discredited by subsequent 'false defectors' deliberately dispatched to undermine his credibility struck many of his critics as inherently improbable. However, Angleton did develop, in November 1967, one lasting innovation, an international channel known as CAZAB, on which to exchange sensitive information about Soviet espionage between specially cleared counter-intelligence specialists.

By 1974, when Washington DC newspaper reports of the CIA breaches of the law, Angleton was dismissed by Director of Central Intelligence Bill Colby. In his retirement, Angleton maintained contact with Golitsyn and leaked some information to trusted authors, but he died in May 1987 a disappointed man, convinced that his methods had served to protect the CIA, preoccupied by the memory of having been duped by his British friend Kim Philby while had had served in Washington between September 1949 and his dismissal in June 1951. During that period of twenty-two months, Angleton and Philby had met on thirteen occasions.

Widely discredited, Golitsyn died in December 2008, but his reputation had been tarnished by several ill-informed allegations, such as the assertion that he had denounced British Prime Minister Harold Wilson as a KGB asset. Accused of being a delusional, paranoid fantasist, Golitsyn gathered together a cadre of adherents who knew and understood his unconventional analytical methodology and, while not accepting all his judgments, came to respect many of his opinion papers, most of which made uncomfortable reading for the West's intelligence bureaucracy.

Among the post-war Soviet intelligence defectors, Golitsyn was unique, both in terms of his personal experience, his knowledge of the KGB's senior management, and the fact that his decision to defect had not been made on impulse. He had planned his desertion for years and had deliberately learned as much as he could about the organisation so he could inflict maximum damage when the moment arrived. His semi-religious conversion had been triggered by an encounter with a Russian Orthodox priest in Vienna, combined by the impact in February 1956 of revelations about Joseph Stalin's crimes

At the age of 26, with the rank of lieutenant, Golitsyn had attended a meeting with Joseph Stalin, Georgi Malenkov and some of the other Soviet leadership. In 1952, he had played a role in the re-organisation of Soviet intelligence and the creation of a counter-intelligence department. A year later, he had been promoted as the head of the American counter-intelligence section, and in 1954 was posted to the Vienna *rezidentura* where he took part in June 1954 in an operation in Linz to kidnap Valeri Tremmel, the leader of the NTS, anti-Soviet émigré organisation, and former chief of police in Nikolaiev during the German occupation of Russia who had participated in the murder of over a thousand Jews and kommissars. During his counter-intelligence briefings he had learned about the fate of Vladimir Skripkin in 1946, and while posted to Vienna he had encountered Piotr Deriabin.

As he would later recall, the material accumulated in secret by Golitsyn would include evidence against

> a senior CIA officer, George Kisevalter, the CIA's star agent Oleg Penkovsky, the statesman Averell Harriman and the spy codenamed GARMASH, all as KGB assets. I also kept a record of the important KGB agents who spied on Soviet writers, artists and intellectuals, including the author Mihail Bulgakov, the poet Anna Akhmatova and the composer Prokofyev. Much of this was gleaned by me in 1961 from one of my colleagues, the KGB officer responsible for monitoring Soviet intellectuals, and I knew it to be of considerable historical importance.[2]

Golitsyn was born on 25 August 1926 in the small town of Pyryatin near Poltava in the Ukraine. His mother, Irina Vasi'yevna Doroshenko, was a Ukrainian who had been orphaned at an early age. She worked in the Ukraine and Moscow in the household of a rich Ukrainian landlord, first as an apprentice and then as a professional cook in Moscow. His father, Mikhail Vasil'yevich Golitsyn, was Russian, and his father had been a serf of a Russian landlord named Golitsyn, from whom he took the name when he was granted his freedom. He became an artisan tanner of fine leather and his son had followed his trade.

Golitsyn's maternal aunt, Ulyana Vasilievna Doroshenko, had been adopted by a wealthy family of Jewish merchants named Milgovsky. She graduated from gymnasium, having received a good private education, and from them she learned Jewish religion, culture and history. When her adoptive parents perished in the Civil War she had come to live with her older sister, where she helped bring up Anatoli and his older sister. In was from her that Golitsyn acquired his knowledge of Jewish history and religion.

At one stage the family ran a café at a busy crossroads, but in 1929 was obliged to abandon the enterprise for political reasons. His father was also sentenced to four months' labour for non-payment of taxes, and during the famine the parents and children experienced hardship and hunger. Eventually, in September 1933 – his father having found work as a labourer – they moved to Moscow to live in the suburb of Zagorodnaya. Like all his friends, Golitsyn joined the Komsomol, the Communist Youth League, and recalled that

> in 1937, when I was aged eleven, I heard a radio program about Stalin's love and care for children and the commentator said that Stalin never ceased thinking about building Socialism and improving the lot of Soviet children. I remember my first thought was fear that Stalin would go to bed and forget about building Socialism when he woke up next morning, and my second was to write to him about our bad living conditions and seek his help. This I did, describing how we lived in one room with ten other families, a total of seventy-five people. It was crowded and noisy, and my mother, a labor heroine, suffered from epilepsy brought on by her accident while building the Moscow Metro. The noise in our room gave her severe headaches so I asked Stalin to give us a separate room where she could live in greater comfort. I showed the letter to an older boy, Zhenya Po3pov, who said it was fine, and I mailed it from Zagorodnaya addressed to Comrade Stalin. Some months later, when I had forgotten all about it, I received a reply from Stalin's secretariat saying that my letter had been passed on to the appropriate authorities, prompting my father to read it out, commenting, 'Tolya has a head.' A year or so later we received our own large room in an apartment with another family in a new house, still on Zagorodnaya, and my mother always said that we owed our new home to 'Tolya's letter to Stalin.

When he finished school at the end of May 1941 Golitsyn was sent to a summer camp before joining the Second Artillery Cadet School in

Moscow at 12 Kropotkina Street. However, in early November, as the Germans approached the city, the entire establishment was evacuated to Leninsk-Kuznetsk in Siberia, where it would remain until spring 1944. When he graduated from the cadet school Golitsyn was assigned to the Odessa artillery school, named for Marshal Frunze, which had been evacuated to an army camp in the Urals near the small town of Sukhoy Log on the River Pyshma. Months later, in December 1944, the school was ordered back to Odessa, the city having been liberated from the German occupation. When, in September 1945, the course was completed, Golitsyn volunteered to join the military counter-intelligence directorate, known as Smersh, and he was transferred to Moscow as a candidate. When Golitsyn completed this course, in October 1946, he was assigned to the NKVD headquarters, in the Lubyanka building. He also enrolled in the NKVD branch of the University of Marxism-Leninism.

> The year I spent in Room 413 was one of the most formative of my career. It was a large room occupied by forty to forty-five officers, nearly a third of the department and among them were the section heads and officers from the American, European, Balkan and Far Eastern sections seated around tables in groups of five or six officers. There were also officers under training before being posted abroad and visiting officers from other sections. In due course I was able to meet and get to know nearly all the 150 officers in the department. My colleagues fell into several recognizable groups, one being the FCD officers who had returned from service abroad, and they were distinguished by their foreign clothes and polished manners. Among them one of the most colorful was Colonel Leonid Morozov, chief of the American section, who had returned from the United States, and he was called 'Count Tolstoy' because of his resemblance to the famous writer. Another was Major Mikhail Sumskoy, head of the British section, who had also been in the United States. He too had been refined by his exposure to western ways and for this reason was known as 'The Diplomat'. Later on, Andrei Vyshinsky, when chief of the Committee of Information, made him his secretary because of his distinguished bearing. Aleksei Vikhranov had served in the Soviet embassy in New Zealand with his 'wife' who was actually a sister of Pavel Fitin's wife. She spoke good English and had been sent to help her 'husband' to handle valuable agents. All the members of this group had a lot to tell us about the FCD and the heads of our department.
>
> The second group consisted of officers who had come from internal directorates of KGB headquarters. They wore good quality, domestically-made suits and bore themselves confidently. They had all the latest KGB news and anecdotes. Mikhail Pazelsky, head of the European section,

had previously worked on Soviet writers and scientists and because of his knowledge of this field he was called 'The Erudite'. Colonel Serafim Gretsch, head of the Balkan section, had worked on the major ministries in Moscow and he had a fund of stories about various KGB leaders including those who had been arrested in the repressions. Mikhail Ivanovich Kozlov, a tall old Chekist with a large wooden face, had spent his early career in the 1930s arresting Soviet diplomats and therefore regarded himself as an expert on Soviet diplomacy. Captain Nikolai Guba kin was a powerfully built officer from the Surveillance Directorate. Nina Yeremei, a buxom peroxide blonde in my section, had worked on coverage of the Moscow telegraph office. Vil Kanata, a witty young officer from the American section, had worked in the Transport Directorate. So had Yevgeni Kashcheyev, a very sociable young officer from the British section, and this last pair were to become my close friends.

The next group comprised of officers who had come from Smersh, the most colorful of whom was Mikhail Shaken, the deputy head of my section and the department's Party leader of the department. The reserve officers who were under training to be sent abroad as SK officers formed another group. Some of them were from the Leningrad branch, some from Tashkent and some from other provincial branches and they were recognizable from their poor quality, domestic suits. Among them was Colonel Aleksandr Likhachev from Khabarovsk who was to be sent Dairen in China. Major Aleksei Makarov from Irkutsk was the first anti-Semite I met in the department and he told anti-Semitic anecdotes about senior KGB officers suggesting that they were Jews.

Members of the last group were known behind their backs as 'The Assassins' or, as Kanata put it, 'the murderers among us'. One of them was Sasha Balakin, a sturdy, 30-year-old athlete from Pavel Soldatov's Partisan Directorate. We were told that he had killed several leaders of nationalist groups in the Baltic area and when I asked him one time how he had done it he told me calmly that he was a member of 'The Forest Brothers', a false nationalist group which had been created and controlled by Sudoplatov. They would establish contact with a genuine nationalist group and when the two met to discuss 'joint actions against Soviet tyranny' they would have a drinking session at night and then 'we would cut their throats'. Then there was Major Viktor Brusov, a man of immense physical strength who was an expert in personally killing German collaborators in occupied Soviet territory. Another was Colonel Nikolai Kiselev, also from Sudoplatov's directorate who had distinguished himself in Yugoslavia by taking over custody of the White Generals Petr Krasnov and Andrei Shkuro from the British and delivering them to Moscow. He told us that, when he arrested General Shkuro, the general asked him if he thought that Marshal Semen Budennyy would give him a squadron to command.

Kiselev had replied: 'I don't know whether he will give you a squadron but he'll give you knouts for sure.'[4]

When in 1963 Golitsyn visited London, as a guest of the Security Service, he was able to shed light on one of the incidents disclosed by Rastvorov:

At the end of 1946, Mikhail Dvizhkov gave me the file on Vladimir Skripkin, a GRU officer, and told me to enter it in the FCD's Special Archives. His only comment was 'the case is closed: the spy has been arrested.' I read the file with intense interest but there were only a few papers on it, beginning with a letter from the head of the KGB's illegals Directorate, Aleksandr Korotkov, to the head of our department, Sergei Fedoseyev, about the recruitment of Skripkin by the British naval or military intelligence service in Tokyo. The letter said that, according to a report received from our agents in London, in July or August Skripkin had visited the assistant British naval or military attaché in Tokyo and had told him that he was the son of a Soviet general, that he was a graduate of the Military Institute of Foreign Languages and that he had been taken into the GRU and sent to Tokyo on a training mission. He had told the British officer that he was disgusted with the Soviet regime and had offered his services to British intelligence. He had described the activities of GRU officers who were known to him and, in particular, had given information on the moral degeneration he had noted in his institute and in the GRU in Tokyo. He had said that, when he returned to Tokyo, he would defect to the British. The British had recruited Skripkin as an agent and had made arrangements to contact him in the Soviet Union, saying a British representative would visit him at his address in Moscow and identify himself by using a password which was given in the KGB letter.

The file contained a report from the KGB's Third (Military Counter-intelligence) Directorate saying that two of their officers, posing as British representatives, had called on Skripkin at his address and had established contact with him ostensibly on behalf of the British. Having accepted them as genuinely British, Skripkin had been arrested, interrogated, tried and sentenced to death. A copy of the ten-page report on his interrogation was in the file and showed that he had admitted to anti-Soviet views and to had confessed to his contact with the British and his agreement to work for them. A memo indicated that the Skripkin affair had been reported to the minister of defense who had ordered that the Military Institute should be purged of 'generals' sons'. As instructed, I entered the file in the Special Archives.[5]

The significance of Golitsyn's testimony regarding Skripkin was not lost on MI5. Golitsyn was certain that the information had originated 'from our agents in London' (rather than a leak in Tokyo or Singapore) and had included the password or *parole* that was to be used as a recognition signal when he was to be contacted in Moscow.

In September 1948 Golitsyn completed his probation as a Soviet Kolony specialist and, having turned down foreign appointments in Ethiopia and Japan, was posted to the Committee of Information the new organisation intended to co-ordinate all Soviet foreign intelligence operations, including the GRU. As Golitsyn would recall,

> Among the people I met briefly in the KI in 1948 were Yuri Rastvorov in the Japanese department who defected in Japan in 1954, and Vladimir and Dousia Proletarsky, using the name Petrov, defected in Australia in the same year.[6]

Of more significance to Golitsyn's subsequent statement that

> before leaving the SK Department for the school in September 1948 I learned of a GRU agent in British intelligence in Turkey who provided information about possible Soviet defectors in Turkey and Iran.[7]

Having turned down postings to Addis Ababa and Tokyo, Golitsyn was sent to the Higher Intelligence School located near the town of Balashikha. Screened by pine trees and tall lilac bushes, the school was known as Scientific Research Institute No. 101, but was known to insiders simply as '101'and was set in the estate of a former landlord some 25 kilometers from Moscow. The original mansion had been replaced by a collection of two-storey wooden huts to accommodate the students attending the two-year course.

While at 101 Golitsyn shared his quarters with Yevgeni Kashcheyev, who told him that 'Igor Gouzenko had compromised a GRU agent in British intelligence and that in 1947 the GRU had an agent in British intelligence in Turkey.'

Kashcheyev also told his room mate that the facility's commandant, Colonel Mitrofan Dubovik, a senior NKVD counter-intelligence officer, had been sent to London during the war to work with a homosexual group of 'special agents'. This was the term used in the KGB for agents in the security and intelligence services.

Another indiscreet disclosure was the reference in one of the lectures to the Finnish Social Democrat prime minister, Mauno Pekkala, who allegedly was a KGB agent codenamed ADVOKAT and run by the *rezident*, Mikhail Kotov, in person.

Golitsyn picked up more tantalizing information when he attended a KGB counter-intelligence course at the Kiselnyy Lande scjool in Moscow in September 1949.

Whereas at Balashikha the emphasis in our training had been on our counter-intelligence methods abroad to the exclusion of the internal sector, at Kiselnyy the emphasis was reversed, concentrating on Chekist methods used against western intelligence services and political opposition inside the country. Our lectures were on three basic subjects, the methods of foreign intelligence services, 'bourgeois nationalists' and anti-Soviet elements inside the Soviet Union; the KGB's methods of countering these forces; and interrogation techniques. The fundamental document on which most of our lectures on the penetration of American intelligence were based was Viktor Abakumov's Order No. 0029 of December 1947, the KGB's first important Cold War directive as the main task of the KGB. The order indicated that during the war the KGB had devoted its main effort to the successful penetration of German intelligence and had neglected the American and other allied services so the order demanded that the KGB should now concentrate on the penetration of the American intelligence service and the other agencies which cooperated against the Soviet Union. It suggested that active methods should be used in devising and executing bold operations aimed at achieving this result and the order was restated in almost every lecture we were given. As a rule, we attended the lectures given to the main course for Party officials and only the lectures on counter-intelligence abroad were given exclusively to our particular course. At that time, between 1949 and 1950, the KGB leadership banned the distribution of important KGB directives, orders or reviews on counter-intelligence matters so we only learned about such things from visiting lecturers who were active senior officers. Order no. 0029 was an exception and the lectures on the American, British, German, French and other western intelligence services were given by the SCD's head, Yevgeni Pitovranov, and the heads of departments in his directorate, Fedor Shubnyakov, Lev Novobratsky and Gleb Strokov, among others.[8]

In particular, Golitsyn later recalled attending a lecture on the subject of penetration operations conducted against Great Britain:

General Lev Novobratsky was head of the SCD's British department before the war and he told us how his department had apprehended a number of British agents in the Soviet Union on the basis of information received from the FCD. One of them was an Indian political émigré named Mukerjee who had been involved in Comintern activities and whom Novobratsky had known. According to him, the KGB had received reliable information that Mukerjee was a British agent so he was arrested and shot. We were also much impressed by Colonel Burdin who gave us many examples of KGB operations conducted to liquidate the Ukrainian underground in Western Ukraine, Poland and Czechoslovakia through the creation of false nationalist groups consisting entirely of Chekists and their agents.[9]

The strategy of creating false opposition groups as a means of infiltrating agents into anti-Soviet émigré had proved very effective before the Second World War, but according to Golitsyn, the methodology was still employed, and still considered highly effective, especially against Ukrainian nationalists.

Colonel Aleksandr Sakharovsky and General Vladimir based their lectures on Vladimir Baryshnikov's counter-intelligence work abroad and on their wartime experience of conducting radio games against the Germans, feeding them with political, military and operational disinformation and dispatching agents to penetrate their intelligence service. Baryshnikov gave an example of a successful agent penetration of a German intelligence school in Austria and later, when I had access to a file on the KGB agent SASHA, I realized that it was to him that Baryshnikov was referring.[10]

The curriculum at the KGB counter-intelligence school really consisted of a series of case histories, highlighting the pitfalls to be avoided and the tradecraft, which had proved most effective.

Colonel Yakov Skomorokhin, then the KGB *rezident* in France, gave a lecture during his vacation on penetration of the French intelligence and counter-intelligence services and told us how an agent in French intelligence had spotted that there was a girl in the French decoding service who was in financial difficulties. Skomorokhin had managed to contact her and took French lessons from her before eventually succeeding in recruiting her and using her to find other candidates for recruitment among the secretaries and translators in her service. Colonel Mitsyuk lectured on the penetration and neutralization of Russian and Ukrainian émigré organizations and Colonel Kristofor Oganesyan, a former KGB *rezident* in Iran, dealt with the Armenian and Georgian equivalents. Colonel Fedor Pilnov, head of the Anglo-American SK Department, gave several talks on preventing defections and he mentioned that his department had received information that a code clerk in the Soviet embassy in London had become a security risk and might defect so the KGB *rezidentura* had been forced to liquidate him. Pilnov also gave another example of a Soviet official who had contemplated defection, but had been lured onto a Soviet ship to be returned to the Soviet Union.[11]

Upon his graduation from the counter-intelligence course in 1950 Golitsyn was posted to the new Counter-Intelligence Directorate's Far East department, which had absorbed the SK section, responsible for the security of Soviet personnel in the region. Golitsyn's assignment was Korea and China.

> SK personnel continued to watch and collect adverse information on Soviet ambassadors and intelligence colleagues and I read a new file on General Terenty Shtykov, the Soviet ambassador in North Korea whose principal misdemeanor was to have as his mistress an eighteen-year-old Russian émigré girl who was suspected of being an American agent. The comical side of the affair was that the SK officer, Viktor Brusov, and the KGB *rezident* Balasanov, codenamed UBEN, hid in the ambassador's apartment and watched the affair taking place from one of his bathrooms. Later Shtykov was recalled from North Korea for his over-optimistic prediction to Stalin that a swift victory over South Korea was assured.[12]

Always inquisitive, Golitsyn's area of interest extended well beyond his SK section, and he often saw telegrams, read files and shared gossip with colleagues on related issues.

> In the course of my work I handled four telegrams and letters from the KGB *rezidentura* in London dealing with British visitors to the Soviet embassy there. The first introduced himself as Sergeant Musgrove from some intelligence unit offering to sell some military information about British troops in West Germany. He was paid, but there was concern in the KGB that he had been sent by the British so a special report was sent to the KGB Chairman. Sergeant Musgrove's approach was probably British-controlled because when, in later years, I discussed the case with the British they showed little interest in it.
>
> The next British visitor suggested a meeting with the KGB in some park in London and he provided some military information. He also asked for a second meeting to take place after his information had been assessed but there was a delay in the KGB over this assessment and the *rezidentura* did not attend the proposed second meeting because a provocation was suspected. Later, when the assessment had been completed, it was found that the information was of great value.
>
> A third visitor offered to sell diamonds and asked big money for them but the *rezidentura* mistrusted him and avoided him thereafter. The last case involved a British subject of Russian origin who applied for permission to return to the Soviet Union to live there. His name was

Dick Sotnikov and he said he had worked as an investigator either in a provincial branch of British counter-intelligence or at Scotland Yard, or perhaps for the South Africans. Once more, the London *rezidentura* suspected a provocation but the SCD was greatly interested in his case and insisted that he be admitted to the Soviet Union. General Serafim Lyalin bombarded our directorate with requests for our agreement and eventually Sotnikov arrived in Moscow where the British department recruited him as a special agent and he was used in recruitment operations against the British embassy in Moscow. His case officer was Bugrov who had fulfilled the same role for Guy Burgess, and after some impressive success he would become chief of the section for active operations against the British in Moscow.

In this same period correspondence passed through my hands showing that the KGB knew that the Canadian ambassador in Moscow was a homosexual and that the SCD was trying to blackmail him on that basis. Colonel Pantlymod Takhchyanov and his agent, a minor Soviet journalist with the cryptonym CHERNY ('Black'), were involved in the operation and, acting on Yevgeni Pitovranov's advice, our section established good contact with the SSD and I myself paid frequent visits to the American and British departments there. At the time the SCD was in disarray, and this was especially true of the American Department. As well as Pitovranov, Leonid Raykhman, who supervised the American and British departments, Norman Borodin, the chief of the American Department, and his deputy, had all been arrested. Raykhman and Borodin were tried by a court of honor in which the prosecutor was Colonel Aleksandr Volkov, and they were accused of groveling before the Americans and of obtaining American goods like cigarettes, records and chewing gum from their Russian agents in the American embassy. Many of their agents, particularly those working against this target, were declared unreliable and were dismissed as agents. Some were even arrested, and Borodin was replaced by Gleb Strokov who had been responsible for the case of Annabelle Bucar.[13]

Even if the case of Sergeant Musgrove attracted little attention from MI5, perhaps for the reasons Golisyn suspected, his reference to John Watkins, the Canadian diplomat (under suspicion of espionage) who would succumb to a heart attack in Montreal in October 1964, was of considerable interest.

As for Annabelle Bucar, she became something of a *cause célèbre* as she had been employed at General Walter Bedell Smith's American Embassy in Moscow in 1947. She had fallen for Konstantin Lapshin, a singer at the Moscow Operetta, unaware that he was working for Colonel Gleb Strokov of the SCD. When offered the opportunity for a secret marriage, sponsored by Lapshin's uncle, Bucar accepted and subsequently refused to return to the United States. In 1952, she was persuaded by the Soviets to write a book, *The Truth about American Diplomats*, critical of American foreign policy, that gave an account of what she claimed was life at the embassy.

While working on SK issues in Korea, Golitsyn was handed the file of a spy codenamed CONSUL, which was highly relevant at the time of his defection in December 1961:

> In 1948 I had been working on counter-intelligence and SK in Korea when George Blake was posted there to work against the Soviets from Seoul, so we had been engaged against one another without knowing it. Then, in December 1951, I found his file, a thin blue folder bearing the cryptonym CONSUL in Krasavin's safe, which described his recruitment by the KGB and opened with a note in Russian addressed to the chief of the Russian security and intelligence service from a detainee in Korea, the British diplomat Blake. In it Blake revealed that he was an officer of the British intelligence service and requested that someone should be sent to discuss discreetly with him his proposed cooperation with Soviet intelligence. The note was full of spelling and grammatical mistakes and was followed by a typed report of eighty to a hundred pages to the Minister of State Security, Viktor Abakumov, from General Belkin about his meetings with, and recruitment of, a British intelligence officer during a special trip he had made to Korea. The report was dated May 1951 and somebody, probably Andrei Krasavin, had crossed out the name Abakumov, presumably after his arrest in August 1951. Belkin reported that:
>
> In accordance with instructions I had several meetings with Blake in secure conditions in the camp where he was held. The meetings took place in conditions which excluded his compromise. Since Blake spoke poor Russian, Lieutenant Aleksandr Chernyshev acted as my interpreter.[14]

The name 'Blake' was written in Belkin's handwriting and the report contained a brief note on Blake's background and family, and his connection with the wartime resistance in the Netherlands, explaining how Blake had joined British intelligence and described where he had worked before his posting to South Korea. An attachment to the report described in a few pages the structure of British intelligence and, according to the document, Blake was willing to work for the Soviet service because he hated the existing class system in England, and because he had become convinced, after the Communist victory in China, that the future lay with Communism. The report did not indicate that Belkin had attached any conditions to his recruitment but said that

Blake had been given the cryptonym CONSUL. Belkin concluded that in case of an emergency, arrangements had been made for Blake to have meetings with two military counter-intelligence officers named Provakov and Layenko, who had helped to organize Belkin's meetings with Blake.

Blake, of course, had never known the names of his two interrogators in North Korea, as he made clear in his 1990 autobiography *No Other Choice*.[14] Accordingly, he did not mention the names of Belkin, Chernyshev, Provakov or Layenko, asserting only that he thought his recruiter later had been the head of the KGB in the Maritime Province. According to Blake, his recruiter introduced him to a fair young Russian with pleasant open features who interviewed Blake's companions, and this description fitted Chernyshev. Provakov, on the strength of his connection with Blake in North Korea, was later transferred to the British section in east Berlin during Blake's tour of duty in west Berlin. Chernyshev was also reassigned to Berlin in 1954. Chernyshev was also present at a meeting of 'technical staff in Geneva during the foreign ministers' conference there in 1954, and doubtless he had been sent there to be in contact with Blake who was involved in MI6's telephone tapping operations there during the conference.

Golitsyn was also indoctrinated into two other important operational files during this period. The first was SYNOK, the codename for 'little son'.

> Kashcheyev described SYNOK as Armand Hammer's illegitimate son, but he may in fact have been his illegitimate nephew. Kashcheyev said he intended to use SYNOK to re-establish contact with Hammer in the United States.
>
> I went through SYNOK's file and noted that he was one of the earliest *stilyagi*. While still a youth in 1944 he had been detained with Anastas Mikoyan's sons for visiting a secret bordello which happened to be the only one run by agents of the KGB's Moscow branch as a honeytrap for members of the Soviet elite. The KGB had considered exiling SYNOK, but decided instead to recruit him as an agent. When General Walter Bedell Smith was the U.S. ambassador in Moscow, SYNOK called on him on the KGB's instructions to ask him to forward a letter to his father or uncle requesting gifts of money and clothing. Bedell Smith had received SYNOK and presented him with a fountain pen.[15]

The second case was SIMA, the codename assigned to Judith Coplon, and Golitsyn was invited to study it by a colleague. Andrey Smirnov, who had explained that Coplon was:

a Justice Department employee when she was arrested with her case officer, Valentin Guichet. This happened in New York and I suggest you examine the contents of the safe and maybe you'll find something of interest for counter-intelligence.' After he left, Krivosheyn and I discussed what we should do about the Coplon file as neither of us realized that the FBI came under the Department of Justice and we thought that Coplon's reports would have been mainly about legal matters. There was also a language problem because my English was very limited, and Krivosheyn observed, 'SIMA is in prison or under FBI surveillance. The FBI has probably set a lot of traps for us. Let's not get involved in the case and waste valuable time.' I admit that we made a big mistake in not exploring the possibilities of penetrating the FBI which Coplon's information might have given us, but I am confident that later in the 1950s the American Department corrected the error and made good use of Coplon's material.[16]

Indeed, Coplon's position in the Justice department had enabled her to alert her Soviet handlers to new espionage enquiries conducted by the FBI, but a tap on her office telephone had revealed her relationship with Gubichev, a member of the UN Secretariat in New York. Coplon was arrested in March 1949 and sentenced to between forty months' and ten years' imprisonment, but her conviction would later be quashed on the grounds that the FBI has employed a wiretap without a warrant.

In 1953 Golitsyn learned about SASHA, a current penetration of the CIA base in Berlin who allegedly had operated against the Abwehr during the Second World War. This investigation would preoccupy the counter-intelligence staff for years, and eventually settle on Igor Orlov, alias Aleksandr Kopatszky, who died in 1982. A decade later the KGB defector Vasili Mitrokhin confirmed that Orlov had been an undetected mole inside the CIA from 1949 until his name leaked in 1978 [16] Golitsyn also saw the file on ALI:

Kashcheyev told me that he was Peter Smolka, alias Smollett, an Austrian Communist who had emigrated from Vienna to London before the war. Kashcheyev showed me a one-page memorandum about ALI's background which described him as 'a member of the original ring of five,' and explained that the original ring of five were the people who had started our successes in England and knew one another. They were Anatoli Gorsky's agents and they had made his reputation because they had penetrated British intelligence.[17]

In September 1953, accompanied by his newly wed wife Svetlana Golitsyn travelled to Vienna to take up a post in the *rezidentura*, located in the Imperial Hotrl. Soon afterwards, the Soviet intelligence community was rocked by a series of defections:

During my time in Vienna I encountered three Soviet officials who in different ways decided to tie their fate to the Americans. One was a GRU officer, Piotr Popov, who volunteered his services to CIA. The second was a member of our KGB *rezidentura*, Pavel Pevnev, who made contact with the Americans later in the Soviet Union, and the third was Piotr Deriabin of our *rezidentura* who defected to CIA in Vienna.

I knew Popov only slightly, having met him several times over meals at the Grand Hotel's restaurant. He knew I was KGB, and I knew that he was GRU and my KGB friend Aleksei Alinin, who worked against the Yugoslavs referred to Popov as 'my GRU rival', indicating that Popov was also working against the Yugoslavs. Popov wore a lieutenant-colonel's uniform and was a short, stocky figure of strong character. His personality was very Russian and natural, without poses or pretensions. He was simple-looking but shrewd and always friendly and smiling, and he once told me that he had just returned from vacation in the Soviet Union. When I asked him how he had spent his time he had replied, with a grin, 'Mostly standing in line.'

We had another meal together shortly after Deriabin's escape, and he remarked 'Kidnaped by the Americans!' still smiling. This was the official explanation of Deriabin's disappearance, but he asked me what was known about Deriabin's desertion and I told him that the investigation was still going on but thus far it had come to light that Deriabin's relations with his wife had been bad. Later I saw Popov at a Party meeting of all the High Commission staff a few months after Deriabin's defection and he and another GRU officer, A. Dolgov, were criticized for not having rejected vigorously enough a suggestion that they should defect, made to them by a British officer at an official reception. The Party leader read a letter from Molotov describing their behavior as indecisive and unworthy of Soviet officers and instructing all staff to be much firmer in rebuffing future approaches. Popov's remained his usual smiling self, but did not speak at the meeting. The last time I saw him was when the KGB and the GRU in Vienna were told in the summer of 1955 to cease their activities against the Yugoslavs because of Nikita Khrushchev and Marshal Bulganin's imminent visit to Belgrade. Greeting Popov in the Hotel Imperial, I joked: 'You're unemployed now, I suppose.' 'No', he smiled, 'they found a job for me in Germany.

The second Soviet intelligence officer who tried to go over to the Americans was a fellow member of the KGB *rezidentura*, Pavel Pevnev, who worked in Georgi Litovkin's German-Austrian group. Codenamed VLAS, he was responsible for the Austrian police and had a dozen agents among the Austrian detectives and so was helpful in gathering information about people we were studying for recruitment. Svetlana and I met him and his wife and they told us they had had a hard time until he had graduated from the Moscow Institute for International Relations and joined the KGB.

After Deriabin's defection to the CIA on 14 February 1954 there was pandemonium in the KGB and the High Commission *apparat*. A day after the defection was confirmed Colonel Aleksei Kurenkov, head of the KGB's German-Austrian Department, arrived in Vienna on Ivan Serov's personal instructions to find out what Deriabin knew and to decide on the counter-measures. Kurenkov called a meeting of all the *rezidentura* and was visibly shaken and upset. Speaking slowly and angrily he said,

> You don't know, you don't have any idea, you don't realize what Deriabin's betrayal means and what damage he may inflict on our Party and our service. For some years Deriabin worked in the bodyguards protecting our Party leaders. If he publishes articles, this alone will be so damaging that I am afraid to speak of what may happen. Deriabin knows about some of our special agents in West Germany. He knows all about our SK work in Vienna: he knows all the SK agents and all the Soviet officials who are under surveillance. He knows all the staff of our *rezidentura* in Austria and many officers in east Berlin. There is a real threat that American intelligence will use Deriabin's information to launch a massive effort to approach, blackmail, recruit or even kidnap our officers and agents. We have begun a special investigation in the *rezidentura* to determine what Deriabin knows about each one of you, to what extent you are compromised and what steps should be taken for your protection. I request your total cooperation with this investigation. You must reveal honestly which of your agents and operations are known to Deriabin. The *rezidentura* and each one of you must reconstruct and regroup your networks. Meetings with agents must be transferred where necessary from the western zones of Austria to the Soviet zone. All meetings should be covered by one or more additional officers. Contact with agents who are not fully trusted should be broken off. Every officer should report to the Imperial after he has met an agent. Every officer should report to the duty officer that he is in his room in the Grand Hotel before midnight. If the Americans try to blackmail or recruit you, report the fact immediately to the *rezident*.

After Aleksei Kurenkov had finished, Ivan Guskov asked for permission to speak and said that some time before the defection he had warned the *rezident*, Yevgeni Kovalev, about Deriabin's suspicious behavior but Kovalev had not paid any attention. Kurenkov replied that Guskov's report on the matter would be re-examined, and then Yevgeni Galuzin, the deputy *rezident*, said the best way to counter the threat of American

Erich and Elizabeth Vermehren, Their defection from Istanbul in January 1944 effectively destroyed the German *KriegsOrganisation* across the Middle East, and proved to be the catalyst for the SD's takeover of Abwehr.

Nicholas Elliott was SIS's Section V officer in Istanbul who engineered Vermehren's defection, whome he condenamed PRECIOUS. The successful exfiltration of Vermehren to Cairo, where he underwent two months of interrogation, established the rest of Elliott's career.

Grigori Tokaev. A leading Soviet aeronautical engineer, Tokaev sought political asylum for himself, his wife and daughter while posted as a GRU officer in Germany in April 1947. Codenamed EXCISE and then STORK, he was deployed to persuade a colleague, Yuti Tasoev, to defect, but he changed his mind after he had been flown to England Tolaev was resettled as Grigori Tokaty and worked a as an academic in London until his retirement from the City University in 1975.

Vladimir and Evdokia Petrov. The NKVD *rezident* in Canberra, Pettrov defected in April 1954 without consulting his wife who was told by the ambassador that her husband had been abducted and probably murdered. Petrov's asylum caused a political storm and prompted a Royal Commission to investigate Soviet espionage in Australia. Numerous CPA members were compromised although no agents were ever prosecuted.

Michael Thwaites. The ASIO case officer who masterminded Petrov's defection, Thwaites was not entirely sure that Petrov was an intelligence professional until after he had been granted political asylum in Australia.

Anatoli Golitsyn, A rare photograph, taken during his visit to Australia to attend the inaugural CAZAB meeting of Allied counter-intelligence officers.

Oleg Lyalin Recruited by a joint MI5/SIS task force in 1971, Lyalin was motivated to defect from the London *rezidentura* by his affair with a colleague's wife. He was a member of the First Chief Directorate's Department V. After he had been granted asylum the Foreign Office initiated a mass expulsion, Operation FOOT, declaring 105 Soviet personnel *persona non grata*. Codenamed GOLDFINCH, Lyalin also identified three of hi agents in London.

Tony Brooks, the SIS officer who teamed up with MI5's Harry Wharton to persuade a member of the London *rezidentura* to defect, and achieved success with Oleg Lyalin. A wartime SOE agent in France, Brooks won a DSO, Military Cross, Legion'd'Honneur and Croix de Guerre. During the Cold War he was posted by SIS to Sofia and Nicosia, and in 1966 served on Lord Mountbatten's committee on prison security following the escape of George Blake.

Arkadi Shevchenko. The most senior Soviet diplomat ever to defect, Shevehenko, passed secrets to the CIA's Ken Millian in New York for nearly three years before he applied for asylum in April 1978. The FBI sought to manage Shevchenko's resettlement by introducing him to a call-girl out of the yellow pages.

Judy Chavez. During his initial resettlement in an apartment in Washington, DC, Arkadi Shevchenko complained to his FBI protection squad about the lack of female companionship. The problem was solved when an escort service was contacted, and Judy Chavez was assigned the task of fulfilling his needs. To the FBI's embarrassment, Chavez later published her story in lurid detail.

Vitali Yurchenko. Formerly the Soviet embassy security officer at the Washingyon DC *rezidentura*, Yurchenko defected in Rome in August 1985 spontaneously. Having compromised several spies, among them Ron Pelton and Ed Howard, he changed his mind and returned to Moscow two months later. One of his debriefing team was Aldrich Ames who supplied his KGB contact with cpies of the daily interrogation reports. Reassured that he was not suffering from stomach cancer, and rejected by his lover, who was in Canada, Yurchenko tolfd his KGB colleagues that he had been abducted and drugged by the CIA, and they pretended to believe him.

Ron Pelton. A former National Security Agency analyst, Pelton was arrested in November 1985 after he had been traced from Vitali's Yurchenko's recollection of Pelton's visit to the Soviet embassy in 1979 when he had volunteered to sell classified information. He was sentenced to life imprisonment but was paroled in November 1015 and died in September 2022.

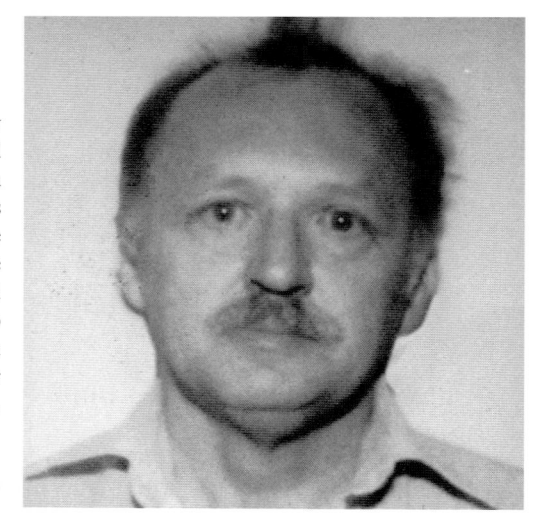

WANTED BY THE FBI

ESPIONAGE; INTERSTATE FLIGHT - PROBATION VIOLATION

EDWARD LEE HOWARD

FBI No. 720 744 CA2

Photograph taken 1983

Aliases: Patrick Brian, Patrick M. Brian, Patrick M. Bryan, Edward L. Houston, Roger H. Shannon

DESCRIPTION

Date of Birth:	October 27, 1951	Hair:	brown
Place of Birth:	Alamogordo, New Mexico	Eyes:	brown
Height:	5' 11"	Complexion:	medium
Weight:	165 to 180 pounds	Race:	white
Build:	medium	Nationality:	American
Occupations:	economic analyst, former U.S. Government employee		
Remarks:	knowledgeable in the use of firearms.		
Scars and Marks:	2-inch scar over right eye; scar on upper lip		
Social Security Number Used:	457-92-0226		
NCIC:	D054071919110810141 9		
Fingerprint Classification:	4 0 1 R 110 19		
	S 17 U 110		

CRIMINAL RECORD

HOWARD HAS BEEN CONVICTED OF ASSAULT WITH A DEADLY WEAPON.

CAUTION

HOWARD SHOULD BE CONSIDERED ARMED AND DANGEROUS AND SHOULD BE APPROACHED WITH CAUTION INASMUCH AS HE HAS BEEN CONVICTED OF ASSAULT WITH A DEADLY WEAPON AND IS PRESENTLY ON SUPERVISED PROBATION

A Federal warrant was issued on September 23, 1985, at Albuquerque, New Mexico, charging Howard with Espionage (Title 18, U.S. Code, Section 794 (c)). A Federal warrant was also issued on September 27, 1985, at Albuquerque, charging Howard with Unlawful Interstate Flight to Avoid Confinement — Probation Violation (Title 18, U.S. Code, Section 1073).

IF YOU HAVE ANY INFORMATION CONCERNING THIS PERSON, PLEASE CONTACT YOUR LOCAL FBI OFFICE. TELEPHONE NUMBERS AND ADDRESSES OF ALL FBI OFFICES LISTED ON BACK.

William H Webster
DIRECTOR
FEDERAL BUREAU OF INVESTIGATION
UNITED STATES DEPARTMENT OF JUSTICE
WASHINGTON, D. C. 20535
TELEPHONE: 202 324-3000

Entered NCIC
Wanted Flyer 524
October 4, 1985

Edward Lee Howard. During his debriefing Yurchenko described a CIA source as a man named "Robert" who had been scheduled for a posting to the CIA station in Moscow and had sold information to the KGB on a trip to Vienna. The CIA quickly identified Ed Howard as the culprit and he was placed under FBI surveillance at his home in Santa Fe. Howard detected the FBI and fled the country. He died in Moscow in July 2002.

Georges Paques. When Anatoli Golitsyn defected in December 1961 he provided the CIA with details of several spies whose reporting he had seen when he had worked in the KGB's NATO section. One of best-placed was Paques who was then deputy chief of NATO's press office who, when arrested, admitted that he had been a Soviet spy since his recruitment in 1958. He was sentenced to life imprisonment and was released in 1970. He died in Paris in December 1983.

Rupert Lockwood. An Australian journalist and Communist Party of Australia activist, Lockwood was exposed ny Petrov as the author Document "J", a series of disobliging personality profiles of senior Australian politicians.

Walter Clayton. ASIO took the opportunity of the Royal Commission to expose Wally Clayton as a Soviet spy codenamed KLOD in the VENONA decrypt. Petrov knew nothing about the VENONA project, which was never mentioned in evidence to the Commission, although its membership was briefed secretly about the source.

approaches based on Deriabin's information would be to regain the initiative. He suggested that each group in the *rezidentura* should examine which of its agents should be briefed on how to respond to an American approach, and asked for recommendations on which of the agents compromised by Deriabin should be transferred to East Germany or Czechoslovakia, out of harm's way. Each group should consider whether there were any known or suspected American agents in Austria who could be detained and interrogated as part of a counterattack on the Americans.[18]

The three defections from Vienna would have a seismic impact on the both the GRU and the NKVD. Especially when the NKVD learned one of Deriabin's motivation:

Deriabin's defection dominated the *rezidentura*'s work for weeks and as the investigation proceeded, officers began to be recalled. The first were Vladimir Pribytkov and the other officers of Deriabin's SK group who were withdrawn to Moscow and reassigned to provincial posts. After Pribytkov's departure, Yevgeni Kovalev told the heads of the different groups that investigation had shown that Deriabin had took off for the Americans when he had discovered that his chief, Pribytkov, had slept with his wife. [19]

There was one further defection in Europe during 1954. A department 13 assassin, Nikolai Khokhlov, who had been deployed against the NTS leadership, as Golitsyn recalled:

While Deriabin's defection was known and much discussed in the *rezidentura*, Nikolai Khokhlov's defection, despite the publicity in the West German press, was kept as secret as possible and was hardly mentioned. I learned of only two cases that had been compromised by Khokhlov and required action to limit the damage. One was a KGB agent, St Poelten's Communist police chief who had helped with Khokhlov's documentation as an illegal. Boris Ivanov of the illegals support group was assigned to this case and he had the policeman transferred from St. Poelten to another town, thus obscuring his connection with Khokhlov, and this successful manoeuver won him a commendation from Ivan Serov. The other case involved an Émigré Department agent named Petlenko with the cryptonym PIT, who was the NTS representative in Beirut and had become known to Khokhlov in the course of his briefing on the NTS and his intended victim, Georgi Okolovich. PIT was instructed to leave urgently for Moscow and he traveled [sic] through Vienna where Krivosheyn and I had lunch with him in the Grand Hotel.[20]

The 1954 defections practically paralysed the Vienna *rezidentura*, as it became obvious that Deriabin had compromised the entire staff, as Golisyn soon discovered.

> I had personal experience of a different aspect of the impact of Deriabin's defection when I paid two visits to DP camps in the British zone. The first visit took place before the defection and I went with two other officers from the Administrative Department to seek out people in the camps who wished to be repatriated to the Soviet Union. We were escorted by British officers who were very friendly and we shared our meals together and enjoyed several agreeable conversations. One evening we were invited to dinner at the officers' mess at Klagenfurt and again we were struck by the spontaneously friendly welcome we received which we found surprising because it was one of the worst periods of the Cold War. During coffee an officer came up and introduced himself as Colonel McDonald. We had an interesting conversation about Soviet-British wartime cooperation, the death of Stalin and the outlook for East-West relations. Of course, we suspected that the colonel was a military intelligence officer because he spoke some Russian and knew something of Russian history. I felt he was studying me for possible recruitment when he produced a list of Russian songs and asked me which ones I would like the band to play. Some of the songs were old Russian romances, some were well known pre-revolutionary songs and many were from the Soviet period. In order to mislead him I deliberately chose my favorites from the Soviet period though I would have preferred some of the older ones. My reaction was, I think, typical of Soviet officials in that period who studiously avoided honest answers in similar situations. In the camps we met a lot of the DPs and we were surrounded by the unfortunates who had lost their country, experienced all kinds of tragedy during the war and had no future. Some were hostile, but others were friendly but scared. A few of the old women simply cried and asked: 'What are we to do?', their main concern being how they would be treated on return to the Soviet Union. 'We don't want to go to Siberia', some shouted. My second visit took place after Deriabin's defection and the attitude of the British officers had changed markedly. They were sarcastic and confrontational, and there were no more invitations to the officers' mess. We interpreted the change as due to Deriabin having identified members of our group, including me, as KGB officers. During our visit to the camps there were threats and provocations against us which, we learned later from our contacts, had been arranged by Lieutenant Scott of British military counter-intelligence. [21]

Gradually the *rezidentura* resumed its operations, but not without much pain. The staff in Vienna was completely re-organised, and there were major repercussions in Moscow:

Headquarters was bursting with activity and news about the Central Committee and KGB reactions to the defections of Deriabin, Khokhlov, the Petrovs and Rastvorov. Ivan Serov had issued orders analyzing the circumstances of the episode and thirty-three Thirteenth Department officers, including its head, Colonel Lev Studnikov, were dismissed or otherwise punished for Khokhlov. Ivan Agayants was 'exiled' to the Balashikha sabool for the Petrovs and the head of his SK Department, Yacov Kozhevnikov, was dismissed. The KGB *rezident* in Tokyo, Aleksandr Nosenko, was retired for Rastvorov and the latter's former chief, Andrei Otroshchenko, was punished. Yevgeni Kovalev, the *rezident* in Vienna, was sent to the research department at Balashikha for Deriabin and there was talk that Serov was blaming Panyushkin for errors in personnel selection which had led to the wave of defections. Eventually Panyushkin left to become head of the Central Committee's Exits Commission which dealt with permission to go abroad but f or some reason there was no order from Serov on the Deriabin case. Even more strangely, Aleksei Kurenkov, the head of the German-Austrian Department, was not punished but was promoted to general and appointed head of the KGB Institute, perhaps helped by important penetrations made in Berlin.

The really exciting news was about the first conference of KGB officers which had taken place in July 1954 when Khrushchev had delivered a six-hour report dealing with the selection, training and use of KGB staff. He said that one single year had shown that the KGB had many rotten apples in its ranks, asserting that five officers of the intelligence service had committed treason and gone over to the enemy camp and asking what sort of people were being selected, trained and sent abroad. He said that the situation in the internal directorates was little better, for the bodyguards were full of parasites, cowards and traitors. Of course, Petr Deriabin had been a ranking member of the bodyguards, and how had the bodyguards behaved at the May Day demonstration at Archangel? There a young terrorist, an army lieutenant named Romanov, had broken away from the demonstration, shouting 'Freedom to the Russian people!' and had started shooting the Party leaders on the reviewing stand with his revolver. He had shot the deputy Party leader and wounded two other, and what had the bodyguards done? Instead of protecting their leaders with their bodies, these cowards lay on the ground trying to save their own lives. Only a major of the border guards who was in the demonstration with his little girl did not panic and showed courage by seizing and disarming the terrorist. The KGB had to be purged of all its Beria henchmen, cowards, parasites and potential traitors. Actually, Khrushchev's reference to five defectors in 1954 was an understatement because two other illegal officers, Yevgeni Brik in Canada and Grigori Bratsikhin in Vienna, had defected.[22]

In September 1955, as the Vienna *rezidentura* was about to be transferred to east Berlin, Golitsyn volunteered for a four-year course at the KGB Institute in Moscow, and it was here that in February 1956 he was informed about Nikita Khrushchev's five-hour, secret speech to the 20th Congress of the Communist Party of the Soviet Union. This was the moment that Golitsyn underwent an ideological conversion, which would quickly be reinforced by the public criticism voiced by the Italian party leader Palmiro Togliati, and then the suppression of the Hungarian revolt.

> Having broken secretly with the Party and the KGB I faced a dilemma in deciding how to fight them effectively, whether from inside the country or from abroad, whether alone or in league with others. To begin with, I thought in terms of creating a small group in the KGB which would work inside the country, but I could see little chance of success. Aware of the KGB's use of provocation, I knew that any colleague I approached would assume (as I would have done) it was a provocation and would report it immediately to his superiors. That would have led to my arrest and my gesture would have been totally futile. I also thought a lot about assassinating one or more Party leaders as I felt that history had justified the assassination of tyrants and morally I was ready for the act. I reflected on my meeting with Stalin, for had I known then all about him and had I broken with the Party at that time I would have had a good opportunity to kill him and I might well have tried. When I heard about a KGB general who shot himself in Ivan Serov's outer office after he had been charged with violations of socialist legality I thought I would not repeat his mistake. I would have shot Serov first because that would have been more meaningful than plain suicide. Students at the institute were used in the protection of the Party leaders during the celebrations in Red Square in May and November and when they visited the sports palace. This gave me the kind of access I needed for an assassination but the difficulty as that, as a student, I had no personal weapon at my disposal. Also, I knew that there were secret metal detectors at the gates into the sports palace.
>
> In Helsinki I had a real chance of killing Nikita Khrushchev when I met him twice in the Soviet embassy in Helsinki in September 1956, or Leonid Brezhnev when I was among those who saw him off at the train station at the end of his visit in 1961, but I knew by that time from the American press that Khrushchev was regarded in the west as an anti-Stalinist reformer and I thought that an assassination of him would be misunderstood in the West and that Brezhnev was not a key target.
>
> The only option that was likely to be effective was to escape to the west and to work with the western intelligence services against the Soviet regime. The sensible course was to prepare myself thoroughly

for defection and leave at a moment of my own choosing and at first the idea seemed full of difficulties, even fantastic but I knew that there had been a tradition of resistance to Soviet tyranny from within the ranks of the KGB and the GRU in the form of defectors. I knew about Grigori Agabekov, Genrykh Lyushkov, Igor Gouzenko and Nikolai Khokhlov, and I also had some personal knowledge of Piotr Deriabin, the Petrovs and Yuri Rastvorov and I knew too how much damage they had done inflicted. I began to revise my opinion of the defectors, and whereas before I had regarded them as weaklings or traitors, I now saw them as patriots and men of courage.

My best hope lay in defecting to and collaborating with the American intelligence and counter-intelligence services and through them I would be able to give western governments secret political information which would help them to understand the situation in the Soviet Union and the Kremlin's aggressive foreign policy. Armed also with extensive information on the KGB I intended to offer myself to the American and other western agencies as a consultant. Secondly, I saw myself as a potential historian of the Soviet secret police system and a specialist on the exposure of its activities either in collaboration with the CIA or independently[23].

Having decided on a future in the West, Golitsyn took a special interest in the way the KGB dealt with defectors, and researched the subject with a special enthusiasm:

Naturally I did all I could to find out what the KGB was doing about the old defectors in the west and in 1956 or 1957 Gribanov's assistant Fedor Scherbak gave our course a report on his trip to the Olympic Games in Melbourne in which he referred to Vladimir Petrov and said that he and his officers thought that the Australians might use Petrov in their provocations against the Soviet athletes. 'However', he said, 'we received information that this would not happen because Petrov had bouts of drinking.' In 1958 I encountered Andrei Smirnov, my former chief in the American Department and he told me that he was on vacation from China where he had replaced Raina as an adviser. We talked about the defections of Yuri Rastvorov and the Petrovs and he confided that he had been punished by Panyushkin for his failure to prevent Rastvorov's defection. Panyushkin, who had received a warning signal about Rastvorov, had sent Smirnov to Japan for this purpose but he had not handled the situation well. When I asked him about Petrov's defection he told me that the FCD had made a thorough investigation of the case for the Central Committee and had concluded that, because Petrov had worked closely under Beria, he had been afraid that he might be punished. The Soviet ambassador in Australia had contributed to the defection by his criticism of some of Petrov's mistakes.

In the same period I met Fedor Shlykov, a KGB officer whom I knew in Smersh school and who had served in Tokyo with Turi Rastvorov. He told me that he had criticized Rastvorov for his western-style behavior at Party meetings in the embassy before his defection, but his criticisms had been ignored. It was only after the defection that his chiefs had praised him for his vigilant attitude, and he had been promoted to the Thirteenth Department. I also met Vasya Savelyev, a KGB officer whom I briefed on SK work when I was in the SK section for Japan, and he told me that both he and the KGB *rezident*, Aleksandr Nosenko (no relation to Yuri Nosenko), had been blamed for having failed to prevent Rastvorov's defection. He said he had received signals about Rastvorov's improper behavior but he and Nosenko had been unable to do anything about it because Rastvorov had boasted that he knew Ivan Serov, and played tennis with him. After Savelyev's recall from Tokyo he wrote a letter to the Central Committee explaining that his inaction was due to Rastvorov's friendship with Serov, but Serov had taken exception and, as Savelyev put it, 'threw me and Aleksandr Nosenko out of the KGB.' For some time Savelyev had endured a hard life, but more recently Gribanov had enrolled him to work against visiting Japanese businessmen.

In 1958 Andrei Sloma, an SK officer in Turkey at the time of Konstantin Volkov's abortive contact with the British there, and whom I knew while I was in the SK Department, told me that he was working as head of the archives at the KGB branch in Lipetsk and had been elected Party secretary of the branch. Knowing that I had served in Vienna he asked me, 'How was it that you failed to prevent Deriabin's defection? If I'd been there it wouldn't have happened', he boasted. He told me that Prybytkov, Deriabin's chief in Vienna, was serving with him in Lipetsk. 'As Party leader I'll finish the career of this womanizer', he said.

In the same year I met Yevgeni Kravtsov the former *rezident* in Vienna, and he told me that, because of Piotr Deriabin, he had been exiled to Balashikha where he was working in the research department. Trying to learn more I asked him why nothing had been done against Deriabin, and he responded 'If I returned to the German-Austrian Department I would liquidate Deriabin within three months.'

At about the time I met Yevgeni Kravtsov I ran into Deriabin's former wife on Gorky Street. She was cheerful and in good spirits, and we exchanged greetings and had a short conversation during which she told me that 'the office' had helped her to get a job working as a typist in the Union of Soviet Writers, and was happy with her work but she had not re-married. Neither of us mentioned her husband.[24]

For the remainder of his course, Goliysyn was a diligent student, and collected information from KGB files that would serve his cause. In late 1956 or early 1957 he read a secret study of up to 500 pages on successful KGB countermeasures against American intelligence activities in the Soviet Union. The principal author of the study was Sergei Fedoseyev, the institute's senior lecturer on American intelligence and it included an account of the successful recruitment of a security officer in the U.S. embassy in Moscow.[25]

Thus, as Golitsyn listened to the authentic case histories recounted by the celebrated Chekists, he began to accumulate the material that he assessed as being the most damaging to the Party leadership.

> Though I had a good deal of knowledge about the KGB, I was not prepared to sit back and content myself with the information that came my way in the normal course of lectures and study so I began to look for leads to or indications of KGB successes in penetrating western intelligence services such as arrests of western agents, other signs of western intelligence failures, awards and special promotions for relevant KGB officers, KGB action against defectors in the west and action to prevent new defections. As a chess player I kept reviewing all possible moves I could make and decided that I could take the initiative in seeking information provided I always had a plausible explanation for my curiosity at the ready.[26]

Between 1957 and 1959, Golitsyn's last two years at the KGB Institute, he took the opportunity, while ostensibly researching a thesis, to acquire even more sensitive information.

> I saw in this a tremendous opportunity to collect information for my mission, and I devoted much thought to the choice of subject for my thesis on which, it seemed to me, the success of my mission would largely depend. Ivanov, the head of Faculty One (KGB methods) tried to persuade me to choose *The KGB's Role in the Wartime Partisan Movement* and he promised to give me access to raw secret files on the subject and told me that the Central Committee was very interested in it. He added that in the long run there was a good chance that my thesis would be published. I politely declined his suggestion, my secret reason being that the subject would not be of compelling interest to the CIA who would get the information anyway if the thesis were published. I wanted instead to find a subject which would give me a pretext to reach into the counterintelligence departments of the First and Second Chief Directorates and pick up information on KGB penetration of the western intelligence services. After much reflection I lit on *The Prevention of Betrayals and Defections by Members of Official Soviet Organizations, Visiting Delegations and Tourist Groups Abroad.*

> I realized that there was a certain risk in choosing such a provocative subject when I was planning my own defection but, in the event, the risk proved justified: in fact I regard this as the most important initiative I undertook in pursuit of material for my mission. It opened vital doors for me and yielded important leads about penetration of the western intelligence services.[27]

To extend his reach, Golitsyn found excuses to attend classified lectures at other KGB institutions:

> There were no lectures for counter-intelligence students at the institute on the methods of Soviet external intelligence: this subject was taught only in the FCD's own school. In order to overcome this obstacle and gain access to textbooks on external intelligence matters I deliberately chose as the subject of my yearly course work for 1957 'the recruitment of agents abroad'. I sought the help of a former FCD officer, Arseniy Tishkov. As I hoped, he advised me to use in my course work cases and examples from the FCD textbooks and gave me permission to have access to them. I was soon able to read books issued at Balashikha by the head of the research and publishing department there, M.A. Burinsky. Among the secret textbooks I read was one on *Methods of Recruitment* by Colonel Kravtsov, one on *Agents of Influence* by Andrei Raina, one on *The Localization of Intelligence Failures* by Ivan Agayants and the memoirs of General Zarubin about his exploits. From these I learned a lot about agents and their recruitment. True, the books gave only the cryptonyms and not the real names of the agents but the background information on concrete situations in which they were involved was to prove helpful to me in my later work with western intelligence services.[28]

It was always intended that after his graduation from the KGB Institute he would return to Vienna but, ironically, this plan was scuppered, albeit unwittingly, by Deriabin who had identified Golitsyn as a member of the 1954 *rezidentura*, which had operated under diplomatic cover in the Soviet High Commission:

> In the closing days of my apprenticeship in KGB headquarters, my colleague Evgenni Ivanov warned me in March 1959 that Petr Deriabin had published excerpts from his forthcoming book in *Life* magazine. In them he had revealed a lot of information about members of the KGB *rezidentura* in Vienna, and he also gave evidence before a Congressional committee in which he referred to me specifically as the case officer for Father Arseni. As a result of the publicity my posting to Vienna as a counter-intelligence officer was canceled.[29]

In anticipation of his graduation and new assignment abroad, Golitsyn prepared himself by making notes and committing important information to his memory:

> I decided to give myself my own exam to find out what I had learned and tried to commit to memory everything of importance. I noted down references in not more than two or three words to important KGB concepts, changes in methods, major recruitments, identities of and leads to agents, significant operations, facts, conversations and names. Then I numbered the references and the total came to 463. That was my rehearsal for meetings with western intelligence services, and then I destroyed my notes. After that I felt satisfied that my studies at the institute and my extra-curricular effort to collect additional information had been successful. I was confident that I had a good understanding of the essence of the KGB's new methods and of its strengths and weaknesses, and I began to develop my ideas on providing western intelligence agencies with a more systematic methodology for the large scale identification of KGB agents.[30]

Having been rejected for Vienna, Golitsyn was anxious to remain in the FCD as this would give him the opportunity to defect, but he only narrowly avoided a transfer to the SCD's Scandinavian Section, which would have involved no foreign travel:

> Next I was offered a post as a senior operational officer or analyst in the NATO section of the Information Department. The idea had no great appeal for me but I accepted the offer because the job would allow me to collect information about KGB sources on NATO. My demotion from deputy head of sektor to senior operational officer did not bother me because my main aim was not to make a successful career in the KGB but to gain information to ensure the success of my defection. My acceptance of the post was made easier for me when Vladimir Legeyev told me that he and Yevgeni Tarabrin were planning to take me out of the Information Department in a few months in order to send me abroad with a counter-intelligence assignment probably in Finland, one of the countries which Tarabrin supervised.[31]

Having joined the FCD's NATO section, Golitsyn was given two months to read himself int the current files, and acquaint himself with the KGB's sources of information:

> For two months I diligently read the section's files and the reports that had been received, trying to memorize the more important ones and to

glean ideas on the identities of the sources who had supplied them. The files showed that since 1957 the section had been receiving from the First Chief Directorate's French Department voluminous quantities of NATO political and military documents, among them, decisions of the NATO Council and records of its meetings, and documents from the NATO Secretariat and its main departments. The section filed the documents in accordance with NATO's own indexing system.

After translation and processing, the documents were sent with a covering letter to the Central Committee, the foreign minister and the defense minister or the chief of the general staff. Usually the covering letters indicated that the documents had been received from Paris but London and Brussels were sometimes mentioned. There were Top Secret NATO and French defense ministry documents on the planning, conduct and assessment of joint military maneuvers in Western Europe. NATO plans for the defense of west Berlin were covered and the texts of warning signals of the imminence of nuclear war were included. There were several reports from French intelligence. Two were translations of original documents dealing with intelligence on Yugoslavia and Poland. There was a French intelligence assessment of Soviet military potential. These documents were received through the KGB's French Department which described the source as in a 'French government organ'. I understood this to mean the French intelligence service. A long NATO document, *Plans for Psychological Warfare against Eastern Europe in Time of War* appeared to have come from a French government source. There were other documents from the French foreign and information ministries. Among the documents received through the British Department were papers dealing with actions of the British Army of the Rhine (BAOR) in the event of hostilities and correspondence between London and Bonn on BAOR's status and expenditure. In the inventory I found mention of a 1958 report from Aleksandr Knrnrkov now in Berlin, about information from HENRY and his five sources. In the section's files I came across a forty-page report from the British ambassador in Moscow, Sir Patrick Reilly, containing an assessment of Khrushchev's popularity. There were copies of letters from the Foreign Office and a number of documents about Bahrein. There were also documents from the Indian High Commission in London dating from 1953 or 1954. The first documents I processed as an analyst were two from the British Admiralty about the naval base on the Clyde. A report was sent to the chief of the Soviet general staff. Kurenyshev and I worked together on a report to the Central Committee and foreign ministry on the French attitude toward West German participation in NATO. It was based on an assessment by the French Deuxieme Bureau: this contained a speech by a former French military attaché in Moscow who might well have been the source of the document. Kurenyshev and I also processed the speeches delivered at the Bilderberg Conference in Turkey in September

1959. One of the subjects discussed was the effects on the west and on western policies of differences between the Soviets and the Chinese. According to Aleksandr Kurenyshev the Bilderberg conferences were held more or less annually in different countries and were attended by influential western personalities. The KGB received the papers on the Bilderberg conferences from two sources, one in London and the other in a West European capital. The Bilderberg papers were taken to Beijing by the chief of Soviet intelligence, Sakharovsky, for the benefit of his Chinese counterpart. Sakharovsky also took with him some NATO and SEATO documents on the Chinese attitude to Tibet and a State Department report on Sino-Soviet differences.

In February 1960 I was given a task which yielded information about an important source in 'British security', the term used by the KGB for MI5. Serov, who had been KGB Chairman and was by then chief of the GRU, complained to the Central Committee that the KGB had stopped sending the GRU information on MI5 operations against GRU officers in London. Serov stated that, when he was KGB Chairman, warnings about such operations were passed to the GRU on a regular basis: now they had ceased. Serov explained this as being due to Shelepin's prejudice against the GRU, probably on account of the Popov case. Serov made two further complaints: he charged that the KGB was not handing over to the GRU agents they had recruited among western military attachés in Moscow and that the KGB was not fully sharing with the GRU the intelligence it received on NATO activities.

Shelepin called on Skryagin, the head of the Information Department, to explain the situation. The latter replied that our department had sent the GRU everything that we had. Shelepin ordered him to supply him with the relevant statistics. The task was passed on to Chernov, the head of the NATO section, who told Bykov to draft a reply covering NATO reports sent to the GRU. As for reports on MI5 operations, Chernov told me to do the job because he had been told that I was a counter-intelligence specialist. He suggested that the best way of getting to the bottom of the problem would be to consult Yevgeni Tarabrin, the head of the British Department, to find out what reports on MI5 operations his department had sent direct to the GRU as well as those sent through the Information Department. I went to Tarabrin who was very helpful. [32]

While serving in the NATO section, Golityn accessed a veritable treasure trove of secret information, and manipulated his unwitting colleagues to learn more about penetrations:

My colleague Aleksandr Kurenyshev became an important source of mine on the affairs of the Information Department. He was a former GRU officer, had served in the GRU's Information Department and had also worked in Canada where he had been responsible for coverage of the local press. According to him, nine Canadian reporters were on the Soviet embassy's payroll, and when he returned to Moscow from Canada in 1956 he had been transferred to the FCD's Information Department because the KGB was short of a military analyst. He was a pleasant, friendly individual who was knowledgeable about the history of the department and its staff because he had served in its Party organization a year earlier. From him I learned that the main NATO source had been providing intelligence on NATO on an ideological basis since 1957, and his case officer in Paris had been Aleksei Trishin. At the end of 1959 the East German leader Walter Ulbricht had included an indiscreet reference to a secret NATO document in a public speech, thereby prompting NATO leak investigation. In consequence, the source had been transferred to the control of a KGB illegal, Olga Shimmel who had for a long time processed reports from the British intelligence services, and was British-born, the widow of a Comintern or KGB officer who had died in the course of his duties.

According to Kurenyshev, before Nikolai Korovin, the head of the British Department, left to become KGB *rezident* in London in 1956, the intelligence output of the department was discussed at a meeting with the Information Department. There had been criticism of the quality of output, to which Korovin had responded: 'But you cannot deny that the milk is flowing.' Kurenyshev also told me that Yuri Modin, who was running a specially [sic] valuable agent in London with Korovin, was sent home by the latter for making a mistake which prejudiced the agent's security. Modin was given a job in the Information Department but he was soon transferred to the Illegals Directorate. Apparently the French section of the Information Department had been receiving a steady flow of Quai d'Orsay documents for the previous fifteen years and Kurenyshev explained how a scandalous situation had arisen over the contents of the special safe in the Middle East section. This contained original documents in Hebrew from the Israeli foreign ministry but because there was no Hebrew translator in the FCD the documents remained untranslated and unprocessed, to the point that so many had accumulated that a second safe had been provided. Eventually the KGB Chairman authorized the employment of a young man from an orthodox family of rabbis in Lvbv as a translator, and I saw him in the department wearing a black suit. He had never been a Komsomol or Party member, he had no friends in the department and nobody trusted him, so he was always alone. But he was energetic, knew the language well and did his job.

From the FCD's monthly secret intelligence bulletin issued for the benefit of members of the Presidium, I learned that secret correspondence between the Italian ambassador in a European country with his foreign ministry on the subject of West Germany's relations with NATO had been obtained. A note on the ambassador's background indicated that he had served previously in Moscow, Paris, London and other capitals.[33]

In later years it would emerge that the agent unintentionally jeopardised by Yuti Modin had been John Cairncross, who had been abandoned at a pre-arranged rendezvous in London. The French spy in NATO would turn out to be George Paques.

In March 1960, Golitsyn was informed that he was under consideration for a counter-intelligence post in Finland, and the following month, after a series of interviews, moved from the NATO section to the fourteenth department, which was responsible for counter-intelligence. In May 1960, he spent ten days at the Ministry of Foreign Affairs' Scandinavian department to support his cover assignment to Helsinki, adopting the name Klimov in the role of attaché.

While at the fourteenth department Golitsyn was assigned temporarily to the American section. He was briefed that most of the agents in Finland were handled by the Scandinavian section of the British department, which employed Finnish speakers, but there were a few agents in the Finnish Security Service and the police. One the agents, codenamed ERIKSON, would later be appointed Heldinki's chief of police.

> Vladimir Klimkin told me that one or two of the agents in the police might be transferred to me. He said that he himself had recruited one of the police agents in Helsinki after the war. His name was Gabrielson and he was a police inspector in Helsinki. His first cryptonym was KUKISHKIN and his current cryptonym was ERIKSON. He was strongly anti-communist and had given the KGB a lot of trouble to begin with but he was eventually broken in and had become a valuable agent after the KGB arranged some life-saving surgery for him in the hospital of a Soviet military base.
>
> Aleksandr Agafonov showed me only three files, the most important of which was the one on Mikko Harrela, codenamed KRISTOV, a Finnish businessman of Russian origin who had been planted on the British. They recruited had him in 1954 to gather information on Soviet affairs during his business visits to the Soviet Union and his showed that in 1955 a British intelligence officer from west Berlin named 'Clemens' had visited Helsinki to brief KRISTOV. The Counter-intelligence Department had planned to detain 'Clemens' secretly and then to try to blackmail him into collaborating. If he refused the plan had allowed for him to be kidnapped and taken to Moscow and Nikolai Makeyev had been sent to Helsinki to carry out the operation, and the *rezidentura* in Helsinki had formed an operational group to abduct the Briton. The group consisted

of three senior Finnish Communist Party officials, two of whom were named Sippola and Lekhtinen. For some reason the operation was not carried out, perhaps 'Clemens' had become suspicious, and the British had broken off contact with KRISTOV. The Helsinki *rezsidentura* ran KRISTOV through a Soviet trade representative, Filippov who had been recruited for the purpose. Agafonov and I decided that I would be in contact with Filippov even though the case did not look promising.

What excited me, though Aleksandr Agafonov paid no attention to it, was that the file contained handwritten notes by KGB officers in Berlin on the information their agent there had given them on personality, weaknesses and so on. The agent was clearly a colleague of 'Clemens' in Berlin and his KGB cryptonym was ENESU. I thought that, if in the future the British had a candid talk with 'Clemens', they might well be able to identify ENESU so I drew up a formal plan of visits I would make to various sections and departments at headquarters to examine ways in which they might be able to help me with my counter-intelligence work in Helsinki. I deliberately made the plan as comprehensive as my situation would allow and among the sections I proposed to visit were the American, British, French and German sections of the Counter-intelligence Department, the relevant SK section to examine whether any of the SK agents in Helsinki could be used for counter-intelligence purposes there, the Finnish group in the Scandinavian section of the FCD's British Department. the FCD archives to study old Finnish cases; the special library to study the training manuals on the main western intelligence services; and the SCD's American and tourist departments. Ostensibly, this was the plan of a diligent KGB officer determined to prepare himself thoroughly for a forthcoming assignment but in fact it was an attempt to collect as much information as possible on KGB agents and penetration of western intelligence services which would be useful after my defection. My scheme was approved by Klimkin himself, which gave me the assurance I needed that my diligence and inquisitiveness would not arouse suspicion.[34]

In anticipation of his posting abroad, Golitsyn attended numerous briefings, one of which was on the sensitive subject of defections:

In Vladimir Klimkin's department I met Chistyakov whom I had known in the SK Department where he had worked on the Soviet colony in Australia, and developed a keen hatred of defectors because of the Petrovs. Klimkin had particular confidence in him and put him in charge of correspondence with Washington on penetration of the CIA. For these reasons I raised the subject of Piotr Deriabin with him and said I was surprised that our service had not succeeded in eliminating him, whereupon Chistyakov had replied, 'I don't understand this myself. We have the opening to do it. We have access to him and we have received two volumes of his CIA debriefings but for some reason we have not taken action against him.'

From Grachev I learned a lot about how the KGB assessed the damage inflicted by defectors and their damage limitation precautions. Grachev told me that a special research group had been set up in 1954 to re-examine all the FCD archives. The group, headed by Grachev, consisted of 500 officers from different departments and its first aim was to assess what the defectors Deriabin, Rastvorov, Khokhlov and the Petrovs knew and had compromised Its second objective was dictated by the political changes which were occurring in Eastern Europe and China. The group was instructed to scour the records for information on all citizens in these countries who had been involved in the past in anti-communist activities or in work for the British, French or other western intelligence services.[35]

The group's third task had been to choose material from the archives, which could safely be used by the KGB in double agent or disinformation operations against the Western intelligence services. According to Grachev, the group completed its work by the end of 1956 when comprehensive damage reports on the defections had been completed. The information collected about agents of Western intelligence services and anti-communists in Eastern Europe and China had been passed on to the security services of these countries and a stack of information had been accumulated about old KGB operations, which could be used in intelligence games against the West. Grachev claimed that, based on the group's recommendations, many changes in KGB methods had been made, particularly in respect of the cover used by KGB officers in legal *rezidenturas*.

When the Golitsyns arrived in Helsinki in July 1960 they still intended to defect, but probably not for some years as his parents were still alive. Initially, Golitsyn was employed as a illegals support officer, in the absence of anyone in that role at the *rezidentura*, and among the many illegals transiting through Finland was another putative defector, Yuri Loginov, who identified 'Klimov' to his CIA handlers as a KGB officer. Golitsyn was indoctrinated into most of the major cases, including that of President Kekkonen.

From 1958 onward the KGB *rezident* Vladimir Zhenikhov ran Kekkonen as an agent and he told me that Kekkonen supplied him with reports from Finnish security on plans for operations to be conducted against Soviet intelligence. Once he allowed me to read one of these reports, which was five or six pages long and concerned a proposal to arrest a GRU officer named Vinogradov for espionage. The report listed recruitment approaches Vinogradov had made to Finnish officers and other evidence of improper collection of military information but, at Zhenikhov's behest, Vinogradov was quietly recalled to Moscow. Kekkonen also gave the KGB copies of reports from Finnish ambassadors and military attachés abroad, and secret information from other government departments.[36]

Golitsyn's plans would change dramatically:

Though I had taken no decision on timing when I arrived in Helsinki everything changed in September 1961 and I decided that I must defect within the next two to three months. My decision was the information Vladimir Zhenikhov had brought back from his visit to Moscow where he had attended a number of high level meetings and a conference of KGB *rezidents*. Mikhail Suslov, Alexander Shelepin, Boris Ponomarev, Nikolai Mironov, Aleksandr Panyushkin and leading members of the FCD had attended the conference and Zhenikhov told us that the new political strategy was now being put into practical effect. This caused me to reflect on all I knew about the new strategy. I thought about the Party's decision in 1959 to assign to the KGB a new political role comparable to that played by the GPU in the 1920s. Related to this were Shelepin's reorganization of the KGB, the creation of the new Disinformation Department and the steps taken to create controlled political opposition. I also thought over what Petr Akorzin had said about the KGB's plans to use their agents in the intellectual field in carrying out the strategy.

As an illegal support officer, I remembered that when Vladimir Novikov returned from his vacation in the Soviet Union in April 1961 I had asked him what was new in KGB headquarters, and he had replied 'they are discussing and planning steps to finish with the United States once and for all.' Novikov did not elaborate but had implied that what was envisaged was large-scale political deception. I recalled also how, a year previously, Zhenikhov had told us that Nikita Khrushchev would brief the members of the *rezidentura* and the diplomatic staff on the new strategy during his visit to Finland. The consul was instructed to prepare a reception room in the consulate where the briefing would take place and the technical officer checked the room for microphones but, to my intense disappointment, Zhenikhov had announced at the last moment that Khrushchev had canceled the briefing because he was tired after a heavy lunch.

Zhenikhov's statement that the strategy was being put into effect crystallized my thoughts for I could no longer sit still and do nothing when the United States was under threat of extinction by new political means The time had come for me to make my escape and convey a warning to the Americans, and if I delayed further it might be too late.

At the same briefing that Vladimir Zhenikhov spoke about the strategy he gave us news about senior KGB appointments, telling us that while General Korotkov, the KGB chief in Germany, was playing tennis with the GRU chief Ivan Serov at the latter's dacha he was summoned urgently to the telephone to be told that the KGB illegal Bogdan Stashinsky, who had assassinated the Ukrainian émigré nationalist leader Stepan Bandera, had defected on the day before the Berlin Wall had been erected, on 13 August 1961.

On hearing the news, Aleksandr Korotkov had collapsed and died from a heart attack. Zhenikhov told us that General Aleksei Krokhin had replaced Korotkov and that General Nikolai Korovin, the former KGB *rezident* in London, had been appointed head of the Thirteenth Department for sabotage, kidnapping and assassinations. There he had replaced Ivan Fadeykin who had been made deputy chief of the Third Chief Directorate (military counter-intelligence) and Zhenikhov hinted that these appointments related to the strategy.[37]

The defection of the KGB professional assassin, and the unexpected construction of the Berlin Wall persuaded Golitsyn that he could not risk any further delay in undertaking his defection, and his account of the final days before his escape makes compelling reading:

My secret intention, after my defection, was to reveal to the world how the KGB had intervened in Finnish presidential elections, how they had distorted the results through bribery and how they had manipulated Kekkonen and other Finnish politicians in their interests, and it was the middle of September 1961 when I decided that the time had come to leave. I broke the news to Svetlana and asked her if she would come with me. She was taken by surprise by my announcement that we would be leaving in two to three months and felt uncertain about it. Our daughter Tanya was in Moscow with Svetlana's parents so Svetlana decided that she must visit them in Moscow before making up her mind. She promised me an answer on her return to Helsinki and I made it plain that my decision was a final one and that if necessary I would have to defect on my own. Svetlana was away in Moscow for a month but I knew she would never willingly betray me. However, I was worried about what might happen if she felt compelled to confide in her family and friends and seek advice from them, but at last she telephoned from Moscow to tell me she was bringing Tanya back to Helsinki. When they arrived we took our usual evening stroll together in the city center and she told me that she and Tanya would be leaving with me.

From that moment on I began to think about our escape in practical terms. I was disgusted by Vladimir Zhenikhov's campaign against the ambassador and refused to take part in his intrigues, but I avoided openly expressing my views. When Zhenikhov made an indirect attempt through Viktor Zegal to involve me against the ambassador I once again declined, quoting to Zegal a Polish saying that 'When the masters fight, the servants lose their scalps.' I knew that Zegal would report what I had said to Zhenikhov and I guessed, rightly, that Zhenikhov would not approach me again.

After I had decided to leave within three months my attitude toward the dispute between Zhenikhov and the ambassador changed, as my sympathies lay entirely with the ambassador and I felt that I should tell him so. I also felt that I should tell Zhenikhov what I thought of his behavior. I still cared about the opinions of my colleagues and I wanted them to remember me after my defection as at least honest enough to stand up for what I thought and capable of telling Zhenikhov to his face what an outright scoundrel he was. I respected the ambassador, Aleksei Vasilievich Zakharov, and knew he had a lot of experience, behind him. He had served successively as deputy minister of foreign trade, Soviet representative in Comecon and deputy minister of foreign affairs and had been ambassador in Helsinki since 1959. From the few personal encounters I had had with him, from his staff briefings and a speech he made at a dinner of the consular corps, I judged him to be a shrewd and intelligent diplomat who loved his young and beautiful wife, who was friendly with Svetlana.

When Svetlana decided that she must go to Moscow to see her parents and Tanya, I had told the ambassador because I thought his approval was required. I said she needed to go 'for personal reasons' and he said he would send a telegram to Moscow. When I mentioned this afterwards to Zhenikhov and he advised me not to await the reply from the foreign ministry, saying that I should not have bothered to ask the ambassador. 'Svetlana can go any day you like' so she left the following day but when, a few days later, I ran into the ambassador in the embassy garden, he greeted me and told me that, unfortunately, he had not yet received a reply from Moscow. I replied, 'But my wife is already there' so rebuked me and demanded 'How could she have gone without my permission?' I told him, as I had originally intended, that I was on his side in the dispute with Zhenikhov, and that I had not taken part in any intrigues against him, but I added that, because of his inhumanly bureaucratic attitude toward my wife's departure, I had changed my mind about him and I called him 'a little despot'. He said nothing but went red in the face and walked away. As far as I know he made no complaint about my remark either to Zhenikhov or to the Party leader.

Zakharov suffered little or not at all from my defection because as I was a member of the KGB *rezidentura*, my defection reflected on Vladimir Zhenikhov. Zakharov remained as ambassador until 1965 when he became head of the Scandinavian Department of the foreign ministry and in 1967 he was appointed deputy Soviet representative to the United Nations.

Next I tackled Zhenikhov with whom I had enjoyed an entirely professional relationship, even though I thought he was a coward and would be unlikely to have me recalled for criticizing him for his intrigues. One day when I had some business with him he asked me to draft a telegram to Moscow requesting that our agent ANNET, whose real name was Koren, should be sent back to Helsinki. ANNET was a beautiful young Intourist guide from Leningrad and I had been her case officer in Helsinki. Yuri Voronin and I had sent her home from Helsinki during Zhenikhov's absence for indiscriminately sleeping around with foreigners and losing interest in her KGB work, but both Voronin and I knew that she was Zhenikhov's mistress. We had sent her packing anyway and had dispatched a suitable telegram to Moscow. I asked Zhenikhov how I should explain to Moscow our request for ANNET's return to Helsinki and he replied, 'Operational necessity'. As calmly as I could I told him, 'You need her back to satisfy your own lust. I won't send the telegram; you'll have to do it yourself.' This took him by surprise and he did not utter a word. It was clearly the moment to attack him for his intrigues against Zakharov and his wife so I told him how disgusted I was, and said he had forgotten that his methods which had once been fashionable would not now be tolerated by the Central Committee. I told him that when I went back to Moscow I would report on his anti-Party behavior to his superiors and, if necessary, to the Central Committee. Even his successes with TUMO and other agents would not save him from censure, and I ended up by telling him that I would submit to him in writing on the following day a request to take a vacation in the Soviet Union. When I handed in my request he read it and replied, 'Because of the election campaign all vacations are canceled. You will get your vacation after the election.' He then told me that, because of our strained relations, it would be better if Yuri Voronin were also present when we had business together, and I agreed. Zhenikhov knew I could make trouble for him so he could not afford to have me recalled to Moscow at that time, and he probably calculated that he would have me recalled after the presidential election when he had gained credit from a Kekkonen victory.

Feeling that I was safe for the immediate future I set about planning our escape. I knew that success depended on choosing the right man in the American embassy to approach, and I already had one man in mind, Frank Friberg, the local CIA station chief. I had first met him at a reception at the Argentine embassy and he had reminded me of the actor Fred McMurray, though shorter. He had come over to me, said 'hello', introduced himself and had moved on. He had appeared friendly, polite and serious and I had sized him up as a man of strong character. I thought even then that he was someone I could turn to in an emergency, and although I knew the KGB had penetrated the CIA, I knew from Zhenikhov that there was none in the Helsinki station. Zhenikhov had confirmed twice that Friberg was the 'CIA *rezident*' and when I had given him information from my low level source on the American Embassy he had expressed a high opinion of Friberg's professionalism. 'They know who our agents are in Finland', he said, 'just as we know theirs.'

I thought out what I should say to Friberg when I approached him and what information I should need to give him to convince him that I was a genuine defector and not a KGB provocateur. I considered various plans for the approach and the escape route, and finally, I fixed on the date of Friday, 15 December in the evening. I knew that the embassy and the *rezidentura* would be inactive over the weekend and that there was little chance of anyone needing me. Escape on that day would give us the best chance of leaving the country before our disappearance had been discovered and I knew how important it was to leave Finland as soon after the initial approach as possible. I knew that the defections of Yuri Rastvorov and the Petrovs had been imperilled by delays in their departures from their embassies in Japan and Australia, and I reckoned that, though risky, the quickest way for us to leave Finland would be by commercial airline from Helsinki airport. I found out that there was a plane leaving Helsinki for Stockholm at 8.15 p.m. on 15 December and I thought I would ask Friberg to take us out on this flight.

Information I had gleaned from Mikhail Kozlov and his pouch proved useful for I knew that the Aeroflot employee Lyubimets was one of his SK informers. I checked that there were no Soviet flights in or out of Helsinki on Fridays so there would be no reason for the Aeroflot representative Utkin, who was a GRU officer, or Lyubimets, to be at the airport on that day. I also reflected on the KGB documents I should take with me, and decided that, though risky, I would have to take the letters from Moscow which indicated KGB penetration of the CIA.

Another of my ideas was to take Kozlov's pouch which contained priceless documents suitable for the public exposure of the more scandalous aspects of KGB activities abroad against Soviet colonies in general and the one in Finland in particular. Kozlov was old and somewhat senile, and thought in terms of the mass repressions of the 1930s and 1940s. Ruining an individual's reputation was no more significant to him than a puff of cigarette smoke and because he could not rely on his memory he kept all the KGB correspondence and copies of his replies, instead of burning them after five months as required by security regulations. I counted over 300 official letters in the pouch and I wanted to take them with me for publication in a book entitled *The SK Line* which would have landed a damaging blow on the KGB.

A few days before our departure Mikhail Kozlov was taken to hospital and I was given access to his pouch but, alas, he reappeared in the embassy on 13 December and I lost access to it once more. Nevertheless, on 12 December, I told Svetlana that we should be leaving in three days' time and I reflected on what to leave behind to mislead the KGB as

I wanted give the impression that I had left, not after long premeditation, but on a sudden impulse prompted by bad relations with Zhenikhov. I also thought out how to handle the question of taking possession of our passports and keeping them safely.

On my last day I spent the final hours at the embassy, and after lunch I told Svetlana to take Tanya to the park near our home at 6.30 [pm] in the evening and wait for me so we would take a taxi together to the Americans.

At 4 p.m. I went to the embassy and spent some time in the consulate, and at 5.30 [pm] I removed our passports from the consulate safe and locked them in my desk drawer, to which only I had the key. I copied into my address book from consular papers the names of KGB and GRU illegals who had required visas and then I went to the *rezidentura* room where about ten officers, including Sergeyev and Zegar, were preparing reports for the following Monday, the day when diplomatic mail was collected for, and received from. Moscow. I asked our code clerk Khokhlov to bring me my pouch which contained my secret documents and I was sitting across the table from Sergeyev when I took the final steps. I wrote out an account of my official expenditure for the first half of December, enclosing a sum of unspent Finnish marks because I was anxious to leave behind no grounds for suggesting that I had made off with KGB funds. Then I took a dozen documents out of the pouch and, when Sergeyev was not looking, slipped them into an inside pocket. I placed inside the pouch some papers I had brought with me from the consulate so that the code clerk would notice no difference in the weight of the pouch when he collected it, and in the margin of a report I had already prepared for my department at KGB headquarters about my low level source on the American embassy I wrote a note complaining that the *rezident* was creating artificial obstacles to my work with my agent by refusing payment to him. I did this deliberately to support the impression that my defection was a spontaneous reaction to the bad relationship with Zhenikhov but when I was about to leave Khokhlov suddenly came in and announced that, on Zhenikhov's instructions, nobody was to leave and everyone was to search his table and his pouch for one of Zhenikhov's telegrams which could not be found. This scared me though I did my utmost not to show it. A cold sweat came over me as I wondered whether Zhenikhov suspected me and wanted me searched. This was the most critical moment in my life, but after a few minutes, all was well. Khokhlov came back to tell us that the missing telegram had been found. After that, I went back to the consulate, picked up the passports and left the building, telling the duty officer on the way out that during the evening and the following day I would be looking after Soviet tourists. I took a taxi in front of the church near the embassy and arrived at the park by 6.30, but Svetlana and Tanya were not there. I found them in the apartment and Svetlana explained she had not gone to the park because she had been expecting me to call her first. She was obviously distraught and I knew how she was suffering at the thought of leaving her parents behind. When she did not go to the park she was probably hoping that I would change my mind and that life would go on as before.

At my suggestion, she wrote out a note addressed to me saying that I could find her and Tanya at the Soviet colony club, and left it in the apartment. I also left behind in a closet a photo of the party at the Lomomatka villa in which I was shown with the hostess and the other guests which I hoped that this would divert the KGB's attention for a day or two when they noticed our absence.

I then called Fred Friberg's home telephone number and a man answered, but I said nothing. I now knew that Friberg was at home so we left the apartment after only fifteen minutes, taking with us nothing but a few family photos and Tanya's favorite toy, telling her that we were going to a party.

Friberg lived in a well-to-do suburb of Helsinki and we hailed a cab and I gave the driver the address. The ride lasted ten to fifteen minutes and we sat in silence, wrapped in our private thoughts. I wondered to myself if perhaps Friberg has gone out since my call, in which case we would have had to try again on the Saturday or Sunday. Certainly there could be no return to the embassy. The cab pulled up in front of the house and I was pleased to note that lights were on, and I saw somebody at one of the windows. I rang the bell and Friberg opened the door, surprised to see the three of us. I did not know whether he recognized me so I said 'I'm Soviet Vice-Consul Klimov and I have come to ask for political asylum from the U.S. Government' to which he replied 'We know you're KGB.' I confirmed this and said that my real name was Golitsyn, and he invited us into the house.

In order to convince Friberg that I was genuine I told him that the Finnish president, Uhro Kekkonen, was a KGB agent of influence with the cryptonym TIMO. Friberg asked if Kekkonen was aware that he was an agent and I explained that Kekkonen had been fully recruited by the KGB, that he fulfilled their instructions and promoted KGB nominees to important positions. I also told him that Vladimir Zhenikhov was his case officer and went on to say that I had significant information in my possession which I would disclose in Washington. I said that I knew that the KGB had penetrated the CIA in Germany through their agent SASHA, and I gave this much information to alert the CIA that I had knew about KGB penetration of the Agency, so proper steps could be taken to prepare for my debriefing. I deliberately did not disclose to Friberg more about my leads to penetration because I did not wish to begin my debriefing until I had arrived in Washington, telling him I would give my information only to the right people.

Friberg suggested that we should be kept in their safe-house in Finland for a month but I disagreed very firmly and asked him to arrange for our immediate departure from Finland, arguing strongly that delay might lead to the KGB discovering our disappearance and taking steps through their agents in the Finnish government to capture us. I said that our defection might also be compromised through SASHA and I urged him to take us out of Finland on the 8.15 [pm] flight to Stockholm that evening because there would be no Aeroflot representatives at the airport. Because of possible penetration I said I thought it would be better if nobody else in his embassy knew of our defection. Friberg was quick to see I was in earnest in my demand for immediate departure and told me I was lucky because he had been due to leave his house for a party given by Finnish friends ten minutes after the time of our arrival. 'Your arrival changes everything,' he said, 'and takes priority. I need to bring in one other man, my assistant, who is reliable. He's Steven, and you've met him.' I said 'No problem, I trust Steven' and Friberg asked for our passports. Ten to fifteen minutes later Steven arrived by car and Friberg gave him our passports, told him to stamp U.S. visas in them, make reservations for the four of us on the Stockholm flight and bring the passports and tickets to us at the airport. At ten minutes before eight Steven joined us outside the terminal building with the passports and tickets. Friberg entered the building with us and we checked in for our flight. When Svetlana and I presented our passports and tickets there was a brief delay as the clerk said he had to make a call to his superiors. Our hearts sank but after a brief conversation in Finnish the clerk said everything was alright and let us through into the departure lounge where there were many passengers waiting. Within ten minutes there was a boarding announcement for our flight. And once the plane was airborne I turned to Svetlana and said 'We've made it. Now we're safe![38]'

The Golitsyn family – mother, father and daughter – would travel over the next four days via Frankfurt, London, Bermuda and New York to Washington DC where the debriefing would begin.

* * *

Friberg had quickly gained Golitsyn's trust, mainly because he had not even attempted to persuade the asylum seeker to return to the *rezidentura* as a CIA asset. He accompanied the Golitsyns to Washington, and remained there for the following four days, introducing him to the Deputy Director of Central Intelligence General Charles Cabell to Jack Maury, then chief of Soviet division, and to his principal debriefer, George Kisevalter, who adopted the alias 'Colonel Mueller'. Established in a safe house in Virginia, conveniently close to the CIA's new headquarters campus, Golitsyn interpreted the documents he had purloined from the *rezidentura* and reeled off details of KGB spies.

> We discussed the bundle of KGB documents I had removed from Helsinki. The first two letters, dated 15 and 21 August 1961, were both circular letters to all *rezidenturas* signed by USOV, the codename of the FCD chief Aleksandr Sakharovsky, on the subject of counter-intelligence. These clearly implied the existence of Soviet agents in western intelligence and counter-intelligence services and highlighted the importance and urgency attached by the KGB to further penetration operations. The first circular, No. 1163 dated 15 August 1961, stated:
> The Collegium of the KGB has examined the state of the service's counter-intelligence work abroad. It has noted the positive results achieved in obtaining information on the activities of the intelligence and counter-intelligence services of the major imperialist states directed against the countries of the socialist camp. Certain *rezidenturas* regularly inform the Center about the activities of these services against the Soviet Union and against Soviet citizens abroad and about the visits of foreign intelligence officers and agents to the Soviet Union and other countries. In a number of cases this has allowed enemy activities to be prevented or appropriate counter-measures to be taken and to achieve a radical improvement in our counter-intelligence work abroad we suggest:
> 1. That a thorough re-examination should be carried out of existing agents among foreigners in all lines of our work in order to choose those who are most able and reliable and who either become recruiters or agents in western intelligence and counter-intelligence services or penetrate those services themselves.
> 2. That *rezidenturas* should take every opportunity to carry out studies in depth of western intelligence and counter-intelligence services, particularly in those sections which work against the Soviet Union and Soviet citizens, and schools which prepare personnel for these services. Particular attention should be paid to operations to penetrate the major western intelligence services especially the Americans through third countries.

The other circular, No. 1240, dated 21 August 1961, stated:

> The intelligence services of the major capitalist countries principally the United States collect secret military information on the Soviet Union especially on its nuclear missiles and new weapons systems: they also try to determine the state of Soviet defenses and make forecasts of future Soviet military potential particularly in new missiles.

Taking account of the importance of these activities, you should:
1. Take every opportunity to collect information about them.
2. Seriously and attentively analyze the possibilities of reorienting those agents of the *rezidenturas* who are connected with enemy special services to collect this type of information.
3. Consider and carry out special operations to widen the access of your agents working in enemy intelligence services so as to cover this requirement.
4. Carry out operations to place your agents in sections of those services which interest us, particularly those which operate directly against us, those which supervise the work of enemy *rezidenturas* abroad which recruit, train and dispatch agents against us and those which collect, analyze and distribute intelligence from them.
5. Step up work on the recruitment of new sources in enemy intelligence services and speed up the recruitment of professional intelligence officers which your *rezidentura* has been preparing. Concerning operations which require decisions from the Center inform us urgently.

Reply to this letter by 10 October.

A third circular, dated 4 March 1961, was signed VOLODIN, the cryptonym of Vladimir Klimkin, head of the Fourteenth Department, instructed the *rezidentura* to collect information on and penetrate the intelligence and counter-intelligence services of the main enemy countries in Finland.

A fourth, dated 6 August 1960 and signed VOLODIN, said that ANTON (Golitsyn) had left to join the *rezidentura* for work against the intelligence services of the main enemy countries. A fifth, dated 7 April 1961 and signed USOV, was a three-page directive on KGB work against foreign tourists in the Soviet Union with a twenty-one page enclosure describing the use made by American intelligence of tourists to the Soviet Union from the United States and other countries.

A sixth letter dated April 1961, reported that, according to reliable agent information, the Americans were developing a new listening device to be used against Soviet embassies abroad. A seventh letter, dated 15 August 1961 and signed MIKHAILOV from Krokhin, the FCD's deputy chief concerned the defection of Rudolf Nureyev showing how the defection had been discussed by the Collegium of the KGB and that criticisms had been made of the KGB *rezidentura* in Paris.[39]

Over the next decade, Golitsyn would disclose much of the KGB's secrets that he had accumulated over the past sixteen years. As well as providing personality profiles of his contemporaries, he helped identify dozens of Soviet spies. Among them

Arne Wuori, a former minister and Finnish ambassador to Britain and the Soviet Union, Mauno Pekkala; a former Finnish prime minister, Gabrielson; the chief of police in Helsinki, Kalle Lehmus, codenamed LEON; the chief of military counter-intelligence; and Kiukas codenamed KORPI, a former minister and head of the passport division in the police. I also mentioned that the KGB *rezident* Zhenikhov was thinking in terms of an assassination of the Finnish social democrat, Vaino Leskinen. I suggested that Friberg should arrange for me to meet Leskinen outside Finland to warn him about the possible threat to his life and to enlist his help in the public exposure of President Kekkonen as a KGB agent before the presidential elections took place.[40]

Within the CIA Golitsyn, now codenamed AELADLE, was handled primarily by Bruce Solie of the Office of Security and by Birch O'Neal and Jean Evans of the counter-intelligence staff. He signed up to a consultancy contract worked on the identification of the elusive SASHA and a dozen other penetration suspects and in the months that followed the CIA and the FBI followed up Golitsyn's clues to individual spies. One, for instance,

an old SCD case in which a code clerk in the U.S. embassy in Moscow after the war, codenamed JACK, had been recruited through blackmail.[41]

Though the case was old it was still significant because JACK had answered questions designed to assist in the construction of a replica of the American diplomatic cipher machine. When identified and traced by the FBI he admitted his guilt.

In other cases, the emphasis was to find the evidence to support the central allegation of espionage, such as the oil tycoon Armand Hammer. Another suspect was the veteran American UPI correspondent in Moscow, Henry Shapiro, codenamed VALERI. According to Golitsyn, Shapiro had been recruited by the CIA, but then 'turned' into a double agent by his colleague Vladimir Kovschuk.

Goltitsyn also tipped off the CIA about Ingeborg Lygren, a valued source inside the Norwegian Security Service:

In 1959 I acquired information in the SCD's Scandinavian section that a KGB officer, Nikolai Krymov, who was responsible for counter-intelligence work against the Norwegian embassy in Moscow, had recruited the female secretary of the Norwegian ambassador in Moscow in 1957 or 1958. She had given the KGB information on American intelligence operations in Moscow and also provided them with her ambassador's cipher but had told her handler that she would not work for the KGB in Norway.

I gave an account of this case to Maury and Kisevalter on 23 December 1961, but I heard no more about it. In June 1964 I mentioned the case during a discussion on Nosenko and as a result David Murphy, the head of the Soviet Division, gave me material on it from CIA files. It was immediately clear to me that Ingeborg Lygren was the individual whom Nikolai Krymov had recruited. She had been the Norwegian ambassador's secretary at the relevant time and she was the only Norwegian who had been involved in American intelligence operations in Moscow, mailing letters in Moscow to CIA agents in the Soviet Union. She was a long-standing member of the Norwegian military intelligence service headed by Colonel Wilhelm Evang and, prior to 1956, had worked as a Russian translator. Evang had chosen her to go to Moscow under cover as the ambassador's secretary and to operate there on the CIA's behalf, locating and filling Agency dead-drops, a task for which she had received specialist training by the CIA in Norway.

She was described as a somewhat unattractive spinster and in Moscow in February 1956 she replaced another spinster, Gunvor Haavik, who had served there for the previous nine years. Information received from the Norwegian embassy in the CIA files indicated that the KGB had begun to study Lygren and plant agents on her shortly after her arrival in 1956. Lygren wanted to learn to drive in Moscow and had applied for a driving instructor from *Burobin*, which supplied services to embassies. At first they were unable to help her but in March 1957 a former commander of a tank regiment, Aleksei Vasilyevich Filipov, was appointed her instructor. Lygren continued her association with Filipov after she obtained her driver's permit in June 1957 because she felt she was not yet a good driver, and he even accompanied her on some of her searches for potential dead-drop sites, but in October 1957 she reported that Filipov had made advances to her and that he was probably working for the KGB, but she said that she could handle the situation. In August 1959 Lygren returned to Oslo.

In November 1964 Inspector Asbjørn Bryhn, the head of the Norwegian Security Service, paid an official visit to Washington for talks with the CIA and FBI. Unknown to CIA's Soviet Division who had been told by Angleton that I was 'on strike', a meeting on 19 November was arranged chaired by Angleton and attended by Bryhn, Sullivan and other FBI representatives, Solie of CIA's Office of Security and me. There it was explained that the CIA had conducted a joint operation in the Soviet Union with the Norwegian intelligence service in which Ingeborg Lygren had been involved, and Bryhn said that this had been brought to his attention when, after Lygren had left Moscow, the Norwegian ambassador had expressed his concern that some sort of amateurish, semi-intelligence operation was being developed that threatened his embassy's integrity. Bryhn said he knew that Lygren had been in contact with some people in Moscow whom he suspected were planted on her, but Evang had retorted that he was pleased with her performance, so the matter had not been investigated further.

I repeated to Bryhn what I had told CIA about the recruitment by Krymov in the period 1957 and 1958 of the female secretary of the Norwegian ambassador in Moscow who had 'special' duties and who had given the KGB information on American intelligence operations in Moscow. From CIA files it was clear that this secretary was Lygren who was the only Norwegian involved in CIA operations in Moscow where she had mailed a number of letters for the CIA.

I also told Bryhn that I had previously given Bruce Solie a lead to a Norwegian agent codenamed NORD. I had recalled seeing Ivan Shishkin, an officer of the FCD's British and Scandinavian Department, which was responsible for Norway, reading the KGB file on NORD, and I knew that 'NORD had passed a NATO document to the KGB in 1960.

In response to this lead, Solie had shown me the CIA file on a Norwegian who had provided services to CIA in Prague similar to those performed for them by Lygren in Moscow. Solie agreed with me that there were indications in this file that this Norwegian was almost certainly NORD and that he had been recruited by the Czechs working in conjunction with the KGB in 1956, that is, before the recruitment of Lygren in Moscow. I pointed out that the Norwegian intelligence service was very small and that NORD almost certainly knew Lygren and could well have given the KGB information about her that was relevant to her recruitment. By recruiting Lygren in 1957 or 1958, the KGB had simultaneously gained access in the CIA, the Norwegian intelligence service and the Norwegian diplomatic service. Undoubtedly the KGB would have tried to exploit their access in each of these fields to extend their penetration further through blackmail or any other available means. Accordingly, I recommended that Bryhn should examine whether anything that had been compromised by the acquisition of the ambassador's cipher might had given the KGB a blackmail hold over any member of the Norwegian diplomatic service. Equally, the further opportunities for penetration of the Norwegian intelligence service which had been opened up by the recruitment of Lygren and NORD should be examined.

It was against this background that it was now possible to understand why, in 1960, Dubensky, the former KGB *rezident* in Oslo who was supervising the *rezidentura* there from Moscow, had told Zhenikhov, the KGB *rezident* in Finland, that he had plans to make further important recruitments in Norway. An officer superior in rank to Lygren and NORD might well have been one of Dubensky's targets and it was obvious that the Lygren case had serious political implications because of Norwegian involvement in the CIA's activities in the Soviet Union at a time when Norwegian membership of NATO was a sensitive matter. The CIA had appreciated the political risks entailed by the operation when they embarked on it and had described it as 'a most explosive operation' if it was exposed.

I suggested to Bryhn that he should check all those who had served in the very small Norwegian embassy in Moscow, which usually consisted of about five people. This recommendation was not made from direct knowledge of the affairs of that particular embassy, but on the basis of a general knowledge of how the KGB operated against the embassies of other small countries like Denmark and Finland.

Bryhn acknowledged that he was aware that the Norwegian embassy's security was very bad and explained that Lygren had been posted there because she had an intelligence background and because she enjoyed Evang's trust. Bryhn wondered whether Lygren, having been recruited in Moscow, was still an active KGB agent in Norway, even if she had declined to spy upon her return home.

From what I had gathered about Lygren's character from the CIA material, I thought she might be prepared to talk in certain circumstances, although she might well have been warned by the KGB that she had been compromised. In any case the first step was to keep her under observation and an FBI representative underlined the importance of coordinating any action against Lygren in Norway with the FBI activities in the United States in linked cases. Finally, it was agreed that Bryhn would research Lygren's case as soon as he returned to Norway.

A few weeks later Bryhn returned to Washington and a further meeting was held on 15 January 1965 at which he told us that Lygren, who was still employed by the Norwegian intelligence service, had been put under surveillance and was leading a lonely existence, with few contacts and she rarely went out socially. She often went to the wine store and occasionally bought a bottle of brandy which she drank in her small apartment. Bryhn also told us that he had established through his own sources that Lygren had slept with Aleksei Filipov in her bedroom in the Moscow embassy, and that her bedroom connected directly through an unlocked door with the room housing the embassy's archives and the safe containing the ambassador's ciphers. Lygren had full access to this safe as well as to the other safes in the embassy, and she had held the keys and known the combinations. Apparently she had often refused to accompany embassy colleagues on Sunday outings, preferring to stay in the embassy of which she would have been the sole occupant. Her access to the premises and the few secrets they contained was therefore often total and unimpeded. According to Bryhn's research, Lygren had arrived in Moscow in February 1956 when her predecessor Gunvor Haavik, who had served there since 1947, returned to Oslo. Lygren had remained in Moscow until August 1959.

It seemed likely that Lygren had been recruited by the KGB in August or September 1957, but a date a few months earlier was also possible, and she was now 'on ice' in Norway. The KGB could have briefed her that she was liable to be approached by the security service, and that she should in no circumstances reveal her recruitment and should stick to the legend they would give her. Bryhn said it was necessary from time to time to blow a case of espionage for political reasons, but he stressed the importance of complete certainty of the facts when questioning Lygren and not to touch on anything which she knew to be untrue or guesswork or speculation. He had to know how many cards he held, such as her access to the embassy safe, her relationship with Filipov and the CIA letters she had mailed.

From the KGB's perspective, Lygren was simply the means to an end, namely the penetration of CIA. She would not have been told directly by the KGB that they had recruited her CIA contact but if she could be induced to give a full account of the way she had been questioned or not questioned about him, important deductions could be made. Similarly, if there had been any changes in the nature of the KGB's interest in or attitude toward her mailing operations that too could be significant. The problem was that she would be afraid to talk. By handing over the ambassador's cipher she had, as Bryhn had told us, laid herself open to a sentence of fifteen years' imprisonment under Norwegian law. In addition, the KGB could have threatened to destroy her, even in a physical sense, if she did so.

The first step should be an interview with Lygren to persuade her to talk, the principal aim of which should be to pursue inquiries into CIA penetration, and not to prosecute the unfortunate Lygren. She was unfortunate because she had not volunteered her services as a KGB agent, but was probably the victim of blackmail and had acted under pressure. She had been weak in falling for Aleksei Filipov but any man or woman who had been placed in a vulnerable situation as she had been could have been recruited by the KGB.

In a discussion of the CIA mailing operation Bruce Solie said that Lygren had mailed thirteen letters to ten different CIA agents in the Soviet Union. The FBI representatives agreed that, with the possible exception of one who had been compromised in a different operation, all these agents had been compromised by Lygren, and one was Lieutenant Kozlov who had been recruited by Igor Orlov in Berlin and was certainly under KGB control before Lygren reached Moscow. To strengthen their hold over her, the KGB would undoubtedly have given Lygren to understand that she was responsible for the compromise of ten agents, whereas in reality all that probably fallen under KGB control before she had mailed the letters. In this connection I had told Angleton earlier that I had learned from a KGB officer named Kalinin who had friends in the KGB's surveillance directorate that surveillance of the employees of the U.S. embassy in Moscow had been suspended for several months in the spring of 1957. I thought this might be relevant to the date of Lygren's recruitment.

On 14 September 1965, Bryhn arrested Lygren and she was formally charged with espionage four days later. He told us that she had made a partial confession, to having handed over a key and safe combination, but then had retracted it and two months later, on 14 December, the prosecutor ordered Lygren's immediate release for lack of evidence.

Several months after Lygren's release Bryhn visited New York and Jim Hunt took us to lunch at the Caravelle restaurant. There were no recriminations, but Bryhn regretted that he had underestimated the KGB and had arrested Lygren over-hastily.

In the spring of 1966 Angleton told me that the Lygren affair had caused difficulties in the Norwegian government and that relations between Bryhn and Evang, which had been strained for many years, had reached breaking point. The DCI wanted Angleton and me to go to Norway to give our side of the story and so, somewhat reluctantly, I agreed to accompany him. In Oslo we were met first by the local CIA station chief, and then by the energetic and impressive Norwegian defense minister who drove us up to a cabin superbly situated in the mountains. There we were awaited by the Chief of Staff, an admiral, and the minister's wife who had prepared a traditional sauna for us.

I gave those assembled a general account of the SCD's offensive against foreign embassies in Moscow and this was followed by a discussion of the Lygren case. Angleton and I gave our version and answered questions from the minister and the Chief of Staff, and the following day the whole party left in the minister's helicopter, Angleton and I traveling [sic] as 'NATO nuclear scientists'.

A few months later a member of the Norwegian parliament visited New York and Jim Hunt took us out to lunch at the Twenty-One Club. The Norwegian MP explained that he was a member of the parliamentary commission investigating the Lygren affair and asked me various questions. Again, I repeated my version of events and he seemed satisfied. Later I was told that both Bryhn and Evang were relieved of their posts, and the NORD investigation had been abandoned. Having learned from the CIA file that NORD had been transferred by the Norwegians to Berlin, I was intrigued by the possibility that he had been involved in Czech operations there, especially since Nalivaiko told me late in 1958 or early in 1959 that the Czechs had penetrated CIA in Berlin.

In January 1977, two years after Angleton's dismissal from CIA at the end of 1974, Gunvor Haavik, Lygren's predecessor as the Norwegian ambassador's secretary in Moscow, was arrested, charged with espionage and confessed. This merely demonstrated the KGB's determination to recruit Western embassy personnel, and certainly did not prove Lygren's innocent.

> Actually, Bryhn gave us details of several other Norwegian officials in Moscow who had been compromised over the years, but not all of them had reported fully and honestly on what had happened. Certainly, as Haavik's successor, Lygren would automatically have been a target for KGB recruitment and Haavik would have been questioned about her. At the very least Haavik would have been able to tell them that Lygren was not a member of the Norwegian diplomatic service, and she may have been briefed officially at some stage that Lygren was a member of Evang's service. The information I had given CIA in 1961 about the recruitment of a Norwegian secretary in Moscow could not have related to Haavik, and had pointed uniquely to Lygren. The Norwegian secretary I knew about had special secret functions which made the case unusually important for the KGB. Lygren had worked for the CIA in Moscow, but Haavik had not.
>
> The CIA later reversed its position on Lygren after Angleton's departure, and went so far as to offer her financial compensation which she declined. I believe she did so because she was fundamentally an honest woman and knew that in her case compensation was not merited. Indeed, I suspected that the KGB had sacrificed Haavik in order to undermine the case against Lygren. By the time they gave Haavik away she was reaching the end of her usefulness to them.[42]

After three months of debriefing, Golitsyn was introduced to the British, in the persons of Arthur Martin and his SIS counterpart, Geoffrey Hinton:

> At my first meeting with the MI5 and MI6 representatives Martin and Hinton on 26 March 1962, they asked me to present my knowledge of British intelligence. Basing myself on the lectures I had attended in the counter-intelligence faculty at Balashikha and Kisel'nyy in 1948–50 where thirty to forty hours of instruction on British intelligence were given,
>
> I began by referring to the Security Service, military intelligence and the Double Cross Committee for double agents. That the Double Cross Committee was near the forefront of my mind when I was asked about British intelligence indications that we were given substantial information on it in the lectures.[43]

Five months later both men were back, to learn what more Golitsyn knew about British cases, and in particular Kim Philby and the university-recruited ring-of-five. On that subject he had little to offer, except the name itself, but identified Peter Smollet as a Soviet spy recruited by Kim Philby. An Austrian by birth, with the name Peter Smolka, he had served as head of the Ministry of Information's

Russian Department. However, he had more to offer in relation to a spy in the British Admiralty who had passed NATO documents to his KGB handlers. When presented with a selection of various NATO papers, Golitsyn correctly selected those that had been handled by a suspect. After a brief investigation in London, a junior civilian clerk, John Vassall, was identified as the spy and arrested.

At the time of Golitsyn's defection, MI5's investigation of Kim Philby and his accomplices had lapsed. During the Malayan Emergency when Arthur Martin had been posted first to Singapore and then to Kuala Lumpur as security liaison officer. The most recent development had been the comments made by Petrov in 1954, which had led to the publication of the notorious White Paper in September 1955. Golitsyn's unexpected appearance and his remarks about a ring-of-five gave fresh impetus to the case and brought Martin to Washington in March 1962 to be introduced to the defector, now codenamed KAGO by MI5.

At some point Goliysyn was confronted with a series of codenames, among them HICKS, STANLEY and JOHNSON, which had been extracted from the 1945 London VENONA traffic, but he was not indoctrinated into the source, and did not recognise any of the cryptonyms. However, he did know about Andrew Rothstein, a British-born journalist, and veteran CPGB member and who was employed for many years as a TASS correspondent. A graduate of Balliol College, Oxford, he also acted as an intermediary between the CPGB and the Soviet Embassy, and as a courier to collect the embassy's funds for the CPGB, Golitsyn claimed that an MI5 officer, Courtenay Young, whom he described as the son of a leading Liberal politician, had been the subject of a recruitment attempt by Rothstein. While it is true that Young was the son of Sir George Young MP, Rothstein's MI5 file only mentions, between 1940 and 1943,

> a considerable amount of evidence on record that Rothstein was engaged in some undercover activity and that he was probably involved in casual espionage on behalf the USSR.[44]

In March 1940, it was learned that Rothstein was trying to find out the new location of Bomber Command and that he was displaying an undue interest in naval and military matters. About this time, he was making enquiries as to where the War Office carried out its secret printing.

Golitsyn's opinion that the ring-of-five consisted of Englishmen who had been recruited while still at university, knew each other, and were probably homosexual, would cause Martin to review the evidence against Philby, and reinvigorate the molehunt. Two important issues emerged. One was a VENONA text from September 1945. Previously overlooked, suggested that an asset in London codenamed STANLEY had submitted a report on the defection and debriefing of Igor Gouzenko in Ottawa. Bizarrely, nobody had connected STANLEY to Philby. Secondly, the telephone tap on Philby, who as a suspect was now codenamed PEACH, showed no contact with the KGB, but did suggest that he was being paid by SIS. In August 1972, this reassessment was underway, Martin was introduced to Flora Solomon, one of Hilby's oldest friends (and possibly an ex-lover). Solomon asserted that Philby had tried to recruit her back in 1935. An ardent Zionist, Solomon had been prompted to contact MI5 through Victor Rothschild because she objected to the pro-Arab, anti-Israeli slant in Philby's articles in the *Observer*. Combined, Solomon's accusation, Golitsyn's knowledge of a ring-of-five and the tentative VENONA clue, there was enough to progress the PEACH enquiry by offering Philby immunity from prosecution.

Meanwhile, Golitsyn's relationship with the CIA became increasingly fraught, and his requests, to visit the White House and to create a campaign group with a $10million budget to expose the Kremlin's machinations. Increasingly disaffected with his office of security minders, Golitsyn moved into a suburban home in Hickory Hill, McLean, and in September 1964 terminated his relationship with the Soviet Division.

Early in February 1963, Golitsyn travelled to England on the *Sylvania* to assist MI5, where he met Arthur Martin, but the visit did not last long. The family moved into a hotel in Torquay, where Tanya attended a convent school, Stoodley Knowle, but by July 1963 word of his visit had leaked to *The Daily Telegraph* so they returned to Miami on the *Queen Mary*. He was accommodated in a more remote safe house, Ashford Farm at Royal Oak on Maryland's eastern shore of the Chesapeake, where he was introduced to James Angleton, and his assistant Ray Rocca.

Under Angleton's sponsorship, Golitsyn began to participate in the investigations, and was consulted on current issues, such as the very recent defection in London of a self-confessed KGB spy, Yuri Krokov, and a potential KGB defector in Switzerland, Yuri Nosenko. Golitsyn denounced both as false defectors who had been dispatched to the west to undermine his own credibility.

The period in which I enjoyed substantial access to CIA information lasted from 1964 to the end of December 1974 and I was given roughly equivalent access to British records from 1970 to 1975, and to French records from 1972 to 1975. But my involvement in American, British and French counter-intelligence efforts was not restricted to those years. The principal condition of my access was that I should not discuss the problems of one country with another, so while in Britain or France I did not report to the CIA and I did not go to these countries as a CIA agent to spy on their internal affairs. My terms were that if particular penetrations were proven, the service or services concerned would share their findings with the CIA and other services as appropriate, and this was acknowledged by Angleton and his staff.[45]

At the height of his relationship with the counter-intelligence staff Golitsyn became the inspiration for the creation in 1967 of CAZAB, an inter-Allied counter-intelligence forum, which exchanged sensitive information between specially cleared personnel. He also participated in a joint investigation, which was codenamed HONETOL, a part anagram of 'Hoover' and 'Anatoli'. Its purpose was to settle the SASHA issue once and for all, but instead it was derailed into a series of debilitating, inconclusive molehunts. Worse, his reinterpretation of some celebrated agents, such as Piotr Popov, Nikolai Artamonov, Igor Kochnov and Oleg Penkvsky as soviet-controlled double agents, made his opinions hideously unpopular.

When Angleton retired from the CIA in 1975, such influence as Golitsyn had ever exercised ceased. He had moved from New York to Miami and was bitterly disappointed. In December that same year, tragedy struck, and Tanya, artistically gifted but very troubled, died in London of a drugs overdose.

In the latter period of Golitsyn's post defection consultancy, when he travelled the world to give presentations in New Zealand, Israel and France, his influence began to wane. He met Vladimir Petrov in Melbourne but found little common ground. In France, where he was hosted by the DST chief Marcel Chalet and his deputy Jacques Sarazon, his analysis of the mole codenamed GARMASH, received a hostile reception. Eventually, devoid of Angleton's loyal support, following his enforced retirement, Golitsyn was sidelined, and then blamed for undermining the credibility of trusted CIA officers and their sources. Nevertheless, he continued to reinterpret counter-intelligence cases, and alleged that he had found evidence to incriminate the American banker and former ambassador in Moscow Averell Harriman, identifying him as a Soviet spy codenamed MAGNATE. When in 1995 the VENONA project was declassified, Golitsyn examined the decrypts and found further evidence to support his increasingly extravagant claims. In 1984, with help from MI5's Arthur Martin and SIS's Stephen de Mowbray, Golitsyn published *New Lies of Old*[46], in which he set to his world view of Kremlin deception, and then followed with *The Perestroika Deception* in 1995.[47]

Golitsyn died in December 2008, and despite his service to the Crown, recognised by the award of an honorary CBE, he was soon under attack from MI5's authorised historian, Christopher Andrew, who denounced the defector as having been at the heart of a delusional campaign to investigate imaginary examples of Soviet penetration. Andrew set the scene by claiming that 'the gaps in the Service's knowledge of the Five and their handlers provided increasing opportunities for a small but disruptive group of conspiracy theorists.' Described as 'the Service's leading conspiracy theorist', Arthur Martin (who was alleged to have been recommended to MI5 in 1946 by Philby) was said to be 'small-minded' and 'lacked the capacity for balanced judgement and a grasp of the broader context.'[48] This was an astonishing verdict to be passed on a loyal, decorated servant of the Crown who had orchestrated the interrogation of Kim Philby in December 1951, extracted confessions from Leo Long, John Cairncross, Michael Straight and Anthony Blunt, and had served with distinction as SLO in Kuala Lumpur during the Malaya Emergency. However, according to Andrew, he had fallen under Golisyn's spell and become irrational in his pursuit of imaginary moles.

Golitsyn had 'sought with messianic zeal sought to persuade both the American and British intelligence communities that they were falling victim to a vast KGB deception from which only he could save them.' He had exercised a 'malign influence on MI5' and was 'troublesome'.[49] Golitsyn's other MI5 acolyte was said to be Peter Wright, the MI5 officer who had retired in January 1976 and co-authored *Their Trade is Treachery*[50] with Chapman Pincher and then *SpyCatcher* with Paul Greengrass. A technician by training, formerly employed by Marconi, Wright had been drawn into molehunting in 1963, and the following year had taken the lead in debriefing Blunt. According to Andrew, Wright's 'conspiracy theories arguably did as much damage to the Service as Blunt's treachery.'

This degree of character assassination in an official or authorised history was unprecedented and bizarre. After leaving MI5 in 1964 Martin had been employed by SIS, and then had worked in his retirement as a clerk in the House of Commons, where he would come to command great respect.

The account of Golitsyn's Machiavellian behavior peddled by *The Defence of the Realm* does a great injustice to Martin and fails to explain that the majority of the MI5 and SIS counter-intelligence professionals who examined the individual pieces of evidence pointing to hostile penetration were convinced that the Security Service had harboured a traitor until at least September 1963. Among those so persuaded were Ronnie Symonds, John Day, Stephen de Mowbray and Geoffrey Hinton. This was not a small clique wedded to a 'monster plot' explanation, confined to one organisation, but twenty-two officers across both services. Indeed, when the former Cabinet Secretary Burke Trend conducted his review of the investigation, he could only come up with a Scottish 'not proven' verdict.

While castigating the 'conspiracy theorists' for not being even-handed in their assessment of the evidence, it can hardly be said that Andrew exercised much impartiality. He gave some (shared) credit to the defector for helping MI5 identify Vassall but says nothing about a second source in the Admiralty, suspected to have been Admiral Colin Dunlop, a distinguished naval officer who had been born in Odessa. Andrew also omits any reference to the American cipher clerk JACK caught by the FBI, nor the NATO spy George Paques.

In Andrew's version of events, MI5 was not penetrated, but simply incompetent. He cites in particular the failure to link the VENONA spy codenamed STANLEY, who had reported on the Gouzenko defection in September 1945, with Philby, who was one of the few SIS officers with the necessary access. He also criticises MI5 for following Golitsyn's assertion about the ring-of-five so literally, that Cairncross had been rejected as one of the candidates for membership on the grounds that he had not been Philby's contemporary at the University of Cambridge.

One of the most frequently repeated examples of Golitsyn's supposed paranoia and unreliability was his role in MI5's investigation codenamed OATSHEAF, which had been initiated after Hugh Gaitskell's doctor had raised concerns about the circumstances of the Opposition leader's death in January 1963. The physician stated that the cause of death was lupus, a condition that affected mainly women in childbearing age in hot climates. There were virtually no examples of elderly men developing lupus in temperate climes. Coincidentally, and entirely independently, Golitsyn had stated that the KGB had been planning the elimination of a European opposition politician so as to replace him with an asset.

Separately, Golitsyn had mentioned that Nikolai Rodin (alias Nikolai Korovin) who had been the *rezident* in London from 1947 to 1952, and again from 1956 to September 1961, had been promoted to head the thirteenth department upon his return to Moscow. As the thirteenth department was known within the KGB as an assassination bureau, MI5 thought it likely that Gaitskell had been murdered and had facilitated Harold Wilson to the leadership of the Labour Party. However, an investigation codenamed OATSHEAF failed to develop any further evidence.

Whilst Golitsyn would often be accused wrongly of alleging that Harold Wilson had been a Soviet spy, he certainly gained notoriety for denouncing another KGB defector, Yuri Nosenko, as a despatched agent, deliberately sent by the Soviets to mislead the CIA and undermine Golitsyn.

Unquestionably Golitsyn was the most controversial Soviet defector of the Cold War era, and proved highly divisive, but he was also hugely productive in the leads he provided. In particular, he would be vindicated regarding the mole codenamed SASHA who had spied from inside the CIA for three decades.

Chapter VI

OLEG LYALIN

*Our intelligence gathering activities in England suffered
a blow from which they never recovered, and the
Lyalin defection sent shockwaves through the Lubyanka.*

Oleg Kalugin, *Spymaster*[1]

Based in the Soviet trade delegation, Oleg Lyalin was a member of the KGB's London *rezidentura* who was persuaded in April 1971 to defect while conducting an illicit affair with his 30-year-old blonde secretary, Irina Templyakova, and to cooperate with a joint MI5-SIS team of case officers. It would be five months before he formally applied for political asylum, at the end of August 1971, as described in his MI5 file, codenamed GOLDFINCH, which opened with a summary:

1. Oleg Adolfovich LYALIN was born on 24 June 1938 at Staropol. His father was an agricultural engineer who suffered expulsion from the Party in 1937, fought with the partisans during World War II and thereafter until his death in 1952 worked in the Chief Planning Department of the City Council of Pyatigorsk.
2. In 1952 LYALIN entered the Higher Marine call in Odessa. He graduated from the school as an officer of the Merchant Fleet in 1959. In 1957, however, he had been recruited as a KGB informant working against western seamen and smugglers in Odessa. In 1958/59 the KGB after trying him on it in an exercise, offered him a job in the illegal net. He was sent to 101 School of the KGB. He passed his 2-year course in 18 months and was then lodged in a private flat for further training.

3. Owing to the breakdown of his first marriage, the plan to place him in illegal work was cancelled and he spent the next 4 years in the KGB. KIAIPEDA, on security work against foreign seamen.
4. In February 1967 LYALIN was sent on a 6 month course at the Department V school near Moscow, where he studied partisan warfare, radio communications, explosives and parachuting. After 18 months of further training and briefing Lyalin was posted to London in April 1969.
5. LYALIN is a captain in the KGB and a Party member since 1960. His motives are personal – dissatisfaction with his career and the desire to marry the wife of one of his colleagues who defected with him.[3]

In the days that followed the defection, the MI5 Security Liaison Officer in Washington DC, Barry Russell-Jones, held frequent meetings with Ed Miller, the director of the FBI's domestic intelligence division, and plenty of transatlantic correspondence was generated by John T. Minnish, the FBI legal attaché at the U.S. embassy in London.

Lyalin's initial plan, when he first encountered his MI5 handlers, had been to persuade the British authorities to declare him *persona non grata* so he could return to Moscow and divorce his wife, but his arrest on the night of 31 August 1971 for drink driving forced MI5's hand. Another factor was a letter written to Lyalin that had been misdirected to the London *rezident*, which indiscreetly disclosed that he had indicated to his wife in Moscow that he was unhappy in London and with the KGB. These unanticipated events combined to frustrate Lyalin's original plan, which MI5 told the FBI, was 'to return to the USSR where he would continue to operate as an agent in place'. However, the case officers who handled Lyalin thought him unstable and considered the idea of running him in Moscow as impractical.

Lyalin's torrid love life was an added complication. While he was having an affair with his secretary, Irina Teplakova, the wife of a colleague, a Soviet delegate to the International Wheat Council described as an 'operational KGB worker', (an occasional co-optee) he was also involved with a married Englishwoman.

Lyalin's value lay partly in his KGB career experience, which had included a lengthy period as an illegal support officer in the first chief directorate's Directorate S (known to insiders as 'Line N') and then his transfer to department V, an even more secret branch of the KGB, which had become notorious when Nikolai Khokhlov had revealed in 1954 that he had been trained as an assassin by the FCD's ninth section. Following Khokhlov's detailed revelations when he defected, the KGB disbanded the ninth section and created a new unit, the thirteenth department ('Line F'), to replace it until it too became notorious when Bogdan Stashinsky defected and described the thirteenth department. Accordingly, in 1969, department V had quietly come into existence, and Lyalin was in an excellent position to identify its key personalities and detail its principal function, to prepare contingency plans for a network of specially trained illegals who would act a saboteur when called upon to do so, perhaps in times of political crisis or even armed conflict. Among the schemes listed by Lyalin was a plan to contaminate the NATO submarine base at Faslane and blame the United States Navy for the contamination, with the objective of undermining the alliance and influencing public opinion in Scotland. It was, stated the FBI Director's assistant Alex Rosen,

> a highly sophisticated and fully developed plan for effective sabotage in England; had personnel in place prepared to carry it out; and had plans for further personnel to parachute into England in time of emergency.[3]

One of the many KGB colleagues exposed by Lyalin was Nikolai A. Kuznetsov, named as head of Department V in the United States. The FBI quickly established his credentials, having already identified him as a KGB officer who had tried to recruit a chemist who was already under the FBI's control:

> Until October/November 1969, the head of Dept. V in the USA was Nikolay Alekseyevitch KUZNETSOV who was in the UN in New York. This was his second posting in the US. On the first, he recruited a technician connected with electronics and computers for which he received a very high decoration. He was not liked in headquarters because he was always emphasising his superior position and the fact that he had been decorated. During this second posting in the US, he produced no practical results and after encountering some 'difficulties' was obliged to return unexpectedly to Russia in October or November 1969 leaving all his possessions behind. LYALIN believes he is now teaching [XXXXXXXXXXXX] believed by LYALIN [XXXXXXXXXXXX].[4]

The NYFO file on Kuznetsov, born 15 October 1921, showed that he had entered the United States on 17 February 1953 as an interpreter attached to the UN secretariat's translation unit. He left fifteen months later, on 13 May 1954, but returned accompanied by his wife Stepanida on 3 December 1954 and stayed for three years, departing on 11 July 1957. His third posting to the United States began on 23 December

1966, as first secretary in the Soviet mission, but he left for Montreal on 15 November 1967. He then returned on Christmas Day 1967 and stayed until 17 September 1968. When he returned home a week after a minor road accident.

Of principal interest to the FBI was what Lyalin had to say about department V's plans for the United States, and the identities of any American citizens recruited by the KGB. This was the issue addressed by a heavily redacted memorandum from Miller dated 14 September 1971:

> [XXXX] also advised that Lyalin furnished information about one [XXXXXXXXXXXXX] Bremen, Germany, and Latvia. [XXXXXXXXXXXXXXX] the U.S. Navy [XXXXXXXXXX] between Germany and Vietnam. He also mentioned a major in the U.S. Army recruited by the Soviets two years ago in Norway who is currently in West Germany. [XXX] has advised that this information has been made available to the Army and the Navy and investigation is now underway to identify these individuals.
>
> Lyalin also named [XXXXXXXXXXXXX] American currently in London who was being assessed by [XXXXXXXXX] of the KGB. [XXXXXXXXXXXXXX] San Francisco people who sent him abroad to avoid the draft. The Chief Resident of the KGB was skeptical about [XXXXX] interest in [XXXXX] and as a result [XXXXX] interest in him has lapsed. We are instructing San Francisco to identify [XXXX] since Bufiles are negative.
>
> Lyalin also mentioned on [XXXXXXXXXXXXXXXXXXXXXXXX] of the U.S. Embassy in London who has been in contact with [XXXXXX] [XXXXXXXXXXX] has advised that both State Department and [XXX] are aware of [XXXX] contacts with the Russians and such contacts are not for intelligence purposes.
>
> Lyalin also mentioned one [XXXXXXXXXXXXXXX] Shell Oil Corporation in London and furnished information to the KGB which he obtained from Shell. [XXXXXXXXXXXXXXXXX] Boston Office has been instructed to identify and develop background information about the activities of this couple in order that consideration may be given to interviewing them.
>
> [XXXXX] is extremely anxious to obtain whatever information is possible which would assist them in determining whether Lyalin is a bona-fide defector and he requested that any information developed be furnished to [XXXXX] through him. He stated the same request was made of [XXXXXXXXXX] will channel information through him to [XXXX] in London.
>
> ACTION: This matter is being followed closely in order that we can develop complete information concerning any Americans involved.[5]

Naturally, the FBI's first concern was the immediate impact on American national security, and what Lyalin could reveal about department V's plans in the United States. As it happened, the FBI was at that time running at least one asset inside the KGB *rezidentura* in New York headed by Vikenti Sobole, and the mole, designated IRONCLAD, quickly alerted his FBI handlers to the drama unfolding in London:

> Source learned that on Monday, 6 September a communication was received by the NY KGB residency from Moscow, concerning a Soviet defection in London, England of a KGB officer assigned to 'V Department' (Sabotage, assassination, etc.) of the London KGB residency. The defector was identified as one LYALIN, first name not recalled by the source. According to the source, the communication indicated the defection occurred during the preceding weekend (4 September 1971) and apparently was [XXXXXXXXXXXX]
>
> Background furnished regarding LYALIN indicated he (LYALIN) had been employed in the London residency since 1969Prior to that time, he had served in the 'S' Directorate (Illegal Support) during the period of 1960–69. Source learned that the communication further indicated that LYALIN defected with the wife of an operational KGB worker assigned to the London Residency, identity of whom was not discussed.
>
> According to the source, the above information was not publicized generally within the KGB Residency but facts relative to the defection were made known to the various Branch 'Chiefs'. Thereafter, KGB officers within each branch were questioned concerning the possibility of LYALIN's knowledge of their affiliation. According to the source, the basis for this questioning was not disclosed to the KGB officers.
>
> Further, source learned through [XXXXXXXXXXXXXXXXXXXXXX XXX] knew of LYALIN and were possibly known to him (LYALIN): [XXXXXXXXXX] source also learned that some other KGB officers within the NY Residency were also mentioned as possibly being known to LYALIN, but these individuals were not identified.
>
> Source also learned that [XXXXXXXXXXXXXXXXXXXXX] is known to LYALIN.
>
> In addition, sources learned through [XXXXXX] that LYALIN can identify some details concerning [XXXXXXXX] operations in London.
>
> According to the source [XXXXXXXXXX] cannot be sure whether LYALIN is in a position to identify him. [XXXXXXXXXXXXXX] who served in London with LYALIN may have mentioned [XXX] as having been [XXXXXX] in the London Residency. [XXXXX] feels that LYALIN undoubtedly knew his [XXXXXX] successor in London as [XXXXXXX].
>
> Source learned that, concerning the reaction of KGB Headquarters regarding the defection. The NY Residency's opinion is that all KGB personnel assigned to the London Residency will be replaced. Concerning those KGB officers assigned to the NY Residency who might

be known to LYALIN, source indicated that the prevalent opinion in the NY Residency is that no immediate action is necessary regarding possible replacement of these officers since the possibility exists that LYALIN might not recall specific names and identities.

Concerning the result of the defection upon current illegal service by the London Residency, source indicated KGB Headquarters will continue the analysis of LYALIN's operational activities while assigned to London will also review the files to which he (LYALIN) had access and, thereafter, formulate the necessary actions regarding the illegal agents known to LYALIN.

Source indicated that the NY KGB Residency was not informed concerning the motivation for LYALIN's defection. Source stated that LYALIN's official cover position while assigned to the London Residency is unknown to the source. Source indicated that LYALIN was a 'rank and file' worker who occupied no supervisory position within the London residency.

Source added that, based on a conversation with [XXXXXXXXXXXXX] source learned that LYALIN entered the KGB in 1960 He was graduated in 1962 from the KGB Intelligence institute 101 and, thereafter, pursued specialized courses relative to 'Line S' techniques for approximately two or three years. In 1969, for reasons unknown to the source, LYALIN was transferred from the 'S' Directorate to Department 'V'.[6]

Although heavily redacted, this report strongly suggests that the source was a senior member of the KGB *rezidentura* whose comments might have made it easy for one of his colleagues to identify him. Accordingly, the report advised that

In the light of this situation, it is again noted that if disseminated further, every precaution is urged to present the above information in such a manner as to fully protect [XXXXXXX]. Contacts with the source regarding this matter are continuing.[7]

The FBI also expressed concern about tasking the source to seek information or to engage in behavior that might compromise him. Nevertheless, in early 1971 the special agent in charge of the New York Field Office informed his director, J. Edgar Hoover, about 'a tentative schedule of meetings with this source for briefing and debriefing' the 902nd Military Intelligence Group, then the United States Army's principal counter-intelligence organisation, formerly known as the Counterintelligence Corps. The 902nd had a reputation for running highly aggressive operations against the Soviets, usually in the form of 'dangles' deliberately deployed to tempt a suspected Soviet talent spotter or recruiter, or via an established double agent, likely a soldier who has been cultivated under the 902nd's supervision.

The precise nature of the relationship between the FBI and the source inside the Soviet Mission to the United Nations is far from clear, but it would appear that the 902nd MI Group was in the final stages of a plan, codenamed IRONCLAD, intended to embarrass the KGB, blow an agent operating on the west coast, and expose the expose the source inside the *rezidentura* who, presumably, FBI knew to be a double agent acting under the KGB's control.

> As the Bureau pointed out, however, in the light of the recent defection in England of an Officer of the 15th Department, OLEG A. LYALIN, this meeting could very well be aborted by the Soviets. In line with this thinking, the NYO wishes to point out that if the meeting is consummated and if the subject does make an appearance, it could be the last opportunity for a long time to take advantage of a situation that could discredit the subject, cause the KGB considerable embarrassment and disrupt the efforts of the 13th Department for an extended period of time.
>
> The NYO agrees with the Bureau that a defection approach to the subject is impractical and unfeasible. Also, the knowledge we might gain, if their operation is allowed to continue, from the handling by the Soviets of the source, in the west coast area seem minimal to the amount of damage we might cause by exposing, not only the subject, but other KGB Officers worldwide, who have handled this source.
>
> The Bureau is requested to make reference to NY TT 9/10/71, captioned 'IRONCLAD IS-R' wherein an informant had had advised that the recent defector OLEG LYALIN had spent approximately nine years in the Illegal Support Directorate before being transferred to the 13th Department, Sabotage and Assassination Group. The NYO has noticed that the submitted communications under separate captions, of information received from [MI5] concerning operations in which LYALIN was privy. The NYO would like the Bureau to consider the feasibility of submitting all information received concerning these departments to a NY control file (captioned OLEG A LYALIN) being opened by this office for receipt of same. In this way the NYO can more properly evaluate this information and can more intelligently submit questions concerning these two Departments in which we have primary interest.[8]

The implication of this plea from the NYFO to Hoover is that Lyalin's defection in London had unwittingly interfered with a well-founded counter-intelligence operation conducted against a department V officer based in the New York *rezidentura* who thought he was managing an asset in California. The NYFO had already assessed their contact as unsuitable for defection and was worried that the KGB would call off the entire 'operational game' in anticipation of Lyalin's compromising the source in New York who was definitely known to him. According to the FBI's informant, 'the subject was among those KGB officers in NY who knew this defector (Oleg A. Lyalin) or were known to him.' The NYFO explained on 24 September that two days earlier Lyalin's colleague had unexpectedly fled the country:

> This departure was obviously in haste as the subject and his wife had taken a new residence in which they stayed for only about a week. He had also indicated to friends that he would remain in the US until the conclusion of the General assembly at the UN. This subject's departure would therefore seem to be linked with the defection of OLEG LYALIN.[9]

While the debate continued between the NYFO and headquarters in Washington DC over how to handle the situation, the FBI continued to receive information from IRONCLAD. Four days later, on 28 September, Hoover was informed that

> Source has determined that the defection of Oleg Lyslin in London, England, has had some effect upon the KGB NY Residency in that regard, source has determined the [XXXXXXXXXXXXXXXXXXXX] have both alluded to the Lyalin defection and in non-specific terms indicated that perhaps KGB should consider the possibility of establishing a special 'service' within the Residency which would analyze the activities, behaviour patterns, weaknesses, etc. of the Soviet personnel with the objective of preventing a similar defection. Source added that [XXXXX] implied that the receipt of a telegram from Headquarters addressed solely to [XXXXXX] outlined this possibility.
>
> Source determined from [XXXX] that he [XXXX] had come to the conclusion that if such a step were taken by Moscow, the special 'service' which would be established within the NY Residency, would probably be composed of personnel assigned to the two Main Directorates, Moscow.
>
> In this regard source feels that [XXXXX] comments might be a prelude to the establishment of more stringent security measures within the Residency
>
> Source feels that the only personnel whom source can trust and [XXXXXXXX]
>
> [XXX] source determined that [XXXXXX] of the NY Residency, had indicated that [XXXX] was not known to OLEG LYALIN, nor did LYALIN know of [XXXX] KGB affiliation.[10]

A few days later IRONCLAD was back in touch with his FBI handlers to report that a senior KGB officer, who had been expected in mid-September on an inspection your, had failed 'to leave the USSR as scheduled'. As reported to Washington, 'source feels that the recent defection in London, England, of KGB officer Oleg Lyalin might have some influence on' the unexpected change in plan.

In another report, IRONCLAD disclosed that the *rezidentura* had been ordered to suspend all operational meetings with its agents:

> The seriousness with which the KGB has viewed the developments in London on the basis of LYALIN's defection is emphasized by the fact that KGB Headquarters has advised [XXXXX] to prohibit intelligence meetings between KGB officers and their most important American agents. This directive was issued by [XXXX] on Thursday, 23 September 1971 and, as a result, only the most insignificant meetings have taken place since that date. There is no indication as to how long this prohibition will be In effect.[11]

The fact that Lyalin had spent some nine years in the KGB's illegals directorate was of great significance to Western intelligence agencies, which knew little about the activities or staff of what was arguably the First Chief Directorate's most secretive branch. Although MI5 and the FBI had some experience of two illegal *rezidents*, Willie Fischer (alias Rudolf Abel) and Konon Molody (alias Gordon Lonsdale), who had been imprisoned in the United States and England respectively, neither had cooperated with their captors. Both men had been thoroughly professional and their silence had been rewarded with their eventual early release in spy-exchanges. Both Soviet officers had won the respect of their interrogators but had whetted an appetite for information about illegal networks that, by their very nature, were potentially vulnerable because of their lack of protection under the Vienna Convention, which protected their counterparts operating under official cover.

The Washington Field Office's interest in the illegals phenomenon prompted the drafting of a questionnaire, which was to be passed to MI5 for GOLDFINCH to answer, and its composition offers an insight into the FBI's understanding of Directorate S's *modus operandi*. Indeed, FBI headquarters considered 'the questions as set up by the WFO are too revealing'.

<u>DEFINITION OF ILLEGAL</u>
Define what the KGB terms an illegal.

TRAINING SCHOOL FOR ILLEGAL AGENTS

I identify and describe individuals who were in training school with you as both students and teachers.

Describe training in selection of drops, meeting places, secret writing techniques, anti-surveillance procedures, communication methods, etc.

PROCEDURES / ORGANISATION

Are third-country nationals used by Soviets in illegal networks in target countries? Are business concerns in target country ever used as part of illegal network?

Where are illegal agents placed in the United States? What are principal targets in the United States? Has the number of Illegal Support officers serving abroad increased or decreased in recent years?

Has the Center taken over the day-to-day direction of illegals so that the duties of Illegal Support officers abroad have been minimized?

How long would an illegal agent reside in [the] target country before he becomes operational? Does this procedure vary with different target countries? How many illegal agents does one Illegal Support officer handle?

Can an illegal agent and his wife enter [the] target country with children?

Do Illegal Support officers and their assigned illegal agents have personal meetings in target country?

What South American countries are utilized to send agents into the United States?

Are Americans recruited in the United States for use as agents in other countries? On [a] large scale?

RETURN TO SOVIET UNION OF ILLEGAL AGENTS

How long would an illegal agent remain out of [a] target country on such a trip?

Is there any pre-set time schedule for illegals to return to USSR for briefing, i.e. 2, 3, etc. years?

How long would an illegal agent remain in [a] target country before returning to the Soviet Union for vacation? For permanent recall? For briefing?

ESCAPE / RECALL FROM TARET COUNTRY

What type of escape training and documentation is given to illegals to leave target country if they believe they are compromised?

In the event that KGB recalled illegal agents from target country in belief their cover had been blown, but it was later concluded that this was not true, would KGB send these same illegals back to that country?

FINANCIAL

Is Swiss bank utilized in funding of illegal agents in the United States?
What is the usual method in funding for illegal agents in target county?

COMMUNICATIONS

Method of communication between center and illegal agent in target country?
Method of communication between support officer and illegal agent?
Are commercial radios adaptable for target country used by Illegal Support officer to communicate with illegal agents in target country?
What makes radio does Center recommend for the use of its illegal agents in target country?
In illegal training school, here is it recommended that illegal agents hide radio schedules, secret writing equipment, etc. when they have set up residence in target country?
Does an Illegal Support officer monitor at one of the legal establishments the same radio transmissions that the illegal agent (whom he operates) receives?

USE OF CP MEMBERS IN ILLEGAL APPARATUS

What is [the] current policy re involvement of CP members in target countries in illegal apparatus, support or recruitment?

USE OF POST OFFICE AND SAFE DEPOSIT BOXES

Are safe deposit boxes used by illegal agents in [a] target country?
Are Post Office boxes used by illegal agents in [a] target country?

SAGOTAGE/DISRUPTION UNITS

In the event of crisis preceding outbreak of conventional war, what action do you think illegal groups took in the United States during the Cuban crisis in 1962?
Are any sabotage units now operational in the United States?
If so, describe organization, equipment, number of agents, procedures, targets.
Are any disruptive units used at this time by Soviets in the United States?
If so, describe organization, procedures, number of agents, targets.

As drafted, the WFO questionnaire was embarrassingly naïve and unrevealed an astonishing ignorance of standard Directorate S procedures dealing with the management of its illegal networks.

Some of the items listed betrayed a very basic lack of knowledge that certainly would have surprised MI5 and doubtless Lyalin himself.

On 16 September, Lyalin's interviews with MI5 analysts yielded a detailed biography, which was circulated to Allied liaison services. It served not only to advertise GOLDFINCH's credentials, but to celebrate the fact that the British had succeeded in running a penetration of the KGB without Soviet interference, Considering that this had not happened since 1947, this represented quite a milestone.

Oleg Adolfovich LYALIN

A RELATIONS

1. Father

Adolf. Born 2878. Died 239.1952 of a heart attack.

Chief engineer of the CALSSYROV (ph) (electrical and engineering equipment for agricultural purposes).

1937: Expelled from Party – reason not known.

During [the Second World] war joined partisan movement, received decorations. Discharged on grounds of health, returned home in 1944 and allowed to join [the] Party again.

1944 until death: Chief of Planning Department of City Council of PIATIKOPSK.

2. Mother

Born 1905 or 2906. Teacher. Graduate of Higher Political School. Party member. Pro-Stalin.

1950s: Separated from husband and went to live in village of MACAVOYS near ARTOL where she was director of a school.

After husband's death in 1952 returned to PIATORSKY and obtained [a] position as a geography teacher.

1954: Accused of collaborating with Germans during the [Second World] war.

1956: Cleared of collaboration charge but was in ill health (only 1 lung) and could not work so retired to TSISIS in Latvia. Visited Czechoslovakia (1964) as Representative of Teachers' Union of Latvia. In receipt of a pension. Refuses to speak to LYALIN because she hates the KGB. As a result of her experience with it when accused of collaborating. LYALIN gets news of her through her sister.

3. Brother

[XXXXX] KHANOKOTSK [XXXXXXXXXXXX].

Graduate of Moscow Aviation Institute [XXXXXX] Institute [XXXXXXXXX] of Radar [XXXXXXXX] Institute, [XXXXX] for the Army on aeroplanes. [XXXXXX] (probably KGB). Lives in Kiev.

4. Stepbrother (Deceased)
   Alexander child of father's first marriage.
   Joined the Airforce. Killed on 2 May 1945.
   [XXXXXXXXXXXXXXX].

5. [XXXXXXXXXXXXXXXXXXXXXXX].

6. [XXXXXXXXXXXXXXXXXXXXXX].

7. [XXXXXXXXXXXXXXXXXXXXXXXXX] Klaypodo.

8. [XXXXXXXXXXXXXXXXXXXXXXXX].

9. [XXXXXXXXXXXXXXXXXXXXXXXXX].

10. [XXXXXXX]rgi Ivanovich SISTRNKO born 11.10.15.
    Identified CO [XXXXXXX] Soviet Russia [XXXXXXXX].

11. O.A. LYALIN
    (1) LYALIN was born 29.6.28 at STAVOPOL but he was not registered until 28.8.1938 and the latter date is therefore his official birthday. During the war years he lived with his mother in German-occupied PIATGORSK In 1950 when his parents separated he remained with his father PIATIGORSK. After his father's death there was very little money and he was obliged to leave school and find work. He continued to attend school in the evenings.
    (2) LYALIN entered the Higher Marine School, KAVOTSK (ph) street, Odessa in 1954 and remained there until 1959. He entered by means of a competitive examination consisting of mathematics, physics, history, literature, and an oral examination in French English or German (LYALIN chose English) Students lived in the School and uniform and leaks were provided free. There were two seasons per year, Spring and Winter, but every year from September to November students were at sea gaining practical experience. LYALIN studied electrical marine engineering, astronomy, physics, and economy of sea transportation. At the end of the course there were two exams: (1) the State exam and (2) Universal Diploma which is a thesis on one particular

subject the student chooses out of five or six set by the Board of Exams. To obtain (1) and (2) is equivalent to a University degree.

(3) In 1957, while still a student, LYALIN was a crew member of a four-masted schooner 'TOVARICH' (a confiscated German ship) making a goodwill tout of Western ports which included a two week visit to Portsmouth, as guests of the Portsmouth Marine School and several Mediterranean ports. In 1958 he visited Kuwait and Suez aboard a tanker. When he left the school in 1959 he served aboard a cargo ship visiting local (i.e. Baltic) ports as third and later second officer until July 1960.

(4) At some time prior to 1959 whilst still a student at the Higher Marine School he was co-opted by the KGB to work against Western seaman and smugglers, (Transportation Department, later 5th Sector Odessa KGB). There was nothing formal about this recruitment. A friend who was already a co-opted worker took him along to the Personnel department of the School where it was arranged. His main qualification for the job was his command of English.

(5) In 1958/59 the KGB sent him on a training exercise to KISEGEV with false documents in the name of OLEF ALEXANDROVICH KISHEEV. His task was to find four named people and collect information about them. Oh his return he was offered a job in the illegal net.

(6) It was the Odessa KGB (for whom he was working as a co-optee) who recommended him for a place in the 101 School. He went for an interview and was accepted. Students lived in at the School. He commenced a two year course at the School in August 1960. This course consisted of Chemistry, Photography, English and 'Tailing'. There was one lecture at the beginning of the course on the structure and purpose of the KGB. Thereafter also six months and one year course at the School LYALIN took his examinations before the end of the course and graduated in October 1961 and was sent to live in a private flat for a few months. There he read the English newspapers and wrote a paper on how to avoid the call-up in the USA. After his graduation it was decided not to use him in the illegal net. He believes this was because of the divorce from his first wife which was pending.

(7) On 29 April 1962 he was posted to Klaypoda where he was in Sub-Division X dealing with foreign seamen. Hs rank was '1 small star'; by the time he left Klaypoda he had '4 small stars'. He was in the same sub-division for the whole of his stay in Klaypoda. The numbering of the sub-divisions changed while he was there and his became sub-division II.

(8) In February 1957 he was sent to Moscow to attend a six month course starting 1 March 1957 at the V Department school at

Calitziner. The school is still called the Calitziner but is now situated in the premises which used to be occupied by the 101 School on the road to BAASIKA 26 kilometers from Moscow. Training at this school consisted of lectures on:

(a) Partisan warfare including organizing a partisan army from a small group, and how to maintain security and prevent penetration by the local secret services or army intelligence. These [XXXXXXXXXXXXXXXXXXXX] Poland and Czechoslovakia.

(b) Radio communications. Two army types of radio were shown, one weighed 24 kilograms and the other 35. They had very good tuning capacities. LYALIN describes a method of using failm to obtain high speed. Coding, decoding and how to use a 'grid' were also taught. LYALIN stated that because of my marine education I know what a radio is and I know how to use it so I was not even attending the lessons' i.e. at the Training Centre.

(c) Explosives. Basic principles and precautions only were taught 'because everybody understand that as soon as you leave the School you will forget about it but it won't take you that long to renew it again.'

(d) A practical exercise in which the students were divided into groups of six and given a direction. The target would be a factory, rocket base, power station or something similar. The group would have to locate and identify the target, give a full description including plans, details of security measures, and how entry might be effected and an assessment of its value as a target.

(e) The same groups of six were given a 'theoretical task'. Each were given two books and a good map of a different place and using only this they had to prepare a plan of where they would land, what equipment would be needed, how many people, etc. Then they were given a place to find and describe fully including how to penetrate it and lastly they blew up a bridge. The last tasks are divided amongst the groups who were supposed to be in radio communication (In fact they had no radio and used telephones). When all the tasks were finished the members reported back to the chief of the group (LYALIN was the chief of his group).

(f) Parachute training. Three rubles per jump were paid as an incentive.

When the course was finished LYALIN returned to Klay Poda.

(9) On 2 May 1968 LYALIN was sent to Moscow and instructed to prepare himself for a mission to Czechoslovakia posing as an

American tourist of German origin. This mission did not materialize as the situation in Czechoslovakia was brought under control and LYALIN returned to Klaypoda in mid-August 1968.

(10) In November 1968 LYALIN was sent to Moscow for training prior to his UK posting. This included visits to most departments at KGB Headquarters although he admits that he managed to avoid some of these. He also received some instruction from the Foreign Trade organization for his cover position. He arrived in the UK on 11 February 1969.

(11) LYALIN speaks good English, some German and a little Spanish and French. He has visited Bulgaria, Turkey, France, Italy, Gibraltar, Sweden, Denmark, Poland, East and West Germany. His service in the UK was hid only foreign posting.

(12) LYALIN's KHB rank is 4-star captain. He has been a party member since 1950. and was the Young Communist League leader in his group at the Higher Marine School.

(13) He has used the following aliases:
Oleg Alexandrovich LYALIN
Aaron Adolfovich STALKASSER
GOTCH (ph nickname)[12]

The purpose of assembling this potted biography was intended partly to alert liaison services to areas of potential interest to them, but mainly to keep a record of the defector's claimed *curriculum vitae* so any subsequent discrepancies might be detected. The interrogation technique had proved useful when in 1964 Yuri Nosenko had been caught out in various contradictions in his KGB career, which to him acknowledging that, for example, he had inflated his rank and exaggerated his status and access to files, motive by a desire to make himself more valuable to his American hosts:

> Until October/November 1969 the head of Department V in the USA was Nikolay Alekseyevich KUZNETSOV who was in the UN in New York. This was his second posting to the U.S. On the first he recruited a technician connected with electronics and computers for which he received a very high decoration. He was not like in headquarters because he was always emphasizing his superior position and the fact that he had been decorated. During his second posting in the United States he produced no practical results ad after encountering some 'difficulties' was obliged to return unexpectedly to Russia in October or November 1969, leaving all his possessions behind. LYALIN believes he is now teaching. The current head of Department V in the U.S. is believed by LYALIN to be [XXXXXXXX] under UN cover in New York.

There are currently two young Department V officers in Washington: They had previously been [a] subordinate to KUZNETSOV. [XXXXXXXXX] prior to going to the U.S. later this year. he will serve under UN cover in New York.

There is a Department V officer in Colombia: he went there in late 1969/early 1970. LYALIN does not know if there is a Department VF representative in Canada. In November 1968 there was someone training to be a member of the Consular staff for Canada. This man might therefore be in Canada.

The 13th Department (now known as Department V) agents in the U.S. about whom LYALIN learned from [XXXXXXXXXXXXXXXXXXXXX] U.K. who up to 1969/70 was in the North and South American subdivision of Department V Headquarters.

[XXXXXXXXXXXXXXXXXXXXXXXXXXXXXX], an Armenian, now an American citizen living in the U.S. He left Armenia many years ago but still has relatives in Russia. He writes to his relatives not to officials and he uses an ancient Armenian language which is difficult to translate as it is not spoken today.

[XXXXXXXXXXXXXXXXXXXXXXXXX].

Note: All three agents mentioned above are American citizens with American passports.

They used their own identities. All three were current cases in 1969/70. [XXXX] was not directly involved in them but heard about them as a result of sharing a room.

1. [XXXXX] has a contact in London who has communist sympathies. The contact shares a flat with a young American. [XXXXXXXXXXXXXXXXX] they advised him to travel to Europe to avoid the draft. Recently [XXXXX] has been holidaying in Morocco. In the U.K. he does occasional jobs to make a living. In places where he works he tries to cause trouble. Inciting strikes, etc. Initially [XXXX] was cultivating his contact with a view to finding out as much as possible about [XXXX], and he met [XXXX] twice. The Resident was [XXXXXX] interest in [XXXX] but he continues to pay attention to the [XXXXXXXXX] was unable to say if there is a homosexual aspect to this case.
2. When [XXXXXXXXXXXXXXXXXXXXXXXXX] was in Norway two years ago [sic] he recruited a major in the U.S. Army. The major was connected with building and reconstruction techniques. He was subsequently posted to West Germany where he continued to be met by someone else. It appears that [XXXX] was on friendly terms with a bookshop owner and he found the American's name on a mailing list for books. He asked the bookshop owner about the major, contrived a meeting in the shop and subsequently

recruited him. LYALIN was unable to supply any further information about this major for the [XXXXXXXXXX].
3. In 1964, the First chief Directorate KGB received a document issued by the 'American Security Service' for its officers on 'What kind of behaviours must be shown towards Russian refugees and refugees originated from the U.S. or from the U.S. zone of Germany. It was distributed to all places where there were Russians who traveled abroad, rig seaports. LYALIN saw a partial translation of it when it reached KLAYPEDA in 1965. The main points that he recalled were:
4. (a) How to criticize the Russian way of life.
    (b) What you may tell a Russian.
    (c) How to treat a Russian refugee or escapee.
5. [XXXXXXXXXXXXXXXXXXXXXXXXXXXXXXXXXXXXXXXXX] between BREMENAVEN, RIGA, VENTSILS and KLAYPEDA, has been a KGB agent since 1963 working to one of LYALIN's former colleagues in KLAYPEDA. [XXXX] has a relative, probably a cousin, whose husband is in the U.S. Nayv working on military transports between HANGENHAFEN [sic] and Vietnam. [XXX] met this American in Germany and obtained from him information about security measures on board ship, cargoes, loading techniques and timetables of his transport which his controller considered very useful. LYALIN could not recall which port the transport sailed but he thought that it could have been a small place in North Germany.
6. When [XXXXXXXXXXXXXXXXXXXXXXXXXXX] Counter-intelligence section in the KGB residency in London, was in the USA (1963–69) he had an agent offering him information about special classified cars. [XXXXXXXXXXXXXX].
7. In July 1971 an urgent report was received by the KGB Residency in London instructing all Pollical Section officers to concentrate on obtaining information on Sino-American relations. [XXXXXXXXXXXXXX] informed LYALIN that he [XXXXXX] London, a JE[XXXXXXXXX] from whom he [XXX] to seek information. This American official had apparently been offered the post of Second man in Singapore but he refused. He told [XXXX] that he was either going to be an ambassador in a very big country or somewhere e else but that he was not going to be a secretary somewhere especially in a place like Singapore.
8. [XXXXXX] has a non-Soviet contact, possibly an American, who returned to London from Geneva on 22nd July 1971. [XXXX] is particularly interested in this person because [XXXX] works in the U.S. embassy, London. [XXXX] has not yet met the girl in the U.S. embassy.

9. [XXXXX] was until Nov/Dec 1970 [XXXX] was in touch with [XXXXXXXX] who was in London from [XXXXXXX] by chance in a café [XXXXXXX] and he passed him technical reports 'to help him'. Before [XXXX] was handed over to LYALIN with instructions to complete his recruitment and bring him under proper control. LYALIN accomplished this in the first two months. [XXXX] provided a large volume of confidential reports from SHELL about the oil industry, e.g. research, developments, production, profits, plans, quarterly progress reports on the Stanley Research Centre, etc. The material was normally collected from him on Friday and returned to him on Saturday so that he could replace it on Monday. [XXXX] motive was mercenary and LYALIN paid him £40 for one year. He signed receipts in the name of [XXXXX] information which from an industrial point of view was considered very good was primarily of interest to the Scientific and Technical Section who were prepared to pay £200 for a complete set of Stanley Research Centre reports. In the second half of 1970 [XXXX] was introduced to [XXXX] of the [XXXX] Technical Section but he did not care for [XXXX] and he left for the U.S. at the end of 1970, without telling [XXXX]. LYALIN does not now know of any attempts to re-establish contact with [XXXX] in the U.S. In LYALIN's view it would probably be necessary to see from [XXXX] employment whether there would be any advantage in recontacting him and if so who, e.g. [XXXX] LYALIN himself would be available to make the contact. LUALIN had received a request from Moscow for [XX] current address. He had intended to establish the address from another of his agents who is in touch with [XXXX].
10. [XXXXXXXXXXXXXXXXXXXXXX] whilst in the UK she appears to have been [XXXXXX] Jesuit Missions at 12 Park Street. New Park Lane, W1 (Tel. No. 493 7811 [XXXXXXXX] went to Boston to live with the wife's parents, but the last that LYALIN heard was that they were looking for a flat.[13]

In addition, Lyalin mentioned a pair of KGB illegals, a husband and wife team, who had arrived in London in mid-1969. He also compromised three of the agents he had run in London, who were promptly arrested. They were a Malaysian clerk, Sirioj Abdoolcader, Kyriacos Costi and Constantinos Martianon.

Abdoolcader, who had been recruited in March 1967 by Vladislas Savin, a fellow 'Line F' officer, was employed by the Greater London Council in the vehicle registration department and had access to details of cars used by MI5 in covert surveillance operations. He had been instructed by Lyalin, to whom he was introduced in 1969, to cultivate Marie Richardson, then a Ministry of Defence secretary working for the deputy director of the Royal Navy's Support and Transport Staff. She had been the subject of an approach while on a cruise to Leningrad in 1969, an incident that she had reported upon her return. Aged 33, Abdoolcader had failed in his pursuit of Richardson, but he nevertheless was regarded as a valuable source by the KGB. He was sentenced to three years' imprisonment.

The other two other KGB agents, Constantinos Martianon and Kyriacos Costi, were Greek Cypriot tailors, brothers-in-law who had been members of the Young Communist League. When questioned they had admitted having been recruited in 1961 during a visit to a Soviet trade exhibition. Aged 27, Costi was sentenced to six years' imprisonment and Martianon to four.

Lyalin agreed to trade information in return for eventual resettlement in the north of England, and he soon supplied a complete order of battle for the KGB in London. He also revealed his own mission, reconnoitered while posing as a textiles buyer across the Midlands, to select targets for attack by special forces in the event of war, including the Fylingdales early warning radar installation in Yorkshire, V-bomber bases, and the London tube, scheduled for flooding by the River Thames after strategically placed bombs detonated. Chillingly, the defector also described a plan to infiltrate agents disguised as official messengers into Whitehall's system of underground tunnels to distribute poison gas capsules. He also identified other members of the London *rezidenturas* who were expelled in Operation FOOT. Codenamed GOLDFINCH, Lyalin's debriefing covered five volumes and was circulated widely among Western intelligence agencies. In Ottawa it was copied by a KGB mole inside the RCMP Security Service, Gilles Brunet, and passed to his KGB handlers.

Lyalin's recruitment was accomplished by Tony Brooks of SIS and Harry Wharton of MI5, supervised by Christopher Herbert, as part of a joint effort to acquire a source inside the *rezidentura*, a highly ambitious goal that could never have been contemplated while there was a suspicion that MI5 had been penetrated. Brooks was a legendary figure, codenamed ALPHONSE who had won a DSO and an MC while organising the PIMENTO resistance network in Toulouse for Special Operations Executive in France during the Second World War. In the early days of the Cold War, he had been posted to Sofia, Belgrade and Cyprus. Wharton was bluff, no-nonsense Yorkshireman, while Herbert had enjoyed an MI5 career that had included a posting to Trinidad as the security liaison officer for the Caribbean. This trio represented the sharp end of a dream team that had been tasked to assemble the complete order of battle of the KGB and GRU *rezidenturas*, and then employ whatever methods they though appropriate to find, cultivate and recruit someone on the inside. It must have seemed a tall order, as such a coup had not been pulled off since 1927.

Lyalin's eventual defection was unplanned, having been prompted by his arrest on drink driving charges by a Metropolitan Police traffic patrol. The detained Lyalin arranged for his handlers to be contacted, and MI5 despatched a team, equipped with the antidotes to various poisons, to extract him from the police station and supervise his asylum. Lyalin and his girlfriend were resettled, and he died in February 1995. While living in England with a new identity Lyalin was the target of a sustained effort by the KGB to trace him, and John Symonds was approached to use his police contacts to establish his whereabouts.

Operation FOOT, initiated and accelerated by Lyalin's defection was the expulsion conducted in September 1971 to expel Soviet intelligence personnel from London, and intended to establish some equivalence in the imbalance that had developed between British diplomatic representation in Moscow and the reciprocal arrangements in London. This had been an objective of MI5 for years, but objections from Downing Street and the Foreign Office had kept the issue off the agenda, until the permanent undersecretary, Sir Denis Greenhill, lent it his support, confident that a joint MI5-SIS operation had acquired a reliable source inside the KGB's London *rezidentura*. His information was considered at a meeting held at the Foreign Office by Greenhill on 25 March 1971 attended by Burke Trend, the chairman of the Joint Intelligence Committee, Sir Stewart Crawford, Sir Martin Furnival Jones of MI5, Sir John Rennie from SIS, and the permanent undersecretaries at the Home Office, Ministry of Defence, and the Department of Trade and Industry. The initiative for removing about 100 Soviets came from Furnival Jones who complained that

> in the last 15 years there had been evidence of penetration of the FCO, the Ministry of Defence, the Army, Navy and Air Force, the Labour Party, Transport House and the Board of Trade. It was difficult to say exactly how much damage was being done. But it was equally difficult to believe that the Russians maintained such a large establishment for no profit. At least 30 or 40 Soviet intelligence officers in this country were actually running secret agents in government or industry.[14]

Following Furnival Jones's presentation, Rennie added that 'the Russians attached high priority to acquiring scientific and technical secrets, and to commercial information with military overtones.' Advocating a mass expulsion, Rennie confirmed that

> our Allies in western Europe, far from viewing our action badly, would probably welcome it. It was clear that the French were concerned about the numbers of Russians in their country, they might emulate our action. This would make it difficult for the Russians to switch their trade[15].

Having examined a table displaying the numbers of Soviet personnel engaged on diplomatic duties in Western Europe, the United States and Japan, which indicated that there were more posted to Britain than anywhere else, the meeting closed with agreement to draft minutes on the subject.

Once the foreign secretary, Sir Alec Douglas-Home, had been convinced of the necessity to restrict the size of the Soviet Embassy in London, and get rid of the disproportionately large KGB and GRU *rezidenturas* that were draining MI5's limited resources, his task was to persuade Prime Minister Edward Heath. On 30 July, he received a memorandum from the home secretary, Reginald Maudling, and the foreign secretary, in which they pressed the case for action:

> Soviet intelligence officers operate under cover of the various Soviet establishments in this country. Apart from the Soviet Embassy (189) there are the Soviet Trade Delegation (121) contract inspectors (73), and other organizations such as TASS, Aeroflot and the Moscow Narodny Bank (134). The total is higher than the Soviet establishment in any other country of Western Europe.[16]

This MI5 assessment would later be disputed by the FBI's mole in the New York *rezidentura* codenamed IRONCLAD. At the end of September 1971, the asset advised his handler that

> the KGB had 50 intelligence officers and the GRU had 35 officers assigned to this residency. Of the 50 KGB officers in the London Residency, 15 were assigned to the Scientific and Technical Branch of that Residency.[17]

Having reluctantly accepted the need for action, but uncertain over the appropriate timing, Heath agreed to have the matter raised privately with the Soviets, who were anticipated, correctly, to be unresponsive. On 4 August, Sir Alec wrote to his Soviet counterpart, Andrei Gromyko, drawing his attention to the problem and illustrating it with a complaint about an application for a visa from a man named B.G.

Glushchenko, together with the statement that he had been nominated to the post of First Secretary at the Soviet Embassy in London.

> This man was in Britain from 1964 to 1968. At that time he was described as the representative of *Aviaexport* at the Soviet Trade delegation, Mr Glushchenko's activities however had little to do with the sale of aircraft. He came to our notice on various occasions; for example, he offered a large sum of money to a British businessman if he would obtain details of certain British military equipment.[19]

Gromyko failed to reply, so it was decided that the announcement would be made on Saturday, 24 September, when the Commons would not be sitting, but at the end of August all the plans were thrown into confusion because Lyalin was arrested on Tottenham Court Road and charged with drunk driving. Fearing he would be sent back to Moscow as soon as his *rezident* learned of his offense, Lyalin used his emergency contact number, and MI5 spirited him out of the police station. However, the news of Lyalin's defection leaked, and was published in the *Evening News* on Friday, 24 September, so Operation FOOT was advanced by twenty-four hours, and handled by Greenhill, as Sir Alec left for New York. Ninety Soviet diplomats were declared *persona non grata*, and a further fifteen who happened to be out of the country, among them Yuri Voronin, the KGB *rezident*, were refused permission to return. Information from subsequent defectors confirmed that foot succeeded in severely disrupting Soviet intelligence operations, and it was used as a model for FAMISH, a similar exercise conducted subsequently in the United States.

In early October 1971 a GRU officer, Anatole Chebotarev, a member of the Soviet Trade Mission in Belgium, and reportedly a friend of Lyalin's, defected from the GRU *rezidentura* in Brussels and was thought to have been quickly spirited to London because his car had been found abandoned at the Channel ferry port of Zeebrugge. A few months later he turned up at the Soviet embassy in Washington DC, seeking repatriation. He was promptly flown back to Moscow under escort where he was convicted of desertion by a military tribunal. He only served a short sentence, and later was pardoned and appointed a French teacher at a school in Ryazin. Although Chebotarev's defection has been linked by the media to Lyalin, there was no such connection. Quite simply, Chebotarev had been stopped by the traffic police while en route to meet an agent, and then had been questioned by the Sureté d'Etat. When offered the opportunity to apply for political asylum, he had done so spontaneously, and been handed over to the CIA.

Lyalin's defection inflicted immense damage on the KGB and wreaked havoc in the third department, which had spent years building up the London *rezidentura*, only to have the entire edifice torn down. Additionally, Lyalin compromised all his colleagues operating under diplomatic cover and effectively terminated the careers of dozens of contemporaries. In these circumstances it was not entirely surprising for MI5 to hear from John Symonds, a former Scotland Yard detective convicted of corruption, that he had been approached by the KGB to use his police contacts to identify one of the Special Branch officers assigned to Lyalin's protection.

Symonds had fled England in April 1972 when two of his CID colleagues, Bernard Robson and Gordon Harris, had been imprisoned for corruption. Symonds had been scheduled to appear as their co-defendant, but his counsel had argued skillfully for a separate trial, but their conviction had persuaded Symonds that he too would be rewarded with a long sentence, so he drove to Morocco where, while trying to find work as a mercenary, he had been cultivated by a Soviet diplomat, doubtless a member of the Agadir *rezidentura*, who was anxious to find Lyalin. Symonds later claimed that he had reported the incident to the authorities in London, without disclosing his whereabouts. In any event, the episode showed that the KGB was in an unforgiving mood as far as Lyalin was concerned. As General Klaugin ruefully recalled in his memoirs, 'the upshot of the Lyalin affair was that dozens of KGB officers were fired or demoted, department V was shut down.'

Chapter VII

ARKADI SHEVCHENKO

Shevchenko's defection, and ensuing denunciation of Soviet foreign policy, was a serious blow, for he had worked at such a high level.

Oleg Kalugin, *Spymaster*[1]

Born in the eastern Ukraine in October 1930, Shevchenko's father was a physician who had been appointed to run a tuberculosis sanatorium on the Black Sea at Yevpatoria. Following the German invasion in 1941, Dr Shevchenko and his staff were evacuated to Siberia but were allowed to return to the Crimea in 1944. Five years later Arkadi graduated from high school and moved to Moscow to attend the State Institute of international Relations, known as MGIMO, a prestigious academic organisation. There he met and married a fellow student, Lina, and he graduated three years later, in 1954.

In 1956, Shevchenko joined the Ministry of Foreign Affairs and his first overseas experience was a three-month posting to the United Nations in New York in 1958, attached to the Soviet Permanent Mission as a specialist on disarmament issues. In 1962, he was sent to Geneva as a member of the Soviet delegation to the UN disarmament negotiations, and in 1963 was promoted to head the Soviet Mission's Security Council Division in New York. He remained in New York until 1970 when he was appointed an advisor to the Foreign Minister Anfrei Gromyko. Three years later, Shevchenko was nominated for the post of assistant secretary general, with the rank and status of an ambassador, and it was this change in allegiance that troubled him as, by convention, UN staff are required to pledge allegiance to the organisation, rather than their country of origin. This, of course, was not the Soviet way, as Moscow regarded the UN institution as an opportunity to extend Soviet influence. In his new role, the UN expected Shevchenko to act devoid of national interest, whereas Moscow required him to continue to further the Kremlin's agenda. The pressure on Shevchenko escalated as he attended a series of international negotiations, the Strategic Arms Limitation Talks, which were intended to introduce bilateral limits on stocks of nuclear weapons. The first stage, the Anti-Ballistic Missile Treaty, was intended to restrict the number of missiles deployed against incoming offensive ballistic missiles. Underlying the talks was the principle of eliminating the need to build more and more missiles to maintain the same level of deterrence. Under the terms of the ABMT each side was required to build only two anti-ballistic missile sites which could be armed with no more than 100 interceptors each. On the Soviet side, the ABM under development was the A-35, destined for launch sites at Kolovos and Checknov while the Americans competed with *Safeguard*, designed by Bell Laboratories but built by Western Eleccric, and equipped with Sprint and *Spartan* weapons, which were deployed in Cavalier, North Dakota and Conrad, Montana. The purpose of ABMT limit of just two sites was to allow one to cover the nation's capital, and the other to protect existing ICBM launch areas, and thereby reduce the risk of an escalating arms race. The document was signed in Moscow in May 1972 by President Richard Nixon and General Secretary Leonid Brezhnev. It was also agreed that both sides would freeze the existing number of launchers, and any new submarine-launched ballistic missiles would require a similar number of land-based launchers to be dismantled. At that time the Soviets had declared a total of 2,568 ICBMs and submarine-launched missiles, whereas the United States possessed 1,754. The disparity in the figures reflected the greater number of free-fall nuclear weapons deployed by the United States Air Force B-52 strategic bombers, and the shorter range missiles located close to Soviet borders. The obvious asymmetry reflected the technical problems encountered by the negotiating teams. For example, the United States wanted to include the new Tu-22 *Backfire* bomber on the grounds that it was capable of delivering a nuclear payload to the continental United States, whereas the Soviet side excluded the aircraft, claiming it did not have the necessary range. The Soviets also attempted, unsuccessfully, to include air-launched Cruise missiles. The only parity was in submarine-launched ballistic missiles, which were frozen at 740.

The issue of verification also became an obstacle, with the Soviets opposed to any on-site inspections, denouncing the suggestion as a breach of sovereignty. A settlement reached on 'national technical means', which was a combination of signals intelligence and overhead satellite surveillance.

The negotiations were long and complex because of the dynamic nature of the technology, the introduction of multiple warheads, the reliability of the integrated radar systems and the use of decoys. As soon as SALT I had been signed, SALT II negotiations commenced to iron out the unresolved issues, and it was during this second round of talks that Shevchenko made an extraordinary contribution. Codenamed DYMAMITE by the CIA, Arkadi Shevchenko was the most senior Soviet official to defect during the Cold War. As a disarmament expert with the rank of undersecretary general at the United Nations, Shevchenko enjoyed access to all but the very highest classifications of Soviet diplomatic telegrams, and in April 1975 he made contact with the CIA's station in New York with a view to defecting. There, in a mid-town brownstone safe house on East 64th Street, he was received by the urbane Kenneth Millian, a former station chief in Argentina and Costa Rica, and latterly chief of covert action for the whole of the Latin American region. For the next thirty-two months his CIA case officer, Millian's deputy, Peter Earnest, liaised closely with him, arranging a regular schedule of meetings every ten days, and both men carried a pager twenty-four hours a day so they could respond instantly if an emergency arose. He also made the arrangements for his eventual escape from his apartment building in April 1978 after he had received an unexpected recall to Moscow 'for consultations'.

Some years later it emerged that the KGB's New York *rezidentura* had become increasingly worried by Shevchenko's behavior, manifested by frequent absences from his office, heavy drinking and unexplained weekend vacations to Florida. The pressure of his double life was becoming a burden for Shevchenko, and the New York *rezident*, Yuri Drozdov, reported his concerns to Directorate K in Moscow where General Oleg Kalugin discussed the problem with the FCD director, Vladimir Kryuchkov, but failed to intervene because of Shevchenko's status and friendship with Andrei Gromyko. However, a further adverse report from Drozdov, who disliked Shevchenko, resulted in the recall.

While Millian's handling of Shevchenko was to be a model of professionalism, the same could not be said of the rest of the team indoctrinated into DYNAMITE, which happened to include a rather second-rate case officer, Aldrich Ames, a man who was widely known to be a heavy drinker, lazy and unreliable. On one occasion, when Ames had completed a rendezvous with Shevchenko, he accidentally left his briefcase, full of highly compromising classified documents on a

New York subway train. Panic ensued, and Ames called an FBI contact who fortunately retrieved the missing item so no harm was done. The incident had no impact on Ames's career, and soon afterwards he was posted to Mexico City.

Thereafter Shevchenko's resettlement, a lonely business because his wife Lina died of an overdose in Moscow soon after his defection, was to cause considerable anxiety. In an effort to supply him with female companionship the FBI searched the Washington DC yellow pages for a suitable escort service. Their eventual choice, Judy Chavez, a 22-year-old Georgetown prostitute, later wrote *Defector's Mistress*[2], much to Shevchenko's embarrassment. She became his constant companion within three weeks of his defection and remained until October 1978, when she sold her story to the media.

Shevchenko's autobiography, *Breaking with Moscow*[3], published in 1985, was criticised in an article in the 15 July 1985 edition of *New Republic* by the American author Edward Jay Epstein who pointed out that certain episodes could not possibly have taken placed as described. He also suggested, incorrectly, that Shevchenko had invented his pre-defection collaboration with the CIA to enhance the interest of his manuscript which, allegedly, did not contain the relevant material when it was first submitted to his original publisher, Michael Korda of Simon & Schuster. He later rewrote it with the help of his American wife, Elaine, whom he married in December 1978, and the revised version was published by Alfred A. Knopf in New York. Epstein dissected the book line by line and concluded that the author had embellished many episodes and invented others to make his story more interesting.

In fact, Shevchenko's story was largely true although he had embroidered some incidents, including the dramatic circumstances of his defection. After twenty years in the Soviet foreign service, including three as one of Foreign Minister Andrei Gromyko's personal advisor, his conversion represented a considerable coup, particularly since Millian and the small circle indoctrinated into the secret had managed the case for so long without a leak. According to Millian,

> the intelligence product was phenomenal. He was much better placed than Penkovsky. It was our first opportunity to get right to the top of the Soviet decision-making machine. He had complete access. .. he could even go into their coderoom and look at all the latest cables.[4]

Shevchenko – whose son, Gennady, and daughter, Anna, stayed in Moscow –lived openly in Washington DC under his own name and married a lawyer. He died in 1998.

Chapter VIII

VITALI YURCHENKO

It was apparent to me when I read the cables that Yurchenko didn't know anything about me so that put my mind at ease.

Aldrich Ames in *Sell-Out* by James Adams[1]

Convinced that he was suffering from the stomach cancer that had killed his mother, a condition that could only be cured in the United States, 50-year-old Vitali Yurchenko defected to the CIA in Rome on 1 August 1985 while on a mission to find Vladimir Alexandrov, a Soviet nuclear physicist who had gone missing. Upon his arrival at Andrews Air Force Base, he was interviewed by Aldrich Ames, and then debriefed by the FBI's Bob Wade at a safehouse in Oakton, Virginia. At its height, the joint FBI-CIA task force involved in debriefing Yurchenko amounted to eleven officers.

Formerly the security officer at the Soviet embassy in Washington DC for eight years, he had been disciplined for calling the police when in December 1976 a CIA retiree, Edwin Moore, had tossed a package of secrets over the fence at the Mount Alto compound. After twenty-two years in the CIA's research division, Moore had accumulated a large quantity of documents that he had valued at $10 million. His initial offer, contained in the bundle thrown into the embassy grounds, included several samples, a price tag of $200,000 and instructions on where to leave the money in Bethesda. The FBI followed up the lead, traced Moore's home in Bethesda, and he was later sentenced to fifteen years' imprisonment but, having suffered a heart attack, was paroled after just three.

Having discussed the incident with the *rezident*, Boris Yakushin, KGB headquarters in Moscow had decided the package was probably a bomb, when, in fact, it contained classified documents. Yurchenko was estranged from his wife and found it hard to support Piotr, his mentally disabled adopted son.

Probably the most important of Yurchenko's 'meal tickets' was his identification of Ronald Pelton, a former National Security Agency linguist who had left the organisation in July 1979 and, in dire financial straits, began to sell classified material in January 1980 to the KGB's Washington *rezidentura*, where the counter-intelligence component was headed by the wily Viktor Cherkashin.

Although the *rezidentura* had been delighted by this unexpected 'walk-in', the staff realised that the FBI's physical surveillance on the front building would have spotted the bearded man as he entered, so elaborate arrangements were made to change his appearance and smuggle him out of the rear exit. Yurchenko, as the embassy security officer using the alias Vladimir Sorokin, had asked a KGB colleague, Gennadi Vasilenko, to shave off Pelton's beard and arrange for him to join a minivan that routinely drove employees home at the end of the working day. Pelton was to lie down in the vehicle, shielded from the FBI's cameras by the other passengers. Trained as a Russian linguist by the United States Air Force, Pelton had served at an intercept site at Peshawar before transferring to the NSA in November 1965. However, he had resigned in July 1979, three months after he had filed for bankruptcy, declaring debts of $65,000, and his financial crisis led him to visit the embassy. The father of four children, Pelton had pursued several money-making schemes, including a fuel-saving device for automobile carburetors, and selling yachts. Separated from his wife, Judith, whom he had married in in 1964 in the town of his birth, Benton Harbor, Michigan, Pelton tried computer consulting and landscaping, but was unsuccessful. In April 1984 he moved in with a girlfriend, Ann Barry, and began to abuse alcohol and drugs.

Over the next five years Pelton met his KGB handler, Anatoli Slavnov, several times, flew to Vienna twice, in October 1980 and again in January 1983, to be debriefed inside the Soviet Embassy compound, and was paid $35,000. Contact was maintained by Slavnov through a telephone call made on the last Saturday of every month to the Pizza Castle restaurant in Falls Church, Virginia. Although Pelton's information was based on his memory, as he no longer enjoyed access to classified information, he had compromised numerous programmes into which he had been indoctrinated while stationed in Pakistan and then during four years in England from 1966 to 1972.

Because Yurchenko did not recall Pelton's real name, the FBI was obliged to identify the voice on the five-year-old recording of the unknown visitor to the embassy who had made a call shortly before his appearance. The mole hunt was conducted by the Baltimore Field Office in an operation assigned the random codename PASSERINE, supervised by Ray Batvinis. The task force consisted of twenty agents and analysts along with Internal Revenue Service agents and postal inspectors, plus about one hundred agents involved in support roles and surveillance. The first objective was to trace the voice, and this was quickly achieved on the very first day of the mole hunt when three NSA employees recognised Pelton on the tape. One of the six teams that interviewed NSA Soviet Group staff was provided with Pelton's name by a colleague with whom he had carpooled over a period of years.

Once the FBI had identified Pelton, and shown his photograph to Yurchenko for confirmation, he became the focus of intensive surveillance over three months which revealed his complicity in a contemporaneous bank fraud, involving $50,000, and he was finally confronted in November 1985 in the Hilton Hotel in Annapolis by Special Agents Dudley Hodgson and David Faulkner who played the tape made five years earlier, on 14 January 1980, of an unidentified man making an appointment at the Soviet embassy. After a second interview later the same day, Pelton offered to act as a double agent to entrap his Soviet contacts but was arrested.

After his conviction in March 1985 Pelton agreed to participate in a damage assessment and he was interviewed at length in a quiet wood cabin on the Naval Air Station Patuxent River in Maryland, conveniently close to his temporary accommodation in the Ann Arundel County Detention Center. The resulting report remains classified because of the many NSA programmes and operational techniques Pelton described. Until the disclosures of Edward Snowden in 2013, Pelton had probably inflicted more damage on the NSA than any other known individual. Although he had spent most of his career in the NSA's Soviet group as a Russian linguist, he latterly had been transferred to a section, which exercised financial control over the NSA's principal projects, and he had been responsible for supervising the budget by moving funds to support under-financed programmes. Inevitably, this position gave him the opportunity to assess the relative performance of particular operations, information that would have been of immense value to the Soviets.

Perhaps the most damaging disclosure was his description of IVY BELLS, an underwater cable-tapping project run in conjunction with the United States Navy, which collected communications traffic at

Soviet naval bases and in Libyan territorial waters. Compromised by Yurchenko, the distinctively red-haired Pelton would be arrested by the FBI in November that year. Convicted at his trial in December 1986, he was sentenced to three life terms plus ten years' imprisonment. He would not be released until November 2015, and he died in September 2022, at the age of 80 in a nursing home in Frederick, Maryland, having converted to Roman Catholicism. He was a gifted pianist and spent his final years living with his son, from whom he had been estranged for most of his life.

Another important counter-intelligence gem was Yurchenko's disclosure that a disgruntled CIA officer designated ROBERT had been in touch with the KGB in Vienna and had compromised several operations run by the CIA station in Moscow. Yurchenko's version of this former employee's behavior neatly dovetailed with a current FBI investigation of Edward Lee Howard, who had been dismissed by the agency in June 1984, shortly after he had been indoctrinated into the station's local assets. At that moment Howard was under FBI surveillance at his home in Albuquerque, but his was able to use his training to evade the watchers and catch a flight to Helsinki.

After the disappointment of his rejection in Montreal, Yurchenko was escorted on a trip to the Grand Canyon and Las Vegas, where he was informed that he was not suffering from cancer. He then began to fret that he would be called to give evidence against Pelton and, to make matters worse, learned that news of his defection had been leaked to the media, probably by the DCI, Bill Casey.

Yurchenko re-defected on 31 October 1985, but not before he had given sufficient information for the FBI to identify a spy in the NSA, Ronald Pelton, and learn the full details of how Nikolai Artamonov had perished. He also mentioned that a KGB colleague, Oleg Gordievsky, had been recalled to Moscow recently because he was suspected of being a traitor, and described a source codenamed ROBERT as having supplied CIA secrets to the KGB. He was also able to clear up dozens of loose ends on other counter-intelligence cases and reveal the KGB's latest tradecraft, including the deliberate brushing of CIA personnel in Moscow with a radio-active spy dust to enable their movements to be monitored.

Unusually, the DCI Bill Casey met Yurchenko several times during his debriefings, entertaining him to dinner twice, and was quite unable to resist spreading the good news of the CIA's impressive coup. Yurchenko was also alarmed when he was told that he might be obliged to appear as a witness in an action brought against the United States government by Ewa Shadrin, the widow of the naval defector Nikolai

Artamonov. Yurchenko, who had been promised total discretion, was understandably dismayed by the leaks and disappointed by his treatment from his CIA Security Division handlers who had failed to show him the respect he felt he deserved, re-defected to the Soviet embassy in Washington DC and called a press conference four days later to complain that he had been abducted by the CIA and drugged.

The heavy drinking counter-intelligence expert had an exaggerated view of what was in store for him and was bitterly disappointed when he was rejected by his former girlfriend, Dr Valentina Yereskovskaya, a beautiful blonde paediatrician and the wife of the Soviet consul general in Montreal. The CIA concluded that it was highly likely that Aldrich Ames, who had been part of his debriefing team, had tipped off the KGB to Yurchenko's continuing interest in the woman with whom he had previously conducted a lengthy and passionate affair and in whom he remained besotted. Accordingly, when Yurchenko unexpectedly turned up on the doorstep or her apartment in Canada in September 1985, she had almost certainly been warned to throw him out, which is precisely what she did, protesting that she had no intention of defecting with her two daughters.

Yurchenko's ludicrous claim to have been abducted and drugged was highly reminiscent of the assertions made by the journalist Oleg Bitov who had gone unpunished after he abandoned his recent defection to England. Although Yurchenko's ploy fooled nobody in the KGB, Vladimir Kryuchkov found it expedient to accept his version of events. After his retirement from the KGB Yurchenko found work as a bank guard in Moscow.

The phenomenon of re-defection is certainly a rarity, but not entirely unknown. In 1947 Yuri Tasoev, who had been encouraged to desert by Grigori Tokaev, was delivered back to his Soviet colleagues, and in December 1955 the GRUs Ivan Ovchinnikov had much the same experience. Born in January 1929, Ovchinnokov, the son of peasants in Selo Tochilnoye, had joined the Red Army in 1944 and, in September 1949, had been posted to the Military Institute of Foreign Languages in Moscow. He later served as a military translator with the rank of lieutenant in a radio intercept regiment based in Stahnsdorf, East Germany. On the night of 4 December 1955, he crossed into the American sector of west Berlin and sought political asylum, asserting that his father had been incarcerated unjustly for thirteen years, a sentence that had killed him. He did not entirely impress his debriefers who could not reconcile his professed attachment to his wife and son, whom he had abandoned. Nevertheless, Ovchinnikov insisted he had been motivated ideologically, and supplied useful information on the

Soviet military and group of Soviet forces in Germany, GRU intercept operations and disclosed details of a KGB signal battalion in Stahnsdorf, which monitored Allied military and diplomatic wireless traffic.

In February 1957, Ovchinnikov was re-interviewed by CIA officers to whom he admitted that his defection had not been ideologically motivated, but economically. A few months later he joined Radio Liberty and began to cultivate a small circle of émigrés that appeared anti-American, anti-Masonic and anti-Semitic. His behavior led to conflict with other Radio Liberty staff in August 1958, Ovchinnikov contacted the Soviet embassy in Bonn to negotiate his repatriation. Two months later he returned to East Germany and upon arrival participated in a propaganda broadcast in which he made a public recantation, Ovchinnikov then dropped from sight, and did not reappear until 1974 when someone with the same name identified himself as editor of *Veche*, a *samizdat* magazine notorious for its anti-Semitism and nationalism, and someone who had spent a decade in the gulag for a political offence.

If Ovchinnikov did serve a term of imprisonment because of his desertion it was most likely because his crime was so egregious there was no opportunity to claim that he had been a victim of an abduction of the kind that enabled Yurchenko to avoid prosecution. It is highly likely that Yurchenko had tried to emulate Oleg Bitov's strategy. The 52-year-old deputy editor of the *Literary Gazette*, Bitov was a KGB co-optee, who defected in Italy while attending the Venice Film Festival in September 1983, only to re-defect to Moscow from London the following August. While in London he wrote a series of articles for the *Sunday Telegraph*, but, conscious of his family in Moscow, made no sensational disclosure. Initially he had explained that his defection had been prompted by his anger over the destruction of Korean Airlines flight 007 earlier in the month. He was critical of the Kremlin, visited the United States as a guest of *Reader's Digest*, but was never going to be in the big league. Without any warning, he had left his flat in East Sheen and abandoned his car, a Toyota Tercel, in Emperor's Gate, near the Soviet Embassy. He claimed at a press conference that he had been abducted by the British Security Service at gunpoint and drugged, but the reality was that he had succumbed to depression, was anxious about his 15-year-old daughter Xenia, and had been unable to complete a contract for the publication with William Morrow in New York and Hamish Hamilton in London, for his memoirs, *Tales I Could Not Tell*, which were to be ghost written by Duff Hart-Davis. After a pub lunch with his SIS handler, Bitov had driven to Kensington and presented himself at the embassy where a member of the KGB *rezidentura*, Oleg Gordievsky, would be informed of his unexpected arrival. After consultations with Moscow, Bitov was issued with a temporary passport and then flown from Heathrow to Sofia and delivered to Moscow. A month after his return Bitov attended a packed press conference at the Ministry of Foreign Affairs' press centre where a nine-page statement was distributed to journalists detailing the 'provocation' and this was followed by publication of a three-part article in the *Literary Gazette*. He was reunited with his brother, Andrei, also a well-known Soviet writer, and in March 1985 engaged in some Kremlin-sponsored propaganda by alleging that the CIA had been implicated in the attempt on the life of Pope John Paul II.

Despite knowing the truth, it seems likely that the KGB management may have found it expedient to present Bitov, who after all was never actually a KGB officer, as a survivor of Western aggression rather than acknowledge that he had simply succumbed to second thoughts. Once reestablished in Moscow, Bitov went to work on *Vek* (Century) a weekly magazine funded by the KGB.

The narrative adopted by the KGB with Bitov and Yurchenko, however improbable, was likely driven by pragmatism, but there was one other reduction that is harder to interpret, although the very unusual circumstances surrounding Yurchenko fueled speculation that he had been sent as a 'false defector' on a mission to sew disinformation and maybe divert attention away from such penetrations as Aldrich Ames, Robert Hanssen, and maybe an, as yet, undiscovered third mole.

The only plausible example of a 'dispatched defector' is Oleg Tumanov, ostensibly a seaman who swam to the Libyan shore from the destroyer *Spravedlivy* in November 1966. He was recruited as an editor for Radio Liberty's Russian broadcasts in Munich, but disappeared suddenly in February 1986, following the defection of Viktor Gundarev to the CIA in Athens. According to his autobiography, *Tumanov: Confessions of a KGB Agent*[2], which was published in 1993 he, like the rest of his family, had been a KGB professional and his unscheduled return to Moscow had brought his penetration mission to a close. However, according to Oleg Kalugin, Tumanov had been a genuine defector who had expressed remorse and disappointment in a letter addressed to a relative but intercepted by three KGB. Tumanov had been traced to Austria by the KGB and pressured into cooperating, the price he had to pay for his re-defection. Allegedly, Tumanov had joined Radio Liberty on KGB instructions, first as an analyst, before he was eventually promoted head of the Russian language service. In Kalugin's version, which occasionally contradicts Tumanov's memoirs, Tumanov recruited two other Radio Liberty employees, and in 1981 arranged for the Radio Liberty building to be moved. While Kalugin avoids mentioning Colonel Gundarev by name, he says that

> a high-ranking KGB official with knowledge of Tumanov's KGB ties defected to the West. Tumanov received a big welcome in Moscow, where the KGB portrayed him as a hero who had infiltrated and exposed that foul purveyor or anti-Communist propaganda, Radio Liberty. Our masters of deception claimed he was a KGB officer who had risked life and limb to work in the West. No mention was made of the fact that, twenty years earlier, he had defected from the USSR.[3]

Kalugin's version, that Tumanov was recruited by the KGB in Austria, long after his defection is supported by his wife, Yeta Katz, whom he had married in 1973. Born in Riga in 1957, Yeta emigrated to Israel in June 1971, and two years later moved to London where she joined the BBC World Service as a secretary working for the head of the Russian service, Anatoli Goldberg. She met Tumanov on one of his visits to London and they were married within a fortnight. He returned to his job in Munich with Radio Liberty and, having sold her flat in London, she joined him there, finding a job at the United States Army Language Training Center at Garmisch-Partenkirchen. At some point, Tumanov confided to his wife that he was a Soviet agent,

> He took the trouble to explain that he really opposes many of the injustices that occur in the Soviet Union and wanted to convince me that his escape from the ship was real. Today I am no longer sure what the truth was.[4]

Yeta continued to work at the McGraw Kaserne base until February 1986 when her husband disappeared and their apartment was raided. Sacked from her job, Yeta travelled to Berlin in 1987 at the request of her KGB handler, and was questioned by the KGB at Karlshorst, but returned to Munich where she was arrested by the German police and detained for six months while under suspicion of espionage. Under interrogation, she admitted having been recruited by the KGB in 1978, after threats had been made about her parents, who were then still living in the Soviet Union. She was convicted of passing biographical data of her language students to the Soviets and was sentenced to five years' probation. She stayed in Germany until 1991 when she moved to Tel Aviv to run a multi-lingual business consultancy. In 2008, she went to live in Moscow, reverted to the name Svetlana Tumanova and now lives in an SVR apartment, reportedly a gift from her Karlshorst interrogator, Vladimir Putin.

Appendix I

VERMEHREN INTERROGATION REPORT, MARCH 1944

While in Cairo, Vermehren was interrogated at length and over a period of two months by Security Intelligence Middle East, which cross-examined him on the structure, staff and agents managed by the Abwehr's branch in Istanbul, known as KONO. Vermehren disclosed that he had acted as a recruiter, case officer and mission planner, supervising espionage operations across the region, working alongside the Abwehr chief in Turkey, Paul Leverkühn, codenamed ALADIN, who was based in Ankara, and his KONO colleagues in Istanbul, Walther Hinz, Gottfried Schenker-Angerer and Robert Ulshofer, who collected military intelligence for Eins Heer (I/H) and Kurt Zaehringer who concentrated on naval information for Eins Marine (I/M).

By the time this report was compiled, SIME had the benefit of three further Abwehr defectors, Willi Hamburger, and Karl and Stella von Kleczowsky.

Copy No:

<u>MOST SECRET</u>

S.I.M.E. Report No. 4

Name: ERMEHREN, Erich

Nationality: German

Date of Interrogation: 11 & 12 March 1944

SPECIAL POINTS

A ABWEHR'S CONNECTION WITH DRUG SMUGGLERS

1. Vermehren states that the Abwehr in Adana and Vermehren ran all the smuggler agents in which are included of course those who smuggle drugs from Turkey into Syria. He says that Abwehr – DI in Istanbul have asked several times for drugs to be sent to them in order that they might supply smuggler agents, but it was only in August 1943 that they received a small consignment weighing one kilo of a medicinal drug somewhat similar to morphia from a Parisian firm, the name of which he does not remember. This consignment of one kilo was worth about TL 750,000 on the black market. It was duly forwarded by I/M in Istanbul to their representatives in Adana and [...] for distribution.

2. Vermehren states that by supplying smugglers with drugs Abwehr hoped to attract some people and induce them to carry out espionage missions for them in Syria in addition to their illicit traffic. He adds that it also gave Abwehr recruiting officials a good cover in that they could pose as drug merchants when dealing with prospective agents. Espionage could then be relegated to second place importance, and only later, when the agent had completed one or two tasks assume its primary role in the man's clandestine journey into Syrian territory.

    Vermehren does not think that any drug smuggling organization was used by the Germans to pay their resident agents in the Middle East.

3. TURKISH DRUG ADDICT
    During his last stay in Germany in late 1943 Vermehren was told by his chief Major KUEBART that he would in all probability be put in charge of a very valuable Turkish source on his return in duty to Istanbul. This source, he was informed, was a Turkish drug addict who had been recruited in November 1943 by [...] KUEBART's personal assistant during his visit to Istanbul. [...] had apparently known the Turk previously when he was in Turkey before the war. and on being contacted in November had agreed to act for the Germans if they kept him supplied with

drugs. Vermehren says that he was not told the man's name and did not get in touch with him in Istanbul but thinks that maybe he would have been instructed to do so had he not come over to the Allies when he did. The agent would have operated in Turkey.

C PERSONALITIES

Vermehren, on being presented with a list of sixty names (Middle Eastern nationals entering Turkey from any direction) and others, gave the following information.

(a) [...] He has already divulged details of this man under reference Report No. 1, para x)

(b) LAPIN [.......] This man made the proposal to KONO in 1942 that he would put his national organization in Syria at their disposal to supply them with military information from that quarter. He was given a large sum of money but his plan never came to anything, whereupon the Germans reduced their payments to him to a small retaining fee, which he still received to this day.

(c) Mohamed Riza GHAFFARI
Vermehren remembers seeing the above's name on a list of Abwehr I/H agents, but states that he is no longer active. And that he knows no more about him.

(d) Parvin WAHASZAIDE
Vermehren considers that the above is probably a German agent, as he has heard the name of WAHASZAIDE mentioned by either HIZ or ULSHOEFER He says they were probably referring to PARVIN who arrived in Turkey from Baghdad in 1942, rather than SULIEMAN WAHASEZAIDE who arrived from Tehran in June 1943. He would have known about the latter's recruitment by his colleagues but states that he has no knowledge of this effect. Vermehren has not heard PARVIS' cover-name 'SEITE'.

(e) Dr. Habib Dr HAHDMAZ
Vermehren knows this Indian's name as he once read part of his translation into German of the Koran. Vermehren suggested that HAMBURGER should be asked about RAHMIA.

(f) Vermehren states that he does not know Mir Hohsen KOUS-SAWSAVIAN, a Persian who arrived in Istanbul in August 1943, representing the HERMAN GOERING-WERKE: Ahmed KHAN, proprietor of the Oriental restaurant in Berlin; Hamdi KHATTIG, an Iraqi employed in propaganda broadcasting under HAHRI, editor of the Persian programme, or Rashid

QESART, Syrian in touch with the German Foreign Office and Ministry of Propaganda.

(g) <u>Mansour and Hussein QASHGAI</u>
Parvis WAHABAIE, during interrogation, had supplied information to the effect that SEILER, then German Consul-General in Istanbul, had given a banquet in honour of the two QASHGAI at the Consulate in January or February 1943, at which certainly Leverkühn and perhaps Vermehren had been present.

Vermehren remembers the occasion but states that he was not invited and that the banquet was a private affair of SEILER's and not an official function. He confirms that Leverkühn was present.

(h) <u>Graf MERAN</u>
Vermehren does not know much about this individual beyond the fact that he is an SD man and at one time was a candidate for inclusion in a special punishment company, owing to his misdeeds. A certain von GEORG apparently spent two months in such a company, in which personnel carried out severe manual duties or handled dangerous high explosives.

Vermehren says that the Kleczkowskis will know much more than he about MERAN, as he was their personal friend.

(i) <u>Organisation 'ARMEN'</u>
Vermehren has never heard of the above. He was shown a photograph of the report from a German agent in the Middle East written on fabric but stated that he had never come across anything like this during his stay in Turkey or elsewhere.

Vermehren did not recognize the names:
   (i) VARICHIAN and
   (ii) ARMAVIR
when these were put to him.

(j) <u>ROSSETTI's wife</u> (Report No. 4, para 9a)
When [Clemens] Rossetti was moved by the Abwehr from southern Italy to Athens, his wife replaced him in the post he had vacated. Vermehren says that she then left Italy for Germany before the Allies had occupied that part of Italy in which she was operating.

(k) <u>ZAMBONI</u>
Vermehren has never heard of this man.

(l) <u>MIRZA KHAN</u>
He has heard of the above and states that he works for ZAEHRINGER Abwehr I/M and is either a Northern Persian or Southern Russian by nationality.

(m) Persian Agent to INDIA
Vermehren states that this agent of [Robert] HINZ (Abwehr I/H) was sent on an espionage mission either early or in the spring of 1943. He traveled [sic] from Turkey to the Indian border, but Vermehren does not know the exact route taken by the agent. At all events, he finally landed up in Southern Persia and approached the Persian (Baluchistan) frontier which he crossed on hearing that there was a large aerodrome nearby in Indian territory. He reached the aerodrome where he was arrested by the local security authorities, roughly handled, and imprisoned by them for two weeks. After which he was released and shipped back into Persia. The agent then made his way to Turkey where he delivered his report on the aerodrome and Persia to the Germans.

(n) KAVAS of the Egyptian Consulate in Istanbul
Vermehren had a contact with this man (see Report No. 4, para 7) and tried unsuccessfully to get hold of secret letters through him.

(o) The DANIELSONS
Vermehren says that he knew the two brothers socially, as his father had been their lawyer, but that as far as he knows they did not work for KONO.

(p) THIRK
ULSHOFER lived in a flat owned by Madame THIRK and Vermehren says that ULSHOFER may have been known to some people as Monsieur THIRK.

(q) HALDUN (Report No. 4, para 11)
The contract with HALDUN was made by one of 'ALADIN's' men. KONO signaled to Berlin the terms of his offer and Vermehren heard that it had been turned down, although he did not see a signal from Berlin to that effect.

(r) Nicolas GALETI Sub-editor of 'BRITANOVA'
Vermehren does not recognize the above's name and added that in all probability KONO had no connections with BRITANOVA. He excepted Abwehr III from this however, whose agents he does not know.

(s) Graf Von MOLTKE
Concerning the above, Vermehren states that he is a well-known international lawyer at present attached to the legal branch of the OKW. His two visits to Istanbul, in July and December 1943 were made in connection with the Danube shipping problem, which was causing the gravest concern to the OKW, the German

Transport Ministry and Foreign Office. Von MOLTKE reviewed the situation and gave advice on the matter. Vermehren also says that he originated a scheme to seize ships formerly owned by countries under Axis control and now flying the British flag in neutral waters, to counteract the seizure of Axis shipping in Allied ports by the British.

On his first visit to Turkey in July Von MOLTKE stayed at Burgas with Dr WILLBRANDT, who is a German emigrant, a very reliable and capable type, very anti-Nazi and likely to return to Germany at the earliest opportunity to fight National Socialism.

On the second occasion in December, he stayed with Leverkühn who, according to Vermehren, esteemed him highly and called him a lever lawyer. and a very honest man with which latter remark Vermehren agrees.

Vermehren gathered from conversation with Von MOLTKE that he was anti-Nazi and thinks that he probably belongs to the anti-Nazi movement in Germany. He supported his opinion by saying that Dr WENGLER, the latter's personal assistant is an ardent and outspoken anti-Nazi. WENGLER accompanied his chief to Turkey in July and paid a second visit alone later in the autumn.

(t) VON TROTT ZU SOLZ

Vermehren states that the above, whose Christian name is Adam, was a Rhodes Scholar and has lived some time in both China and America. He is strongly opposed to the Nazi Government, but politically ambitious and at the moment holds the appointment of personal assistant to head of the Indian Department of the German Foreign Office. This department is interested in information of a military and political nature obtained on India through diplomatic channels, e.g. through the Afghans. It is also concerned with propaganda to India.

During his visit to Turkey in June 1943, VON TROTT ZU SOLZ stayed with Leverkuehn [Leverkühn], with whom he had been working before the war, for part of the time. Leverkuehn [Leverkühn] wanted him to be attached to the German Embassy in Turkey as Secretary, dealing with American and Allied policy. The Foreign Office would not release him however and Gesandter [Erich] WINDELS, last German minister to Canada, was given this post. It was thought that WINDELS would have gained some knowledge of USA policy while holding his appointment in Canada.

Vermehren states that 'ADAM' is anti-Nazi and very probably connected with an anti-Nazi movement in Germany. It is also probable that this movement includes amongst its members, General [Franz] HALDER, who Vermehren considers to be a most valuable man for post-war Germany. Vermehren says that no-one knows where HALDER is at the moment. Vermehren gives 'ADAM' the highest recommendation, adding that he will not do the same as he has done and come to the Allies, as he considers himself too valuable to the opposition in Germany itself.

'ADAM' has an elder brother and a younger brother names JOACHIM. Vermehren knows them both and has a high opinion of them. The eldest, before the war, worked as a workman in a Berlin suburb to study working class conditions and feeling. During the war he became a Welfare Officer (before Vermehren's time) but was eventually transferred to the Russian front on account of his anti-Nazi views. Vermehren last heard of him in Germany where he was recovering from a wound received in battle. He has been converted to Roman Catholicism

Vermehren states that JOACHIM, the youngest brother, is now in Holland as a lieutenant in command of a company of Free Indians, He has also been converted to Roman Catholicism. Vermehren says that 'ADAM' is well on the way to embrace the same faith.

All the VON TROTT ZU SOLZ brothers are in touch with an anti-Nazi German author named ERNST JUNGER.

NB. In regard to the above information concerning VON MOLTKE, and the VON TROTT ZU SOLZ brothers in sub paras (n) and (t), it is Vermehren's wish that it should be handled with the utmost discretion in order to avoid harm coming to those whom he mentions at the hands of the Nazis.

(u) MRALAREN OYSU (Report No. 1, para 12i)
Vermehren states that the above had not been told of his proposed employment as courier between Baghdad and Istanbul in the spy-ring organized for Iraq and Iran by him (Report No. 1, para 12h and i). He said he knew of OYSU's willingness to work, as he had already consented to smuggle things through to Syrian and Iraq for the *several* people.

Vermehren does not think that OYSU was involved in the reported smuggling and espionage organizations in which a 'MAHMOUD' in Istanbul sent letters to Mohamed FARAH and his associate HAGOP GULBENKIAN in Aleppo. Vermehren does not know these two last-named individuals. But has something to say on the subject of 'MAHMOUD' in Istanbul.

(v) Mahmoud Al ANGERER
HASSAM SIRRY (see Report No. 2, para 3c; Report No. 3, paras 2, 3b, 12, 19c(ii)) told Vermehren that he had heard from his

friend YALINTIRK (Report No. 3, para 2) that an ABUBAKR in Istanbul had been receiving letters written in the style of a mother addressing her son and apparently concerning life on a farm in Syria. The contents of the letters were suspicious in that they contained many figures, disguised for example in this manner: 'Our sow has had so many piglets and our hen has laid so many eggs in the past week.' Vermehren thinks that the ABUBAKKR in question may be Mahmoud Al BUBAKR, and he may also be identical with the MAHMOUD in para 3.

(w) <u>SABRI KIPEL</u>

Vermehren says that he had the above on his list as a prospective agent but had never actually contacted him. He hoped that HASSAN SYRRY would be able to investigate the possibilities of using this man.

Vermehren states that KIPEL has not worked for KONO.

4. Vermehren volunteered the following names and produced the following information on them:

(a) <u>ALI SHINAS</u>

The above is one of HINZ's agents. Vermehren knows nothing at all about him.

(b) <u>ABDUL KERIM</u>

This man is either HINZ's or ULSHOFER's agent. Vermehren does not know anything else concerning him.

(c) <u>MARSHANI</u>

The above is a Circassian living in Istanbul employed by Abwehr I/H for a long time, at least since 1942, as a recruiting agent. Vermehren states that he was an unsuccessful one, however and is an irresponsible type who, by failing to keep an appointment would ruin the prospects of recruiting a good agent. MARSHANI is a paper or cotton merchant by trade.

Vermehren states that he trained this man for an espionage mission to Egypt and the preparations for his journey were almost complete when Vermehren came over to the Allies. MARSHANI was to report on military matters in secret writing and would have been given matches. He was also instructed to recruit resident German agents and amongst Circassians in Cairo and Alexandria.

(d) <u>SICHERHEITSDIENST AGENTS</u>

5. Vermehren states that AHMED SAABRY (REPORT No. 2, para 4a) was a paid SD agent,

6. The remainder of the Germanophile clique (reference Report No. 2, paras 3–5). That is, ABUBAKR, HASSAN SIRRY, HASSAN AL FENDRE and Prince MANSOUR DAOUD before he went over to the Italians, were all Abwehr agents but nevertheless interested in FAST of the SD who could possibly provide them with a political future. Vermehren says that Prince DOUAD of the above clique was a paid Abwehr I/H agent although he too knew FAST.

E GERMAN W/T AGENTS

Vermehren was asked whether a German W/T agent before being sent on a mission to the Middle East was given a 'pep talk' by hid instructor saying that he would soon be a link in a large German W/T network supplying information to the Germans from all quarters of that territory.

Vermehren replied that although he did not know from personal experience what happened, he imagined that the agent would be given an underrated rather than exaggerated version of the extent of German W/T activities in the Middle East.

F KONO'S RELATIONS WITH REPRESENTATIVES OF COUNTRIES OTHER THAN TURKEY

7. Vermehren states that he knows of no contacts between KONO and: The Hungarians; the Romanians; the Spaniards; the French.

8. With regard to the Italians, he says that HINZ exchanged military information with Lt. ANDORA. He had no Italian contacts himself and knows of none with Abwehr other than those he has already given (Report No. 4, para 8).

9. Vermehren states that Leverkuehn [Leverkühn] encouraged political interaction with the Japanese Press Attaché AOKI, mainly about America.

10. As far as the Russians are concerned, HAMBURGER told Vermehren of a White Russian agent. Vermehren cannot remember his name but thins he was a special envoy of General WRANGEL. He knows where he lives because HAMBURGER drew him the following plan:

11. (a) Regarding the Afghans, Vermehren says he asked Leverkuehn [Leverkühn] if he could approach the Afghan Minister in Ankara. Leverkuehn [Leverkühn] replied that he was already looked after by the SD.
    (b) The elder HAMATA has a cordial contact with his Afghan Minister.

(c) Vermehren says that a few days before he left Turkey, ULSHOFER went to Ankara to try and recruit Afghan agents.

12. The only contact with Iraqis known to Vermehren is SCHENKE-ANGERER with the Iraqi Consulate (see Report No. 3, para 16b(ii))

G GERMAN PENETRATION OF THE BRITISH INTELLIGENCE SERVICE

13. Vermehren states that he has already given all the information he could about German penetration of the British organizations in Turkey to another officer. He was therefore questioned no further on this matter.

E GERMAN PENETRATION OF THE AMERICAN O.N.I.

14. YOLLAND, Elmer (?) American Report No. 1, para 12e)
The above is about 33 years of age and was originally teacher at the American College in Istanbul, but attached to the ONI and the American Consulate General as a political commentator. He was a friend of LEHMANN, former head of ONI and became a great friend of Georg STREITER, correspondent of the *Berliner Borsenzeitung*, who took over the editing of the paper *Boyoglu* after the Italian collapse. He was an SD man.

15. Vermehren described Yolland as very queer, an egoist, well-informed and 'brainy'. He had been in Germany before the [Second World] war and was an idealist who wanted to end the war and start an era of the common man. To this end he began in April 1943 to visit STREITER's house almost every night to give him information about American opinion, what the American Consulate and Colony in Istanbul were thinking and what German propaganda would suit the American public. He also gave information about Anglo-American quarrels in the Middle East and asked for German books and press material in return. Vermehren often saw him at Streiter's house and listened to him sometimes for hours at a time discussing how he could get visas to visit Hungary, where his family were. His father had been a professor for 15 years. Once only did he give military information; He told Vermehren one night that that morning a very high British intelligence officer had visited the ONI and asked for maps of Sofia, Budapest, Vienna and Stuttgart, apparently for bombing purposes,

16. In August 1943 the ONI staff was out down, [Harold] LEHRMANN was sent home and Yolland lost his job there. STREITER then asked KONO to take him over and KONO

began to pay him TL 200.a month. Vermehren received his information for three weeks; then HOEBKE, KONO's driver, who spoke excellent English and had little to do, saw Yolland daily. Yolland's information was all passed to WINDELS (the last German Minister to Canada) who had come to Istanbul to start an Embassy Information Department. KONO reported that this information was getting less but might improve and should be kept going, as WINDELS liked it.

Vermehren believes that Yolland was paid latterly by the German Embassy and no longer by KONO.

Sometime in or after August 1943 HAMBURGER told Vermehren that Yolland had been discovered by the Americans to be working for the Germans, but the Americans, though they were ashamed of his treachery and tried to 'cut' him, still employed him. HAMBURGER would know more of what the Americans thought of Yolland.

Yolland knew DIZLINGER of the SD. But Vermehren does not know whether he gave DIZINGER information.

17. ALADIN had his own man in the ONI but not very highly placed. Neither this agent nor ALADIN had much respect for the ONI.

I   THE FADL CASE (Report No. 1, para 12g; Report No. 2, paras 11g & r)

18. The following is a summary of information in the above case obtained from Vermehren by Captain [Desmond] Doran of SIME on 4th March 1944.

Once SHAHAB made his original approach to the German Embassy in Istanbul in 1940 or 1941 requesting to be sent to Germany for propaganda work. The offer was turned down by the German Foreign Office, who arranged that he should be put in touch with the SD.

In the summer of 1942, the Abwehr in Istanbul borrowed SHAHAB for sending to Egypt to put into operation a W/T set controlled by Father DEMETRIUS.

On SHAHAB's arrival in Cairo however, he was unable to obtain the W/T set. As a result of information s0upplied to him by the SD, he contacted MOHSEN FADL an SD. agent and AZIZ FADL, and arranged for the operation of a W/T link.

MOHSEN FADL had been recruited and despatched to Egypt by Graf Meran of the SD.

After SHABAS had returned to Turkey Prince MANSOUR DAOUD's mother-in-law was sent to Egypt with instructions and secret ink for the FADLs.

In November 1942 HASSAIN SIRRY was sent with money, a code, instructions in secret writing and perhaps white-headed matches for the FADLs. He was to deliver these through Prince MANSOUR's mother-ln-law who was still in Egypt.

In February 1843 MAHMOUD MAHI SIRRY was dispatched to Egypt to deliver a secret ink letter and EP 500 to be paid in installments on receipt of instructions from Turkey depending on the efficiency of their work to the FADLs. SIRRY was also to carry out an espionage mission of his own, supplying military and shipping information from Alexandria.

19. H1LMI BEY

After being informed during Captain Doran's interrogation that a certain HILMI had at one time contacted the FADLs in Egypt, Vermehren now expresses the opinion that the HILMI who works as Vice Consul in the Egyptian Consulate at Istanbul is probably identical with this man. He says however that he never sent HILMI BEY to Egypt and that, if the FADLs were indeed approached in this manner, it must in all likelihood have been the SD who had given HILMI his instructions He also considered it probable that AHMET SALABRY recommended this man as an agent to the SD. Some indication of HILMI's activities for the SD were given by the fact that he told the Abwehr after he had contacted them in Paris that he had a message from Egypt for them but had destroyed it. Vermehren adds that HILMMI BEY is a specialist in money transactions on the black market. Vermehren was asked whether he agreed with the assumption that it was HILMI BEY who had informed FAST of the SD of HILMI's arrest by the British in 1943, after which FAST gave the news to him. (see Report No. 3, para 15b. Vermehren admitted that HILMI possibly had heard through the diplomatic courier and had been FAST's source, but pointed out that if this assumption was adopted it would mean that the SD had possessed a sure channel through whom they could also arrange to pay their resident agents in Egypt or elsewhere. Vermehren imparted however, that the SD experienced the same difficulties as the Abwehr in remunerating such agents. Indicated that the odds were that HILMI had been FAST's source or not.

20. <u>MANSOUR FADL</u>

Vermehren states that the above was an agent of the SD when he arrived in Egypt in 1941. MANSOUR FADL. He does not think he was a paid agent however, owing to the difficulties in establishing communications between a resident agent in the Middle East and the Abwehr or SD in Turkey. Vermehren added that as [Erwin] Rommel was expected to occupy Egypt at that time, many agents would have to be rewarded by the Germans in the political field.

It appears that the Paris names were given to Prince GAMAS by the SD in Turkey for use in an emergency when no other suitable bodies could be found by the Abwehr.

21. <u>COF IN CAIRO (see Report No. 1, para 12)</u>
Vermehren says that this man's [...]. The Abwehr had devised a plan whereby [...] was to travel to Egypt in October or November 1942, contact the FADLs and give them a photograph of [...] who was also known to [...] would then have got in touch with the last named and instructed him to pay 31,000 to the person. I assume destroyed the photograph before entering Syria or else the Abwehr gave up the plan and nothing ever came of it.

22. <u>OTHER MEN TO HAVE BEEN CONTACTED BY PRINCE SHAHAB (Report No. 1, para 12)</u>
Vermehren previously referred to another Egyptian who was to be contacted by SHAHAB in addition to Father DEMETRIOUS. Vermehren was asked for more details but could only say that an elderly Egyptian aristocrat, prominent politically, who was to have supplied the information which would have been communicated to the Germans by some of DEMETRIOUS's W/T sets. When SHAHAB arrived, he found that this man had been arrested and interned with the priest.

23. <u>COMMENTS AND RECOMMENDATIONS</u>
Vermehren has probably given most of the important information in his possession but his capacity to recollect odd facts which may be important is not yet exhausted. He should therefore remain available for the submission of further names and queries which may occur in investigating German intelligence activities against the Middle East.

SIME
J.F.E Stephenson, Captain
19 March 1944
H.F.M. Eadie, Captain

Appendix II

MI5 STUDY OF SOVIET DEFECTORS, 1948

A STUDY OF DEFECTORS FROM THE USSR

The object of this paper is to draw certain general conclusions about the subject of defection. For this purpose, the records available to us of Russian defectors have been studied. It is often dangerous to deduce generalities from the study of particular cases, but in our opinion common factors do emerge clearly from the stories of the defectors.

For the purpose of this paper a defector is assumed to be one who abandons the Russian service and who offers the information in his possession to a foreign power.

The cases of the following Russian defectors have been studied:

	Defected
Eugene PIK	1927
Grigori BESSEDOVSKI	1929
George AGABEKOV	1930
Walter KRIVITSKY	1937
Alexandre BARMIN	1937
Leon HELFAND	1940
Ismail AKHMEDOV	1942
Victor KRAVCHENKO	1944
Igor GOUZENKO	1945
Constantin VOLKOV	1945
Kiril ALEXEEV	1946
Michel KORIAKOFF	1946
YURCHENKO	1946
Mikhail DENISOV	1946
Vera TAKACS	1946

Andre JURACHOW	1947
Alesander KRAVCHENKO	1947
'S'	1947
Vasili SHARANDAK	1947
Grigori TOKAEV	1947

It will be seen from the above list that the period of time covered is twenty years, 1927 to 1947. We must point out that we are unable to say definitely that all important cases of defectors have been studied by us. For example, in 1931 according to newspaper reports of the time, the defector BESSEDOVSKI had founded in Paris an 'Association of Non-Returners' or defectors' club of which the membership was said to be about one hundred. We have no information about these men nor do we even know if they ever existed.

The summaries of information about all the defectors listed above, with the exception of JURACHOW and 'S', can be found in the Appendix to this paper.

It may at first appear that twenty cases in twenty years is a small number. In this connection it should be remembered that for many years the frontiers of Russia have been virtually sealed, and nobody has been allowed to leave the country until a careful investigation has been conducted into his political reliability. All the defectors studied were serving abroad at the time of their defection, Furthermore, within the USSR and Soviet citizens abroad, so rigid a watch is maintained upon each individual that the majority of those who are at all discontented with the regime are almost certain to be arrested or recalled to Russia before they have a chance of developing into even potential defectors.

II REASONS FOR DEFECTION

The examination of a defector's reasons for his action is by no means a simple matter. It will usually reveal however an immediate cause such as his having been recalled to Russia from his post abroad shortly before he defected. Further scrutiny of his case shows in many instances a more deep-seated reason, often of long standing. These long-term reasons are in some instances caused by disillusionment with the increasing discrepancy between the Stalinist regime in Russia and the original conception of the USSR or by a realisation of the contrast between life at home and life in a democratic country. Such a disaffected state of mind may lead to the thought but not always to the action of defection, and if it should become known to the Soviet authorities it may be the cause of the recall to Russia which impels a man to take the decisive step. Not all defectors have latent feelings of disaffection, though nearly all, however strong their desire to break with the Soviet system, receive some outside stimulus before they defect.

It is often said in disparagement of defectors from the Russian Service and their motives that as they are already under sentence of recall fear is the true reason for their action. Should their recall be due to their having fallen under suspicion because of their dissident views or because of some breach of discipline, the best they could expect on their return to Russia would be disgrace or imprisonment; execution or exile to Siberia would be the more likely fate. We do not consider however that the existence of an immediate cause of defection should necessarily be regarded as a reflection upon the validity of the long-term reasons described below, a Russian who openly breaks with his Government not only exposes himself to mortal danger – TROTSKY, AGABEKOV, Ignace REISS, KRIVITSKY and probably VOLKOV paid with their lives – but may also suffer throughout his future life from misgivings as to whether in breaking with his Government he has not also been a traitor to his country. A Russian with a real love of Russia must feel that in defecting from his Government he renounces his country forever, and in order to do this the requirement of an outside stimulus to push him over the brink is understandable; also any defector who has left members of his family behind him in Russia must realise that his defection places them in danger.

BESSED0VSKY, KRIVITSKY, BARMIN, HELFAND, AKHMEDOV, GOUZENKO, ALEXEEV, KORIAKOV and TOKAEV are known to have been recalled to Russia immediately before they defected, making nine out of a total of twenty.

Our records of some of the others are not complete, and it may well be that the number of those recalled is even larger.

The very nature of the USSR as a totalitarian police state holding rigid ideological and economic tenets from which no divergence is tolerated is bound to foster dissatisfaction among those who must suffer from its implementation. From about 1923, the year of the second Soviet constitution, the ideological split between Stalin and Trotsky became increasingly marked until it culminated in 1929 with Trotsky's banishment from the USSR. In 1937 with the great purge of the Red Army and the Intelligence Service directed against so-called Trotskyist elements it became clear that nobody whose views were suspect or whose abilities, real or imaginary, offered a threat to the Soviet system, would be spared. Thirty-five thousand Red Army officers were purged at this time. Walter KRIVITSKY and Ignace REISS who expected to be affected by the purge fled from the Soviet Intelligence Service as a result of this KRIVTTSKY to become a defector but REISS to meet his end at the hands of Soviet assassins in Switzerland. BARMIN who defected in the same year said that the recent Moscow trials had filled him with horror. HELFAND, who broke with the Soviet in 1940, said in the letter which he wrote to Molotov at the time that the old revolutionary pioneers to whom he claimed to belong had been liquidated in every sense of the word. The Russo-German pact of 1939 had further disillusioned him; he felt that the Stalinist Government no longer stood for the aims to which he had devoted his life. TOKAEV, the most recent defector, also expresses strong dissatisfaction with the regime. He defected just in time to avoid arrest.

TOKAEV further states that there are many people with his views in the USSR and that conspiratorial groups exist to some extent. Though we have not enough evidence to confirm this there are signs that a purge is in progress and sudden recalls of Russians from Germany are fairly frequent. If the Soviet Security efforts are not completely successful, therefore, we may hope to receive other defectors of this type and should expect some of them to be of considerable importance.

In addition to the purges and repressive measures described above, resulting in the complete lack of freedom of the individual, the economic difficulties of the USSR have necessitated harsh measures which have affected successive classes of the population and have kept the standard of living of the majority of the people exceptionally low. Such measures as the collectivisation of farms have caused misery and suffering for the entire peasant class. As a result, to avoid general discontent, Soviet propaganda has painted an entirely false picture of Western Democracy and the position of the worker. Both Victor KRAVCHENKO and GOUZENKO, who defected on their first visit to a foreign country, have emphasised their amazement on discovering the contrast between the Western Democracies as they are and the account given of them by Soviet propaganda and between the standard of living at home and abroad. GOUZENKO has expressed this attitude of mind admirably in his statement before the Royal Commission, which is given in full in the Appendix.

TOKAEV has also said that while in Berlin, where he got to know the British, American, French and other Western Europeans, he realised the utter falseness of Russian propaganda. This realisation seems to have seen the initial factor in shaking the faith in the Soviet system of those Russians who were paying their first visit to a foreign country.

AGABEKOV and TAKACS and DENISOV defected because the exigencies of Russian service interfered with the course of their love affairs. AGABEKOV had fallen in love with an English girl, and for her sake he abandoned his post and openly broke with the Soviet Government. TAKACS and DENISOV, both of whom worked for the Russian Intelligence Service, were refused permission to many, and finally when they were even forbidden to meet they decided to defect together. In addition, SIIARANDAK, who was not anxious to return to Russia as he was able to enjoy a much more comfortable life in Hungary, was confirmed in his desire to desert by the fact that he had fallen in love with a Hungarian girl whom he wished to many.

It is interesting to note that in not one of these cases have we any evidence that the defectors had been recalled to Moscow or otherwise threatened in any way.

Our information about KORIAKOV is scanty, but we have been told that he had been planning for some time to abandon his post owing to his religious convictions. He escaped from the Russian Embassy in Paris in 1946 after he had been recalled to the USSR.

III METHODS OF DEFECTION

After he has made up his mind to defect, the defector is faced with the very difficult problem of how best to carry out his intention. Seven of the defectors studied have chosen countries other than the one where they were employed for their action, as they presumably thought that they could thus reduce the risk. Only one minor character successfully carried out his intention of defecting to the British. Three others attempted to do so, but one was recalled to Moscow before negotiations were completed and the other two were handed over to the Americans. TOKAEV, who chose the Canadians, in fact found himself in British hands. Four defectors therefore chose the British, of whom only one was handled by us; we 'know of no defections in British territory.' The comparative unwillingness of defectors to approach the British may be explained by the fact, pointed out by SHARANDAK and TOKAEV, that there is a general impression among Russians, fostered by Soviet propaganda, that the British hand back defectors. This depression may have been confirmed by the Russian interpretation of the Yalta Agreement.

TOKAEV, who chose the Canadians in Berlin as the recipients of his defection, has given his reason for doing so as follows:- firstly, he is violently opposed to the Potsdam Agreement; secondly, he had heard that the British hand defectors back; thirdly, he was opposed to the 'materialistic' outlook of the Americans; fourthly, among the French there are 'too many people like Thorez and Duclos'. He therefore chose the Canadians as being ideologically closest to the British and as not having been signatories of the Potsdam Agreement.

Of the remaining defectors, six defected in Paris, three in America, three in Germany, two m Austria, two in Czechoslovakia, one in Canada and one in China.

Having selected the recipient and the locality most suited to his purpose, a defector, in most cases already under surveillance, must first succeed in eluding watchers; secondly, he has the by no means easy task of persuading someone to accept and protect him. and of convincing then that his story is a true one. He is not often [sic] able to plan his action long enough in advance and must therefore trust to luck as to whether he will be well received.

As a rule a defector does not know whom he should best approach, which makes his task difficult. Five men defected in France, and were helped in their initial approaches to the French Government by the White Russian colony in Paris; ALEXEEV in America was also assisted in establishing himself by a White Russian organization; AKHMEDOV throw himself on the mercy of the Turks, Victor KRAVCHENKO and GOUZENKO both decided to approach the American and the Canadian Press respectively with their stories. They were not as successful as they had hoped they would be; KRAVCIIENKO had to tell the newspapers far more than he had intended to do before they would take any interest in him, and GOUZENKO had no success at all with the Canadian newspapers he approached.

VOLKOV approached the British Embassy in Istanbul with a

sensational catalogue of information which he proposed to provide in return for protection and remuneration. He was however recalled to Moscow before a decision was made about him **TAKACS** and DENISOV offered themselves to a British representative in Prague who arranged for their handling by the Americans.

Since the end of the war the majority of defections, as would be expected, have taken place in the field. The defector's task is a much easier one under such conditions. His problem consists not so much in finding anyone to accept him, but simply in reaching territory where he can make contact with Western Forces, and once he has reached such territory the risk of his being assassinated or arrested before he can carry out his intention is small.

GOUZENKO and Alexander KRAVCIIENKO share the distinction of being the only two defectors known to have made careful preparations to bring with them info mat ion and documents of value to offer to their protectors. During the last few weeks before his departure from the Russian Embassy in Ottawa, after he had made up his mind to defect, GOUZENKO selected a number of documents from the files which he took: with him when he left.

Alexander KRAVCHENKO deferred his defection for some months so that he might have an opportunity to obtain more information about Russian Intelligence Service activities to give to the Americans as a proof of good faith.

IV RECEPTION

From the defector's point of view, it is clearly desirable that he should be received into protective custody as soon as he raises his approach, otherwise he runs the risk of being removed or liquidated in the interval which may elapse between his first contact with foreign representatives and the couplet eon of negotiations. Disadvantages to the recipients in accepting a defector at face value certainly exist, and in particular a

British Liaison abroad, such as the Embassy at Istanbul approached by VOLKOV, rarely has the machinery necessary to cope with immediate acceptance and evacuation. In VOLKOV's case the delay which was necessary before a decision could be reached proved too long and the opportunity was missed. Although the British representative in Prague was not able to handle the evacuation of TAKACS and DENISOV he could and did put then in touch with the Americans who, as their zone of Germany borders upon Czechoslovakia, were able to make the necessary arrangements,

J'ield conditions would seem to be the most satisfactory for the reception of defection. Facilities are usually available for evacuation if necessary, and the keeping of a defector under close control until his story has been checked and the avoidance of political repercussions through premature publicity are also far easier to arrange in the field.

In GOUZENKO's case we have an interesting example of the reaction of the public to a defection. After the difficulties he encountered from the Press and Canadian Government Departments, he was forced when his situation became desperate to turn to ordinary Canadian citizens who were his neighbours. They accepted his story, gave him shelter from his pursuers and then sent for the police to whom he was at last able to give his information.

Reception arrangements must of necessity depend upon political expediency, the expectation of a worthwhile return in valuable information, and upon facilities available to the recipient; but it is clear that while delay in acceptance nay not necessarily be fatal, an expeditious decision is certainly desirable.

V REACTION OF THE SOVIET AUTHORITIES

The attempt made by the Soviet authorities to repair or counteract the harm which a defector may do is usually rapid and forceful. To this end, kidnapping and assassination were frequently used expedients in the early days, There the physical recovery of the defector dead or alive has proved impracticable, some form of defamation of character is the most common alternative. This may serve several purposes – as an effort to retrieve the defector, as in the attempts made to use the accusations of stealing brought against GOUZENKO and ALEXEEV as a reason to demand that they be handed over to bade to the Soviet authorities, and as a means of discrediting him personally both in the eyes of his protectors and of the Russian people. The TAKACS and DENISOV case shows an interesting development of this discrediting technique in which an attempt was made by means of a planted document to persuade the British that they had simulated defection on the instruction of the Russian or Hungarian Intelligence Service.

TOKAEV was asked what measures the Russians would be likely to take to prevent defection. He said that the authorities would never allow the public to know that there were people who would be willing to cross the frontier, consequently nothing would be done to oppose it openly. As already explained, however, constant vigilance is maintained with a view to preventing the possibility of defection, and it is one of the tasks of the Russian Intelligence Service to keep an ever-open eye on such matters.

VI SUBSEQUENT HISTORY OF DEFECTORS

It is hardly necessary to point out that the solution to a defector's future can never be an easy one. He cannot feel that he is safe from the fear of assassination, and security precautions to avoid murder are hardly compatible with a normal working life. To avoid the dangers which threaten him he is forced to use such expedients as the adoption of a false name and a life of strict seclusion. He is also faced with the necessity of making a living for himself and his family; this is not an easy matter. Those responsible for his disposal must consider the fact that if he is not adequately protected the fate which may befall him will discourage those who might have followed his example. If he is left with no resources he presents a security risk.

The stories given in the Appendix will show the various attempts to solve this problem. It is not surprising that a number of defectors have found the most satisfactory solution to their material difficulties in the writing of their memoirs, either as articles for the Press or as books. PIK, BESSEDOVSKY, AGABEKOV, BARMIN, KRIV1TSKY, Victor KRAVCHENKO, GOUZENKO and KORIAKOFF have all taken this course.

VII INFORMATION PROVIDED BY DEFECTORS

Of the twenty defectors who form the subject of this paper, eleven can be said to have been reasonably fully exploited from our point of view. These are AGABEKOV, KRIVITSKY, AKKMEDOV, Victor KRAVCHENKO, GOUZENKO, ALEXEEV, DENISOV, TAKACS, Alexander KRAVCHENKO, 'S' and TOKAEV. Of the remaining nine, PIK was regarded as an unsatisfactory and dishonest informant; BES5EDOVSKY's newspaper articles were of some use to us and it is not thought that he possessed much additional information of interest to an Intelligence Service.

BARMIN's information was never seen by us. In view of the fact that he had been engaged in Intelligence work from 1919 this seems unfortunate. HELFAND was seen by British representatives at various times since his defection and has produced a good deal of valuable information about Russian Intelligence activities. Constantin VOLKOV was of course only able to offer a tempting catalogue; in the case of KORIAKOV and YURCHENKO we have seen no product.

In the eleven exploited cases we do not think that there can be any doubt that the dividend was a very valuable one. Even where it was more of historical than current interest it has been of the greatest assistance in giving us a picture of the development of the Russian Intelligence Service and the Soviet regime, AGABEKOV, KRIVITSKY, AKHMEDOV, GOUZENKO, DENISOV, TAKACS, Alexander KRAVCHENKO, SHARANDAK and 'S' were all in a position to know at first-hand about the particular sections of the Russian Intelligence Service in which they worked, and in several cases had a far wider knowledge. The more spectacular results of information provided by KRIVITSKY and GOUZENKO were the trial and sentence of a Foreign Office cypher clerk for espionage on behalf of the Russians and the breaking up of a Russian Intelligence Service network in Canada. Twenty persons, one of them a Canadian Member of Parliament and many holding positions in connection with Canadian administration and atomic research, were tried for supplying; information to a foreign power, and GOUZENKO's evidence also led to the trial and conviction in this country of Dr Allan Nunn MAY.

AGABEKOV and AKHMEDOV provided information on Russian activities in the Middle East and Turkey and the latter has recently given information which even after six years this led to a spy ring which recently came into operation in the Western Hemisphere; DENISOV, TAKACS and SHARANDAK on Hungary, and Alexander KRAVCHENKO and 'S' on Germany. TOKAEV, as a high-ranking aircraft expert, is in a position to provide both technical information and accounts of the intentions and methods of the Politburo.

There are inherent dangers in the acceptance of information from defectors, particularly where the information cannot be checked and is not supported by documents. There is a great temptation for a defector both to over-state his own position and to embroider and colour his facts to suit himself, but not as many defectors as would be expected seen to have succumbed to this temptation. There is also a temptation for the subsequent users of the information to be too much impressed by it and to regard later material which may reach then from a different source as incorrect because it does not coincide with the defector's story.

In spite of these and other drawbacks, there is no doubt that the defectors whose cases form the material for this study have provided information of enormous value to us. They have been, in fact, a major if not the chief source of our knowledge of the Russian Intelligence Service, and in the absence of other sources they are likely to be so for some time to come.

VIII THE FALSE DEFECTOR

Those responsible for handling defectors have generally, we think, adequately borne in mind the dangers of an agent being planted in this guise. It has been pointed out that the 'arranged defection' of a Russian official fortified with a quantity of true information and documents might be accompanied by a story of sympathisers still in the Diplomatic and Intelligence Services of the USSR. The country which gives such a defector shelter might be touted to use him not only as a short-term source of information but also as a long-term agent, and the latter case might provide a penetration opening for the Russian Intelligence Service. Also, a skilled Russian agent posing as a defector would be likely in the course of his interrogation to learn a good deal about the methods, targets and personalities of the Intelligence Service handling him, and the knowledge already in its possession.

We know of no proven case of the acceptance of a defector who later proved to be false and in the lack of any information about an operation of this nature it is not possible to say how it would be organised or to estimate the likelihood of its success. Recently there was a suspicion that an attempt was being made to introduce to us a false defector, but we have few details and cannot comment upon the story.

Clearly precautions should be taken in each case, including a careful check of the defector's story against all other sources. It is felt that the risk of a false defector being undetected or, if undetected, of his do in; any serious donation can be made very small by proper handling. In our opinion the existence of such risks should not unduly influence us against receiving a defector since we stand to gain much more than we may lose with him.

IX TREATMENT OF DEFECTORS

It seems clear to us from all the cases we have studied that the quality of the information provided by a defector, and consequently the advantage to be gained from him, is to a large degree affected by the way in which he is handled. The Security Service, however, has had very few direct dealings with any of the defectors whose cases have been studied and has therefore practically no first-hand experience of handling them. Defectors are a vital source of information and as sources of information they present a unique psychological problem. Only if considerable attention is given to the psychological aspects of each case can a defector acquire that feeling of trust in his interrogator which is of such assistance in the future conduct of the operation.

It should be remembered that almost any man who has defected, whatever nay have been his reasons for doing so, has been through a period of intense and often prolonged nervous strain. There is bound to be a reaction after the defection has been successfully completed and for some time such a man is likely to be in an abnormal state of mind, Some defectors have abandoned the service of their country and come to us because of a genuine conviction that loyalty to the Stalinist Government is no longer compatible with the best interests of Russia and the world. With such men, every effort should be made to confirm in them the feeling that in giving us all the information in their possession they are actively attacking the Stalinist regime and furthering the interests of their countrymen. They are bound to suffer from doubt and recrimination as to whether they have acted rightly and should these doubts persist they may materially affect the amount of information which a defector may give. They may even lead to a complete revulsion of feeling and a desire to return to his masters, Furthermore, it would appear that in most cases, whatever may have been his real reasons for defecting, the subject will want in self-justification to convince his interrogators and incidentally himself that his true motive was selfless and ideological. In our opinion nothing should be done to prevent his taking this view; it is important that he should mint a in his self-respect, since we are largely dependent upon his goodwill and gratitude in obtaining information from him.

There has been a notable absence of cynicism amongst some of the most important Russian defectors and it is felt that cynical approaches should be avoided as they are distasteful and incomprehensible to those who are not of a cynical turn of mind. Many defectors have an exaggerated sense of their own importance; it is felt that allowances must be made for this in appropriate cases, and the defector should be treated, so far as possible, as a person of importance and integrity. Some care may have to be taken to make the defector-feel that he is meeting men of high status, but it is not suggested that action along these lines should mount to over-indulgence. Indeed, this would be disastrous since the relationship between the defector and his questioners should, at any rate on the surface, be one of mutual respect. A show of firmness when this is necessary can only do good.

Consideration must also be given to other matters. There is a marked contrast between the feverish activity which loads up to a defection and the comparative idleness which often follows it. It would seem inadvisable to leave a man too much alone and with too much time to think in the early stages after his defection. If he can be kept busily employed writing his story and talking to his interrogators he is less likely to indulge in dangerous recriminations and second thoughts. Besides, the feeling that he is doing useful work is exactly what is required to help him to justify his action to himself.

Steps should of course be taken to minimize the worries a defector may have about the safety of his family and himself, and the problem of his future.

The remarks above are intended to apply primarily to such defectors as have or can believe that they have a disinterested and respectable motive for their action. Men who throw themselves on our mercy only because they fear for their personal safety are unlikely to present such a complicated problem, since all they are likely to expect or receive from us is asylum and protection, and since if they threaten to prove intractable we can simply withdraw our protection without much loss to ourselves.

Our opinions on the handling of defectors are not intended to advocate in any way the least relaxation of security precautions to establish whether a defector is genuine, and efforts to ensure that even if he is not he can do little harm. A genuine defector will expect and appreciate that to protect ourselves we must go to considerable lengths to establish his reliability; but there is a difference between this and giving a man the impression that he is constantly regarded with suspicion. Sooner or later the investigations into his reliability should be presumed to have been completed and from his point of view he should cease to be treated as a suspect, This of course does not mean that those handling him will forget the possibility that he may have boon planted; it is plainly a question of a change of attitude in interrogating him. A risk always exists in the acceptance and exploitation of Russian defectors; the defector may be a brilliant plant, or he may at a much later date resume work for the Russians. This risk can be minimised by reasonable security precautions, but it cannot be eliminated. A too great insistence upon the risk may, by antagonising a genuine defector, destroy all the value which might have been gained from the operation.

X SUMMARY

In this paper we have illustrated by the stories of the defectors the points which we consider to be relevant to the subject of defection. They can be recapitulated briefly as follows

1. The repressive measures introduced in the USSR in the course of the past twenty years have affected successive classes of the Russian people and have given then cause for that dissatisfaction with the Soviet regime which engenders the desire to defect.
2. Defectors are almost unanimous in claiming that dissatisfaction with the regime was the main reason for their action. An additional impetus however is almost always present in the form of fear, love, or a desire for the western way of life.
3. The possible consequences to a man's family should they be in Russia are a considerable deterrent to defection – and worry about the' may affect his value after defection.
4. It is most important that, if he is to be accepted at all, a defector should be received with despatch and given immediate protection. Otherwise the opportunity of taking advantage of his offer may be

missed, and his failure should it become known will be a deterrent to other potential defectors.
5. The reaction of the Soviet authorities to a defection is prompt and energetic. In the early days they resorted to kidnapping and assassination to recover the body before much harm could be //done, and also preferred criminal charges with requests for extradition. This latter expedient, which has become the most common in recent years, also served the purpose of an attempt to discredit the defector both in the eyes of his protectors and if necessary of his compatriots.
6. The solution of the defector's future is bound to be a difficult problem. He fears assassination or kidnapping and is faced with the necessity of earning a living, Those responsible for his disposal must consider the fact that if he is not adequately protected the fate which nay befall him will discourage those who night have followed his example. If he is left with no resources he presents a security risk.
7. The information provided by defectors has been of a very high quality and of the greatest value to us. Though the danger of a penetration agent disguising himself as a defector must, of course, be borne in mind, adequate security precautions and careful checking of his story should prevent him from doing serious damage even should he remain undetected. Where there is reasonable expectation of advantage to ourselves, our decision as to the acceptance of a defector need not be unduly swayed by the fear of attempted penetration.
8. A great deal depends on the way in which a defector is treated. An attempt must be made to anticipate his fears and worries and to eliminate them when possible. Many difficulties such as those which have marred the late stages of past defections can be avoided if firmness and understanding are used from the start, and if an atmosphere of mutual respect can be established between the defector and those who are handling him.

Appendix III

DEFECTOR CASE HISTORIES

Eugene PIK
Grigori BESSSEDOVSKY
George AGABEKOV
Walter KRIVITSKY
Alexandre BARMIN
Leon HELFAND
Isnail AKHMEDOV
Victor KRAVCHENKO
Igor GOUZENKO
Constantin VOLKOV
Kiril ALEXEEV
Michel KORIAKOV
YURCHENKO
Mikhail DENISOV
Vera TAKACS
JURACHOW (no history)
Alexander KRAVCHENKO
'S' (no history)
Vasilyi SHARANDAK
Grigori TOKAEV
Eugene PIK

Grigori BESSEDOVSKY

Grigori BESSEDOVSKY was born in 1896 at Poltava in the Ukraine and was of Jewish extraction. He took part in the revolution and served in the Red Army as Political Commissar for one of the Soviet Regiments which were fighting General DENIKIN's forces. Later he was elected President of the Economic Council of the Poltava district and was a member of the All-Ukrainian Central Executive and of the Central Committee of the Ukrainian Communist Party.

BESSEDOVSKY was stationed in Vienna in 1921 to 1922 as head of the Consular Section of the Legation of the Soviet Ukraine and he was Counsellor of the Soviet Legation in Warsaw during the years 1923 to 1925.

He was sent in the sane capacity to Tokyo in 1926 following his failure to obtain a visa for the United States in December 1925. During his time at Warsaw he was said to have kept in constant contact with the Vienna centre of the Third International and to have been in charge of the activity of the Executive Committee of the Third International in Poland.

In October 1927 BESSEDOVSKY had been appointed Counsellor to the Soviet Embassy in Paris. He was said to be a notorious terrorist and a member of the Ukrainian Section of the GPU.

In October 1929, BESSEDOVSKY defected from the Soviet Legation in Paris. According to his own account he was proposing to go on leave at the end of September 1929 and for ideological reasons decided to take advantage of this never to return. There is also a suggestion that he was already in touch with the French Police. On the 2nd October 1929 ROIZENMANN, a member of the Control Commission of the Communist Party, arrived from Moscow with specific instructions to bring BESSSEDOVSKY back. BESSEDOVSKY was summoned and in a most uncomfortable interview his return to Moscow was demanded. He refused and on ROIZENMANN's instructions was virtually arrested. He succeeded in escaping by climbing over two walls and he obtained Police protection to remove his wife and child from the Embassy, A week after his flight, BESSSEDOVSKY stated that he would place all information that he had in the possession of the French Government. Attempts to kidnap his son had already taken place. Later in August 1929 there were indications that Moscow and the Paris Embassy were very upset by the BESSSEDOVSKY scandal and that immediate steps were to be taken to render him innocuous.

In January 1930 BESSSEDOVSKY was tried in Moscow for the misappropriation of more than £3,000 belonging to the Soviet Embassy in France.

He was sentenced in absentia to ten years imprisonment. He himself alleges that the money charge against him was a fabricated one; his reasons for defecting were, he said, ideological but there was a suggestion that one of the reasons for his action may have been frustrated ambition – he had hoped to be Ambassador in Paris.

BESSSEDOVSKY continued to live in Paris where he formed an Association of Non-Returners for deserters from the Soviet regime, He also ran a garage and a number of taxis. An attempt on his part to come to the United Kingdom in November 1930 was unsuccessful, He was regarded as absolutely unprincipled and untrustworthy in every way and at this time was said to be extremely talkative and indiscreet, a bad judge of people and entirely surrounded by a number of suspicious GPU individuals. His Defector's Society according to the *Evening News* had a membership of about one hundred in 1931, was particularly directed against Stalin, frankly revolutionary and militaristic and designed to overthrow the Soviet Regime.

After his defection in 1930, AGABEKOV, revealed that he had at one time been ordered to go to Paris and liquidate BESSSEDOVSKY but for some reason unknown to him the order was changed.

In August 1932 BESSSEDOVSKY was in touch with Arthur BAY, a White Russian in Germany who for many years worked for the German Intelligence Service.

Many of BESSSEDOVSKY's collaborators in the White Russian Non-Returners Organisation were suspected of being GPU agents, and in 1938 he was supposed to be in touch with the German Intelligence Service, During the war BESSSEDOVSKY remained in Prance where he was active in the Resistance Movement and he is reported to have been pardoned by the Soviets as a result of this work. In 1945 he was reported as a Soviet agent in Prance who had been assigned to the collection of information on the American Army. BESSSEDOVSKY now lives in Cannes and since the end of 1946 reports have been received to the effect that he has been producing the Russian 'hand-outs' for the Press as part of a Soviet Press deception scheme.

A report in April 1948 states that BESSSEDOVSKY, although not admitting that the articles in Paris newspapers for which he was responsible are Soviet 'hand-outs', makes no bones about his contacts with members of the Soviet Embassy.

Geogri ARUIUNOV"@ AGABEKOV @ OUSEPIAN @ AZAVOV

George AGABEKOV (whose real name is ARUTIUNOV) was born at Askabad in 1895. He left the second course of the Tashkent Institute of Oriental Languages to join the army on the outbreak of [the First World] war. In 1913, he joined the Communist Party and after a certain period of service with the Central Administration of the CHEKA in Moscow, he was sent as GPU *rezident* to Bokhara. Later he held various positions under the OGPU in Turkestan, Afghanistan and Persia until November 1929 when under the name of OUSEPIAN he was appointed rezident of the OGPU in Istanbul for Turkey, Greece, Syria, Palestine and Egypt.

> When he was in Istanbul AGABEKOV was anxious to learn English. In the course of his enquiries as to who could teach him, he met an English family by the name of STREATER. Isobel STREATER who was then aged twenty, fell in love with him almost at once and he with her. AGABEKOV became engaged to her in spite of her parents displeasure, and as a result of this association he approached the British authorities in Istanbul in February 1930 with an offer to disclose the methods whereby the OGOU was rapping correspondence between the Foreign Office and British Embassies and Legations in Egypt and the East. In his approach he stated that he had become engaged to Isobel STBEATER and had no wish to return to Moscow.
>
> This approach does not seem to have met with any success and in June 1930 the STKEATERs sent their daughter Isobel to Paris to stay with a married sister in an attempt to break up her love affair with AGAH£K0V. Isobel arrived in Paris on the 22nd June 1930 and AGABEKOV followed her on the 26th. He revealed his Secret 3ervice past to her relations and announced that he had decided to leave his post, had prepared the manuscript for a book of disclosures and had abandoned his parents in Russia all because of his love for Isobel, whom: he wished to marry immediately. At his request Isobel had smuggled into France his manuscript and £200.

AGABEKOV wrote to the White Russian paper *Les Demieres Nouvelles* telling then that he had defected and that he was about to write a book. He was interviewed by the press – the *Morning Post* in July 1930 stated that he ascribed his change of heart and life to his recognition of the following facts

> Under the slogan of 'freeing the oppressed East', the Soviet Government are undertaking an Imperialist policy in China, Persia, Afghanistan and in the whole Near East. During the last two years the revolutionary spirit in the USSR has turned into bureaucracy and servility. Among the loaders the question of revolution has resolved itself into a struggle for fat jobs. The result of Stalin's government is permanent hunger in such an agricultural country as Russia,

AGABEKOV was seen and courteously received by the Prench Prefecture. He also got in touch with BESSSEDOVSKY who had defected in 1929 in Paris and founded the Association of Non-Returners. AGABEKOV gave a great deal of information to the French during his stay in Paris, and this information was passed to the British Intelligence Service.

On the 12th August 1930 AGAHEKOV was expelled from France. The reason given for this action was that after a long test and analysis of his information, the French had found that he had not added materially to what was already known. They also said that he had lied on certain points and that they had concluded that he was a provocateur. It transpired, however, that the chief reason for his expulsion was the commotion caused by Isobel's parents who succeeded in setting strong representations made to the French by the British Consul. The impression given to British Intelligence was that the French having got what they wanted out of AGABEKOV and finding that he was a nuisance, seized upon the pretext offered by the STHEATERs in order to get rid of him.

AGAHEKOV took refuge in Belgian, where he was frequently interviewed by a member of the British Intelligence Service to whom he gave copies of his memoirs in installments. AGABEKOV's reminiscences were published in French early in 1931.

In late August 1935 *The Daily Telegraph* published a story to the effect that AGAHCKOV had offered to lay bare the secrets of the Soviet espionage system in return for news of Isobel, from whom he had heard nothing since his arrival in Belgium. He is also reported to have said that as he had definitely forsaken the Soviet service in order to follow the dictates of his heart, the unkind treatment which he had received at the hands of European authorities, might prevent the powerful OGPU's agents iron carrying out their intention of deserting the Soviet cause.

Isobel was taken back to Istanbul by her family and in October 1930 she succeeded in sending to AGAHEKOV a letter and a ring through the intermediary of a friend in London. Isobel said that her letters were being opened by the authorities in Istanbul, and she was afraid that her father would take measures through the Turkish police to prevent her leaving the country. In November 1930 *The Daily Telegraph* reported that Isobel was rumoured to have left her house in Istanbul and gone to join AGABEKOV in Brussels. It is not known when they were married but in January 1932 the *Daily Mirror* published a photograph taken in Brussels of AGABEKOV and Isobel, who by then had become his wife.

In 1931 the Soviets concocted an elaborate plot to kidnap AGABEKOV. The main idea was to lure him to Bulgaria on the pretext of helping a rich woman to escape from Russia; he would then be enticed on board a Russian ship. AGABEKOV, it is alleged, saw straight through this story, but accepted the proposal with a view to compassing the destruction of the Russian agents involved. He went to Sofia in November 1931, told his story to the Chief of the Bulgarian Security Police and asked for his protection if he should go on to Vania. AGABEKOV then returned to Belgium and had more discussions with the Soviet intermediaries. On Christmas night 1931 he arrived at the Athenee Palace in Bucharest with one of the Soviet agents. After a very complicated few days in the course of which Soviet agents arrived in Constanza from all sides with the object of either assassinating or kidnapping AGABEKOV, about twenty OGPU agents and informers implicated in the plot were arrested in Rumania in January 1932.

The fact that the kidnapping attempt was a genuine one was considered by the Romanians to be completely confirmed by other sources to which they had access. They therefore regarded it as out of the question that AGABEKOV might still be in Soviet pay.

In October 1935 AGABEKOV was arrested by the Brussels Police, the charge according to the Press being that of being in possession of stolen bonds. However, it later transpired that in fact he was arrested and sentenced to four months imprisonment for receiving stolen bonds. There were no political charges. In August 1936 he was reported to be under an expulsion order from Belgium and he applied for a visa to come to England to visit his wife. The expulsion decree was suspended and on the 7th January 1937 he was again arrested in Brussels on a charge of stealing by means of false keys, receiving and passing under a false name. He was released on 18 December 1937 and the Belgians report that since March 1938 he had disappeared, and according to certain journals he had been kidnapped and probably killed by agents of the GPU.

In January 1940 Isobel applied for an exit permit to go to Brussels, 'In order to take up in person enquiries which are already on foot with regard to my husband's disappearance.' The application was refused as official enquiries were said to be already underway.

Permission was finally granted for Isobel to go to France in May 1940; by this time she had seen an account in *Les Deernieres Nouvelles* of 1938 in which one, V.L. BURTZEFF, an elderly Russian, said that AGABEKOV had been kidnapped and killed by CHEKA agents. Isobel was anxious to try and find BURTZEFF and see if he could give her any more information.

A report which we received in May 1942 stated that AGABEKOV had left Belgium in 1937 or 1938 and had gone to Spain where he was reported to have done valuable work for Franco. Since then nothing has been heard of him and it is believed that he is dead.

Isobel, his wife, worked as a private secretary from 1937 to 1942, and from 1942 to 1945 she was a corporal in the WAAF. From 1945 to 1946 Isobel AGABEKOV was with the United Nations War Crimes Commission, and in November 1946 she obtained employment at the Foreign Office.

Walter KRIVITSKY

Walter KRIVITSKY was born in Krivoyrog, South Russia on 15 January 1890 and christened Walter GINZBURG. His father was probably a Jewish émigré from Posen, which was then German; his mother was a Slav.

He was educated as a mining engineer, then studied civil engineering at Ekaterineslav. In the 1914 to 1918 war [First World War] he held a non-commissioned post in the Tsarist Engineers and entered the Red Army in November 1917. He joined the fourth department of the Red Army Intelligence about 1919. He was a specialist in German military espionage and was responsible for many years for that work. From 1935 to 1937 he was given a much wider commission embodying responsibility for Soviet secret operations in all Western European countries.

In the autumn of 1937 KRIVITSKY was operating in Paris, at that time Stalin's purge of the Red Army was at its height. Many Russian agents and a number of KRIVITSKY's colleagues and friends in the fourth department had been executed.

In July 1937, one SPIEGELGLASS, chief of the foreign section of the NKVD arrived in Paris with the task of assassinating Ignace REISS, a disaffected Russian officer who was thinking of defecting. He handed this task over to KRIVITSKY who warned REISS of the plot. Ignace REISS escaped to Switzerland but was there assassinated by two Soviet agents. SPIEGELGLASS discovered that KRIVITSKY had warned his friend and in August 1937 KRIVITSKI was ordered to return to Russia. Aware that the tine for his liquidation at the hands of the OGPU had arrived, he temporized, meanwhile making plans to remain in France and defect from the Soviet Union.

In December 1937 KRIVITSKY asked for permission to remain in France as a political émigré. His open letter reported in *The Times* of 9 December 1937 was as follows:

> For eighteen years I faithfully and conscientiously served the Bolshevik party and the Soviet authority, being firmly convinced that at the same time I was serving the cause of the October Revolution and the interests of the entire working class.
>
> The latest events, however, have convinced me that the policy of the Stalin Government is not only continually tending more and more against the interests of the Soviet federation, but also against those of the whole labour movement. In the Moscow trials, especially in the secret trials, the best representatives of the Bolshevik Old Guard have been condemned as spies and agents of the Gestapo. Stalin has not even

hesitated to decapitate the Red Army and has ordered the execution of its best and most talented leaders.

He has accused them of treason but in reality it is precisely his policy which is undermining the military power of the USSR, its national defences, its economy and its finest achievements in all departments of Soviet construction. Every fresh case, every fresh shooting has shaken my faith more deeply. I have sufficient sources of information to know how the trials are being got up and that innocent people are being killed. By remaining abroad I hope to assist in the rehabilitation of the tens of thousands of so-called spies who in reality are the most devoted fighters for the cause of the working classes.

While he was in Paris KRTVITSKY gave to the Surete secret evidence which helped to secure the conviction of the wife of the kidnapper of the White Russian General Miller, He met Leon Blum who introduced him at the American Embassy, and Mr. Bullitt, who had been American Ambassador in Moscow from 1933 to 1936, thought that he would be a problem for Cordell Hull to see. Mr. Bullitt sent him to the United States with a temporary passport for display and a *laissez-passer diplomatique* to be used at the customs in case of emergency. His wife and small son accompanied him to America and in April 1939 he published a series of articles in the *Saturday Evening Post*. These articles he later extended into a book *I Was Stalin's Agent* which he wrote with the assistance of a journalist named LEVINE, and which was published in America and in England.

In July 1939, the Communist paper *New Masses* launched a savage campaign in its pages to the effect that KRIVITSKY was really an Austrian denizen of Paris night clubs called Samuel GINSBURG who had never been a general in the Army. KRIVITSKY was branded as a Trotsky and LEVINE as a notorious anti-Soviet fascist.

In September 1939 LEVINE went to the British Embassy in Washington and told them a story obtained from KRIVITSKY about a member of the Foreign Office Cypher Department who was working as a Russian agent. This story was pursued and resulted in the arrest and conviction of the Foreign Office employee in question who had a long record of espionage for the Russians.

In November 1939 it was suggested that KRIVITSKY might be brought over to Europe for interrogation. The State Department had already made energetic use of him as an informant and he had given evidence before the House Committee on Un-American Activities. Negotiations for inviting KRIVITSKY to cone to England were put under way and it was agreed that as suggested by his lawyer KRIVITSKY should be given a letter of introduction to Herbert Morrison so that the latter should be responsible while he was in England, It was also arranged that his wife and son should reside in Canada while he was away and should be very carefully guarded.

KRIVITSKY arrived in England on the 19th January 1940. He knew that he had been invited to London by some official authority, department unspecified, and that he was wanted to give the fullest possible information about Soviet military intelligence activities in the United Kingdom. He stayed in London for one month during which time he was exhaustively interrogated by this Office and provided an enormous body of very valuable information.

He returned to Canada on the 15th February 1940, travelling on a British passport in the name of Walter Thomas. Money was sent to him in Canada. For this money he signed a receipt in the name of 'Walter Thomas' and the money was deposited at the Royal Bank of Canada in Montreal.

By November 1940 KRIVITSKY had succeeded in entering the United States, and was living in New York in hiding with his family. On the 10th February 1941 he was found shot dead in a hotel bedroom in Washington.

The circumstances of his death pointed to suicide and he left suicide notes, one to his lawyer Louis Waldmann, one to a friend, Miss Suzanne LaFollette, and one to his wife. KRIVTTSKY had spent the week end before his death with friends in Virginia, and it was there that he had bought the. 38 automatic with which he was shot and which was found in his room after his death. Many people hold the view both from the tenor of his notes and from the fact that he had lived in constant fear of liquidation by the Soviets, that he would never willingly have committed suicide, and that in fact, whether he shot himself or whether he was shot, his death showed that Stalin's agents had finally been successful in settling accounts with him.

Alexandre BARMIN @ LETA @ Ian KARLOVIAST

BARNIN was born at Moguilev on 16 August 1899. According to information from a reliable source, at the beginning of 1919 he followed a course of lectures on military espionage at a special school founded by the Red Army Intelligence and passed out first. Soon afterwards under the name of Ian KARLOVIAST he joined the counter espionage service and was instrumental in securing the arrest of ASTROV, one of the principal leaders of the insurrection of the Russian Anti-Soviet Party at the end of 1919. In 1920 he was sent to Latvia as a secret agent of the Third International but to escape arrest by the local police he hurriedly returned to Moscow. He remained there until 1928 working in the counter espionage section under ULITSKI and at the same time underwent training at the Commissariat of Foreign Trade. At the beginning of 1929 he was sent to Paris as sub-manager of the General Import Section of the Soviet Trade Delegation, subsequently becoming manager; in reality however he acted as secret representative of the OGPU. When General KOUTIEPOFF was kidnapped, BARMIN, on the evening of 2 February 1930, displayed such haste in burning certain papers in his office that he narrowly escaped setting the building on fire. As a punishment he was transferred to Milan where he became involved with an Italian woman and was subsequently recalled to Moscow.

In 1931 the Third International, because of social conflicts, strikes etc., arrived at a special decision regarding Belgium, and at the end of that year BARMIN was sent as Soviet representative for foreign trade to Belgium and Luxemburg, Holland being included from May 1932 onwards.

In February 1932, BARMIN applied for a visa to come to the United Kingdom. He urgently wished to see a Mr KHASANOV, president of a metal firm who was then in London for a few days. According to the Belgian authorities BARMIN was an OGPU agent and was considered dangerous. He had only a monthly permit for Belgium and they were anxious to expel him but he had influential friends. His visa was granted and he came to England for four days in April 1932.

In October 1932 we heard that BARMIN had been recalled to Russia and it was doubtful whether he would return to Belgium. We have no more news about him until December 1937 when he defected in Paris. It then emerged that he had been First Secretary at the Soviet Legation at Athens from 1935 until March 1937 and then Charge d'Affaires there.

It seems that BARMIN, although not technically summoned back to Moscow, was ordered by the Communist Cell of the Legation in Athens to drink tea with a Soviet Captain in his ship in the Piraeus. For some days BARMIN hedged by asking the Captain to come to him instead, and eventually he went to the French Legation, asked for a visa for France and reached Paris. In an impassioned defence of his refusal to return to Russia, BARMIN said that he had devoted nineteen years to service of the Soviet Government,

> the recent Moscow trials have filled me with stupefaction and horror, at first I did violence to ray conscience and resigned myself to events ... but the events of the past few months (months which I have spent in France

on sick leave) have taken away my last illusion. I obey the dictates of ray conscience in breaking with this Government. I have considered the dangers to which I expose myself by acting thus. I sign my own death warrant and expose myself to the attacks of hired assassins ...

In March 1938 BARMIN asked for a visa for the UK for two or three months in order to write a book. His request was refused as it was thought that a visit from him would be likely to have undesirable results. OGPU agents anxious to liquidate him would be attracted to Britain and we should have to give him police protection which might not be successful.

In August 1938 he applied for a visa for three weeks. We were informed that when he had arrived in France he was believed to have been protected by two ministers; probably Max DORMOY and Pierre COTY. He was granted permission to work and was then employed in the Commercial Department of Air Prance at Le Bourget. He wished to publish his memoirs in England under the title *Twenty Years in the USSR*. There is no sign of BARMIN ever having come to England in this connection, nor have we seen a copy of his book.

There is some suggestion that at one time BARMIN was employed by the Americans but dismissed by them in 1944. We have no more recent information about him at the present time.

Leon Borisovich HELFAND

HELFAND was born on 10 December 1900 at Poltava. He arrived in France on 19 March 1926, travelling on a Soviet passport visa'd by the French Embassy in Moscow on 23 January 1926. He was first employed as a clerk at the Soviet Embassy in Paris, subsequently as Chief Secretary at the Soviet Consulate, finally returning to the Soviet Embassy as Second Secretary.

His rapid promotion was said to be a reward for his devotion to the Communist cause. In July 1929 ho was reported to be in close relation with the leaders of the French Communist Party and with those of the French revolutionary Trades Union, and furthermore he was strongly suspected of being in charge of the dissemination of Communist propaganda in Syria and Morocco. HELFAND lived at the Embassy and was feared by his colleagues there who nicknamed him 'Eye of Moscow'. According to the defector BESSEDOVSKY, the Englishman who offered to sell the Foreign Office cypher to the Soviet Embassy in Paris was interviewed by HELFAND, Early in 1930 it was reported that HELFAND had been appointed to replace YANOVITCH at the Soviet

Embassy in Paris but he disappeared after the affair of the kidnapping of General KOUTIEPOV. His membership of the GPU was stated to have been confirmed.

In May 1930 the *Echo de Paris* published information given by Vladimir BOURTZEFF on the KOUTIEPOV affair, alleging that HELFAND and ELLERT effected the kidnapping of KOUTIEPOV, that HELFAND had left Paris urgently on 28 January1930 and that both HELFAND and ELLERT had arrived in Berlin from Moscow on 22 February1930. In Berlin they were said to have held a meeting with two Swiss and one Hungarian agent to discuss the formation of a new GPU organisation.

HELFAND next worked at the Commissariat for Foreign Affairs in Moscow and between 1930 and 1932 he was known to various members of the British Embassy there. One of them said that HELFAND had the reputation of being a GPU stalwart and was said not only to have been concerned in the kidnapping of KOUTIEPOV, but also to have been responsible in the early days of the revolution for a number of peculiarly brutal murders.

He always gave the impression of being anti-British. On the other hand Ire Ingram was thought to have obtained a good deal of information of various kinds out of him. He was described as a very intelligent Jew.

In April 1938 the *Volkischer Beobachter* stated that a Bolshevik Legation was in prospect for Madrid and that Leon HELFAND was proposed as Ambassador. HELFAND was at that time Counsellor at the Soviet Embassy in Rome and was, in May 1937, contemplating a visit to England during his leave. Although no objection was offered to the grant of a visa, he did not attempt to come.

In August 1940, we heard that HELFAND had come to be on bad terms with GORELKIN, the Soviet Ambassador in Rome, and that there were indications that he also fell into disfavour with Moscow. At the end of July 1940 he gave up his post in Rome and decided not to return to Moscow. He was reported to have proceeded to the USA where he intended to take up private employment. In an explanation of his action which he sent to Molotov, he stated his conviction that the co-operation of Soviet Russia with Fascists and National Socialists could not but result in the downfall of the USSR and the destruction of the revolutionary achievements of the country. So much progress had been made on the downward path he averred, that the old revolutionary pioneers in Russia, to whom he claimed to belong, were being liquidated in every sense of the word, HELFAND informed Molotov that had he been a single man he would have returned to Moscow in spite of the certain fate in store for him, but he considered that he owed it to his wife and child to seek safety abroad. He maintained that he harboured no malice against the present holders of power in Soviet Russia and that he had no intention of taking up any subversive activity against his country. He appeared to hope that these assurances on his part would induce the Soviet authorities to postpone his liquidation, although he professed not to be unduly worried about this.

Early in 1941 HEFAND, who had gone to ground in New York under an assumed name, was contacted by Gallienne of the British Consulate in New York, and produced a good deal of valuable information about Soviet Intelligence activities.

We heard from a source in touch with Czechoslovak circles in September 1944 that one of the chief Soviet agents behind ELAS was a certain HELFAND who had been connected with the General KOUTIEPOV affair, It seems likely, however, that this source was mistaken as in February 1945 HELFAND was still living in New York, very profitably engaged with a shipping firm with Egyptian connections and similar commercial activities.

In February 1947 HELFAND answered a questionnaire about certain, natters relating to Soviet Intelligence activities which had been submitted by the British Intelligence Service.

Ismail AKMEDOV @ Georgi NIKOLAEV

AKHMEDOV was born in Orsk in 1900. His father and mother were teachers and were 'lost' during the October Revolution. At the age of fourteen AKHMEDOV joined the Komsomol and in 1920 he entered the Institute of Eastern Languages where he studied Arabic and Persian. In 1921 he was sent to Bukhara as a propagandist and at the same time he entered the Communist Party, In 1925 he went to the Military Electrical School in Leningrad and graduated in 1929 with the rank of Lieutenant of the Signal Troops.

During his interrogation by the Americans in 1947 AKHMEDOV said that his first rude awakening to the menace of Communism occurred in 1929 when thousands and thousands of peasants were purged because they had not entered the collective farms. This statement and other statements of his during the 1947 interrogation do not however appear to have come to light until five years after his defection, and it is difficult to say whether they are genuine feelings of long standing or whether he has found time during five years to read *I Chose Freedom* and generally to think up reasons other than immediate fear to advance in explanation of his defection.

In 1931 AKHMEDOV entered the Military Electrical Academy of the Red Army in Leningrad, graduating in 1936 with the rank of an Engineer Captain specialising in wireless. During the 1946 interrogation he made the statement that during this study he had an opportunity to compare Western democracy with Communism and knew that he preferred Western democracy but he had to wait until he had an opportunity to break with the Soviets, The only way he could break with the Soviets that he knew of was to join the Soviet Intelligence Service.

In 1936 he was appointed as an engineer to the Red Army's Central Institute of Experimental Radio and Electricity. This was at the time of the military purge and as many first ranking engineers had been arrested he was appointed to the post of chief of the First Section of this Institute. He worked there for nearly two years and in 1933 was sent to study at the General Staff of the Russian Army. He was there for two years and was taught how to organise Army operations, to prepare and provoke wars and to organise Intelligence Service work in foreign countries.

In 1940 AKHMEDOV graduated from the General Staff Academy with the rank of major and in September of that year, according to the 1947 interrogation, he was appointed to the post of the Chief of the Fourth Division of the Intelligence Department of the General Staff of the Red Amy.

AKHMEDOV's personal history as given to the Turks and passed to us in 1942, contains some discrepancies including the statement that in 1939 he served temporarily on the Finnish Front, and was then Staff Officer in the Operations Section South West Front during the advance into Bessarabia,

In June 1941 AKHMEDOV was sent to Berlin under cover of Vice President of TASS in Berlin under the assumed name of Georgi NICOLAEFF. His task was to verify a message which had been received stating that Germany was about to declare war on Russia and to attempt to establish a network in case a state of war should arise. Two weeks after his arrival war was declared and he was interned in Germany, He was exchanged with Germans interned in Russia and in July 1941 he arrived in Turkey.

Upon his arrival there he was appointed Press Attaché in the Soviet Embassy at unlearn and was simultaneously ordered by the Intelligence Department of the General Staff to organise and direct military intelligence against Germany.

We have two stories on the reasons for AKHMEDOV's break with the Soviets in 1942. One is to the effort that at the time of the Soviet attempt on von Papen's life in Ankara about May 1942, AKHMEDOV telegraphed on his own initiative to Stalin recommending that PAVLOV, the organiser of the plot who had sought refuge in the Soviet Consulate, should be handed over to the Turks. As a result he received a severe reprimand from Moscow and was summoned there to answer additional charges for associating with Poles, Czechs and other so-called 'Allied canaille'. AKHMEDOV realised that he was in danger and sought refuge with the Turks who hid him away in a village called Sparta.

In the 1947 interrogation no mention is made of the PAVLOV incident, and AKHMEDOV's reasons for his defection are given as a combination of the disgust with the continual conflicts caused by the three channels directing Soviet Intelligence within Turkey, and the culmination of a long disillusionment with the Soviet regime.

Elaborating more fully (in 1947) on his break with the Soviets, AHMEdOV stated that his reasons for defection were political and began with the purge of the peasants and were accentuated by the military purge in 1936. He stated that he was opposed to the Communist way of thinking on questions of philosophy, economics, politics and social problems, and that living in a foreign country even for a short time had opened his eyes and given him the opportunity of choosing between freedom and Communist slavery.

When AKHMEDOV was seen by a representative of British Intelligence in June 1947 he made a good impression and seemed to be a conscientious informant. The Americans had also been taking an interest in him and interrogated him fairly extensively. It seems possible that some of the information which he produced on operations against the USA, which were being run from the Fourth Department may lead even after six years to a spy ring still operating in America.

Victor Andreevich KRAVCHENKO

Victor KRAVCIIENKO was born on 11 September1905 at Dnepropetrovsk. His father was an anti-Tsarist mechanic who was engaged in revolutionary activity in 1905 and 1906 who had never been a Communist. In 1922 KRAVCHENKO joined the Komsomols. From 1926 to 1928 he served in the Red Army and in 1929 joined the Communist Party and entered the Technical Institute at Kharkov. During the time of the purge of 1937 he was denounced by political enemies and questioned by the NKVD. He was cleared in 1938 and in 1939 became director of the largest secret metallurgical construction in Siberia. He fell under suspicion again and was sentenced to a year's hard labour. He went into the Red Arry instead but was released in 1942.

He arrived in Canada on 13 August 1943 as Engineer Inspector of Material for the Metals Division of the Soviet Purchasing Commission in the USA. While he was in America he decided to defect from the Russian Service but on the advice of certain friends he thought that he would have to take some action which would appeal to the American public. He believed that all he would have to do would be to approach an important newspaper and simply say that he had resigned. In fact the newspaper was not very interested until KRAVCHENKO would give an outline for his reasons. He had previously intended to write his whole story later in the form of an indictment, but he was in fact forced to say more than he had intended to at the moment of his defection. When he resigned in the first week of April 1944 he said:-

> I can no longer support double-faced political manoeuvres directed at one and the same time toward the collaboration with the United States and Britain, and at the same time pursuing aims incompatible with such collaboration. Collaboration with the democratic countries cannot be pursued while the Soviet Government and its leaders are in reality following a concealed policy of their own, designed to accomplish purposes at variance with their public professions.

When asked why he had defected KRAVCHENKO said that his visit to the USA, his first to a foreign country, had crystallized views and sentiments he long had felt in Russia

On 7 April 1944 the Soviet Embassy in 'Washington stated that KRAVCHENKO had lied in saying that he was in charge of the Metals Division, in fact he was neither a member of the Purchasing Commission nor in charge of the Metals Division. Being on military service and having been sent for temporary work at the disposal of the Purchasing Commission in the US in the capacity of one of the Inspectors of Pipes, KRAVCHENKO had been instructed to return to the Soviet Union to continue his military service. Two weeks before the date of his expected departure to the USSR to serve in the Red Amy KRAVCHENKO, according to the Russian Embassy, betrayed his military duty and became a deserter having refused to return to his motherland for military service and to cover his desertion he made slanderous statements about the USSR on the pages of certain New York newspapers.

KRAVCHENKO denied the accusations of desertion and said that he had never been recalled to Moscow, The FBI had several interviews with him and he provided them with a good deal of information. He was, however, extremely nervous, saying that he would commit suicide rather than fall into Russian hands and the FBI consequently had to be very cautious in their dealings with him. He was living in hiding but actively negotiating with American publishers and was also in close touch with a number of Social Democrats, many of foreign nationality or extraction.

In addition to giving information to the FBI, KRAVCHENKO wrote and published his widely read indictment of the Soviet system *I Chose Freedom*.

Igor GOUZENKO

Igor GOJZENKO was born in 1919. He was educated in primary and secondary schools and later entered the Academy of Engineering in Zoscov, but after two months he was sent to a special school conducted under the aegis of the General Staff of the Red Army. GOUZENKO never became a member of the Communist Party but he became a lumber of the Komsomol at the age of seventeen. According to him it was not usual in peace time to admit any but Communists to the special Academy which he attended, but during the war owing to the shortage of suitable candidates it was decided that Komsomols might go there for training.

From this school he was sent to the main Intelligence Division of the Red Army in Moscow and was then sent to the front in May 1942 where he remained for about one year. The Soviet authorities decided towards the end of 1942 that GOUZENKO should be sent abroad; his 'documentation' took approximately six months to complete and included a very careful investigation of him by the NKVD.

GOUZENKO arrived in Canada in June 1943 to act as cypher clerk for the military attaché, Colonel ZABOTIN, who was appointed at the same time. About September 1944 a telegram was received by Colonel ZABOTIN indicating that GOUZENKO's return to Russia was required, but owing to representations made by the Military Attaché this did not take place.

A few months previous to September 1945 GOUZENKO carelessly left drafts of two confidential despatches lying around where they were found by a charwoman and turned over to one of the Embassy officials. This individual took the matter up with GOUZENKO who, realising the seriousness of the position, implored him not to cake a report about it, The man promised to do his best but some time later GOUZENKO received instructions to return to Moscow and a new cypher clerk was sent out. The latter was supposed to take over GOUZENKO's duties immediately but ZABOTIN did not consider him sufficiently qualified and left, the seals in the hands of GOUZENKO. The formal transfer was to take place on 6 September 1945.

Originally GOUZENKO apparently intended to comply with his instructions and he bought some clothes to take back with him to Russia, Then it seems he began to have doubts. He was certainly afraid of being liquidated should he return. His wife and child were with him in Canada and it seems that the fact that nothing had happened to Victor KRAVCHENKO encouraged GOUZENKO to feel that he also had a chance of defecting.

GOUZENKO says that he had for some time been having a struggle with himself as to whether he should return to Russia. When he arrived in Canada he was impressed by the complete freedom of the individual which he found existing and which was utterly foreign to his experience in Russia and foreign to the information which he had received in Russia as to life in the democratic countries. He was impressed with the things that were on sale in the stores and with the fact that those things were there to be purchased by anybody who wanted to buy them.

He was also greatly impressed with the freedom of the elections in Canada and the contrast between the system of nominating candidates and voting in Canada, and the system he had known in Russia where one name only appeared on the ballot. He also says that he had seen how the Canadian people had sent supplies to the Soviet Union and collected money for the welfare of Russian people while all the tine members of the Russian Embassy were developing under cover counter-espionage activity directed against Canada.

During the last few weeks prior to his departure from the Embassy on the 5th September 1945 GOUZENKO selected a number of documents which he left in their places in the files, turning over the edges or corners in order that he might take then out quickly at any time. On the 5th September he left the Embassy with the documents about 8 p.m. and went to the *Ottawa Journal* where he spoke to a woman reporter. It did not take her long to realise that this story was too hot to handle and she advised him to go to the Justice Department.

On the next day GOUZENKO, accompanied by his wife and son, went to the Justice Building and spoke to the private secretary to the Minister of Justice, to whom he also showed his documents. The private secretary asked GOUZENKO to wait and spoke to the Under-Secretary of State for External Affairs. GOUZENKO was finally turned away with veiled accusations that he was after all in possession of stolen documents. Again he tried the Press, this time the *Citizen* and was referred to the Royal Canadian Mounted Police. By now he must have become somewhat flustered because the only thing that emerged clearly was that he wanted to become a Canadian citizen. Consequently he was sent to the Crown Attorney at the Court House. lie spoke to the latter's secretary who, sensing the news value involved, called up *Le Droit* and then the *Citizen,* luckily without success.

Hastily, GOUZENKO returned to his apartment and at once he noticed that the place was being watched. Soon after he and his family had gone into his flat there was a knock on the door and his name was called. He did not answer but unfortunately his child ran across the room, GOUZENKO went out through the back door to the next-door apartment and asked his neighbours whether they would be willing to keep his child for the night in case anything should happen to him and his wife. Eventually the whole GOUZENKO family took refuge in the flat of another neighbour and their next door neighbour went by bicycle to get the police. The police arrived and interviewed GOUZENKO who said that he was a member of the Russian Embassy who had information of value to Canada and wanted police protection. The police arranged to watch the apartment building and to come up if their help was needed.

Between 11.30 [pm] and midnight, a party of four Russians, among them PAVLOV the Second Secretary and head of the NKVD in the Embassy, and ROGOV the Assistant Military Attaché, broke into G0UZENKO's empty flat. The police were summoned and arrived to discover them ransacking the apartment. After arguments with the police the Russians left and the GOUZENKOs spent the remainder of the night with their neighbours under police protection.

On the following morning GOUZENKO was taken to the office of the Royal Canadian Mounted Police where he turned over his documents, told his story and asked to be kept in protective custody as he feared for his safety and that of his wife and child.

On the 8th September the Soviet Embassy sent a note to the Department of External Affairs informing them that GOUZENKO had failed to report for work on 6th September. They stated that it was later discovered that GOUZENKO had stolen some money belonging to the Embassy and had hidden himself together with his family. Complaints were also made about the rude behaviour of the Canadian Police to the Embassy officials and the Embassy asked that urgent measures should be taken to seek and arrest GOUZENKO and to hand him over for deportation as a capital criminal. In a further note a week later, the Embassy again asked the Government of Canada to apprehend

GOUZENKO and his wife and without trial to hand them over to the Embassy for deportation to the Soviet Union. GOUZENKO denied the allegation forthwith and although the Department for External Affairs asked the Embassy for particulars of the money stolen, these were never forthcoming. In the opinion of the Royal Commission these circumstances disposed of the theft suggestion.

On the 10th October 1945 GOUZENKO made a formal statement before the Royal Commission:

I, Igor GOUZENKO, wish to make the following statement of my own will:

> Having arrived in Canada two years ago, I was surprised during the first days by the complete free don. of the individual which exists in Canada but does not exist in Russia. The false representations about the democratic countries which are increasingly propagated in Russia were dissipated daily, as no lying propaganda can stand up against facts.

During two years of life in Canada, I saw the evidence of what a free people can do. That the Canadian people have accomplished and are accomplishing here under conditions of complete freedom – the Russian people, under the conditions of the Soviet regime of violence and suppression of all freedom, cannot accomplish even at the cost of tremendous sacrifices of blood and tears.

The last elections which took place recently in Canada especially surprised me. In comparison with the then system of elections in Russia appear as a mockery of the conception of free elections. For example, the fact that in elections in the Soviet Union one candidate is put forward, so that the possibilities of choice are eliminated, speaks for itself.

While creating a false picture of the conditions of life in these countries, the Soviet Government at the same time is taking all measures to prevent the peoples of democratic countries from knowing about the conditions of life in Russia, The facts about the brutal suppression of the freedom of speech, the mockery of the real religious feelings of the people, cannot penetrate into the democratic countries.

Having imposed its Communist regime on the people, the Government of the Soviet Union asserts that the Russian people have, as it were, their own particular understanding of freedom and democracy, different from that which prevails among the peoples of the western democracies. This is a lie. The Russian people have the same understanding of freedom as all the peoples of the world. However, the

Russian people cannot realise their dream of freedom and a democratic government on account of cruel terror and persecution.

Holding forth at international conferences with voluble statements about peace and security, the Soviet Government is simultaneously preparing secretly for the third world war, To meet this war, the Soviet Government is creating in democratic countries, including Canada, a fifth column, in the organization of which even diplomatic representatives of the Soviet Government take part.

The announcement of the dissolution of the Comintern was, probably, the greatest farce of the Communists in recent years. Only the name was liquidated, with the object of reassuring public opinion in the democratic countries. Actually the Comintern exists and continues its work, because the Soviet leaders have never relinquished the idea of establishing a Communist dictatorship throughout the world.

Taking into account least of all that this adventurous idea will cost millions of Russian lives, the Communists are engendering hatred in the Russian people towards everything foreign.

To many Soviet people here abroad, it is clear that the Communist Party in democratic countries has changed long ago from a political party into an agency net of the Soviet Government, into a fifth column in these countries to meet a war, into an instrument in the hands of the Soviet Government for creating artificial unrest, provocation, etc, etc.

Through numerous party agitators the Soviet Government stirs up the Russian people in every possible way against the peoples of the democratic countries, preparing the ground for the third world war.

During my residence in Canada I have seen how the Canadian people and their Government, sincerely wishing to help the Soviet people, sent supplies to the Soviet Union, collected money for the welfare of the Russian people, sacrificing the lives of their sons in the delivery of these supplies across the ocean – and instead of gratitude for the help rendered, the Soviet Government is developing espionage activity in Canada, preparing to deliver a stab in the back of Canada – all this without the knowledge of the Russian people.

Convinced that such doable-faced politics of the Soviet Government towards the democratic countries do not conform with the interests of the Russian people and endanger the security of civilization, I decided to break away from the Soviet regime and to announce my decision openly.

I am glad that I found the strength within myself to take this step and to warn Canada and the other democratic countries of the danger which hangs over them.

(Sgd) GOUZENKO.

I have read the foregoing translation which was made from my original statement in Russian, and have found it to be correct.
October 10th 1945

(Sgd) GOUZENKO.

In the course of his interrogations GOUZENKO produced a vast amount of information supported by documents covering the existence of a collate Red Amy network operating in Canada. He appeared before the Royal Commission, which was set up in February 1946 to examine this information, and was considered to be a most reliable and informative witness. As a result of his defection twenty persons, one of them a Canadian Member of Parliament and many of them holding positions in connection with Canadian administration, atomic energy etc., were tried for supplying information to a foreign power. One at least of the Russian espionage service networks in Canada was thus entirely broken up and his evidence also led to the trial and conviction in this country of Dr Allan Nunn MAY. In the opinion of the Royal Commission GOUZENKO by his action in defecting and in providing all the information in his possession had 'rendered great public service to the people of this country and thereby has placed Canada in his debt'.

In December 1946, GOUZENKO read an agreement with the *Cosmopolitan* magazine to publish his memoirs in serial form. He was of course a completely free agent in any question relative to his private interests and it was anticipated that since the espionage trials in which he was giving evidence were completed, he would take up residence in Canada. His articles appeared during 1947 but we have not seen them there.

In April 1947 the *Daily Graphic* Inside Information reported that GOUZENKO had been made a British subject by the exercising of an old prerogative of the Crown. In an earlier newspaper reported through the *Evening News* it was stated that he might leave with his wife and two children for another British Dominion to live on the £25 a month annuity, which had been bought for him by an anonymous Canadian.

Constantin VOLKOV
On 24 March 1945 Mr. Page, British Vice Consul of Istanbul, received the following letter:-

Dear Sir, I should be very much obliged if you would receive me at the British Consulate to-day or to-morrow evening at 10 o'clock, I want to speak to you on important and urgent business.

Would you kindly let me know whether you can receive me, As a confirmation of your agreement, please send me your visiting card by courier or ring the Consulate up (the telephone number is 42610), addressing the man on duty in such a way:

The British Consulate requests your Consul to call upon us for negotiations regarding the Soviet citizen by the name of Beorgence'.

Please note that if the presence of an interpreter is necessary, it is desirable that he should be an Englishman,

Hoping to hear from you soon, I am very truly yours. (The visiting cord of Consul VOLKOV a member of the Soviet Embassy was attached.)

After consultation with Mr. Hurst, Mr. Page decided to ignore this letter. On 4 September 1945 VOLKOV arrived at the British Consulate in Istanbul and saw Mr. Page. He was brought by an official of PCO, to Mr, Reed of the British Embassy, VOLKOV said that what he had to tell Mr Reed was of a strictly private nature and the official was sent away.

VOLKOV introduced himself as the Deputy Chief of the Soviet Security Service in Turkey and without further preliminaries said he had some information of great importance to give to Mr, Reed. He alleged that he would be able to provide information on Soviet Intelligence activities directed against Britain. Mr. Reed asked him why he was telling him this, to which he replied that he had quarrelled with his Ambassador and other members of his Embassy and could not stand it any more. He became quite excited at this juncture – although both before and afterwards he remained sitting very quietly – talking very fast and never looking at Mr. Reed. This made him at times difficult to understand but Mr. Reed says that he seemed normal, sober and composed.

VOLKOV then told Mr Reed that he had an empty flat in Moscow in which he had left a suitcase containing the names of Soviet agents in the UK and a great deal of other information connected with Soviet activities. It could be arranged for somebody to go and collect this suitcase which was supposed to contain only private papers. This all seemed so extraordinary to Mr. Reed that he told VOLKOV that he was not particularly interested in what happened in Moscow, but would like to know exact details of the work against Britain, VOLKOV refused to give these details until Mr. Reed could confirm that the British were 'interested' in the information he had to give, lie was not asked for a definition of the word 'interested' but was told the conversation would be reported to Mr. Reed's superiors.

VOLKOV begged that if any account of the conversation were sent to London it should go in writing and not by telegraph and that the information he had given should be restricted to the minimum number of people, what he had to say he wished to say only to Mr Reed. Mr. Reed was not to telephone VOLKOV who would come and see him again in a few days' time.

He was asked if he were [sic] not running a considerable risk in making these visits but he said that he was not – that he was not being followed or watched and that only his wife knew what he was up to. He then went away.

On the 13th September 1945 – nine days after his interview with Mr. Reed – VOLKOV handed to Mr. Page a long letter addressed to Mr. Reed, In this he asked for the following guarantees:

1. The maintenance of absolute secrecy with regard to proposal. The non-despatch of any record about the natter either by radio or telegraph.
2. All agreements with your Management must be conducted directly and without the participation of any third parties.
3. The loss of my post and situation must be worthily compensated by an immediate payment to me of at least £50,000 sterling. I consider this sun as a minimum, considering the importance of the material and evidence given to you, as the result of which all my relatives living in the territory of the USSR are doomed.
4. The offer to me of a refuge and also a guarantee of full safe conduct. I beg you to communicate to me your decision either provisionally or definitely by the 25th September or at the latest by 1st October 1945.

In return for these concessions, VOLKOV offered a long catalogue of information which he represented himself as able to provide. He said that he himself had been an official of the NKGB Intelligence Service since the Autumn of 1936. There is no doubt that had he really been able to provide all that he offered, the information would have been of inestimable value.

Late in September and early October three telephone calls were made to the Soviet Consulate in an attempt to get into touch with VOLKOV, The first was answered by the Russian Consul General, the second by a man speaking English who claimed to be VOLKOV, but clearly was not, and the last by the Russian telephone operator who said that VOLKOV had left for Moscow.

Enquiries showed that VOLKOV and Mrs. VOLKOV had in fact left by air for Russia on 26th September 1945 in a plane which was carrying a Doctor and two persons who \ were described as Diplomatic Couriers, but who had not formerly appeared on any Soviet courier lists.

Kiril Mikhailovich ALEXEEV

ALEXEEV was born at Lebedian on 1 June 1908. He was at an elementary school until 1923 and from 1923 until 1925 he attended art school in Moscow. In 1925 he entered the Central Institute of Labour and took courses in plumbing, finishing in 1926 as a qualified plumber. He entered the Metallurgical Technicum in 1927 and studied in the Construction Division, graduating in 1929 as a technician. In 1930 he enrolled in the Mining Academy in Moscow in the Metallurgical Division and graduated in 1935 with the degree of Metallurgical Engineer, In that year he married Antonina Ivanovna, o fellow student who was also in her last year, Antonina was the daughter of a roan who had been an active Bolshevik prior to and during the revolution, but who was never an official of the Party, He was arrested in 1937 by the NKVD and charged with being an enemy of the people. His daughter was told that he had been banished for ten years without right of correspondence; she eventually found out that he had been executed.

After his marriage ALEXEEV stayed on at the Mining Academy assisting the professors until 1937 when he received that degree of Candidate of Technical Science, In 1937 he was appointed chief engineer for the building of an ammunition factory near Moscow. He refined there until 1940, was transferred to another factory, and when the war broke out in 1941, was sent to the Construction Bureau No.1 in Moscow as chief engineer. He worked on various assignments as a general metallurgical engineer and never saw active service with the Amy.

ALEXEEV says that both he and his wife were brought up in the Greek Orthodox faith. During his youth ALEXEEV was a member of the Komsomol and from 1937 he was subjected to considerable pressure to join the Communist Party, In 1939 he became a candidate, but realising that he would never become Party Member he says that he destroyed his candidate documents and membership book in about 1935 or 1940.

ALEXEEV says that from an early age he was dissatisfied with life in the USSR because of the extreme strictness of the regime. He explains that while a young man of twenty-four or twenty-five years of age he had begun to realise that life under such a system of government was impossible. During the war it became increasingly clear that no changes in the regime were to be expected; this realisation brought matters to a head and he made a final decision to break. He states that he merely wanted to be able to live and work under a democratic system; that is, a system by which his children could be brought up properly. He and his wife had agreed on this subject and felt that they could not bring up their children in the way they considered to be right in the USSR.

In the autumn of 1943 ALEXEEV decided to try for a foreign assignment. He had heard from one of his brothers of the possibility of a vacancy in Mexico. He obtained two affidavits testifying to his character (one of them by somewhat underhand methods) and in addition he was helped by his spotless employment record. In November 1943 he was investigated by the NKVD and the foreign Section of the Central Committee. According to ALEXEEV, it is possible that the records of his purged father-in-law were not found at this time because they had been in the Ukraine and might have been destroyed during the German invasion.

The ALEXEEVs passports, which were not diplomatic, were issued in March 1944. ALEXEEV's idea at that time was that he and his family would live in Mexico for a while, where they would acquire some friends and learn the language. He claims, however, that always in the back of his mind there existed the great desire to go to the United States where he would easily be able to obtain employment because of his training.

In the United States he felt that his children could be brought up properly and that he and his family could be respected and desired members of society.

He added that he felt that he would be able to obtain money front the sale of a rotary motor which he had designed; he did not expect to participate in politics once he settled in the United States.

Antonina Ivanovna confirmed that she and her husband first decided to try for a foreign assignment in the Autumn of 1943. Life was very difficult in Moscow and they wanted to go abroad. She says that she and her husband discussed leaving Russia for good but never actually made up their minds until his recall in 1944, the main deterrent being her mother who was still in Moscow. Antonina states that lots of people in Russia want to get out of the country and try their best to do so.

ALEXEEV and his family arrived in Mexico in July 1943. Before leaving Moscow he had been briefed on his duties, which were to be those of assistant to the Commercial Attaché. He also says that he was called before a chief of the NKVD. known to him as Georgi NIKOLAEVICH who proposed that he should spy upon OUIMANSKY, the Russian Ambassador in Mexico. ALEXEEV told the NKVD man that he would not spy upon Russians; he promised, however, that he would report any anti-Soviet activities which he night observe. While he was in Mexico in December and again in January he was twice asked whether he had anything for Georgi NIKOLAEVICH, It was during ALEXEEV's service in Mexico that Constantin OUMANSKY was killed in a plane crash, While he was at the Embassy in Mexico, ALEXEEV was allowed to buy a car with his own money and he took possession of it in July 1946.

The ALEXEEVs, in spite of a warning that they had received before leaving Moscow, were friendly with several foreigners in Mexico, among then a Jugoslav called Adolpho WEISSMANN. They were again warned during their Mexican assignment that they were not to associate with foreigners but ALEXEEV was under the impression that the Embassy did not know of his contact with WEISSMANN. In September 1946 the order for ALEXEEV's recall to Moscow reached the Soviet Embassy. He was relieved of his regular duties and an accounting was made to his superior of all funds in his possession. Then his recall first came through it was anticipated that he might have to travel through the USA to join a Soviet ship so arrangements were made with the American Embassy for a transit visa. In the meantime ALEXEEV succeeded in selling his car. He states that he and his wife had definitely decided not to return to the Soviet Union; Vie felt that on return to Russia he would be more or less permanently isolated as he was not a Party Member and as ho bad been in contact with foreigners whilst in Mexico. Towards the end of October a Russian ship arrived at Veracruz and arrangements were made for ALEXEEV and his family to leave on her. At this tine he became aware that he was being watched. He succeeded, however, in persuading the Russian Embassy doctor that his daughter was not well enough to travel and the ship left without him. Throughout the month of November ALEXEEV had been trying unsuccessfully *to* persuade his Ambassador to let him travel through the USA, but during the last week of November he heard that another Russian ship was about to put in at a Central American port.

With the expected arrival of the second ship, he decided, that his last chance had come, and on the 26th November he went to the American Embassy, collected his transit visas and obtained, tickets on a plane leaving for America the following morning at 5 a.m. He and his family successfully escaped on the plane; the only two persons who knew of their plans were the Jugoslav Adolpho WEISSMAN who gave then the name of a friend of his whom they could contact in New York, and another friend of theirs, a middle-aged woman called Dvoira WAISSMAN.

On arrival in the USA ALEXEEV contacted an anti-Soviet newspaper through which he got in touch with a White Russian organisation which has assisted other Soviet escapees, such as deserters from Soviet ships. He and his family were taken to an establishment run by this organisation in the country, but they did not feel safe there and moved to a hide-out in New York,

On the 30th December 1946 ALEXEEV issued a brief statement through a lawyer:-

> all my life I have worked for the Russian people ... but it has become clear to me that my work, like that of the whole Russian people is beneficial to the Soviet regime and not to themselves. No section is more exploited or rather enslaved ... millions of guiltless men have been put into concentration camps until the entire Soviet Union is a concentration camp ... even men belonging to the nearest entourage of the dictator do not feel safe. That is why the great majority of the Russian people hate the Soviet regime ..., and this is the reason why I cannot return to my homeland end doom my family.

The FBI interrogated ALEXEEV in December but were able to get very little out of him owing to his nervous state of mind and fear of liquidation. His lawyers were attempting to obtain legal sanctuary for him. On the 1st January 1947 the Soviet Embassy in Washington made a formal request to the State Department for ALEXEEV's apprehension and delivery to them as a criminal who had embezzled official Soviet fluids in Mexico. ALEXEEV denied this allegation, but for a time his fate hung in the balance. On the 21st January 1947, the State Department refused to extradite ALEXEEV.

ALEXEEV was again interrogated by the FBI in January 1947 when he amplified and in some cases corrected the information he had previously given. At this second interview ALEXEEV and his wife stated that his brothers and sisters and her mother were probably already in prison. He was anxious that if possible enquiries should be made about them.

Michel KORIAKOFF

This case was first brought to our notice in November 1946 by a neighbour of this Office, who had heard through a White Russian newspaper in Paris and through her friends, that an official of the Soviet Embassy in Paris named KORIAKOFF had disappeared without trace in circumstances which suggested that he was severing all connection with his own people.

In March 1947 we succeeded in obtaining his story from the Americans. Captain Michel KORIAKOFF was on the staff of VESTI s RCDINI, a Russian language newspaper published in Paris by the Russian Embassy. While stationed in Paris he apparently wrote a book entitled *Why I Refused to Return to Soviet Russia* based primarily on his religious convictions, and decided to join the ranks of Soviet citizens in exile. His escape was precipitated by the fact that on 18 March 1946 the Chief of Personnel of the Russian Embassy summoned him and informed him that he would be on his way to Moscow that day, accompanied by a Captain of the Russian Repatriation Commission, Accompanied by the Captain and Major BERESIN he was escorted to his hotel and given fifteen minutes to pack. On the pretext of collecting his pay from the Embassy he created an opportunity of eluding the Captain, escaped through the side door and disappeared into the Metro,

He was first brought to the attention of the Americans in Paris through the efforts of Miss Sophie ZERNOVA who directs the Centre d'Aide Pour Les Refugies Russes in Paris. It is not thought that the Americans took any active part in the protection of KORIAKOFF although he was apparently interviewed on one or two occasions concerning the internal organisation, personalities and activities of the Russian Embassy in Paris. He did not, to our knowledge, make any appreciable contribution to information already in our hands on this subject, although he did confirm in a rather superficial manner the relationship of the Press and Propaganda Sections of the Embassy with Émigré and French Communist Party organisations.

A new non-Soviet Russian weekly *Russkaya M'isl* which started publication in April 1947 published in its three first numbers extracts from a book written by KORIAKOFF. The whole book was being published in installments in the French paper *Cahiers du Monde Nouveau* under the title *Why I am not Returning to Russia*. We have not seen KORIAKOFF's book but it seems clear that his motives for defection were mainly religious.

Major YURCHENKO

In April 1947 we heard from Austria that YURCHIENKO, who was the Russian equivalent of DAPM in Vienna had defected. He was said to have made contact with the Americans and to have reached the. American Zone of Germany. In May 1947 it was learned that he had not defected to the Americans but to the French. This information was confirmed in June and YURCHENCO was stated to be in Paris under the protection of the French. Nothing more is known about his defection nor have we received any information produced by him.

Mikhail Filipovich DENISOV

DENISOV was born on 23 August 1923 in Totischehevo, Lev Tolstoi county, Rezan district. In 1924 the family moved to Moscow where his father was a driver for the military motor pool for Soviet ministers.

From 1929 until 1939 DENISOV went to school in Moscow and then entered the Aviation Technical School. At the outbreak of [the Second World] war he was sent to an aviation plant in Moscow where he worked as a locksmith until October 1941, He then worked at another plant in Kuibyshev until his call up into the Red Army in June 1942, He was sent to the Military Institute of Foreign Languages of the Red Army in Stavropol and while there in September 1942 he Joined the Komsomols. He started by learning German but after a month switched to Hungarian, studying at the school until April 1944 when he was commissioned as a junior lieutenant.

He worked as an interpreter for various sections of the Red Army Intelligence Department on the Ukrainian front and in February 1945 moved with the 4th Ukrainian Front Headquarters to Stanislava, later to Proskerov and then to Ivunkachevo. From Ivfunkachevo he was transferred to Debrecen and the Allied Control Commission in Hungary, In June or July 1945 he was assigned to the Soviet Embassy in Budapest as personal interpreter for the Minister. In Budapest he met Vera TAKACS and on 31st January 1947 he was sent back to Moscow because of his relationship with her.

From February 1947 until the beginning of April, DENISOV was in a reserve battalion of Red A ray officers in Moscow. On the 15th April he was assigned as an interpreter of the Intelligence Department Red-Bannered Danubian Fleet at Ismail on the north of the Danube, and on 11 May 1947 he was sent back to Budapest.

When his request to marry TAKACS was repeatedly turned down by the Soviet authorities and he was forbidden even to see her, they made up their minds to escape together. They decided to go through Czechoslovakia since the Soviets would never think of looking for them there as the logical place for them to go would be Austria, On the 15th August 1947 they left Budapest for the frontier where they were helped by a Black Marketeer. On the 16th August they illegally crossed the border into Czechoslovakia, and on the evening of the 17th they reached Prague, having travelled by train. They spent the night with a Czech woman, and on the next day went to the British Embassy, of which they had found the address in the telephone book. They wanted to see the British Military Attaché believing that in exchange for the information they had to offer, the British would help them out of Czechoslovakia and possibly find then a job. Instead of the Military Attaché they saw the Air Attaché, who told them to come back at 3 o'clock in the afternoon. On their return they met two men in civilian clothes who arranged to meet them that evening at a bridge in Prague. Frou there they were taken by car to a house where they spent a day and a half, after which they were told by one of the men that since the British had no border with Czechoslovakia they would turn them over to American representatives. On the 20th August 1947 they were taken by car out or town, transferred to a jeep driven by an American captain, crossed the border and went to Regensburg.

As previously stated in the section on Vera TAKACS, DENISOV provided extensive and valuable information to his American interrogators. The motive for his defection would appear to be his love for Vera TAKACS.

Veronika (Vera) Feodorovna TAKACS

Vera TAKACS was born on 26 December 1916 in Astrakhan, Russia. Her parents were divorced in 1920 and in 1921 her mother was married again to a Hungarian. She went with her mother to Budapest and became a Hungarian citizen, attending high school for four years. She then went to a school for actors where she learned dancing and acting, got a job with a cabaret and, accompanied by her mother, travelled extensively, appearing in Belgrade, Zagreb, Rome and other cities. She returned, without her mother, in Italy until 1934 or 1935 then went to Egypt and Syria, back to Italy and to Malta. In 1937 she decided to give up the stage and settle down. She had not lived a very moral life and had become the mother of an illegitimate child when she was seventeen.

She returned to Budapest, went to live with her parents and learned shorthand and typing. She worked at a medical laboratory until January 1942 when she became secretary to a well known construction engineer who was also a deputy in the Hungarian Parliament. She worked in this man's office throughout the German occupation until the arrival of the Russian Army.

At the beginning of 1944 when the Germans occupied Hungary Vera became worried about the conscription for labour of all foreign, nationals and naturalised citizens, and for this reason and to get a home and a name for her child and herself, she married a Hungarian,

Istvan TAKACS. Her carriage broke up, however, and she found herself alone again.

A few days after the Russian occupation of Budapest in January 1945, TAKACS was arrested and although her papers were in order she was detained because she had been born in Russia and spoke Russian. After a short time in a detention camp she was taken to the office of Captain ABRAMOV of 126 Battalion NKVD Frontier Troops where she was thoroughly screened and asked to become an interpreter. She went to Austria and Czechoslovakia with ABRAMOV but she finally complained to high ranking officers of his uncontrolled and licentious behavior, and in the summer of 1945 she was sent back to Budapest where she became interpreter at the Inspektsya. At some time in the latter half of 1946 she met Mikhail DENISOV, a young Russian who was also acting as interpreter in Budapest, When TAKACS met DENISOV, seven years younger than herself, she decided that he was her man and she was ready for any sacrifice in order to hold him. Unfortunately the Russian authorities did not approve their marriage; she was more than willing to become a Soviet citizen and live in Russia as DENISOV's wife. When she learned that this was impossible she saw no alternative but to get away from Hungary with DENISOV, especially as it became increasing difficult even to carry on their affair.

The escape of TAKACS and DENISOV in August 1947 is described in the note on the latter. They both gave a very great deal of valuable information to their American interrogators. In TAKACS's interrogator's opinion the fact that she escaped mainly for personal reasons did not diminish the value of the information given. She advanced ideological reasons for her flight from Soviet tyranny and attempted to establish that no personal affairs had influenced her decision.

Alexander KRAVCHENKO

Alexander KTAVCHENKO was born on 14 June 1925 in Svenigoroda, Kiev in the Ukraine. His father was a farmer who settled there during the 1917 revolution. Alexander KRAVCHENKO attended public school from 1951 to 1938 and graduated from Kirova school in June 1941. During his school years he was a convinced Communist and an avid reader of Marx, Lenin and Stalin.

After graduation he helped his father on the farm until June 1942 when he was sent to Germany as a slave labourer. He worked as a mechanic in a German factory in Ludwigshafen until he was liberated by the American Amy on 24th March 1945.

In June 1945 Alexander KRAVCHENKO was transferred at his own request to a Russian repatriation camp. Out of this camp he was recruited into a SMERSH unit because of his language qualifications – he speaks German fluently with only a slight accent. In February 1946 Alexander KRAVCHENKO came to the NKVD, first in Frankfurt on the Oder, later in Eberswalde and finally in Potsdam where he worked as an interpreter with the so-called Investigation Section of the Operational Sector.

His pre-occupation with English language studies combined, with certain careless remarks, yielded him the reputation of being pro-western. Owing to the shortage of experienced interpreters, he escaped imprisonment, but he sensed that his days of freedom were numbered. By December 1946 he had realised that his ideas and ideals were not in accord with those of the Soviet Government and that he could not reconcile his conscience with the methods used in the work with which he was connected. He decided to defect to the American authorities, offering to tell them everything about his work with the Russian Intelligence Service. He hoped in return to be given an opportunity to emigrate to America and start a new life there. At first he had planned to desert on the spur of the moment, but he realised that he actually knew very little about the MGB, and he feared that the American authorities would not believe his story unless he could prove by giving facts that he was sincere. He therefore decided to remain in his job for the time being and to keep his ears and eyes open. Wlicreas before he had kept very much to himself he now made every effort to be sociable, engaging in political discussions with his colleagues although always being careful not to reveal his real feelings, and making a point of listening to telephone conversations, collecting names and photographs of Russian Intelligence Service personnel and noting in code the licence numbers of cars assigned to his Sektor.

KRAVTCHENKO originally planned to take a boat kept for recreational use to the Wannsee and turn himself over to the American authorities there. He was however unable to do this and he therefore decided to make his escape during the next duty trip away from Potsdam.

In June 1947 he went with his officer to Halle to carry out an interrogation there. In order not to arouse suspicion he only took enough luggage for two days, but he made sure that he had in his possession all the photographs and other material which he had collected. After their job was completed KRAVCHENKO left his officer in a suburb of Berlin on the pretext of wanting to visit a friend and promising to be back in Potsdam that evening. He immediately proceeded to the

American Sector in Berlin where he reported to an American MP and successfully completed his defection on the 19th June 1947.

In the opinion of the American Field Representative who interrogated him, Alexander KRAVCHENKO is an unusually intelligent person considering both age and background. He seemed to be endowed with an remarkably retentive memory for even insignificant details. At the same time he displayed outstanding judgement in conveying the kind of information which he believed to be of counter-espionage interest.

A large volume of background information enabled the Americans to check up on most of the facts related by him and in almost every instance they were confirmed by previous information. There were no indications that Alexander KRAVCHENKO had been planted on American Intelligence for deception purposes. He provided them with a great deal of information on the re-organisation of the Russian Intelligence Service in Germany, the structure of MVD. Operational Sectors, MGB. Sections, personalities etc.

Vasilyi Mikhailovich SHARANDAK @ Laszlo BAKSA

SHARANDAK was born on 8 May1923 at Olkhovata, the son of an agricultural labourer who in 1922. benefited from Lenin's distribution of land and was able to settle on a snail farm of his own. In the 1930s their farm became part of a collective farm and as a result the family lived in extreme poverty and semi-starvation.

From 1930 to 1933 SHARANI1AK went to elementary schools and in 1939 he obtained a scholarship at a pre-medical high school where he stayed until the outbreak of the Russo-German war. While at school he became a member of the Komsomols and, though not an active member, he believed in Communist doctrines and had various discussions with his father who did not share his views and who often recalled the better days of Tsarism.

After the Germans invaded the Ukraine SHARANDAK remained on the faro with his father until 1942 when he volunteered for work in Germany. He was put in a party of Ukrainian slave workers and sent to Austria. The conditions were not at all what he had expected and he made several unsuccessful attempts to escape. As a result of one of these he was in prison in Hungary under the false Hungarian name of BAKSA from May 1943 until the day before the Russian troops arrived in Sopron, 29 March.1945. After his release from prison he stayed in Sopron where he met and fell in love with Maria GRASZLI, a Hungarian girl to whom he became engaged.

From about April 1945 to July 1947 SHARANDAK was employed as Hungarian interpreter with different security units of the Russian occupation forces in Hungary. This suited him well as he wanted to stay in Sopron with his fiancée and had no desire to go back to Russia. Simultaneously with his work for the Russians he was engaged on the Black Market with the full knowledge of his employers both on his own and on their behalf.

SHARANDAK states that since the end of the war it was his firm intention to settle in Hungary. He worked for the Russians whilst they were there because he was thus able to avoid military service or repatriation, but he had always intended to desert at the last moment before the Russian withdrawal. At the beginning of 1946 he started to prepare the ground for staying behind. He registered with the police in Sopron under his alias of BAKSA and managed to obtain other documents in the same way.

In June 1947 SHARANDAK was employed at the Russian Security Headquarters in translating denunciations of persons suspected of espionage on behalf of the Western Allies. One of these reports was about a Professor VOLAND who was employed as a translator at the British Mission. SHARANDAK was struck with the idea that he might exploit this information and in this way get in touch with Hungarians connected with the Mission. He decided to call on Professor VOLAND to inform him that he was under Russian supervision and eventually to offer his services. The visit was not a success as SHARANDAK did not even see V0LAND and was received with suspicion. He realised how ill advised his action had been and decided to desert before there were any repercussions.

In July 1947 he went to Sopron to make further preparations for his desertion and made up his mind not to return to Security Headquarters. He hid in Budapest until early August, but realising that he could not do this indefinitely he went back to Sopron to hide with his fiancée's family. One of his Black Market friends assured him that he would get him across the frontier, if not straight to the British Zone, at least to Vienna, His friend failed him, however, and meanwhile Russian enquiries about his disappearance had led then as far as the flat where he was hiding. On the 30th August 1947 he crossed the frontier on foot and on the 3rd September reached the British Zone and at Hartberg reported to the British. He appears to have had some misgivings as to whether the British might not return him. There were rumours, he said, that Russian deserters were being handed back.

SHARANDAK's interrogator says that he has a natural intelligence, a love of adventure and a dislike of regular work. So far as the motives for his defection are concerned, he has in his possession photographs which show that before the war his family were living in extreme poverty. The news which he has since received from home has not held out any hopes of betterment. It is believed that the fact that he enjoyed a much higher standard of living in Hungary than he could expect in Russia, together with the fact that he had volunteered to work in Germany, were the most important contributing factors to his decision. He appeared to be genuine in his bitter feelings against the present regime in Russia but holds no definite alternative political views, nor has he any religious convictions.

Throughout his interrogation he was fully co-operative and provided voluminous though fragmentary information on what he knew of the organisation and functions of the Russian Army Security Service in Hungary. He intends to join his fiancée in Hungary as soon as possible and to settle there under a false identity. He believes that there are no prospects for him elsewhere but that in Hungary through his connections he could easily find some means of livelihood.

Colonel Grigorii Aleksandrovich TOKAEV

TOKAEV was born on 13 October 1909 near Vladikavkaz in the Caucasus, he is of Oasetian origin which he describes as a small minority of Indo-Iranians living in the Northern Caucasus. Son of a peasant family, he had the normal up-bringing of a Caucasian peasant and although he attended the usual village school and later graduated to secondary schools etc, he was in his early years, almost entirely self-educated. He joined the Communist Party in February 1932 having previously been a member of the Komsomol.

In May 1932 he obtained nomination as a student at the Zulcov Military Air Academy in 'Moscow where he studied for five years, qualifying as an 'aero-constructor' in 1937. He was appointed an engineer in the aero-dynamics laboratory in the same Academy, eventually becoming the head of the laboratory. In December 1940 he was transferred to the appointment of deputy head of a department in the Academy and on 16 April 1941 he became a Doctor of Science which he describes in German as 'Kandidat Technischer Wissenschaften' of the same Academy. In November 1942 he became 'Dozent in Flugzeugbau' and was appointed lecturer and in November 1944 he was appointed senior lecturer – honorary title of professor – at the Academy. During this period he lecturcd to other institutions, and had attained the rank of Engineer Lieutenant-Colonel.

At the end of the [Second World] war, on the 28th June 1945 TOKAEV arrived in Germany on appointment to the 'Abteilung Luftwaffe' at the SJ'A Karlshorst, Berlin, remaining there, however, only five weeks. On the formation of the Allied Control Authority Secretariat (US Sector of Berlin) who was appointed Joint General Secretary of the Russian element of this Allied Secretariat, where he remained until 6th March 1946. During this period he had occasion to meet a large number of British, American and French officials, and he realised for the first time in his life that these people were human beings and moreover gave an impression of freedom of thought and action which was quite contrary to his Soviet up-bringing. At this time TOKAEV apparently had several conversations with his Western friends about possibilities of visiting their countries.

On the 6th March 1946 he transferred at his on request to the SFA. Although he had been extremely interested in the work of the Allied Secretariat and above all with the contacts he had been able to make there, he realised that he was not a cleric but a technician, hence the request to be returned to the duties with which he was familiar.

In the SFA he had the general assignment of collecting all possible information on German aero-dynamics, In addition he had certain subsidiary tasks from time to time. As examples of these he gave:-

a. To discover in detail the organisation and structure of the German Luftfahrtforschung Akademie which is next due to the GAP Ministry in Berlin, This task was on direct instructions from MALENKOF in Moscow.
b. To examine and obtain all available information on the project SANGER. This was a so-called project thought up by SANGER for a supersonic long range very high altitude jet propelled bomber which had been discovered by TOKAEV and a few more engineers in 1945 Moscow expressed great interest in this project.
c. To try to persuade SANGER and certain of his colleagues to transfer to Moscow; this again was on direct orders from MALENKOV. VOSNESENSKY and General SEROV but TOKAEV was unable to carry out this assignment.

Throughout the whole of his service in Germany he was consultant on air development matters to Marshal SOKOLOVSKY, He was taken to Moscow by the Marshal on two occasions to act as his advisor at conferences in the Politburo.

In October 1946 TOKAEV, was called to Moscow by the Soviet Foreign Office as consultant in the preparation of the air clause of a German peace treaty. He was required to prepare a report stating which German aircraft experts were still in Germany and which had been taken to the West.

In April 1947 TOKAEV was again summoned to Moscow where he was told by VOSIJSSENSKY, a member of the Politburo, Deputy Prime Minister, and chairman of the State Planning Commission –

'Comrade TOKAEV we have asked you to cone in order to have your views on SANGER's project; they say you are opposed to it; Is that so or not? Give us your observations'.

TOKAEV expressed his views which were briefly that SANGER's project did not exist – that the material described *as* a project only represented rough notes and an interrupted formulation of an interesting idea. It would require extensive and very serious research to build such an aeroplane as SANGER had visualised. Out of the discussions arising from this meeting a project was formulated which included the following:-

> The Soviet of Ministers of the USSR directs:
>
> A Commission is to be created composed of the following, Colonel General YAKOVLEV, Engineer Lieutenant Colonel TOKAEV, Academic an ICELDISH and Professor KISHKIN.
>
> This Commission is to proceed to Germany to carry out research for further details and specialists dealing with SANGER's project. On completion of this task the Commission will submit a reasoned report on the practical possibility of realising SANGER's project.
>
> Marshal SOKOLOVSKY is to afford the Commission all possible assistance.

On the following day TOKAEV was taken to see Stalin, MOLOTOV, MALENKOV, ZHADANOV, BULGAXIN, VOROSHILOV, MIKOYVN, BERIA, V0SNESENSKY and SHVERNIK.

Stalin asked TOKAEV about SANGER's project and TOKAEV again repeated his reservations. Under Stalin's direction it was there and then arranged that the Commission with General SEROV instead of General ZIKOVLEV should be set up and should present its report by the 1st August. While TOKAEV was in the room. 'Stalin telephoned SOKOLOVSKY, told him that TOKAEV's chief in Germany, KUTSEVALOV, was being removed, and said that TOKAEV was to be made deputy to whoever took charge of the Air Department. On the next day, the 10th April 1941, the Commission left for Germany.

General SEROV and TOKAEV immediately had a sharp dispute about the former's treatment of one of the German scientists. Next SEROV on his own initiative appointed to the Commission Stalin's son, a man of whom TOKA.EV had a very low opinion, At the end of April a telegram was sent to Stalin stating that the Commission had so far failed to find any further materials or specialists on SANGER's project, TOKAEV at the same time, with the knowledge of the Commission, sent his own telegram to the effect that his attitude to the SANGER project remained unchanged, and that in his opinion the methods of the Commission were all wrong.

TOKAEV was immediately summoned by SOKOLOVSKY who told him that MALENKOV was very displeased by his behaviour and that he was to drop his obstinacy and his personal intrigues. MALENKOV had instructed SEROV, KELDISH and KISHKIN to proceed to Moscow and the work of the Commission was to be handed over to General ALEXAHDROV. TOKAEV refused to work under ALEXANDROV whom he considered quite unsuitable and who he personally disliked. Marshal SOKOLOVSKY flew into a terrible rage and in spite of his objections, TOKAEV started work with the Commission under ALEXANDROV on the 3rd May 1947. The burden of the work of the Commission fell on TOKAEV's shoulders. Meanwhile LANGE, one of the German scientists working for the Russians, had drawn up a plan for starting; a construction office to design an elaborate supersonic aircraft. TOKAEV protested against this plan as he did not think LANGE and his team were capable of designing such a plane, Moscow, however, approved the aircraft and asked that a Russian report should be provided regarding the LANGE Group's proposals. TOKAEV met the LANGE Group and after a long exchange of ideas, the Group presented an ambitious programme of work. This was forwarded to Moscow together with TOKAEV's comments which were to the effect that he did not consider that the LANGE Group was worthy of any serious attention.

About two weeks later TOKAEV was informed that he was relieved of work on the Corliss ion. He became aware that he was falling under suspicion and furthermore a number of his friends and colleagues were disappearing. He asked Stalin's son whether he could be received by Stalin to talk about the work of the Commission, but he was told not to worry. He also wrote a request to be allowed to return to the USSR.

In July 1947, General SEROV unexpectedly arrived back in Germany and told TOKAEV that they must start looking for specialists in designing jet-propelled aircraft engines, TOKAEV said that he had been removed from work on the Corliss ion and he again asked to be allowed to return to Russia. SEROV, however, said that he was to stay in Germany and continue work on the LANGE/SANGER project. TOKAEV also became involved with an attempt to get another German scientist, Professor TANK, to come to Russia, This negotiation was a most complicated one (TANK was a suspected British agent) and as a result of this it seems that TOKAEV fell more and more under suspicion. TANK had in fact been in contact with the British authorities. To suspect TANK was, therefore, reasonable? and it may well have been reasonable for the Russian Security authorities to suspect TOKAEV, if they had already evidence that he was disloyal to the regime.

TOKAEV, according to his own statements, had long been anti-Stalin and he had been involved with an anti-Stalin underground movement in Russia and in Germany. He went on leave to Moscow in September 1947 and there he obtained certain information about arrests of fellow conspirators which led him to believe that he would soon be caught himself. It was a matter of time before his underground connections would be discovered and his involvements with the suspect TANK would be another nail in his coffin. He therefore hurried back to Germany and decided to try to defect.

After considerable thought he chose the Canadians to defect to as opposed to the British, Americans or French, for the following reasons:-

1. He is violently against the Potsdam Agreement.
2. He had heard in Russia that the British hand back defectors.
3. He was opposed to the materialistic outlook of the Americans.
4. Among the French there are too many people like Thoress and Duclos.

He therefore chose the Canadians as being ideologically closest to the British and as not having been signatories of the Potsdam Agreement. In about September 1947 he wrote and sent through the ordinary mail a letter to the Canadian Military Mission in which he said that Officer 'X', a high ranking Russian Officer, asked for asylum for himself and his family and promised to respect Canadian laws. He said that he would telephone on a given day, but no call was received from him. Later he wrote another similar letter which was handed to the Persian Mission with the request that it be delivered to the Canadians.

By October 1947 the net had started to close around TOKAEV. He had been questioned about what he knew of the underground organisation, was under constant surveillance and indeed was more or less under open arrest.

On the 13th October 1947 he again asked in writing to be sent back to the USSR and was told to prepare for his departure. On the 21st October he was informed that he was released from duty. TOKAEV started 'preparing to leave for Moscow', but in the meantime he was also trying to get in touch with the Canadian Military Mission to whom he had written over a month earlier, An officer who knew of TOKAEV's difficulties went to an address in the French Sector in Berlin and telephoned the Canadians. Two days later he was flown back to the USSR with his family, and TOKAEV never learned the result of the telephone call. He then decided that he would have to take a risk; he asked an unknown German to telephone the Canadians and ask for their decision. An appointment was made for the following day and after various elaborate and efficient arrangements, TOKAEV, his wife and small daughter, were removed by air. It was not until the last minute, after he had entered the plane, that he discovered that in fact it was the British who were in charge of his escape. He was horrified at this discovery and expected at any moment to be put down at a Soviet airport. However, he has expressed the greatest satisfaction at his subsequent treatment by us and says that he now realises that the story that the British hand back defectors must have been Stalinist propaganda.

TOKAEV has been extensively interrogated, has provided a very large amount of technical and political information and his interrogation is still in progress. He has been a very difficult man to exploit. First, he is fanatically anti-Stalin and is anxious that we should immediately carry out his plans to help bring about the downfall of the Stalin government, plans of a propagandist nature whose implementation could not be countenanced. The refusal to carry them out has caused TOKAEV to have frequent bouts of annoyance, in which he refuses to cooperate in his interrogation. Secondly, he has consistently refused to cooperate in any attempt to contact and use his alleged former fellow conspirators for intelligence purposes.

During his first interrogation TOKAEV was asked why he had defected. He did not reply for some time, saying that he was not really quite clear in his own mind yet as to why he had taken the step. He gave several reasons,

a. He had belonged to a small Indo-Iranian minority, for many years domiciled in the Caucasus, whose national characteristics and in fact whose existence had been destroyed by the Soviet regime.
b. He has been fortunate in that he had a good education and obtained a position of importance in his 'particular profession'.

He therefore lived in a way far superior to the greater majority of his fellow countrymen. Tie could not, however, help realising that the majority of the subjects of the USSR lived in a state of complete squalor in order that the aims and objects of the Stalin regime might be carried through – in other words, that his people were being betrayed by their government to further their own ends. He learned while in Berlin to despise Russian propaganda, he realized its utter falseness. He got to know British, American, French and other Western Europeans. He realised that the propaganda regarding Western Europe and the United States as put out in every Russian newspaper, every radio programme, every theatre and in every book was false.

c. He realises that the Stalin refine has systematically endeavoured to seal off Russian thinkers from all civilizing influences; that any section of the community which believes in being unable to carry out its tasks efficiently without some contact with the outer world is liquidated. In this connection he mentioned that there has recently been a systematic purge of all scientists of international reputation. That he himself was under suspicion and that unless he took this opportunity of deserting he would not get a second chance.

d. He has a child. He wants her to have a free education, not the hopelessly biased and propagandised one that she would get in a Russian school.

TOKAEV has given all his interrogators the impression that he was fanatically anti-Stalin. He said that he would never do anything against his own people, but that he was prepared to do anything in his power to destroy the present Russian Communist regime; that the Russian nation fought the war in order to destroy Hitlerism and oppression and semi-slavery; they fought it with their allies in the hope that on victory being obtained they would have the same privileges and freedom as their allies. This hope was never realised – their position now is worse even than before the war.

After his defection TOKAEV was anxious to go somewhere where he could live as a free man and where he could work towards the destruction of the present Russian regime in order that some day he may return to Russia and find it a country where man is free.

NOTES

Introduction
1. See Aooendix II.
2. *The Storm Petrelss* by Gordon Brook-Shepherd (London: Collins, 1977)
3. *The Storm Birds* by Gordon Brook-Shepherd (Weidenfeld & Nicolson, 1988). See also *Of Moles and Molehunters: A Review of Counterintelligence Literature, 1977-93* (CIA Center for the Study of Intelligence, October 1993 by Clrvrland Cram.
4. *Ibid.* p. 32
5. *Ibid.* p. 41
6. Volkov letter first reproduced in *Historical Dictionary of Cold War Counterintelligence*, (London: Rowman & Littlefield, 2007) p. 286; \Adso FCO138/193 (declassified October 2015.
7. Patrick Seale, *Philby: The Long Road to Moscow* (London: Penguin, 1978)
8. *The Defence of the Realm* by Christopher Andrew (London: Allen Lane, 2009) p. 345
9. *Ibid.*
10. *A Spy Among Friends* by Ben Macintyre, (London: Bloomsbury, 2014)
11. *MI6* y Keith Jeffery (London: Bloomsbury, 2016)
12. *The Swird and the Shield: The Mitrokhin Archive* by Christopher Amdrew & Vasili Mitrokhin (New York: Basic Books, 1999)
13. *KGB: The Inside Story* by Christopher Andrew & Oleg Gordievsky (London: Hodder & Stoughton, 1990) p. 305
14. *The Defence of the Realm*, p. 344
15. *The Swird and the Shield: The Mitrokhin Archive*, p. 138.
16. *A Spy Among Friends*, p. 96
17. *Stalin's Agent* by Boris Volodarsky (London: OUP, 2015). p. 395
18. *The Secret History of the Five Eyes* by Richard Kerbaj (London: B;ink, 2022). p. 99.
19. *Kim Philby* by Tim Milne (London: Biteback, 2014). p. 160

Chapter II Grigori Tokaev
1. Guy Liddell Diaries, 26 November 1947
2. *More Cloak than Dagger* by Molly Sasson (Ballarat, Austrli: Conner Court Publishing, 2005).
3. *Betrayal of an Ideal* by Grigori Tokaev (Indiana University Press, 1955)
4. *Comrade X* by Grigori Tokaev (London: Harvill Press, 1956):

Chapter III Yuri Rastvorov
1. *SpyCatcher* by Peter Wright & Paul Greengrass (New York: Viking, 1987). P. 286:
2. Cleveland Cram correspondence, 15 February 1985
3. *Ibid.*

Chapter IV Vladimir Petrov
1. *Empire of Fear* by Vladimir Petrov (London: Andre Deutsch, 1956)
2. Petrov's MI5 file at KV2/342 to KV2/3488

Chapter V Anatoli Golitsyn
1. *Defence of the Realm*, p. 503.
2. *Checkmate* by Anatoli Golisyn. Unpublished memoirs
3. *Ibid.*
4. *Ibid.*
5. *Ibid.*
6. *Ibid.*
7. *Ibid.*
8. *Ibid.*
9. *Ibid.*
10. *Ibid.*
11. *Ibid.*
12. *Ibid.*
13. *Ibid.*
14. *No Other Choice* by George Blake (London: Cape, 1990)
15. *Checkmate* by Anatoli Holitsyn.
16. *The Sword and Shield: The Mitrokhin Archive* by Christopher Andrew and Vasili Mitrokhin, p. 195.
17. *Checkmate* by Anatoli Golitsyn.
18. *Ibid.*
19. *Ibid.*
20. *Ibid.*
21. *Ibid.*
22. *Ibid.*
23. *Ibid.*
24. *Ibid.*
25. *Ibid.*
26. *Ibid.*
27. *Ibid.*
28. *Ibid.*
29. *Ibid.*
30. *Ibid.*
31. *Ibid.*
32. *Ibid.*
33. *Ibid.*
34. *Ibid.*
35. *Ibid.*
36. *Ibid.*

37 *Ibid.*
38 *Ibid.*
39 *Ibid.*
40 *Ibid.*
31 *Ibid.*
32 *Ibid.*
33 *Ibid.*
34 *Ibid.*
35 *Ibid.*
36 *Ibid.*
37 *Ibid.*
38 *Ibid.*
39 *Ibid.*
40 *Ibid.*
31 *Ibid.*
32 *Ibid.*
33 *Ibid.*
34 *Ibid.*
35 *Ibid.*
36 *Ibid.*
37 *Ibid.*
38 *Ibid.*
39 *Ibid.*
40 *Ibid.*
41 *Ibid.*
42 *Ibid.*
43 *Ibid.*
44 Andrew Rothstein's MI5 file is at KV2/1577
45 *Ibid.*
46 *New Lies for Old* by Anatoli Golitsyn (New York: Dodd Mead, 1984)
47 *The Perestroika Deception* by Anatoli Golitsyn (London: Edward Harle, 1996)
48 *Defence of the Realm* by Christopher Andrew, p. 504.
49 *Ibid.*
50 *Their Trade is Treachery* by Chapman Pincher (London: Sudgwich & Jackson, 1982

Chapter VI   Oleg Lyalin
1 *Spymaster* by Oleg Kalugin (New York: Smyth Gryphon, 1994) p. 131:
2 FBI Fie No: 105-82555-2ND – NR5762
3 *Ibid.*
4 *Ibid.*
5 *Ibid.*
6 *Ibid.*
7 *Ibid.*
8 *Ibid.*
9 *Ibid.*
10 *Ibid.*
11 *Ibid.*

12 *Ibid.*
13 *Ibid.*
14 National Archives, PREM 15/1936
15 *Ibid.*
16 *ibid.*
17 FBI Fie No: 105-82555-2ND – NR5762
18 *Ibid.*

Chapter VII Arkadi Shevchenko
1 Oleg Klugin in *Spymaster* p. 212
2 *Defector's Mistress* by Judy Chavez (New York: Dell, 1979)
3 *Breaking with Moscow* by Arkadi Chevchenko (New York: Alfred Knopf, 1985)
4 Ken Millian correspondence

Chapter VIII Vitali Yurchenko
1 *Sell-Out* by James Adams (London: Penguin, 1995)
2 *Confessions of a KGB Agent* by Oleg Tumanov (New York: Edition Q, 1993)
3 Oleg Klugin in *Spymaster* p. 196
4 Yela Katz (Svetlana Tumanova), *Israel Hayom*, 29 March 2023

INDEX

13th Department, First Chief Directorate 147
902nd MI Group 146

A Spy Among Friends (Macintyre) xxii, 245
A Study of Defectors from the USSR (MI5) xv
A-35 missile 166
Abakumov, Viktor 94
Abdoolcder, Sirioj xiii
ABM, *see* Anti-Ballistic Missile.
ABMT, *see* Anti-Ballistic Missile Treaty..
Abubakr 14–17, 184
Abwehr I (intelligence) 3–5, 7, 100, 177, 184–85, 188–89
Abwehr II (sabotage) 9
   Defectors from, *see* Kurt Beigl; Willi Hamburger; Otto John; Cornelia Kapp; Karl von Kleczkowski; Stella von Kleczkowsky; Peter Schagen; Hans Ruser; Erich Vermehren.
   See also, KONO; Zossen.
Abwehr III (counter-espionage) 6, 181,
ACAMEDICIAN (NKVD codename for bank employee) 78
Adams, James 169
ADVOKAT (KGB codename for Mauno Pekkala) 93
Aeroflot 162
Agayants, Ivan (KGB officer) 105

Agabekov, Georges (Soviet defector) 107, 190, 192–93, 197–98. 203, 205–208
Agents of Influence (Andrei Raina) 110
Ahdmaz 179
Ahmed, Saabry 184
Akhmedov, Ismail 190, 215–17
ALADIN (Abwehr agent) 8, 177, 181
Alangerer, Mahmoud 183
Alexandrov, Vladimir 169
Alexeev, K**iril 190, 227–30**
ALI (KGB codename for Peter Smollet) 100
Ali, Shinas 184
Alinin, Aleksei (KGB officer) 101, 132
Allyson, Maria IEvdoki Petrov's alias) 82
Allyson, Sven (Vladimir Petrov's alias) 82
ALPHONSE (Tony Brooks' SOE codename 160
Aman (Israeli Military Intelligence Service) 86
Ames, Aldrich 167–69
Andora, Lt. 185
Andrew, Prof. Christopher xxii,xxiv, 138, 245–46
Andrews Airforce base 169
Angleton, James 86–87, 129, 132–44
ANNET (KGB codename for Koren) 121
Anti-Ballistic Missile (ABM) x,,166
Anti-Ballistic Missile Treaty (ABMT) x, 166

Antonov, Victor Mikhailovish (NKVD codename IGNAT) 74
Aoki (Japanese press attaché) 195
Armavir 180
ARMEN (Abwehr network) 180
ARTIST (Abwehr officer Johnnie Jebsen) xiii, 5
ARTIST (NKVD codenamefor Herbert Tattersell) 78
ASIO, *see* Australian Security Intelligence Organisation.
Astrov, 211
Auenrode, Ludwig von (Abwehr codename LUDOVICO) 10
Australian Security Intelligence Organisation (ASIO) x, 39–43, 45–87
    Director-General, *see* Charles Spry.

B-52 strategic bomber 166
Bacva, Aza 19
Bagley, Pete\ ix
Bajanov, Boris (Soviet defector) xix
Baksa (alias of Vasili Sharandak) 236
Balassanov,96
Baltimore Field Office 171
Bandera, Stepan 119
BAOR, see British Army of the Rhine.
Barmine, Alexandre 190, 211–13
Barras 80
Baryshinkov, Vladimir 95
BASK (NKVD codename for Jack Hughes) 76
Batvinis, Ray (FBI officer) 171
BBC World Service 176
Bdul, Kerim 184
Beaumont College 16
Beckett, Dr. H.C. (ASIO source FRANKMAN) xiii, 48–58
Bedell Smith, Gen. Walter 97
BEF, see British Expeditionary Force.
Beigl, Kurt (Abwehr defector) xiii, 1, 14–16
Belkin 99

BEN (NKVD codename for Alf Hughes) 78
Beria, Lavrenti xx,31, 240
Berlin Wall 119
Berliner Borsenzeitung 187
Bermuda 85
Bernie, Frances \ \9nkvd codename SISTER) xiii, 41, 77
Bessedovski, Grigori 190, 204–205
Bessedovsky, Gregory (Soviet defector) xix, 190, 191, 197, 276.
Betrayal of an Ideal (Tokaty) 22
Bettaney, Michael xxv
Bevin MP, Ernest 22
Bialoguski, Dr Michael (ASIO source DIABOLO) ix, 45–68
Bing, Geoffrey 21
Bitles, B. 80
Bitov, Oleg (KGB defector) 173
Bitov, Xenia 174
BLACKGUARD viii, 7
Blake, George (KGB codename CONSUL) 98
Bogomolz, Viktor 10.
Borodin. Norman 97
Bourtzeff, Vladimir 214
Boyoglu 187
Bratsikhin, Grigori (KGB illegal) 105
Breaking with Moscow (Shevchenko) 168
Brezhnev, Leonid 106
BRIDE (original codename for VENONA) 82
Brik, Yevgeni 105 (KHN illegal) 105
Britanova181
British Army of the Rhine (BAOR) x, 112
British Expeditionary Force (BEF) x 17
British Security Service (MI5) xi- xxv, 2, 5–6, 9, 22, 27, 20–21, 29–31113, 138–139
    Director-General, see Martin Furnival Jones; Roger Hollis; Percy Sillitoe; Dick White.
    Seputy D-G, *see* Guy Liddell.

Security Liaison Officer Canberra 39; 83, Washington, 142.
And Golitsyn 92, 113, 134–36, 140; *Walter* Krivitsky; Oleg Lyalin,; Gordon Lonsdale; Vladimit Petrov; Yuri Tasoev; Grigori Tokaev; Tayiana Rezun; Vladimir Rezun.
Study of Soviet Defectors xi, 190–345.
VENONA 39.
British Secret Intelligence service (SIS) xiv- xv1, 134, 138, 161
Chief of, *see* John Rennie; Stewart Menzies.
Section V 3
CAPULET 20;ELLI 31 EXCISE 21; GOLDFINCH 141; HARLEQUIN 5; JUNIOR 9; KAGO 136; PEACH 136; PRECIOUS 3; REDWOOD xv ;STORK 19
See also Nicholas Elliott; Tony Brooks; Machlachlan Silverwood-Cope. Vladimir Skripkin.
Brook, 81
Brook, Robin 21
Brooks, Cyrus 21
Brooks, Tony ix,, 140
Brooks, Tony (SIS officer) 160
Brook-Shepherd, Gordon xix-xxiv, 245
Bruce Lockhart, John 18
Brusov, Viktor 96
Bryhn, Asbjørn 129
Bucar, Annabelle 97
Buchenwald concentration camp 16
Bulganin, Marshal 23
Bulgarian Security Police 208
Burgess, Guy xxiv, 42, 82, 97
Burgess and Maclean 1955 White Paper 135
Burhop. Eric 79
Burris, Maude 31
BURTON (NKVD codename for bank employee) 78
Butkov, Mikhail (SIS codename NORTHSTAR) xiv, xxiii,
Byington, John M. 34

Cabell, Gen. Charles 125
Cairncross, John 115
Calwell, 81
Camp 020 7
Camp Peary 87
Canberra Times 61
CAPULET (MI5 codename fot Yuri Tasoev) xvi, 20
Casey, Bill 172
Catterick, HMS 84
CAZAB 87, 136
Central Intelligence Agency (CIA) 31,
See also Director of Central Intelligence.
Piotr Deriabin; Anatoli Golitsyn; Viktor Gundarev; Nikolai Khokhlov; Stanislas Levchenko; Yuri Nosenko; Yuri Rastvorov; Arkadi Shevchenko; Bogdan Stashinsky; Vitali Yurchenko.
Counterintelligence Staff
Chalmers, Ian xviii
CHARLIE (NKVD codename for Rex Chiiplin) 75
Chavez, Judy 168
Chebotarev. Anatoli 163
Cherkashin, Viktor 170
CHERNY 97
Chernyshev 99
Chernyshev, Aleksandr 98
Chiplin, Rex (NKVD codename CHARLIE) 74
Christie, John (GCHQ officer) 77
CIA Office of Security 87,
CIB, *see* Commonwealth Investigation Branch.
City University 23
Clay, Gen. Lucius 21
Clayton, Wally (Soviet spy codenamed CLOD xiii, 74
Clem, Stanley A. 20
Clemens, Hans ((KGB codename ENESU) 114
CLEVER (NKVD codename for Rogers) 79
CLOD, see Wally Clayton..

Colby, Bill 87
Combined Services Detailed Interrogation Centre (CSDIC) x, 7,
Committee of Information (CI) x, 35, 93,
Commonwealth Investigation Branch (CID) x
Communist Party of Australia (CPA) x,xiii, 39
Comrade X , (Tokaty) 22
CONSUL (KGB codename for George Nlake) 98
Coplon, Judith (NKVD codename SIMA) 100
Coty, Pierre 213
Counter-Intelligence Corps (CIC) 34
Counterintelligence Staff xix
    Chief of, see James Angleton.
Cowgill, Felix (SIS officer) xiii, 1
CPA, see Communist Party of Australia.
Cram, Cleveland (CIA officer) ix, 32, 245
Cranfield College, 23
Crawford, Sir Stewart 161
CSDIC, see Combined Services Detailed Interrogation Centre.

Dachau concentration camp 16.
Daily Telegraph xix, 80, 91 136, 174, 207
Daily Worker 23
Danielson 181
Das Reich 2
Day, John (MI5 officer) 139
DCI,, see Director of Central Intelligence.
D-Day 17
Defector's Mistress Chavez) 168
Defence of the Realm (Andrew) xxiv, 85, 138, 245–47
DELFTER, see Erich Vermehren.
Demetrius, Father 187, 189
Deniken, Gen. Anton 204

DENIS (NKVD codename for Allan Dalziel) 41, 78
Denisov, Mikhail 190, 232=33
Department V, First Chief Diretorate 156
Deriabin, Piotr (NKVD defector) xix-xx, 84, 88, 101–105–10. 116–17.
Deuxieme Bureau 112
Dew, Det. Insp.22
DIABOLO, *see* Dr Michael Bialoguski.
Direction de la Surveillance du Territoire (DST) x, 137
    Chief of, *see* Marcel Chalet.
    See also GARMASH.
Director of Central Intelligence (DCI).*see* Bll Casey; Bill Colby; Dick Helms.
Directorate K, First Chief Directorate 158, 167
    Chief of, *see* Oleg Kalugin..
Directorate S, First Chief Directorate 149
Displaced Person (DP) x
Divischok, Vintoss V. (NKVD codename PETCHEKO) 76
Dixlinger (SD officer) 187
Dolgov, A. (GRU officer) 101
Dormoy, Max 213
Doroshenko, Irina 88
Douad, Prince Mansour 185
Douglas-Home, Sir alc 162
Doyle, David ix
Doyle, Hope ix;
DP, *see* Displaced Person.
DREADNOUGHT (MI5 codename for Ivo Popov) 5.
Drozdov, Yuri (KGB officer) xov, 167
DST, *see* Direction de la Surveillance du Territoire.
Dubuvoi, Petr 19
Dudley Hodgson, (FBI officer) 171
Dunderdale, Wilfred (alias "Mr Douglas") 21,

Dunlop, Adm. Colin 139
DYNAMITE (CIA codename for Arkadi Shevchenko) xvi

Earle, George 8
Earnest, Peter (CIA officer) xiv
Ehy I am not Returning to Russia (Koriakoff) 231
Elliott ,John (ASIO officer) 77
Elliott; Nicholas (SIS officer) ix, 3
Empire of Fear (Petrov) 38
Empire of Fear (Petrov) 84
ENESU (KGB codename for Hans Clemens) 116
Ennis, Maj. Rose Esther Ennis 34
ENORMOZ (NKVD codename for atomic weapons research) 77
Epstein, Edward Jay 168
ERIKSON (KGB codename) 115
ERIKSON (KGB codename for Erik Gabrielson) xiv
EVA (NKVD codename for H.M. Kristisen 79
Evang, Wilhelm xiv, 129–34
Evans, Jean (CIA officer) 128
Evatt, D.r Herbert xiv, 41, 43, 70, 73, 80
EXCISE (MI5 codename for Grigori Tokaev) xiv, 21–22

Fadeykin, Ivan (KGB officer) 119
Fadl, Mohsen 187, 189
Falaise, SS 42
False ddefector 199
Falstein, 81
FAMISH 163
Farah, Mohamed 183
FAREWELL (codename for Vladimir Vetrov) xiv
Fasi 185, 195
Faulkner, David (FBI officer) 171
FBI Counterintelligence Reader, 36
FBI,, *see* Federal Bureau of Investigation.
FCD, *see* First Chief Directorate.

FCO, *see* Foreign & Commonwealth Office.
Federal Bureau of Investigation (FBI) x-xiv,, 26, 81, 86, 128, 131–32, 139–48, 167–70
    Diirector of, *see* J. Rdgar Hoover
    See also Kitil Alexeev; Judith Coplon, Willie Fischer; HONETOL; Edwrd L. Howard; JACK; IRONCLAD; Victor Kranchenko,; Oleg Lyalin; Edwin Moore; Ron Pelton.
    See also New York Field Office; Washington Field Office.
Fendig, Phillip (CIA officer) xiv
Fergusin (NKVD asset codenamed RAFAEL) 78
FERRO (NKVD codename for Ric Throssel) 74
Filipov, Aleksei Vasilyevich (KGB officer) 129, 132
Finnard, 81
First Chief Directorate (FCD) , x, 112, 142, 149, 168
Fischer, Willie, alias Rudolf Abel) 149
Fitzharding, 81
Focke-Wulf 18
FOOT (mass expulsion, 1971) xx,iii, 161, 181, 190, 206, 208, 310
Foreign & Commonwealth Office (FCO) x, xviii, xxii-xxiv, 18, 20, 23
    Cypher Department 210;
        Northern Department 22; *See also* Information Research Department; John King.
FRANKMAN (ASIO codename for Dr H.C. Beckett) xiv.
Fraser 80
Freund, Hans Milo 6
Friberg, Frank (CIA officer) xiv, 121
FRIEND (NKVD codename for Koaki) 79
Furnival Jones, Sir Martin 161

G-2 (U.S. army intelligence) 34
Gabekov, George 205–208
Gabrielson; 128
GAF, see German Air Force.
Gaitskell, Hugh 139
Galeti, Nicolas 181
Galrielson, Erik (KGB codename ERIKSON) xiv
Galuzin, Yevgeni (KGB officer) 102
Garbler, Pul (CIA officer) xiv, 86
GARMASH (Soviet spy) civ, 88, 137
Generalov, Nikolsi 52
Georg, von. 180
German Air Force (GAF) x, 24
Gestapo 209
Ghaffari, Mohamed Riza 179
Ginzburg, Water (real nme of Walter Krivitsky) 209
GIRLFRIEND (NKVD asset POIRUGA) 78
GLEN (NKVD codename for Filip Kislitsyn) 57
Glushchenko, B.G. 163
Gmirkin, Vasia 86
Godova, Galina Andrevna 36
Goldberg, George (CIA5- officer) xi, 86
GOLDFINCH (MI5 codename for Oleg Lyalin) xv, 141
Golitsyn, Anatoli (KGB defector codenamed AE;LADLE;SAWDUST) xiii-xiv, xx, 37, 85–140, 247
Gordievsky, Oleg (SIS codenamed OVATION) 175
Gouzenko, Igor (GRU defector) xiv, 15, 41–42, 66, 93, 107, 136, 190–98, 203, 219–25.
Government Communications Headquarters (GCHQ) 76
Gray, Robert (CIA officer) xiv, 86
Greengrass, Paul 138
Greenhill, Sir Denis 161
Gromyko, Andrei 162
GRU, see Soviet Military Intelligence Service.

Gssan al Fendre 185
GUGB, see Soviet Intelligence Service x
Guichet, Valentin (KGB officer) 100
Guinness, Alec xviii
Gulbenkian, Hagop 183
Gundarev, Viktor (KGB defector) 175
Guskov, Ivan (KGB officer) 102
Gutvakh Aleksandr Mikhailovich 81

Haavik, Gunvor (KGB spy) xiv
Haavik, Gunvor xiv
Hahdmaz, Dr Habib 179
Hahri 179
Halder, Gen. Franz 183
Haldun 181
Hamata 185
Hamblen, Derek (MI5 officer) xiv, 39, 81
Hamburger, Willi (Abwehr defector) 1, 5–6, 8, 13–14, 117179, 185, 187
Hammer, Armnd (KGB codename SYNOK) 99, 128
Hansen, Georg 6
Hanssen, Robert 175
HARLEQUIN, (SIS codename for Major Richard Wurmann) 5
Harris, Gordon 164
Hart Davis, Duff .174
Hart, Herbert (MI5 officer) 7
Hartley, Christopher 19
Hayter, William 22
Helfand Leon 190, 213–15
Helms, Dick (CIA officer) ix
Herbert, Christopher (MI5 officer) xiv
Heth & Co., A.M. 21
Heth, Edward 162
Hibbard, L.U. 81
HICKS (KGB codename for Guy Burgess) 135
Hill, Jim (NKVD codename TOURIST) xiv
Himy Bey 188

Hinton, Geoffrey (SIS officer) 134
Hinz, Walther (Abwehr officer) 177, 181
Hiroshi Shoji 33
Hitler, Adol 17
Hiuse Committee on Un-American Activities 210
Hoebke 187
Hollis, Roger (MI5 officer) 39
HONETOL 86
Hook, Jack 80
Hoover, J. Edgar (FBI Director) xv, 86, 137, 246–48
Houghton, Hrry xxv
HOUSE PARTY 20
Hovanesian, Artush (KGB defector) xx
Howard, Edward Lee (KGB codename ROBERT) 172
Hughes, Jack (NKVD codename DASK) 76
Hughes, Sgt. Alf (BEN) 78
Hunt, E. Howard (CIA officer) xiv
Hunt, Jim (CIA officer) xiv, 133

I Was Stalin's Agent (Krivitsky) 219
Imperial College, London Univesity 23
Information Research Department (IRD) 22
International Wheat Council 142
IRD, *see* Information Research Department,
IRONCLAD (FBI codename for KGB source) xiv, 145, 147–49, 162
ISOS (Abwehr decrypts) xi, 5, 7,9,
Ivanov, Boris (KGB officer) 103
IVY BELLS (NSA operation) 171

JACK (KGB asset) 128
Jarkov 63
Jebsen, Johnnie (SIS codename ARTIST) xiv, 5, 12,
Jeffery, Keith xx, 245
JIC, *see* Joint Intelligence Committee.

JOE (NKVD codename) 78
John Paul II, Pope 175
John, Otto (defector) 1
JOHNSON (KGB codename for Anthony Blunt) 135
Joint Intelligence Committee (JIC) xi
Junger, Ernst 183
JUNIOR (SIS codename for Hans Ruser) xiv, 9
Jurachow, Andre 191

KAGO (MI5 codename for Anatoli Golitsyn) 135
Kaiser, F 79
Kapp, Cornelia 6
Karlow, Peter (CIA officer) xiv, 86
Karlowviast, Ian (Alias of Alexandre Barmin) 211
Karpinsky, 62
Kartseva, Evdokia Alexeevka (Mrs Petrov) 35
Kashcheyev,Yevgenni 93
Katz, Yeta 176
Keggett, George L(MI5 officer) xv
Kekkonen, Urho xiv, 85, 117–19, 121. 124, 126
Kellar, Alex (MI5 officer) 17
KGB Line X (science and technology) x-ix,
KGB, *see* Soviet Intelligence Service,
KGB: The Inside Story (Andew & Gordievsky) xxiii, 245
Khan, Ahmed 179
Khan, Mirza 181
Kharkovetz, Georgi (NKVD officer) 42
Khattig, Hamdi 179
khokhlov Nikoolai (NKVD defector) xix, 103, 105, 107, 123, 142
Khrushchev, Nikita 105
KI, *see* Committee of Information.
KIN (NKVD codename for Boris Yartsev) xv, 42
King, John xv,
Kipel. Sabri 184,

Kisevalter, George (CIA officer) xv, 86
Kislytsin, F\filip (NKVD codename GLED) 63
KISS (SIS double agent) xv, 7
Kiukas (KGB (codename KORPI) 128
Kleczkowski, Karl von (Abwehr defector) 1, 6, 8, 137, 180
Kleczkowski, Stella von (Abwehr defector) 1, 6, 8, 137, 180
Klimkin, Vladimir 115
Klimkin, Vladimir (KGB codename VOLODIN) 127
Klugin, Oleg 141
KO, *see* KriegsOrganisation.
Koaki (NKVD assrt codenamed FRIEND 79
Koblensky. Leo von 7
Koester 10
Koenig 6
Komsomol (Young Communist League) 36
KONO, see KriegsOrganisation NeheOrient.
Konon Molody (alias Gordon Lonsdale) 149
Korda, Michael 168
Korean Airlines flight 007 174
Koren (KGB asset codenamed ANNET) 121
Koriakoff, Michel 190, 230–31
Korovin, Nikolai (KGB officer) 114
KORPI (KGB codename for Kiukas) 128
Kotov. Mikhail 93
Koussawsavian, Mir Hohsen 179
Koutiepoff, Gen. 212
Kovaleski, Fred 36
Kovalev, Yevgenni (KGB officer) 103
Kovalski, Pavel CIA officer) xv
Kovich, Dick (CIA officer) xv, 86
Kovschuk, Vladimir 128
Kowalski, Fred (CIA officer) xv
Kozlov, Mikhail (KGB officer) 121
KRAB (NKVD codename for S.B. Kristisen) 79

Krasavin, Andrei 98
Kravchenko, Alesander 191, 234–36
Kravchenko, Victor 190=91, 217–19
Kravtsov Yevgenni (KGB officer) 108
KriegsOrgaisation Portugal 9–20
KriegsOrganisation (KO) x
KriegsOrganisation NeheOrient (KONO) 2, 3, 14, 17
Kristinsen, Wilbur (NKVD codename MASTERCRAFTSMAN)) 78
Kristisen, H.M. (NKVD codeame EVA0 79
Kristisen, S.D. (NKVD codename KRAB) 79
KRISTOV (KGB codename for Mikko Harella) 115
Krivitsky, Walter 308–11
Krivitsky, Wlter xviii,xxix-xx, 190, 192, 197–98, 209-
Krokhin, Aleksei (KGB officer) 119
Kryuchkov, Vladimir IKGB officer) 167
Kuebart Wilhelm (Abwehr officer) 178
KUKISHKIN (KGB codename) 115
Kurenkov, Aleksei 102
Kuzichkin, Vladimir (SIS codenamed REDWOOD) ic, xviii
Kuzichkin, Yuri ix
Kuznetsov, Nikolai (KGB ofiicer) xv
Kuznetsov, Yuri (KGB officer) xv

Lapsjin, Konstantin 97
Layenko, 99
Legeyev, Vladimir (KGB officer) 111
Legge, Jack 80
Leggett, George MI5 officer) 77
Lehmann, Harold 186
Lehmus, Kalle (KGB codename LEON) 128
LEON (KGB asset Kalle Lehmus) 128
Levchenko, Stanislav xix
Leverkühn, Pand (Abwehr officer) 2–4, 6–7, 177–160. 180, 182. 185
Levine Isaac Don 210
Leydin 62

Liddell, Guy xv
Lifanov, Nikolai 52
Life 36
Lissner, Ernest J. 34.
Literary Gazette 174–75
Litovkin, \Georgi (KGB officer) 101
Llandaff Castle, SS 83
Lockwood, Rupert (NKVD spy codenamed WARREN) xv
Lockwood, Rupert WARREN) xiv
Loginov, Yuri (KGB officer) xv, 87, 117
Lonsdale, Gordon (alias of Konon Molody) 149
LUDOVICO Abwehr codename for Ludwig von Auenrode) 10, 15
Ludwig, Thomas 6–7, 15
Lyalin, Oleg (KGB defector codenamed GOLDFINCH) xv
Lyalin, Serfim 96–97
Lygren, Ingeborg xv, 128–32

Macartney, Hope 36
Macintyre, Ben xxiii-xxiv, 245
Maclean, Donald xxiv, 42, 82
Magan, Bill (MI5 officer) 17
MAGNATE (KGB codename for Averell Harriman) 137
Major, David ix Maury, Jack (CIA officer) xv
Makeyev, Nikolai (KGB officer) 115
Malenkov 23
Malenkov, Georgi 88
Mao, Sedong 22
Marshall, William xxv
Martianon, constantinos (KGB spy) xv
Martin, Arthur (MI5 officer) ix, 17
Marwitz, Admiral von der 4, 6
Masao Mitsuhashi 34
MASINT, *see* Measurement and Signature Intelligence.
MASTERCRAFTSMAN (NKVD codename for Wilbur Kristiansen)) 78

Mata Hari 46
Maudling, Reginald 162
Maury, Jack (CIA officer) xv
May, Alan Nunn 224
Mayer, Otto 7
Mayhew MP, Christopher 22
McInnes 80
McKell, 81
McLean 80
McNamara, George (KKVD codename DAILOR) 78
Measurement and Signature Intelligence (MASINT) xvii
Menzies, Sir Robert 42
Menzies, Sir Stewart 21
Meran, Graf 180
Methods of Recruitment (Kravtsov) 109
MGIMO, *see* State Institute of International Relations,
MI5, see British Security Service.
MI6 (Jeffery) xxiii-xxiv, 245
MICHAEL (NKVD codename of Vladimir Petrov) 75.
Michel. Werner 32
Mikko Harrela, Mikki KGB codename KRISTOV) 115
Miller, Ed (FBI officer) 142
Miller, Ed (FBI officer) xv
Miller, Forbes 80
Millian,Ken ix
Mills, Bruce 79
Milner, ian (Soviet spy) xv , 43
Ministry of Foreign Affairs (MFA) 165
Minnish, John T. (FBI officer) 142
MIT, *see* Turkist Intelligence Service.
Mitrokhin, Vasili (KGB defector) xv, 100, 245,
Modin,Yuri (KGB officer) ix, 114
Mole Relief Act 87.
Moltke, Graf von 181
Montebello atomic test site) 38
Montgomery, Fld.-Mrhl. Sir Bernard 20

Moore, Edwin (CIA officer) 169
Morris, Dave 79
Moscow Narodny Bank 162
Mossad (Israeli Intelligence Service) 86
Mowbray, Stephen de ix
Moyzisch, Ludwig 6
Mrshani 184
Mukerjee 94
Murphy, David ix, 86, 129
Murphy, David (CIA officer) xv, 86
Murray, Ralph 22
Musgrove, Sgt.. 96
MVD, *see* Soviet Intelligence Service.

NASA, *see* National Aeronautics and Space Administration ii
National Security Agency (NSA) xii, 370-71
NATO, *see* Norrth Atlantic Treaty Organisation.
Naval Air Station Patuxent River, Maryland, 171
Near East Division 87
New Lies for Old (Golitsyn) 86
New Republic 168
New York Field Office (NYFO) xii
New York Times 36
Nicolaeff, Georgi (alias of Georgi Akhmedov) 216-17
NID, *see* Naval Intelligence Division.
Nikolai Mironov, (KGB officer) 118
NINA xv, 46
Nixon, \President Richard 166
NKVD, see Soviet Intelligence Srvice,
No Other Choice (Blake) 99
Nobinuri Higurashi, 33
NORD (KGB asset) 139
North Atlantic Treaty Orgnisation (NATO) xi
North Korea 96, 98
NORTH STAR (SIS codename for Mikhail Butkov) xviii
Northern Department 22
Nosenko, Aleksandr 33, 108

Nosenko, Yuri (KGB defector) xv, xix, 3, 87, 129, 236, 140, 156,
Nosov, Fedor (NKVD officer) 39
Novikov, Vladimir (KGB officer) 118
Novobratsky, Lev 94
NSA, *see* National Security Agency.
NTS, *see* Union of Ukrainian Nationalists.
Nureyev, Rudolf 127
Nval Intelligence Division (NID) xii
NYFO, *see* New York Field Office.

O'Neal, Birch (CIA officer) 128
O'Sullivan, Fergan (NKVD codename TOURIST) xv
OATSHEAF139
Of Moles and Molehunting, (Cram) xix
Office of Naval Intelligence (ONI) 186
Office of Strategic Services (OSS) xii, 86
  X-2 95
Office of War Information (OWI) x
Oflag VIB
Oganesyan, Kristofor 95
OKW, *see* Wehrmacht High Command.
Oldfield, Maurice (SIS officer) 17
OLGA (NKVD codename for Ross Maie Ollier) xv, 40
Ollier, Rose Marie (NKVD codename OLGA) xv
Olsen, C. 80
Orlov, Alexander (NKVD defector) xix
Orlov, Igor (alias Aleksandr Koptszky) 100
OSS, *see* Office of Strategic Services.
Oswald, Lee Harvey xx
Ousepian (alias of Georges Agabekov) 206
OVATION (SIS codename for Oleg Gordievsky) xviii

Ovchinnikov, Ivan (GRU defector) 173–74
OWI, *see* Office of War Information.
Oysu, Mralaren 184

Page, Hamilton 224, 226
Pakhomov, Ivan (NKVD officer) xv
Palestine 22
Panyushkin, Aleksandr (KGB officer) 118
Papen, Franz von 3, 13, 217
Paques, George (KGB spy) xv, 85, 115, 139,
PASSERINE (FBI codename for Ron Pelton) 171
PEACH (MI5 codename for Kim Philby) 136
Pekkala, Mauno (KGB codename ADVOKAT) 93
Pelton, Ronald 170–71
Pendred, Lawrence 19
Penkovsky, Oleg (GRU officer) xix-xx, 08, 88, 168
Petrov, Evdokia (NKVD defector) xx, 35, 37–246
Pevnev, Pavel (KGB codename VLAS) 101
Petrov, vladimir (NKVD defector) xx, 34, 35–84, 93, 105,107, 116–17, 122, 135, 137,246
Pfeiffer, Erich 6
Philby, Kim (KGB codename STANLEY; MI5 codename PEACH) xxxiii, xxii, xxiv,16, 47, 67, 86, 134–36, 138–39, 245
Pik, Eugene 190,
Pilnov, Fedor 95
PIMENTO (SOE network) 160
Pincher, Harry Chapman 138, 247
Pitovranoc, Yevgeni 94, 97
Pitovranov Yevgenni 97
Plaitkais, Janis 42
Plans for Psychological Warfare against Eastern Europe in Time of War (NATO) 112

Plettenberg, Elizabeth von 2
POIRUGA (NKBD asset codenamed GIRLFRIEND) 79
Ponomarev, Boris(KGB officer) 118
Ponsonby, Myles (SIS officer) 17
Popov Ivo (MI5 codename DREADNOUGHT) 5
Popov, Dusan (MI5 codename TRICYCLE) 5
Post-Hostilities Planning Committee 38 39
Powell, Geoffrey 79
PRECIOUS (SIS codenme for Erich Vermehren) xv
Pribytkov, Vladimir (KGB officer) 103
Proletarsky, Vladimir (Vladimit Petrov) 35
Provakov 99
Public Law 96–450 (Mole Relief Act) 87
Putin, Vldimir 176
Putron, Owen de 19

Qashgai 180
Qashgai, Mansour 180
Qesart, Rashid 180
Queen Mary, RMS 136
Quentin Johnson (CIA Officer) xiv

Radio Liberty 174
Radio Security Service (MI8) 276
RAE, *see* Royal Aircraft Establishment.
RAF Northolt 19
RAF, see Royal Air Force.
RAFAEL (NKVD codename for Fergusson) 78
Rainia, Andrei (KGB officer) 107, 110
Rastvorov, Tatyana, 36
Rastvorov, Turi xix-xx, 20, 37, 55, 84, 102–102, 105–208, 117, 122, 246
Ravensbruck concentration camp 16,
Raykhman, Leonid 97

RCMP, *see* Royal Canadian Mounted Police.,
Reader's Digest 174
REDWOOD (SIS codename for Vladimir kuzichkin) ix-xviii
Reed, Ronnie \9mi5 officer) 78
Reilly, Patrick 112
Reiss, Ignace 192
Rennie, Sir John 161
Rezun. Tatiana (GRU officer) xix, xxi
Rezun, Vladimir (GRU officer) xix. xxi
Richards, Ron (ASIO officer) xv
ROBERT (KGB codename for Edward Lee Howard 172
Roberts, Douglas (SIS officer) 17
Robertson, James (MI5 officer) 82
Robson, Bernard 164
Rodin, \Nilolai (alias Nikolai Korovin) 149
Rogers (NKVD asset codenamed CLEVER) 79
Roncalli, Angelo 3
Rosen, Alex (FBI officer) xv
Rossetti, Clemens (Abwehr officer) 181
Rothschild, Victor 136
Rothstein, Andrew 135
Royal Air Force (RAF) xii
Royal aircraft Establishment (RAE) xii
Royal Canadian Mounted Police (RCMP) xii, 221
Royal Commission on Espionae (Candian) 224
Royal Commission on Espionage (Australian) 40
Royal Commission on Espionage (Cnadian) 42
Rtamonov, Nikolai (Soviet defector) 172.
Ruser, Hans (SIS codename JUNIOR) xiv
Russell-Jones, Barry (MI5 officer) 142
Russia Today. 23

"S" 191
Sadovnikov (NKVD codename SAEED) xvi, 75
SAEED (NKVD codename of Sadvnikov) 75
Safeguard missile 166
SAILOR (NKVD codename foe George McNamara) 78
Sakharovsky, Aleksandr 126
SALT I 167
SALT II 167
SALT, see Strategic Arms Limitation Treaty (SALT) xii
Sänger, Eugn 19
SASHA 86, 95
Sasson, Dr Molly ix
Savelyev,Vasya (KGB officer) 108
Savin, Ladislas 159
SAWDUST (CIA codename for Anatoli Golitsyn) xvi
Scarlett; John ix
SCD, *see* Second Chief Directorate
Schagen, Peter 1
Schenker-Angerer, Gottfried (Abwehr officer) 7–8. 177, 186
Scherbak, Fedor (KGB officer) 107
Scotland Yard 164
SEAMAN (NKVD codename for Vladimir Petrov) 82
SEATO, *see* South-East Asia Treaty Orgaisation.
SD, *see* Sicherheitsdienst.
Second Chief Directorate (SCD) xiii, 109
Second Chief Directorate (SCD) xii
Secret Intelligence Service (SIS Section V 3
Security Intelligence Middle East (SIME) x, 7, 177
Seiler 180
Sell-Out (Adams) 169
Serov, Ivan 105
Serov, Ivan 23
Shadrin, Ewa 172
Shahab, Prince 187

Shapiro, Henry (KGB codename VALERI) 128
Sharandak, Vasili 191, 236–38
Shashinsky, Bogdan (KHB illegal) 119
Shelepin, Alexander (KGB officer) 118
Shergold, Harold (SIS officer) 17
Shevchenka, Lina 165
Shevchenko, Anna 168
Shevchenko, Arkadi (CIA codename DYNAMITE) xvi
Shevchenko, Elaine 168
Shevchenko, Gennady 168
Shigeru Takamore 33
Shin Bet (Israeli Security Service) 86
Shlykov, Fedor (KGB officer) 108
Shtykov, Terenty 96
Shubnyakov, Fedor 94
SIA, *eee* Soviet Intelligence Agency.
Sicherhetsdienst (SD) 6, 16–17
Sillitoe, Sir,Percy (MI5 D-G) 39
Silverwood-Cope, Machlachlan (SIS officer) 31
SIMA (NKVD codename for Judith Coplon) 100
SIME,, *see* Security Intelligence Middle East.
Simons, Martin Frncis (alias of Yuri Rastvorov) 32
Simpson, Colin 80
Sirry, Hassam 183
SISTER (NKVD codename for Frances Bernie) xvi
Sjimmel Oga (KGB illegal) 114
SK, *see* Soviet Kolony
Skomorokhin, Yakov 95
Skripkin, Vladimir (NKVD officer) xvi, xx, 32, 36–37, 88, 92,
Skripkin, Vladimit (KVD officer).xvi
Slavnov, Anatoli (KGB officer) 171
Sloma, Andrei (KGB officer) 108
SMERSH 235
Smirnov, Andrei 99
Smolka, Peter (alias Smollett, KGB codename LI) 100

Sobole, Vikenti (KGB officer) 145.
Sogolow, Alexander (CIA pffocer) xvi
Soiegelglass, Sergei 209
Sokolovsky, Marshal 239
Sokolovsky, Marshal Vasili 19
Solie, Bruce (CIA officer) xvi
Solie, Bruce (IA officer) 128
Solnikov, Dick 97
Solomon, Flora 136
Sorokin, Vladimir (alias of Vitali Yurchenko) 170
South-East Asia Treaty Organbisation (SEATO) xii
Soviet Film Distribution (VOKS) xii
Soviet Intelligence Agency (SIA) xii
Soviet Intelligence (KGB; NKVD; MVD) *passim.*
Soviet Kolony (SK) 83, 93
Soviet Reparations Committee 20
Soviet Trade Delegation 141
Special Branch 22
Special Operations Executive (SOE) 160
Spry, Sirr Charles (ASIO D-G) 39
SpyCatcher (Wright & Greengrass\0 138
Stalin, Josef 22
STANLEY (KGB codename for Kim Philby) 135
Stashinsky, Bogdan (NKVD defector) xvi
State Institute of Internatioal Relations (MGIMO) xi, 165
STEPAN (NKVD codename for "STANLEY) 78
Stiebel, Pamela (MI5 officer) 77
STORK MI5 codename for Grifori Tokaev) xvi, 19
Streater, Isobel 206
Stretter, Georg 186
Strokov, Gleb 94
Sullivan, Bill (FBI officer) xvi
Sunday Express 21
Suslov, Mikhail (KGB officer) 118
Symonds, John 164

Symonds, John ix
Symonds, John xvi
SYNOK (NKVF codename forArmand Hammer) 99, 128

Takacs, Isfan 234
Takacs, Vera 190, 233–34
Takhchyanov, Pantlymod 97
Tales I Could Not Tell (Bitov) 174
Tank, Prof.. Kurt 18
Tarabrin, Yevgeni (KGB officer) 111, 113
Tasoev, Yuri (GRU defector codenamed CAPULET) xiii, xvi, 20–21, 31,173
TASS News Agency xv, xix, 21, 42, 47, 55. 73135, 162, 276
Tattersell, William Herbert (NKVD codename ARTIST) 78
Taylor, 79
TECHNICIAN (NKVD codenme for Allan Dalziel) xvi
Templyakova, Irina 141
Tenant, C.R. 78
Tennequist (NKVD asset codenamed TIKHON) 78
TEODOR (NKVD codename for K. Turnbull) 89
*The German Secret Service in Turkey,*SIS Digest 3
The KGB's Role in the Wartime Partisan Movement 109
The Localization of Intelligence Failures(Agayants) 109
The Mitrokhin Archive (Andrew & Mitrokhin) 245
The Perestroika Deception (Golitsyn) 86
The Prevention of Betrayals and Defections by Members of Official Soviet Organizations, Visiting Delegations and Tourist Groups Abroad. 109
The Storm Birds (Brook-Shepherd) xix, xxi

The Storm Petrels: The First Soviet Defectors 1928–1938, (Brook-Shepherd) 245
The Truth about American Doplomts (Bucar) 98
Their trade is Treachery (Pincher) 138
Thirk (alias of Robert Ulshofer) 181
Thomas, Walter (alias of Walter Krivitsky) 211
Thompson, Drew ix
Throssel, Ric (NKVD codename FERRO) 74
Thwaites, Michael (ASIO officer) ix, xvi, 43, 69
Thwaites; Michael ix
TIKHON (NKVD codename for Tennequist 78
Tishkov, Arseni
Tito, Josip 22
Togliati, Plmiro 106
Tokaev, Grigori 191, 238–4
Tokaev, Grigori (GRU defector codenamed EXCISE; STORK) xvii
TOURIST (Soviet codename for Jim Hill) xiv-xvi, 78
Tpkaev, Bell 19
Tremmel, Valeri 88
Trend, Burke 139
TRICYCLE (MI5 codename for Dusan Popov)
Trotsky. Leon 18
Trott xu Solz, Adam von 183
Trott zu Solz, Joachim von 183
Tsarev, \Oleg ix
Tu-22 *Backfire* bomber 166
Tumanov, Oleg 175
Tumanov: Confessions of a KGB Agent, (Yumanov) 175
TUMO (KGB codename for Uhro Kekkonen) 121
Turkist Intelligence serviceb (MIT) x
Turnbull, K. (NKVD asset codenamed TEODOR) 79
Twenty Years in the USSR (Barmin) 213
Tyupanov, Col. 22

U-177 84
UBEN (KGB codename for Balasanov) 96
UCHIDA (NKVD codename for Yuri Rastvorov) 34
UDS (NKVD codename for Don Woods) 78
Ulbrivht, Walter 114
Ulshofer, Robert 177
UN, see United Nations,
Union of Ukrainian Nationalists (NTS) xi
United Nations (UN) xii, xxi, 72, 120, 147. 165,
United Nations War Crimes Commission 208
United Press International (UPI) xii
UPI, see United Press International.

VA:ERI (KGB asset Henry Shapiro) 128
Valintirk 184
Varichian 180
Vasilenko, Gennadi (KGB officer) 170
Vassall, John (Soviet spy) xvi
V-bomber bases, 160
Veche, 174
Vemehren, Michael 16
VENONA 38
Vermegren, Isa
Vermehren (Abwehr defector codenamed PRECIOUS and DELFTER) cvi.
Vermehren, Erich ix
Vermehren, Petra 2
Vetrov, Vladimir (KGB officer codenamed FAREWEELL xiv, xvi, xix
Vienn Convention 149
VLAS (KGB codename for Pavel Pavnev) 102
VM, see V-Mann (Abwehr agent).
V-Mann (VM) xii
VOKS, see Soviet Film Distribution,

Voland, Prof. 237
Volkov Konstantin (NKVD officer) xx-xxiv, 37 , 97, 190, 192, 195–98, 203, 224–27,
Volkov. Konstantin 224–27
Volkova, Zoya xxi
VOLODIN (KGB codename Vladimir Klimkin) 127
Volor, Frantislika 86
Voronin, Yuri (KGB officer) xvi, 121
Voroshilov, Marshal Kliment 25

WAAF, see Womens Auxiliary Air Force.
Wade, Bob (FBI officer) 169
Wahabaie,Parvis 180
Wahasnzaide, Parvin (codenamed SEITE) 179
Waldmann, Louis 211
Walsh, Gen. Robert 20
WARREN (NKVD codename for Rupert Lockwood xvi, 75
Washington Field Office (WFO) xii
Watkins, John 97
Wehrmacht High Command (OKW) xii
Wengler, Dr 183
Wesselow, Peter de (MI5 officer) xiii
Westcott, 81
WFO, see Washington Field Office.
Wharton, Harry (MI5 officer) xvi, 146
White, Dick (MI5 officer) 76
Wiggins, Betty 20
Wilson, Haarold 86,87
Windels 187
Windels, Erich 183
Winterbotham, Fred 19
Womens uxiliary Air Force (WAAF) xii
Woods, Don (NKVD codename UDS) 78
Woomera Guided Missile Rnd 38
Worth Priory. 16
Wrangel, Gen. Piotr 185

Wright, Peter (MI5 officer) ix, 31, 138, 246
Wuori, Arne (KGB asset) 128
Wurmann, Richard (SIS codename HAREEQUIN) 5

Yakushin, Boris (KGB officer) 170
Yarotsky, 19
Yartsev Boris (NKVD officer) xvi
Yartsev, Brois (NKVD codename KIN) xv
Yereskovskaya, Dr Valentina 173
Yolland Wdgar 186
Young, Courtenay (MI5 officer) xvi
Young, Sir George 135
Younger, Kenneth 21
Yurchenko, Maj. 190, 231–32

Zabotin, Col. Nikolai 219
Zaehringer, Kurt (Abwehr officer) 181
Zamboni 181
Zarubin, Vasili 109
Zernova, Sophie 231
Zhenikhov, Vladimir 117
Zhukov, Marshal Georgi 18
Zhukovsky Air Force Academy 18
Zossen 6